AF506032

Wild Visions

Wilderness as Image and Idea

Wild Visions

BEN A. MINTEER, MARK KLETT, AND STEPHEN J. PYNE

Yale UNIVERSITY PRESS | NEW HAVEN & LONDON

Foreword by Roderick Frazier Nash

Support for the publication of this book was provided to Ben Minteer as a Fellow of the Center for Humans and Nature.

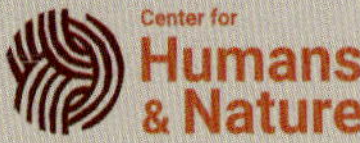

Published with assistance from the foundation established in memory of Calvin Chapin of the Class of 1788, Yale College.

Copyright © 2022 by Ben A. Minteer, Mark Klett, and Stephen J. Pyne. All rights reserved.
This book may not be reproduced, in whole or in part, including illustrations, in any form (beyond that copying permitted by Sections 107 and 108 of the U.S. Copyright Law and except by reviewers for the public press), without written permission from the publishers.

Yale University Press books may be purchased in quantity for educational, business, or promotional use. For information, please e-mail sales.press@yale.edu (U.S. office) or sales@yaleup.co.uk (U.K. office).

Designed by Monograph / Matt Avery
Set in Chaparral, Blanchard, and Macklin Sans type by Monograph
Printed in China.

ISBN 978-0-300-260724 (hardcover : alk. paper)
Library of Congress Control Number: 2021952937
A catalogue record for this book is available from the British Library.

This paper meets the requirements of ANSI/NISO Z39.48-1992 (Permanence of Paper).

10 9 8 7 6 5 4 3 2 1

Contents

Foreword

RODERICK FRAZIER NASH

This important book concerns the dance between wildness and civilization over the past ten thousand years of history on earth. Nothing was "wild" before then because nothing was tamed or controlled. But after herding and agriculture began, it made sense to think about those parts of nature that had their own "will" as distinct from those that had been bent to follow the will of people. The word "wild" is a contraction of "willed." Wilderness literally means a self-willed place. The rise of modern civilization (repeated in North America over the past four centuries) could be thought of as a push-ing back of wildness. Fields were fenced, pigs and goats appeared, horses' wills were broken with ropes and spurs, and wild people were conquered. Even nonliving components of the natural world such as rivers came to be thought of as wild or, if dammed, harnessed in the service of technological civilization.

But how far was too far? When did progress turn into destruction and in the process violate the rights of nature? Ben Minteer, Mark Klett, and Stephen Pyne explore in this book various shades of wildness in the American West. Their work points to the question of how we want to occupy this planet in the future. In this effort they have guidance from Thomas Cole, whose paintings made in the 1830s showed the rise and fall of an overly populated, overly controlled "empire" that cut off its wild roots. Cole had Rome in mind, and so did Henry David Thoreau. More recently, the sociobiologist E. O. Wilson proposed that humans allow wild nature half of

Roderick Frazier Nash is Professor Emeritus of History and Environmental Studies, University of California, Santa Barbara, and the author of *Wilderness and the American Mind*. Yale University Press published the first edition in 1967 and the fifth edition in 2014. Nash is also the author of *The Rights of Nature: A History of Environmental Ethics* (University of Wisconsin Press, 1989).

the earth. My book *Wilderness and the American Mind* makes repeated appearances in the pages that follow; in the fifth edition, the epilogue looks out a thousand years to a low-impact, high-technology future I call "Island Civilization." Human presence is imploded. The point is to leave most of the planet self-willed.

This book suggests that Aldo Leopold's "mountain" (described on page 11) and even Edward Abbey's solitary desert (in Ben's essay that begins on page 94) have room enough for a restrained civilization. And yet we are at a crossroads, looking for a direction to turn. The ideas that follow are essential for humanity finding its way.

Wild Visions

Overlook

Layout

BEN A. MINTEER

Some years ago, I was invited to write an essay on the writer and wilderness activist Edward Abbey for a collection assessing his literary and philosophical importance.[1] Abbey was a brilliant but often divisive figure whose book *Desert Solitaire* remains one of the most powerful statements in American wilderness philosophy. I'd always admired his ability to drill down to the bedrock of our environmental ethics and the bluntness of his view that wilderness protection was a fundamental obligation of any society that would deem to call itself civilized. He seemed to understand better than most what was at stake.

And yet I'd also grown uncomfortable with him over the years. Although I would recommend *Desert Solitaire* to students and friends interested in nature writing and the wilder parts of the desert Southwest, the persona Abbey created as his popularity grew in the 1970s and 1980s—that of a swaggering, rhetorical bomb thrower who took great pleasure in offending just about everyone—started to wear me out. So, too, did the offhand misogyny in works like his satirical novel *The Monkey Wrench Gang,* a defect that the book's memorable comic escapades and enviable sense of place just can't wash away.

But it wasn't only that. I'd also found myself moving away from what originally attracted me to Abbey in the first place: his attitude toward the wilderness and the quasi-religious zeal in which he defended it. It probably boiled down to a difference in philosophical temperament and interest. My own pragmatism proved to be an increasingly bad fit with Abbey's polemics and the radical biocentrism that dripped from his pages. Like others, I also worried that such a single-minded focus on the wild stood in the way of a more inclusive environmentalism, one that made room for rural, suburban, and urban landscapes and the communities they supported—if only because the fate of the wild was, and is, bound up with the fate of these other parts of the landscape. Unlike Aldo Leopold, who wrote lyrically and forcefully about the wilderness and wildlands but never forgot that it was but one type of land use among many, Abbey seemed to have little useful to say about the challenge of living sustainably in places where the wild was not the dominant force. In fact, he had much to say that seemed to hurt the cause.

As we'll see later, I now think I was wrong about much of this. But getting back to that assignment, as I was struggling with what I wanted to write about Abbey, I came across a photo of him taken near the end of his life that's partly responsible for the book you now hold in your hands. It appeared in the gallery pages of an Abbey reminiscence written by his friend Jack Loeffler, a black-and-white picture of a smiling Abbey standing with two others and bearing the credit line "Photo by Mark Klett."

Mark, as it turned out, was a colleague of mine at Arizona State University, and I'd gotten to know him a little over the years, though I wasn't aware of his Abbey connection. Since I was flailing around trying to find a line to pursue in my essay, I sent Mark an email asking if he'd be up for sitting down with me to talk about the photo and how his path ended up crossing with Abbey's. "The beer is on me," I said. If you know anything about Abbey, you know that this was a fitting form of payment.

The rest of the story is picked up later in this book ("Edward Abbey's Wild Visions"). But in the course of my conversation with Mark about his time with Abbey a couple of unexpected things happened. I'd originally thought I'd gather some useful detail and background that I could lightly sprinkle into my essay, which I was still envisioning as an academic analysis of Abbey's moral philosophy and its contemporary relevance. Yet, as we talked, I realized that Mark's experience with Abbey was really the story I was most interested in telling, especially the occasion that drew the writer and the photographer

together for a week in the Southern Utah wilderness more than thirty years ago. After a series of fits and starts, I finally had my way in.

Although Mark and I talked a lot about Abbey that evening, our conversation also took some turns into a few side canyons. We eventually ended up reflecting on the many parallels between landscape photography, particularly in the American West, and the development of environmental thought (particularly environmental philosophy and history) in the 1960s and 1970s. It became clear that both traditions had gone through a similar series of growing pains, self-criticism, and attempts at reconstruction, roughly around the same time. I started to think that these parallels might be worth a closer look, and I made a mental note to return to them when I got the chance.

Around the same time, I was wrapping up a collaborative anthology with another ASU colleague and friend, the environmental historian and chronicler of wildfire Steve Pyne. That book, *After Preservation,* was a meditation on the idea of the Anthropocene: the recently proposed name for our current geologic period signifying the outsize impact of humans on the planet. Steve and I were interested in how the idea was being received by the environmental community, especially its implications for the preservationist movement, which seemed to have a lot to lose in the face of competing claims about the fundamental humanness of the non-human. Mark ended up contributing the perfect cover photo for the collection. The stars for a larger collaboration by the three of us had started to align.

American ideas and images of the wilderness have evolved dramatically over the past one hundred and fifty years, from a view of wild country as an inviolable, even mythical "place apart" to one that exists only within the matrix of human activity and societal choice. This shifting understanding has in turn provoked complicated questions about the importance of the wild in modern environmentalism, as well as new aesthetic expectations as we reframe the wilderness as (at least to some degree) a human creation.

For example, how do our celebrated traditions of wilderness photography fit with this more clear-eyed view of the history and degrees of human influence and the retreat of outmoded myths of "untrammeled" nature? Can we cultivate a responsible environmental ethic and aesthetic that lies someplace between—or maybe outside of—the extremes of the (purely) wild and the (completely) wrecked? If so, how might this steer future environmental thought and photographic practice as we move deeper into a human-dominated age?

This book is our attempt to explore these and other questions, both in text and in pictures. Although there are some excellent works exploring the role of photography in American environmentalism, this book is distinctive in its focus on the wilderness and especially its union of historical and contemporary landscape photography and environmental thought. While it grew out of our earlier conversations and collaborations, the innovative layout and conceit of this book was also inspired by the "Exhibit Format" series popularized by David Brower during his tenure as executive director of the Sierra Club in the 1960s. The original Sierra Club books created the new genre of "environmentalist coffee table book" by showcasing the work of photographic luminaries such as Ansel Adams, Eliot Porter, and Philip Hyde. In the process they presented a distinctive and, today, controversial view of wild landscapes as pristine environments threatened by human activities and encroachment. *Wild Visions* updates this classic form, using the conventional photo book format to explore not just the historical and more familiar expressions, but also alternative views and ideas that help us appreciate the changes in representing and valuing wild landscapes over time.

Furthermore, this is a true collaboration. Mark oversaw the photos, and for the most part the texts are jointly written by Steve and me, although there are a few exceptions (as noted). One of them is the thoughtful essay ("Cultivating Wildness") by Gavin Van Horn from the Center for Humans and Nature, which we are proud to have as a partner on the publication of this volume.

Although the book ranges across a wide historical, intellectual, and artistic territory, the words and images should be thought of as a curated collage rather than a systematic survey. That is, we haven't attempted a comprehensive chronicle of ideas or images, but rather a perspective on the subject informed by our interests, backgrounds, and judgments, both individual and collective. So, for example, even though much of the book follows a kind of loose chronology, the discussion is organized more thematically and visually. The first half of the book explores historical roots and trends in the emergence of wilderness as an idea and as an aesthetic practice, including the relationship between landscape painting and photography in the nineteenth century, the rise of wilderness advocacy in print and pictures, the heyday of Ansel Adams, Eliot Porter, and classic wilderness imagery, and the slow churn of U.S. wilderness policy culminating in the Wilderness Act of 1964. We then consider the parallel disruption and critique of the wilderness ideal in photography and environmental thought in the last decades of the twentieth century before exploring, in the final section, attempts to restore, remake, and rethink the wild—both photographically and philosophically—in a time defined by the ubiquity of the human presence. Often the wild is viewed in binary terms: it's either revered as sacred and ecologically pure or dismissed as profane and fallen as a result of human activities. In this book we hope to show the possibilities of avoiding this binary in depicting the wild even as we acknowledge the lasting allure of its appeal.

Not surprisingly, the discussion is largely preoccupied with work coming out of the American West, a focus that mirrors the classic way of packaging wilderness photography and environmental history. Our intention is not to contribute to the long tradition of ignoring other regions in the depiction of the wild so much as it is to provide a design that parallels the familiar Sierra Club series. It's an approach that allows us to shift historical and compositional ground while holding the geographical context mostly constant (there are a couple of important outliers along the way). As you'll see, focal landscapes in the wilderness tradition recur. Chief among them is Yosemite, which serves as a kind of type location for a key set of ideas about the wild and as a nexus of modernist and postmodernist depictions in art and photography, from the vast canvases of Albert Bierstadt and the celebrated prints of Ansel Adams to contemporary re-imaginings by a new generation of landscape photographers.

At the same time, we've tried hard to capture a compelling variety of perspectives and visions toward the wild in these pages, and to put the words into a kind of dialogue with the pictures. Toward that end, many of the chapters are accompanied by an "About the Gallery" conversation among the three of us, where we explore the interplay of text and photography further while also discussing the rationale for our aesthetic and thematic choices. We see these conversations as something akin to a readers' (and viewers') guide; or, harkening to our ways of experiencing wild places, serving a kind of "docent" function in the book. They lead you from essay to image while allowing you to form your own responses to both. Throughout, we've sought to draw attention to the ideas, figures, and works that the three of us think are important in understanding the arc of the American wilderness narrative. As you'll see, it's an arc that has started to bend in some exciting and unexpected directions.

This book arrives at a time marked by a deep sense of unease and uncertainty about how we should think about and represent the American landscape, wild and otherwise. Some of the legends of wilderness preservation, such as John Muir, have in recent years found their legacies called into question as a more unblinking view of their racism, which ranged from "casual" to pervasive, has emerged.[2] The result has been a difficult moral, cultural, and political reckoning over the history, voices, and values of American environmentalism. Interestingly, these winds of change are also whipping across landscape photography, as questions of race, ethnicity, and gender increasingly figure into artists' choices about the meaning and form of the environment they choose to reveal in the image. It's a reminder that any discussion of "our" wilderness values and experiences must be mindful of the plural histories and relationships different communities have had with what we traditionally call "wild" on the American landscape. We don't pretend to have resolved these tensions in this book. But we've tried to strike a balance between presenting the tradition of wilderness photography and thought that has exerted great influence in shaping the wilderness in modern imagery and imagination, while also pointing out some of the tradition's biases and blind spots regarding what the American wilderness means, what it should look like, and who it's for.

Ed Abbey certainly had his thoughts about such questions, many of which haven't aged well. But on this one point I'll let him have the last word in my introduction (no doubt he would've liked that). Writing about the wild landscapes sprawled across his beloved Colorado Plateau—home to Arches, Zion, and the Grand Canyon—he reminded us that, "Despite the best efforts of a small army of writers, painters, photographers, scientists, explorers, Indians, cowboys, and wilderness guides," the meaning of the wilderness was "still beyond the reach of reasonable worlds. Or unreasonable representation. This is a landscape that has to be seen to be believed, and even then, confronted directly by the senses, it strains credulity."[3]

Abbey's probably right about this, but we're pressing ahead anyway. It's good to have you with us.

Picture

MARK KLETT

As Ben Minteer has written, he and I first began a conversation about Edward Abbey that quickly moved into discussing environmental history and the ways photographers have depicted the western landscape in particular. Some time later, Ben had a related discussion with Steve Pyne, and the two of them proposed to me a collaboration, a book, that would attempt to link the parallels between environmental thought and photography.

At first, I imagined that Ben and Steve were asking me to contribute my work alone to this proposed project. And in full disclosure, my own images are among those works included here. But it was clear from the outset that tracing the history of our respective fields would mean that no one person could represent the complexity of ideas that follow the trajectory of images related to the "wild."

Thus, for this book I took on the job of selecting the visuals you see on these pages. It's a role in which I'm not completely comfortable, because I am simply not a professional curator. As Ben has suggested, this book is not intended to be a survey of what has been done by photographers over the past hundred and fifty years; rather, in selecting photographs and discussing them with my co-authors, I hoped to explore many of the directions photographers have taken to represent their relationship to the land, the culture, and their roles as image makers. In the end, I edited a selection that spoke to me as a practicing landscape photographer and educator, one that represents my own, not impartial perspective on the themes and issues Ben and Steve discuss in the text. For my part of our collaboration, I relied upon a personal history of what I experienced as the "wild" from a practice spanning forty years.

My approach to selecting images for this book relied on a personal knowledge of places in the American West. The intersection of wild lands and photography has been central to my practice. For over forty years I've explored the region, and steeped myself in its geography as well as the natural and cultural events that have shaped the land and driven the forces of change. My perspective has been shaped by my college training as a geologist, and my early work on the Rephotographic Survey, a project that revisited and then repeated the landscape views of more than a hundred and twenty sites that were first photographed for the western surveys of the 1860s and '70s. Later, other projects I did, often in collaboration, revisited historic images made in places like Yosemite and Grand Canyon National Parks. One project even addressed places that were drowned by the dam that flooded Glen Canyon on the Colorado River, and were of sites that are no longer accessible. All of this work involved research into the past, using historic images as a basis for making new work, and thinking about photography of place as a reflection of time and change, as well as examining methods of representation. So the way photographs in this book were selected might best be seen as a reflection of my own research-based artistic practice.

Over the decades I've had the privilege of knowing dozens of colleagues who share my love of the region, and who explore the contemporary West with great passion and intellect. At the same time, I've taught hundreds of students, and many have gone on to become professional colleagues. It was from some of these acquaintances and former students that I have chosen photographs to include in this book. Yet there were others included whom I did not know, but have become acquainted with their work through teaching classes in landscape photography while looking for new work to show my students. I am indebted to one of my former graduate students, Josh Haunschild, who helped research and bring to my attention photographers whose work I had not yet seen, and whose vision clearly seemed to contribute to the concept of this book.

Although it is not a comprehensive selection, I think the work included addresses many of the changes in approaches, attitudes, values, and shifts in methods used by photographers over time. It was my purpose to include as many photographers and as much diversity of individuals, ideas, and approaches as was practical. Unfortunately, this approach also limits the ability to more fully represent the depth of each individual's practice. For more about the individual photographers included and their work, the book's appendix contains further information on them.

It's an ongoing argument whether the work of photographers simply reflects the culture in which they live, or if their personal perspectives actually help to define it. One thing is certain: photographs are multi-layered and do much more than describe the subjects depicted (and sometimes more than the photographer intended). They are read by viewers in ways that one cannot predict, and the value and understanding of a work often changes over time. Yet something remains universal about the process photographers go through to make their images, and a quote from the mid-nineteenth century explains what has not changed in more than a century and a half of photography:

Nothing is so beautiful as the truth, but one must choose it.[1]

The photographs in this book come from what photographers have chosen to represent as their experience of the land, their concerns, their passions and their commentary, and always from their unique moment in time. There may have been a beginning to this visual legacy, but there will hardly be an end. I hope this volume will contribute to the ongoing dialogue between image maker and image reader about the land we live in, and the wild as we perceive it. This is a conversation that is sure to continue through the cultural and technological changes in photography in the years ahead.

Print

STEVE PYNE

I'm a print guy, mostly. Words, not images, are my instinctive medium. So it seemed appropriate that "print," even if it refers to the reproduction of a photo, should be my byline for explaining how I came into this project and what I hope to contribute to it. The fundamental creative tension in *Wild Visions* is the dialogue between Ben and Mark; their conversations never failed to captivate me. I've contributed to the text and in the pauses between their exchanges, but at times served more as a commentator and sidebar.

My own intellectual coming-of-age story with the wild is simple. A few days after I graduated from high school in Phoenix, I found myself on a fire crew at the North Rim of Grand Canyon National Park. I returned for fifteen summers. My adult life began with those experiences. Everything I've written traces its pedigree to the questions raised by fire and the canyon. Even my Ed Abbey connection comes from those days, since for twelve of those summers I was fire crew boss and for two of them, when Ed staffed North Rim Tower, I was nominally Ed's supervisor.

When I began in June 1967, it was four years after the publication of the Leopold Report, and three following the passage of the Wilderness Act. The controversy over building dams at Marble and Bridge Canyons, in the greater Grand Canyon, was just winding down. The idea of the wild was in the air, which on the North Rim (8,000–9,000 feet) was thin but heady. By the time I returned for my second summer the National Park Service had, in the name of naturalness, recanted its all-suppression, all-the-time fire policy in favor of a program of fire restoration.

The rest of the year I went to college, and then to graduate school. The American Civilization program at the University of Texas at Austin had only one core requirement, a field of study in intellectual and cultural history, and you had a choice of two professors; I took William Goetzmann. I learned about the history of ideas and how to think about thinking. A field of study on the American West, taught by John Sunder, introduced Roderick Nash's *Wilderness and the American Mind*, then in its second edition. Here was something I could relate to. It explained how the ideas that swirled around the Grand Canyon's controversies had evolved.

So I learned in Austin that ideas mattered, and at the canyon that ideas had practical consequences. In June 1967 I was taught that fire suppression took precedence over every other park activity except for "the safety and safeguarding of human life." You attacked every fire and stayed with it to the last smoke. In June 1968 I was taught that smoke was as much a part of the rim as cloud was of the canyon. Our new charge was to put good fire back into the woods. Clearly, ideas had significance: the vision of an untrammeled wild had changed what critics had assumed was an immutable commitment to fire exclusion by the federal fire agencies.

In the coming seasons I learned one more thing. Ideas were just words and images unless they were translated into deeds. Season after season, the park struggled to establish a bona fide fire management program, and then just quit. Other concerns—the congestion of river traffic, the throngs of visitors, the desperate drought of water on the South Rim—were more pressing. The North Rim's forests were an accident of political geography, not integral to the canyon. The rim was not legal wilderness; what its fire policy should be was a matter for discretion by the National Park Service. The park decided it had other priorities. It was relatively easy to create a wilderness by legally gazetting borders. It was impossibly tricky to manage it with something as vexing and shape-shifting as free-burning fire.

I ended my summers on the North Rim in September 1981. But I found a surrogate in the White Mountains of Arizona. The landscape had a similar elevation and a comparable forest, with volcanoes instead of canyons. We bought a lot on the south end of Alpine, a hamlet amid the Apache National Forest, and built a cabin. I go often. It's a good reminder of where I came from.

Alpine is Aldo Leopold country. He spent his early years as a forest ranger here. On nearby Escudilla Mountain he wrote about Arizona's last grizzly. On the east fork of the Black River, about a thirty-minute drive south of Alpine, he shot a she-wolf whose dying eyes flashed green fire, a scene he later made famous in "Thinking Like a Mountain," imprinting the wolf into the living emblem of the wild. The region still bears his influence. A little south of Alpine, Mexican grey wolves have been reintroduced. Farther south lies the Bear Wallow Wilderness. The fires that he helped suppress in his early years are, in the name of naturalness, beginning to return.

In June 2011 they returned with vengeance. An abandoned campfire deep in the Bear Wallow Wilderness boiled out of its borders and raced across 538,000 acres, one headfire flying toward our cabin like an arrow. The cabin escaped with hardly a scorch mark—I'd spent twenty years preparing for such a burn. The vegetation took a serious hit, particularly old oaks and young aspen. The bigger challenge, however, may have been to the ideas bequeathed by Leopold, which might be bundled under a general notion of the wild. The Wallow fire burned over both wilderness and backcountry, over wolf-kill and wolf-introduction sites. Red fire met green fire.

The wild could not be abstracted from people. A careless backpacker kindled the fire. The fire threatened small towns, and not just new exurbs; Alpine had been established thirty-three years before Arizona became a state. Amid an Anthropocene in which megafires could ramble over such vast acreages, what did old notions of wilderness mean? If all we wanted was the Wild, we got it with leaping flames and smoke palls well beyond any pretense of control. If what we wanted was a bundle of ecological and cultural goods, then we could well watch it lost piece by piece, or just swallowed in a giant gulp of flame. I wondered if I was not back on the rim and once again watching the irresolvable drama involved in trying to make an ideal real.

The vision inherited from the narrow reading of Leopold could no longer encompass the panorama of threats and responses. It was good to have both the Bear Wallow Wilderness and Mexican grey wolves in the mountains. I feel better even if I only conjure them up from time to time in my mind's eye. We need the wild. But it is no longer enough. The Old Wild like the Old West has passed. I live in a New West, in some ways better and some ways worse, and welcome a New Wild, different from the old but just as distinct, and compelling, and vital.

Discovery
Documentation
Defense

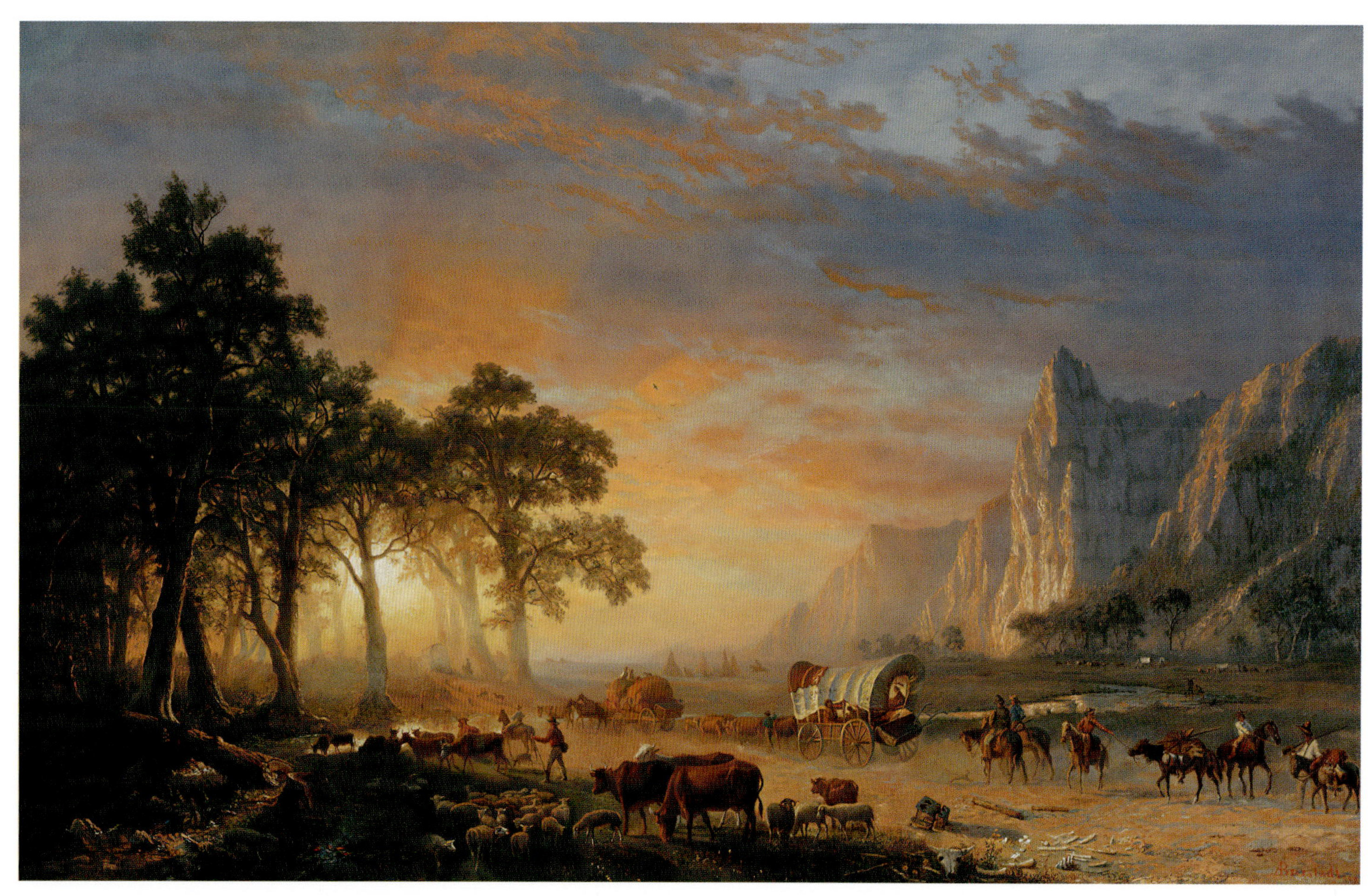

 1. Albert Bierstadt (1830-1902), *Emigrants Crossing the Plains,* 1867 (Oil on canvas, 60 × 96 inches, National Cowboy and Western Heritage Museum, Oklahoma City)

Creation Story

"Wilderness" is an old word that, in the late nineteenth century, acquired a new meaning in the American context. By the time of the Wilderness Act (1964) it served, in select minds, as an informing narrative for the American experience. The wild became inextricably intertwined with a national creation story.

The historical circumstances were the westward expansion of the young American republic (plate 1). Early colonists had spoken of wilderness and deserts and dark, desolate places. New England Puritans had famously pursued an "errand in the wilderness." But wilderness was a murky Other, or more, a vast geographic Otherness, that contrasted with civilization. Much as we measure heroes by the power of their rival villains, so early settlers could measure their triumph against the challenges of the wild. The wild was what you saw on the other side of the frontier; it was what settlement vanquished, as woods, prairies, and wetlands were converted to farms, pastures, and towns.

America, as Walt Whitman famously observed, has multitudes, and that includes multitudes of origin stories. America's indigenous peoples had theirs, and so did the newcomers, whether they came by choice or in chains. But as the country became a political entity, it sought a collective creation story. The Pilgrims offered one; the American Revolution another; but not until James Fenimore Cooper transformed Natty Bumppo, the Leatherstocking, from comic diversion into a protagonist and moral guide did the frontier and its pioneers begin to claim priority. At that point what the pioneers confronted mattered to the narrative. In retrospect it is possible to identify a succession of prophetic voices (including most notably Henry Thoreau's) that urged, as George Catlin did in the 1830s, that some places be set aside to preserve the memory of what had been transformed. Still, it was not an idea taken seriously at the time.

Explorers, often accompanied by artists, added to the imagery. Things began to change with the advent of photography and the completion of the transcontinental railroad in 1869. The West became more accessible, revealing glimpses of itself

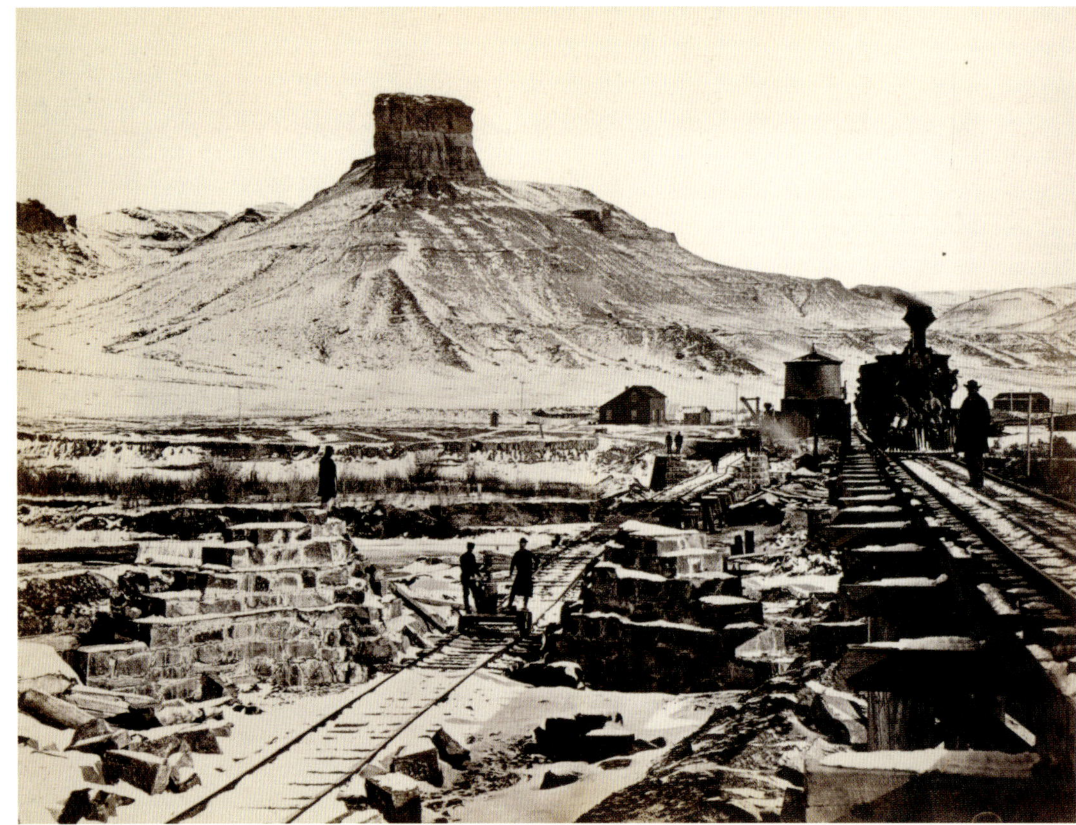

2. Andrew J. Russell (1829–1902), *Construction of the Railroad at Citadel Rock, Green River, Wyoming*, 1869 (Albumen print, Library of Congress, Prints and Photographs Division, Washington, D.C.)

in the pictures made by photographers employed by Union Pacific and Central Pacific, especially A. J. Russell (plate 2). Russell's images circulated in a variety of formats, including as album plates, stereographs, and glass lantern slides. His book *The Great West Illustrated* (1869) reproduced dozens of photographs from his work with the Union Pacific in the 1860s, documenting the region's rugged topography for curious Easterners while also showing, as Martha Sandweiss writes, how American technological power could unlock the nation's vast material treasure.[1] Yet the geographical regard was far from even; western lands east of the 100th meridian, such as the midwestern prairies, lacked the aesthetic qualities and sublime features that would come to define the wilderness in the American environmental imagination.[2]

At the same time, the earlier impulse to appreciate the wild as something more than a commodity persisted. By the late nineteenth century it found celebrated spokespersons like John Muir, and in the mid-twentieth, Aldo Leopold. As less and less land appeared untouched by the rush of frontier settlement, the more what remained seemed precious, and not just on aesthetic grounds. The historian Frederick Jackson Turner, for example, drew a direct connection between the wilderness experience and the shaping of a distinctive political character. His "frontier thesis," originally put forth in a series of essays published in the 1890s, argued that the struggle against the wild inspired an independence and aptitude for self-governance that forged American democracy.[3]

By the mid-twentieth century wilderness had, to some minds, become an indispensable part of a founding dialectic that had made America what it was. In 1964, the same year that President Lyndon Johnson signed the Wilderness Act, Roderick Nash completed his doctoral dissertation, published three years later as *Wilderness and the American Mind*.

His thesis, and the place of wilderness in the American experience, could not be more starkly stated. "Wilderness was the basic ingredient of American culture. From the raw materials of the physical wilderness, Americans built a civilization. With the idea of wilderness they sought to give their civilization identity and meaning."[4] In this recasting the frontier shifted from a contest between pioneers and indigenes, or between an American republic and European empires, or

between old aristocratic societies and a newly democratic one, and metamorphosed into a dialectic between nature and people for which "wilderness" emerged as a common medium. The interaction of civilization and wilderness, with each creating the other, made America.

Wilderness was thus at the nuclear core of the American experiment. While there were many arguments for wilderness preservation—the wild as a lab, as a gym, as a sanctuary, as expression of American exceptionalism—Rod Nash's emphasized a cultural cause. The argument would hinge (eventually) on paradoxes about whether the wild was a physical setting or a state of mind, but an emergent America needed distinctive national symbols, and by the post–World War II era, wilderness had shouldered its way to the table of claimants. As the wilderness idea had grown, so had America as a global power. Its preserved specimens of the wild were what this civilization had that Europeans did not. Yellowstone, Yosemite, Grand Canyon—these were what America boasted of in place of a Roman Colosseum, an Acropolis, a Mont Saint-Michel. It helped that those same mid-century decades had been a time of restrictive immigration and assimilation that let the country meditate on what its identity should be.

But there were also acts of profound historical and cultural omission, the neglect of challenging wilderness narratives that put the lie to the received story of a pristine, people-free, pre-European landscape. The Native American presence was all but expunged from the emerging Euro-American wilderness myth, an erasure of a dynamic and shifting mode of human management of the environment, from earthworks and forest clearing to the use of fire and wildlife management.[5] For example, the Yosemite region, one of the iconic wilderness settings in the American environmental imagination (then and now), bore the influence of the Southern Sierra Miwok, whose activities played a part in shaping the historical ecological conditions of the Sierra Nevada. It was an inconvenient truth for wilderness founders like Muir, whose celebration of an untouched Eden meant that the original myth of the wild hinged on a historical inaccuracy. When joined by bigoted views toward Native Americans, it was not merely ethnocentric but, for future generations, embarrassing.[6]

Still, America's frontier continued in the postwar era, now sprawling through business, institutions, and military posts around the world. But while it looked outward to project its power, America looked inward to decide who it was and to celebrate its presumed exceptionalism. It found land. And especially, it found wilderness.

From Grand Manner to Grand Canyons

Before there were photos there were paintings. When early photographers sought to present landscapes, not just simply document their contents, when, that is, they behaved like artists not as traveling reporters, they saw those prints through a lens shaped by the landscape painters before them. They framed the scenes in the same way. They assumed the same aesthetics, a comparable sense of the sublime. Art came from art. What painters did in oils and canvas, photographers did with emulsions and paper.

The vision of an American landscape as unsullied wilderness, as unfallen nature, was the result of a happy accident that saw an aesthetic turn merge with a nationalistic one. The pedigree of the aesthetics is readily traced. In the late eighteenth century portraiture had enlarged into vast canvases on complex historical subjects, usually drawn from classical sources, such as *The Oath of the Horatii* and *Marius amid the Ruins of Carthage*. The early Enlightenment was an age of neoclassicism (self-consciously referred to in Britain as an Augustan Age).

The earlier models were adapted into more contemporary events such as *The Death of General Wolfe* and *The Raft of the Medusa*. They were carefully balanced compositions, and they were morally charged images, intended to inspire and, in the fullest sense, to serve didactic purposes. In the hands of Sir Joshua Reynolds the result became known as the Grand Manner. The best-known practitioner in the Americas was Benjamin West.

But West, born in British North America, was an awkward model because he had fled the New World for the Old after the American Revolution. In Britain he served the aristocracy and the state. Americans wanted comparable canvases but better suited to the politics and novel landscapes of their fast-growing republic. Instead of human history they turned to natural history. In America's great expanse of fresh countryside they found the sublime. The Grand Manner morphed into a tradition of American landscape.

The usual chronicle grants Thomas Cole and *The Oxbow*, which he painted in 1836, credit as the font (plate 3). The scene

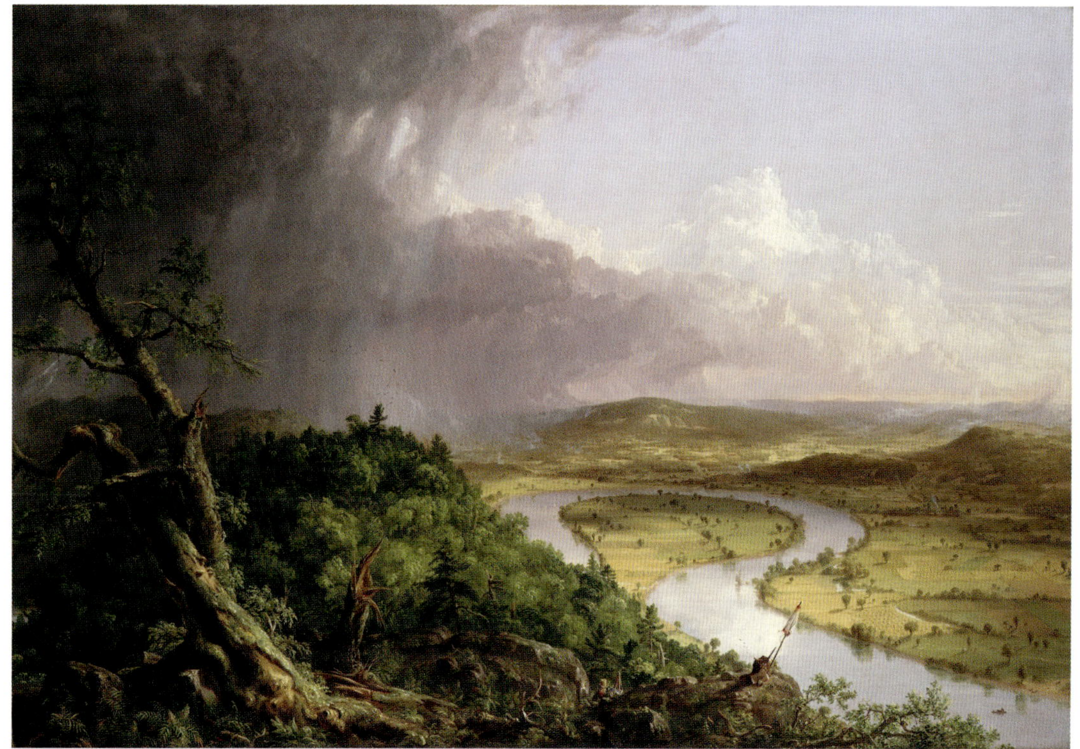

3. Thomas Cole (1801–1848), *View from Mount Holyoke, Northampton, Massachusetts, After a Thunderstorm—The Oxbow,* 1836 (Oil on canvas, 51½ × 76 inches, Metropolitan Museum of Art, New York)

is not wholly wild—it shows farms along the Connecticut River, after all. But the lightning-split tree in the foreground moves the scene well beyond the traditional pastoral. Cole's students and emulators relocated slightly west, to the Hudson River valley, founding America's first internationally recognized school of art. Some painters, like Frederic Church, went farther afield, following Alexander von Humboldt to South America and other explorers to Jamaica and Greenland. And some, like Albert Bierstadt, went west, where the land seemed still dewy with

the Creation and radiant with a kind of naturalized and nationalized religiosity (plate 4).

Here, the timing was ideal. The same year as *The Oxbow,* an uprising split off a big chunk of Mexico into Texas, giving rise to the expression "manifest destiny," and the War Department established a special branch, the Corps of Topographic Engineers, to map and inventory the new lands being added to the national estate. The corps' expeditions expanded dramatically after the Mexican War. Their exploring companies often included artists, of varying skill, so that their inventories included images—drawings, sketches, sometimes fully realized landscapes.

But artists didn't need official expeditions. In 1830 George Catlin traveled to the plains to record, primarily through portraits of Native Americans, what he feared would be a vanishing way of life; when he returned in 1838, he created a museum and gallery for his hundreds of paintings. Similarly, the Swiss artist Karl Bodmer accompanied Prince Maximilian zu Wied-Neuwied from 1832 through 1834 to the plains; and in 1837 Alfred Jacob Miller joined William Drummond Stewart, a Scottish laird, on travels to rendezvous with trappers of the Rocky Mountain fur trade. Collectively, these artists invented western art, among it a tradition of western landscape.

Taken together, they found land, access, aesthetics, and an audience—the citizens of a young republic, eager for emblems of what their grand experiment stood for. Young America had pristine nature. America's peculiar national art was the landscape art that expressed a prelapsarian world, seemingly unmediated by institutions or human contrivance. These were New Worlds preserved, at least on canvas.

Despite their cumbersome apparatus, glass-plate photog-

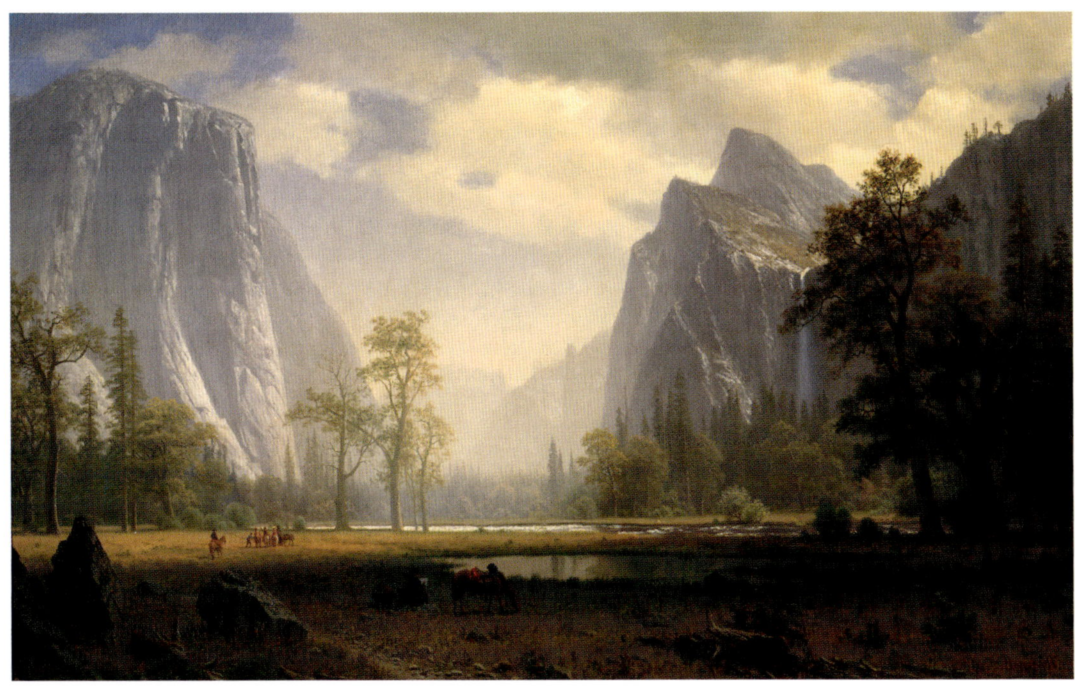

4. Albert Bierstadt (1830–1902), *Looking Up the Yosemite Valley,* ca. 1863–1875 (Oil on canvas, 35⅞ × 58 inches, Haggin Museum, Stockton, California)

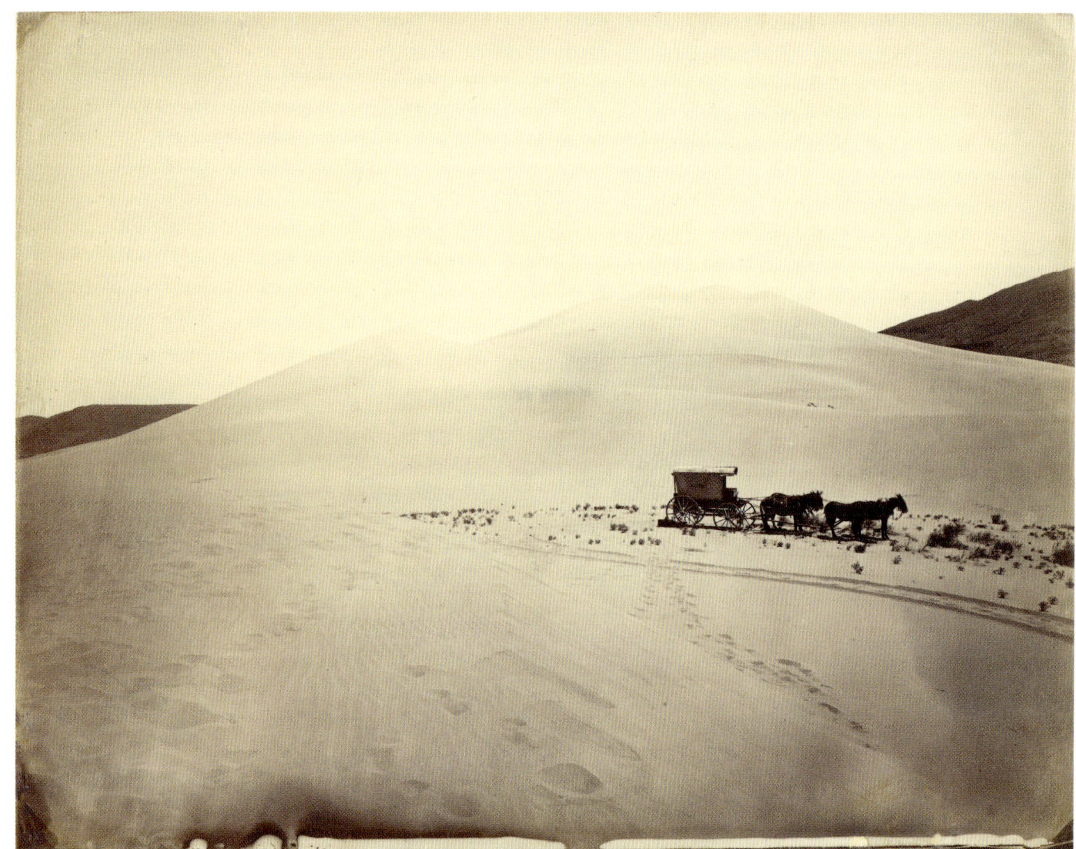

5. Timothy O'Sullivan (1840–1882), *Desert Sand Hills near Sink of Carson, Nevada,* 1867 (Albumen silver print, 8¾ × 11½ inches, The J. Paul Getty Museum, Los Angeles). The footsteps visible in the scene suggest how O'Sullivan went back and forth to the wagon with his wet-plate negative to make this photo.

raphers often attached themselves to the Great Surveys of the post–Civil War era, documenting an American West as both a place of exotic grandeur and as a land ripe with future commercial opportunities. It was work that demanded artistic vision and practical inventiveness in equal measure. Timothy O'Sullivan, who accompanied both the Geological Exploration of the Fortieth Parallel and the Geographical Surveys West of the 100th Meridian, traveled with his own rolling darkroom, a mule-drawn wagon the photographer had converted from a Civil War ambulance (plate 5).

Landscape was still a popular art form. Photos could appear alongside paintings in the narratives and atlases of survey reports; the most famous were probably the operatic canvases of Thomas Moran for Yellowstone and the Grand

Canyon, which appeared with photos by W. H. Jackson and Jack Hillers. The two visions seemed to merge in the magnificent panoramas of William Henry Holmes, so meticulously detailed that they seemed to be drawn through a camera's lens (plate 6).

One of the more striking mirror images can be seen in Jackson's and Moran's depictions of the Mountain of the Holy Cross in the Sawatch Range of the Colorado Rockies. The painter was apparently so impressed by the photographer's image from 1873 that he set out to visit and create his own rendition (plate 7, plate 8).

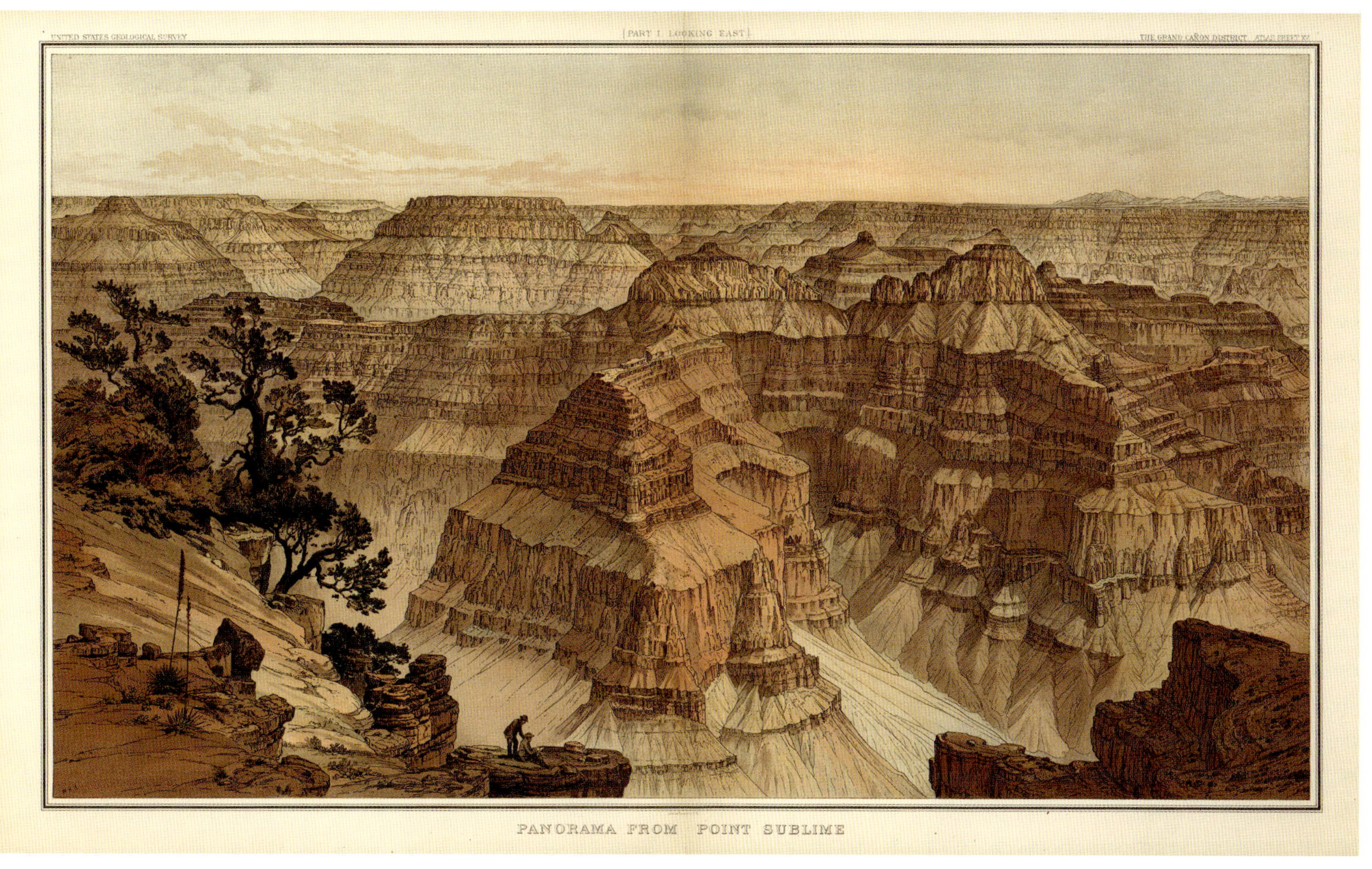

6. William Henry Holmes (1846–1933), *Panorama from Point Sublime* (looking east), 1882, from the *Atlas* to Clarence E. Dutton, *Tertiary History of the Grand Canyon District,* Monograph 2, U.S. Geological Survey (Library of Congress, Geography and Map Division, Washington, D.C.)

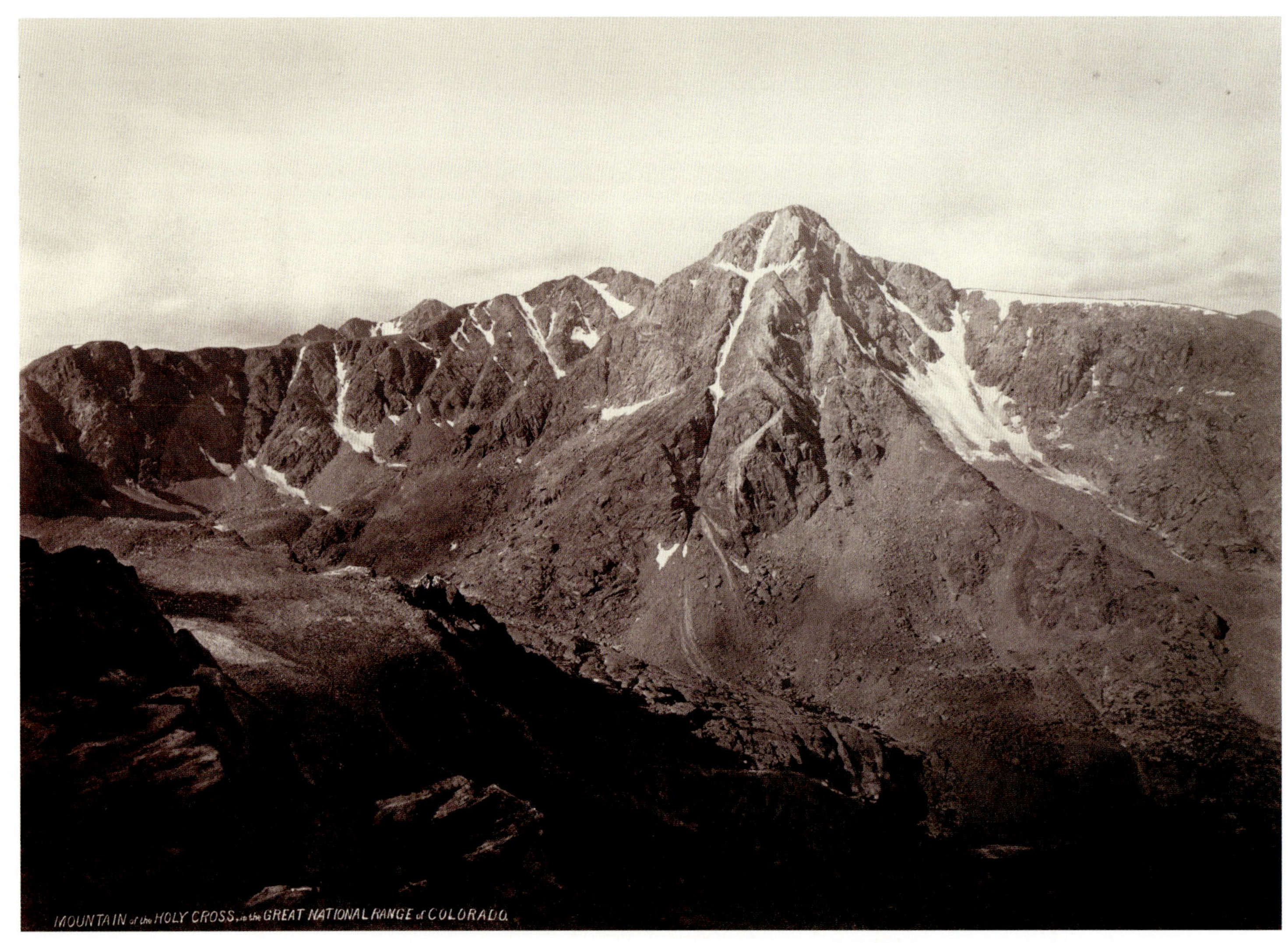

 7. William Henry Jackson (1843–1942), *Mountain of the Holy Cross,* Colorado, 1873 (Albumen silver print, 9¹¹⁄₁₆ × 13¼ inches, The J. Paul Getty Museum, Los Angeles)

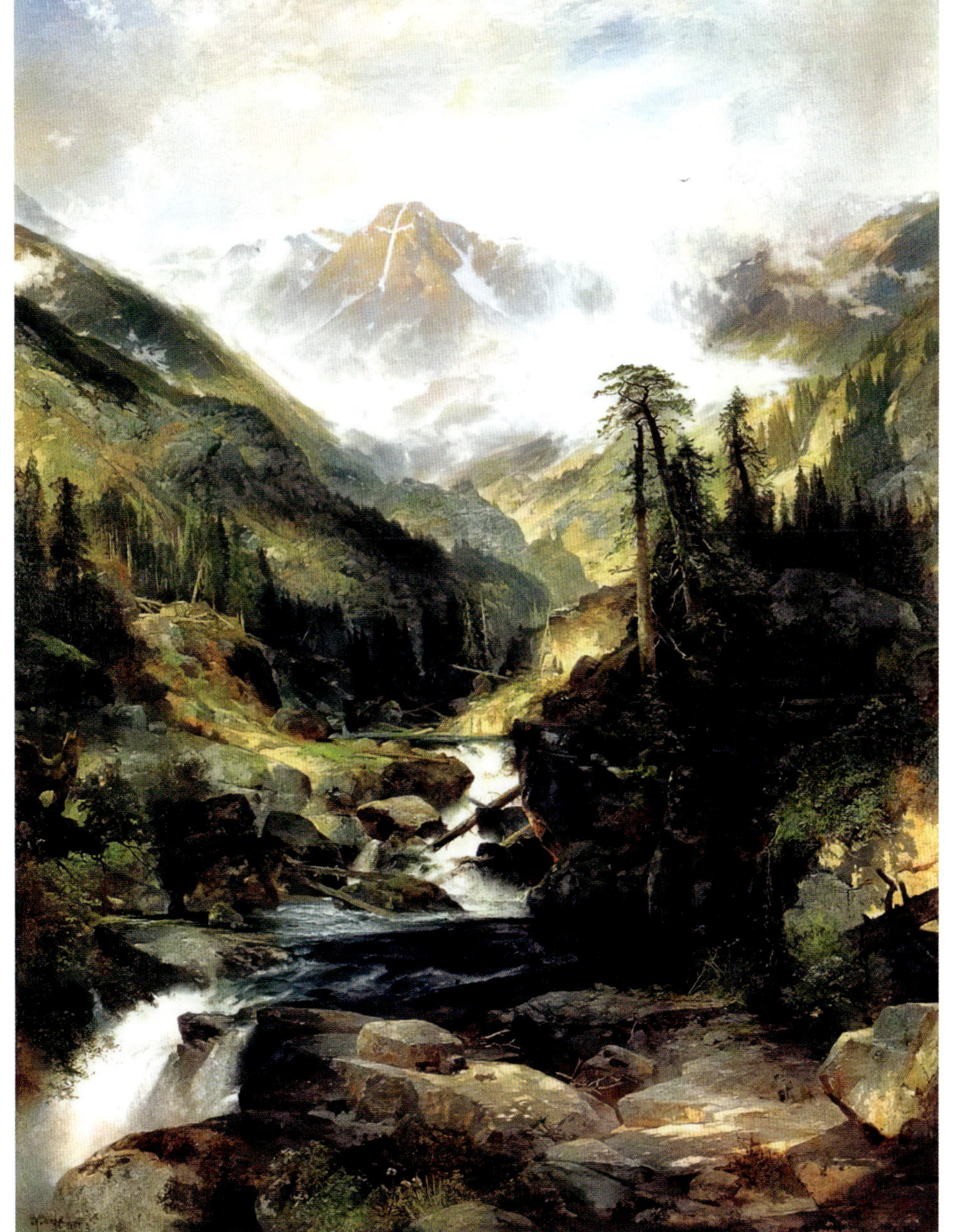

8. Thomas Moran (1837–1926), *Mountain of the Holy Cross*, 1875 (Oil on canvas, 86½ × 77⅛ inches, Autry Museum of the American West, Los Angeles)

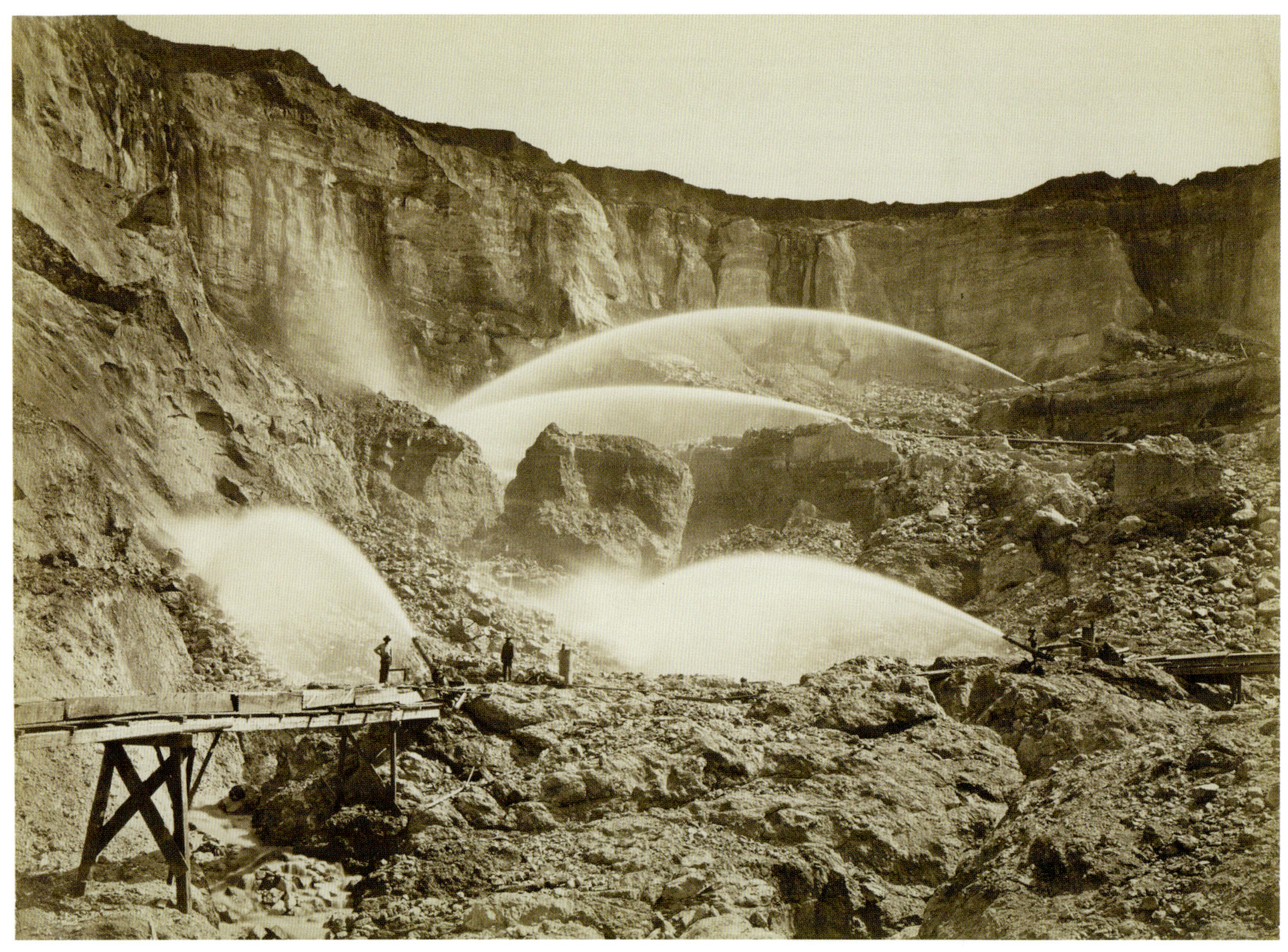

9. Carleton Watkins (1829–1916), *Malakoff Diggings, Nevada County, California*, 1879–1881 (Hearst Mining Collection, Bancroft Library, University of California, Berkeley)

As the images found an audience, they began to shape public attitudes in complex ways. In many cases, they stirred a sentiment toward appreciation, and a desire to protect those remarkable tall trees, peaks, and waters. Carleton Watkins's iconic photographs of Yosemite Valley in the early 1860s, for example, are credited with playing an important role in its designation as a preserve by President Abraham Lincoln in 1864. The Yosemite Grant Act, which also put the nearby Mariposa Big Tree Grove into state hands, created a template for the establishment of national parks in the decades that followed.[1]

The flip side of preservation, though, was exploitation, and Watkins would also capture the accelerating industrialization of the western landscape in the years that followed, a photographic record of technological marvels running alongside nature's own (plate 9). If the early landscape photographs were an introduction to the monumental scenery and wonders of a vista new to most Americans of the time, they also served as celebrations of human ingenuity and engineering might, pictorial paeans to the untapped economic potential of the newly revealed (to Euro-American eyes) West.[2]

Eventually the movement faded. Modernism challenged both the geographic representation and the Romantic aura of those classic landscapes, which faded from prominence. The art of western landscapes became popularized and commercialized into postcards and picture magazines, and eventually into the motion pictures of Hollywood westerns. By then the monumental landscapes were being reserved as parks, national forests, and later wilderness. When a new wave of landscape photographs emerged through people like Ansel Adams, they still echoed, even if in black and white, the aesthetics, assumptions, and ethics of those who had first rendered the American scene into visual art.

Visual Art as Reportage and Advocacy

The grand landscape panoramas were art, of course. But they were also reportage and often an alloy of advertising and advocacy. The primary reason for transporting artists (and later photographers) on expeditions was to visually document the peoples, objects, and scenes encountered. A lot of what was published was drudgery—a record of what was seen, including such mundane objects as shards and rocks. Some of it failed even that task (Lieutenant Amiel Whipple sourly declaimed that the only thing Heinrich Möllhausen ever painted accurately was a Navajo blanket). Some participants, that is, failed both as recorders and as artists.

But outside the pale of the Hudson River, beyond the Shenandoah, across the wide Missouri, what artists saw and rendered into paint and print was novel, and visual journalism was a task expected by the American public. Revealing the unknown was as important as recreating the sublime, and often seemed the same. The public paid to visit Catlin's museum, or to walk through the cyclorama of Frederic

Church's Mississippi River. They went to galleries as they would a circus, to see the curiosities and be awed by the unexpected. Artists were also explorers: they announced discoveries of the previously hidden.

Before Yellowstone's geysers could be celebrated, they had to be found (plate 10). The transfiguration from artifact to art happened subsequently in a studio. Later, after the monumental vistas had hardened into icons, photographers like Eliot Porter looked for the still-hidden niches and scenes overlooked in the first rush of revelation—micro-scenes that miniaturized the monumental. Once unveiled, the question shifted to understanding the scene and deciding what to do with it. Here, again, art assisted by segueing into advocacy.

Thomas Moran's paired paintings of the Yellowstone and the Colorado canyons were deliberately promotional. The first celebrated the Geographical Survey of the Territories under Ferdinand Hayden; the second, the Geographical and Geological Survey of the Rocky Mountain Region under John Wesley

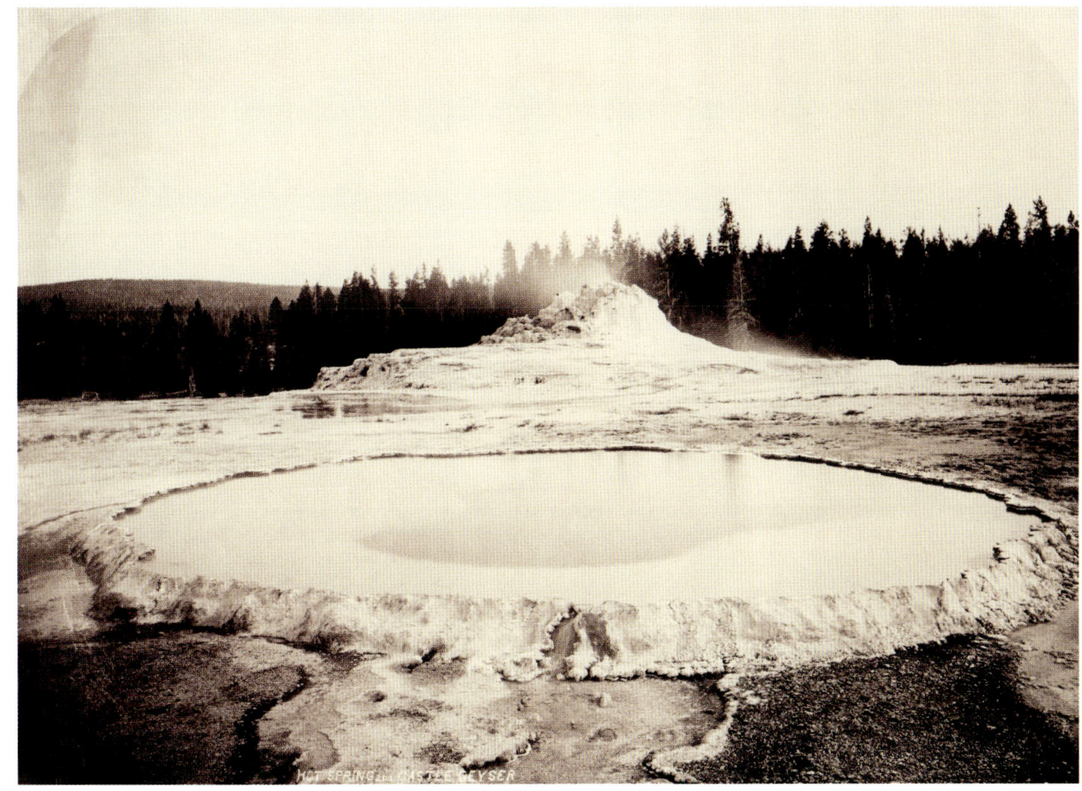

10. William Henry Jackson (1843–1942), *Hot Springs and Castle Geyser*, 1872 (Gelatin silver print, 5⅞ × 8½ inches, Amon Carter Museum of American Art, Fort Worth, Texas)

Powell. Congress bought both canvases and hung them in the Capitol. The effect was to advertise equally the surveys and the nature they used to claim attention.

As with Carleton Watkins's photos of Yosemite Valley in the early 1860s, Moran's works contributed to arguments for preservation, almost immediately at Yellowstone, with the nation's first national park created in 1872. The second came much later, after political squabbles were worked through, and after William H. Holmes, once a Hayden Survey artist, later one for the U.S. Geological Survey, still later curator for the National Gallery, organized an exhibit of canyon art in 1918 to promote the establishment of a national park. The park's organic act followed the next year.

The model of artistic activism for wilderness preservation would be repeated again in the 1930s, when Ansel Adams made a series of pictures documenting the remote Kings Canyon region south of Yosemite. Adams, whose early musical ambitions soon became overtaken by his love of photography, joined

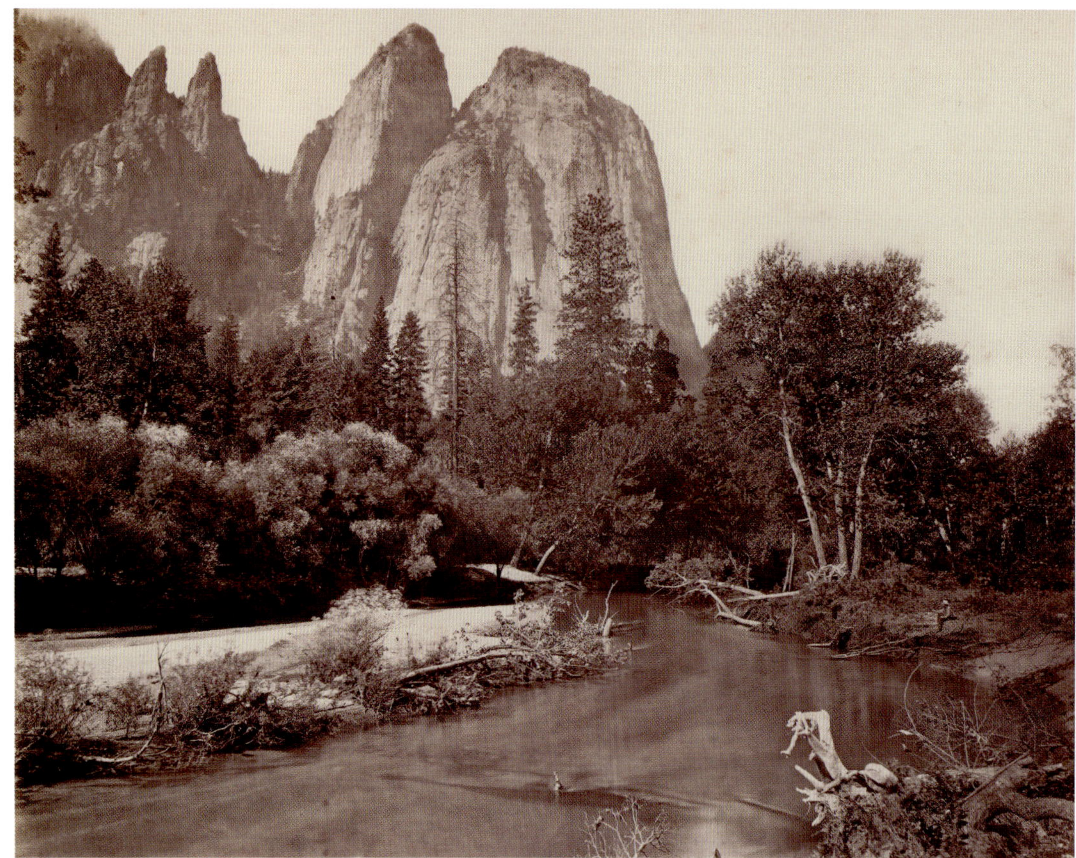

11. Eadweard Muybridge (1830–1904), *Cathedral Rocks, Valley of the Yosemite,* 1872 (Albumen mammoth plate print, Eadweard Muybridge mammoth plate photographs of Yosemite, PC-RM-OV-Muybridge, courtesy, California Historical Society, OV-RM Muybridge_003.jpg)

the Sierra Club in 1919 when he took a job as a custodian of the LeConte Memorial Lodge in Yosemite, which served as the club's valley headquarters.[1] After an early flirtation with pictorialism, a photographic movement defined by soft images and textured prints that resembled etchings, Adams emerged as a full-blown modernist by the late 1920s, and he began to produce images displaying the straight style, sharp focus, and mastery of light and shadow that became his aesthetic calling card (plate 11, plate 12).[2] Adams's pictures were undeniably awe-inspiring; with the publication of the Sierra Club books in the 1960s they became canonized. But they also created a set of powerful expectations about the wild as a sublime and dramatic photographic subject, with implications for how we should relate to it.

Adams's photographs of the Kings River Canyon began to appear in the *Sierra Club Bulletin* in the mid-1920s; a decade later the club was pushing for the area's protection in the midst of a struggle between the U.S. Forest Service and the National Park Service over its management as a wilderness park.[3] Recognizing the power of Adams's pictures and seeing an opportunity to move the legislative needle, the club asked Adams to attend a parks conference in Washington, D.C., in January 1936 to lobby Congress for the establishment of Kings Canyon National Park. As he recounted many years later: "I ventured into the strange wilderness of our nation's capital with a portfolio of photographs under my arm, visiting congressmen and senators in

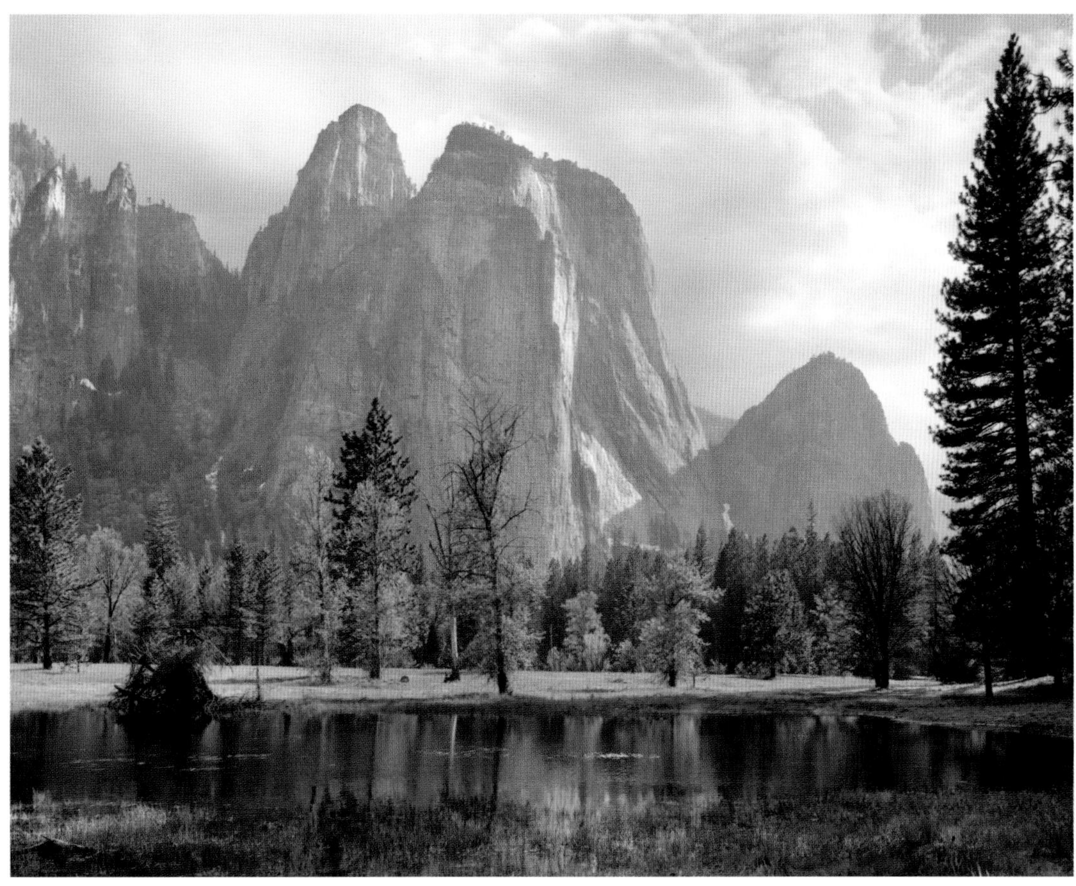

12. Ansel Adams (1902–1984), *Cathedral Spires and Rocks, Late Afternoon, Yosemite National Park,* 1949, gelatin silver print, printed 1960. In this photograph Adams has refined away much of the roughness of Muybridge's photograph from the same location (shown in the previous plate) and provided a more commanding sense of scale. Also, unlike Muybridge's image, which captured a human figure in the lower right corner, Adams's scene carries no visible trace of human presence, a motif that reinforced his presentation of such places as uniquely pure and pristine. (Smithsonian American Art Museum, gift of Bernie Stadiem, 1992.20.1; courtesy of the Center for Creative Photography, © the Ansel Adams Publishing Rights Trust)

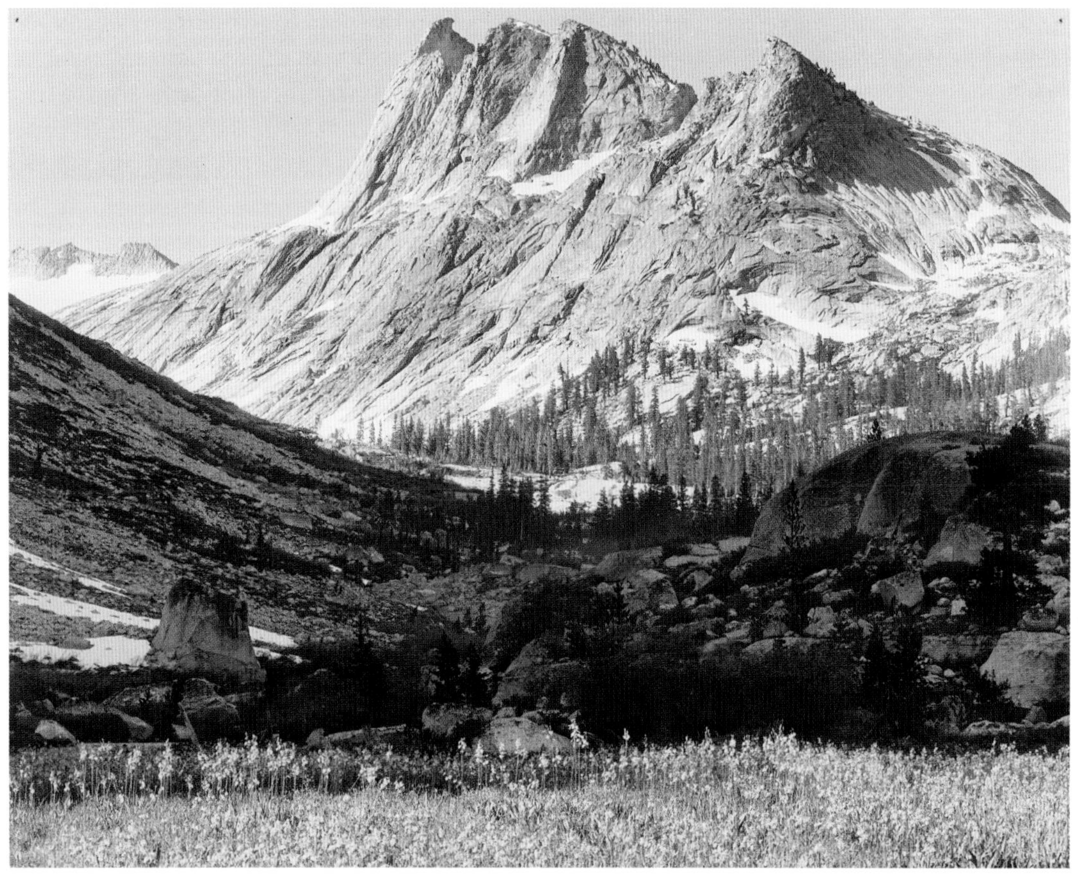

13. Ansel Adams, *Boaring River, Kings Region, Kings River Canyon (Proposed as a national park), California,* 1936 (National Archives and Records Administration, College Park, Maryland)

their lairs. I boldly proclaimed the glories of the High Sierra and showed my pictures with the unabashed confidence that they would prove our contention" (plate 13).[4] Adams was by then well aware of the power of imagery to shape political judgment regarding nature preservation, having noted the influence of pictures made by Watkins and Jackson on the preservation of Yosemite and Yellowstone, respectively.

In 1938, Adams published his first book of landscape photography, *Sierra Nevada: The John Muir Trail,* which included many images from the Kings River Canyon area. He sent a copy of his new book to the director of the National Park Service, who in turn shared it with the interior secretary. It eventually ended up in the hands of President Franklin D. Roosevelt, who in 1940 signed legislation creating Kings Canyon National Park.

Although it's too simplistic to draw a direct line from pictures to policy, the photographs clearly had an influence, and collected in book form, a publishing-as-advocacy precedent was set. As Arno B. Cammerer, director of the Park Service during the campaign to protect the area, wrote to Adams, "So long as that book is in existence, it will go on justifying the park."[5]

Meanwhile the surveys published official reports and accompanying atlases, often with dramatic illustrations of the wonders they had discovered. It was an old practice, used to great effect for the voyages of Captain James Cook and perhaps most spectacularly realized in the multi-volume *Voyage to the Equinoctial Regions of the New Continent* published by Alexander von Humboldt. It was a durable strategy for rallying elite (and public) enthusiasm. Well before the early 1950s, however, the tradition was looking more than a little shopworn as a vehicle for publicizing geographic discovery; Antarctica, the deep oceans, and space were more likely to involve moving pictures or images from robots.

But as a strategy for promoting America's natural wonders it was ready for an upgrade as the Bureau of Reclamation made plans that threatened to submerge existing parks. The breakthrough event was a proposal to construct a dam at Echo Park, then part of Dinosaur National Monument along the Colorado-Utah border, a fossil-rich array of canyons and mountain areas traversed by the Green and Yampa Rivers. Some forty-three years after the clash at Hetch Hetchy, in which Yosemite Valley's geologic twin was submerged, it appeared that the same issue had returned. A key component of the environmentalist pushback was a book, *This Is Dinosaur: Echo Park and Its Magic Rivers,* published by Alfred A. Knopf in 1955. The driving force behind both the campaign and the book was David Brower,

then the Sierra Club's executive director. Brower asked the novelist and historian Wallace Stegner to edit the book with the hope that it would tip the scales in the preservationists' favor.

It was a hybrid volume—hybrid in its design, half modern, half echoing the style of the classic reports of explorers; hybrid in its theme, that heritage as well as wilderness was at risk. If a second national park could be violated, then none were safe. Photographer Philip Hyde provided many of the book's photographs, including a memorable picture of Steamboat Rock, which would become one of the park's most familiar landmarks.

A documentation of the beauty of a remote and little-known western landscape, *This Is Dinosaur* was also a plea for restraint in the nation's hell-bent drive to develop the remains of the American West. Although the editor Stegner emphasized that the wilderness at Echo Park was not to be shielded from all human use and enjoyment—he celebrated its ruggedness and remoteness as supplying a special kind of recreational and cultural value—he reminded readers that some uses, such as damming and flooding to create a reservoir, were destructive and likely permanent. And he warned of a tendency to "over-engineer ourselves" to the point that "the open and the green and the quiet, might not survive the bulldozer."[6]

Text and image reinforced one another to illustrate what was at stake at Dinosaur. As the historian Mark Harvey writes, the book also solidified the connection between the wilderness and the protection of the national parks and provided an interlinked visual and textual argument for preservation that defined much of the ethos of wilderness activism for generations.[7] The publisher agreed to provide a copy of the book to every member of Congress; unlike the tale of Hetch Hetchy in Yosemite, the Echo Park dam proposal died.

The same strategy for advocacy, though on a wider geographical scale, returned in 1960 with *This Is the American Earth*, a collaboration between Ansel Adams and Nancy Newhall (who provided the text), an expensive and exquisitely produced volume inspired by an earlier exhibition of Adams's photos at the LeConte Lodge in Yosemite. Published by the Sierra Club, the book celebrated a vision of wild nature that Adams became well known for—dramatic, sublime, and largely devoid of human presence. But it also issued a warning about the wild's fragility and tenuousness in the face of steamrolling urban sprawl and commodity production. If we weren't solicitous of the scattered wild remnants we had left, wrote Justice William O. Douglas in a blurb on the book's back cover, there would be only "sadness and tragedy ahead."

The success of *This Is the American Earth* spurred Brower's Sierra Club to begin publishing a series of large-format coffee-table volumes, gorgeous with color images, to promote wilderness. The impulse quickened when the Bureau of Reclamation prepared to dam the Colorado River above and below the Grand Canyon, but within the historic dimensions of the river for someone rafting through it. Again, with the text-and-image books as promotional instruments, the environmentalists triumphed. A pristine image of a pristine place, pivoting on a clever figure of speech, could defend wild places against the grubby calculations of engineers.

Although the "Exhibit Format" series waned by the late 1960s (coinciding with Brower's departure from the club), the use of landscape and wilderness photography as environmental and political advocacy by no means disappeared. In the following decades artists grew and diversified the tradition, from documenting the scarring of the American Southwest by military testing to recording the aesthetic, ecological, and cultural impacts of mining, pollution, fossil-fuel dependence, and human-driven climate change. In a number of cases these contemporary wilderness and landscape photographers have maintained the thematic tradition of the older Sierra Club volumes in their presentations of natural beauty in peril, even as their projects have taken on the aesthetic and political concerns of the current scene. And they continue to work at the photographer's task articulated by Ansel Adams more than half a century ago; namely, to reveal natural beauty and the duty to preserve it, as well as to stir, as he put it, "the deepest concern about our hazardous tenure on the planet."[8]

For the public, the Sierra Club books, particularly their stellar images, helped identify the kinds of places worth preserving.[9] But they also had a problematic consequence for the moral and aesthetic appreciation of the environment beyond the traditional wilderness vista. By implication, they suggested that places less pure, less transcendent, less aesthetically mesmerizing, might not be worth saving. Like America's lands, aesthetics was polarizing into the purely wild and the purely built. As time wore on it was clear, too, that they left us in a kind of metaphysical and practical bind: Adams's pictures, and those of many of the photographers working in the Sierra Club style, tended to narrow the options for interacting with the wide nature that filled the lens; we could either be tourists who briefly step in and out of the picture, leaving little trace, or despoilers threatening its very existence. It wasn't always clear how we were to fit into the scene in the more harmonious and durable way that Adams and his Sierra Club allies envisioned.

But wilderness was also only a sliver of American nature. Other places, even those inhabited by people, even those built by people, might also hold environmental and aesthetic interest and be worthy of attention. As we'll see, photographers working in this mode continued a legacy of reportage—this is what the western landscape is like; but as they turned away from the spectacular and toward more vernacular settings, the frame of reference shifted. They did not invoke the sensibility of the sublime, except in its ambiguous appeal to awe. Just as the task of protecting or in many cases restoring such places required many kinds of techniques and land designations, so the task of valorizing them demanded other images and other words.

About the Gallery

BEN A. MINTEER (BAM): Mark, in this chapter we talk about Ansel Adams's work as representing the "Sierra Club style" of landscape photography. How do you see that style?

MARK KLETT (MK): Actually, I hadn't thought of a "Sierra Club style" as it relates to the individual photographers. For example, I think Ansel Adams was pursuing his own vision, and used the technical methods he became famous for to make compelling photographs that satisfied his creative needs.

BAM: The Sierra Club Exhibit Format books ended up featuring the work of many other photographers, including Eliot Porter and Philip Hyde, who had their own techniques and styles. Porter, for example, was a pioneer in color photography and often worked close-up, zooming in on smaller natural features. But does a "Sierra Club style" signal any dominant aesthetic tradition to you—or maybe a technical one? The union of landscape photography and environmental advocacy also comes to mind when we think about the work of these photographers in the Sierra Club folio series. So maybe it's "all of the above"?

MK: As the work was published and was made accessible to a large audience, the publications themselves perhaps took on a particular look and presence that helped to define how we see the work. I do think the act of making a book also influences a photographer's practice because it focuses the work for an intended audience.

BAM: So it's a case where some of us writing in environmental studies circles who look at these texts as signifying a fairly coherent series have projected back onto the individual photographers—a sensibility that comes more from our reception of the books, maybe, than anything the individual photographers were actually doing. Still, I'm intrigued by what you say about focusing the work for a particular audience, something Adams was a master at doing, right?

MK: I think the photographers were very much engaged in the environmental messages you're receiving from the books, but the creative process is not as simple or linear as pasting those concerns onto an image. The making of the photograph and the later editing and presentation of the work are separate parts of the creative process.

Regarding how he made his photographs, Adams is thought of in the photographic community as an expert at his craft, and he's best known for the idea of "pre-visualization." That is, he was able to use his technical expertise to visualize what the final print would look like at the time he made his initial exposure in the camera. I think this is where the art of photography resided for him, in the transformation of the scene into an image he visualized in his mind, through the intentional control of the photographic process. This kind of technical mastery is sometimes considered a West Coast American tradition in photography, but it did have enormous influence in the field everywhere.

STEVE PYNE (SP): So you think he visualized not just the photos, but also their reception? And his own?

MK: I do wonder if Adams could have pre-visualized the trajectory of his career and its influence on the environmental community. My guess is that he had strong feelings about wild places that influenced his practice, even early on, and that later in his career he was able to use the photographs he'd been making for decades to sharpen his message and affect a larger public audience. It's a question I would refer to the photo historians.[10]

But I'd be curious how the Sierra Club folio series affected the thinking of people in your field, Ben and Steve. When you look at pictures like this, do you think transparently of the place and its issues, or do you consider how the photograph makes a statement? Not just as the record of a place, but as the vision of an individual maker?

BAM: Well, for a long time, I probably thought mostly of the place and the arguments that played out in these scenes, as you say. I do think it can be difficult for those coming more from

the text side of things in environmental studies to also see these events and places through the photographs, that is, as expressions and artistic visions valuable for their own sake as well as their service to a particular cause or campaign.

SP: I wonder if we're wrangling with disciplinary divides. Artists are naturally inclined to emphasize their individual visions. Scholars are always looking for patterns and trends, and can dismiss (perhaps too flippantly) personal distinctions as the narcissism of small differences. I'm inclined to trace the Sierra Club books to the reports of western explorers and William Holmes's 1918 exhibit of Grand Canyon art at the National Portrait Gallery, where aesthetics and advocacy merged. I think there is a strong sense that the Sierra Club books not only shaped an era but serve as useful emblems for it.

BAM: When I look at the following gallery, images such as David Hanson's photo of mining scars in Colorado (plate 15) and Subhankar Banerjee's work (plate 17), which effectively ties preservationists' fight against the development of the Arctic National Wildlife Refuge to Alaskan tribes' natural and cultural heritage, the link to Ansel Adams's use of photography to press for environmental protection seems clear.

And yet photos like Hanson's, as well as those by Sharon Stewart (plate 16), Victoria Sambunaris (plate 18), and Terry Evans (plate 19), seem more confrontational and, well, angrier than Adams's images of, say, Kings Canyon. The celebration of natural beauty has receded in this newer work and the link to action seems more present, more in-your-face. How do you see pictures like these fitting in the earlier photographic advocacy tradition of Adams and others working in his style?

MK: Maybe you're right to think that the tone of the work has become more strident today, and perhaps it should. But of course advocacy has been a part of photographic tradition since the early days of the medium. In this chapter we also see a William Henry Jackson photograph of Hot Springs and Castle Geyser (1872). As we've discussed, Jackson's photographs played an important role in convincing Congress to create the first national park in Yellowstone. From history we understand that photographs have the power to convince viewers that one place is beautiful enough to protect or preserve, or more recently, that another place has been devastated by human abuse that needs to be addressed. Without images that show us these things, how will we develop empathy for the places we cannot see or visit?

SP: Unless you have lived and are rooted in a place for a long time. These images are necessary because we are dealing with people confronting landscapes as newcomers. They don't have an organic connection to these lands. They have to find alternatives if they wish to preserve fragments of it. Images are great ways to do that.

MK: I still think photographers work to exercise their personal visions of the world, but it's always been interesting to me to see how an audience interprets photographs, and that has changed over time. For example, if a photograph shows a landscape stripped of trees, littered with stumps, with a smokestack belching black smoke, we might interpret that image negatively from our twenty-first-century perspective.

But from a nineteenth-century perspective such a picture may have been seen as a good thing—nature was being tamed, and progress was being made toward achieving national destiny (a dual reading we can see, for example, in some of Carleton Watkins's work). So if we reversed the question, and could somehow go back in time and show Terry Evans's photo of a North Dakota oil pad to one of William Henry Jackson's contemporaries, that person might think it was a wonderful sign of civilization's advance.

SP: I think the growing consensus about an Anthropocene, of humanity's capacity to remake the earth from its atmosphere to its oceans to the biosphere, is breaking down the old dichotomies. It's not about people or the wild; it's all about people doing stuff everywhere at various intensities. Contemporary images will show this sensibility.

MK: We know now that encouraging preservation is only part of what photographs can do. It's no longer a matter of setting aside for posterity lands that are beautiful or worthy of scenic wonder. The lands we inhabit every day are more often the subjects of contemporary photography, as those places often struggle with environmental dangers. And I think there's a heightened feeling by many photographers that we need to act more quickly, that timeliness is critical.

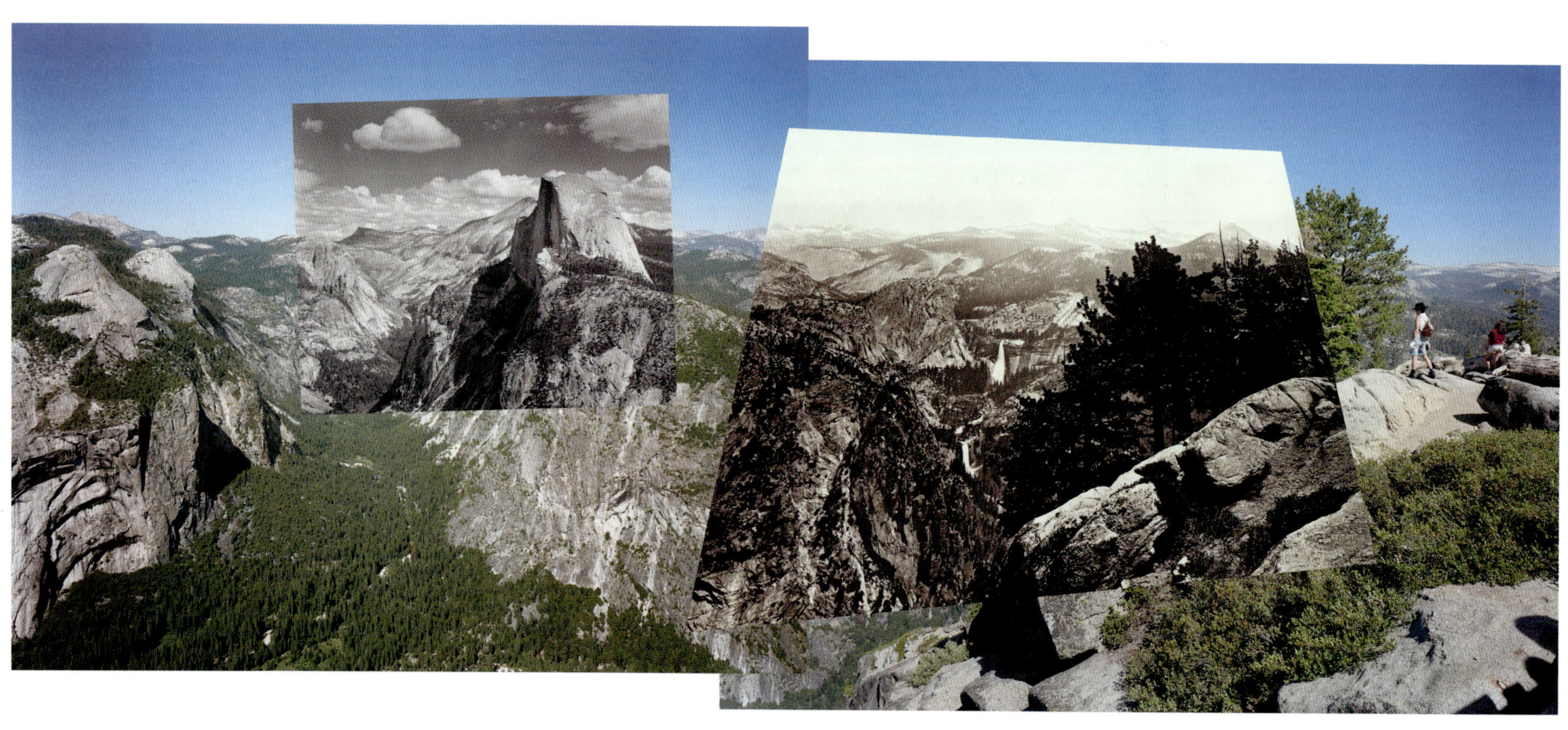

14. Byron Wolfe and Mark Klett, *View from the Handrail at Glacier Point Overlook, Connecting Views from Ansel Adams to Carleton Watkins*, 2003

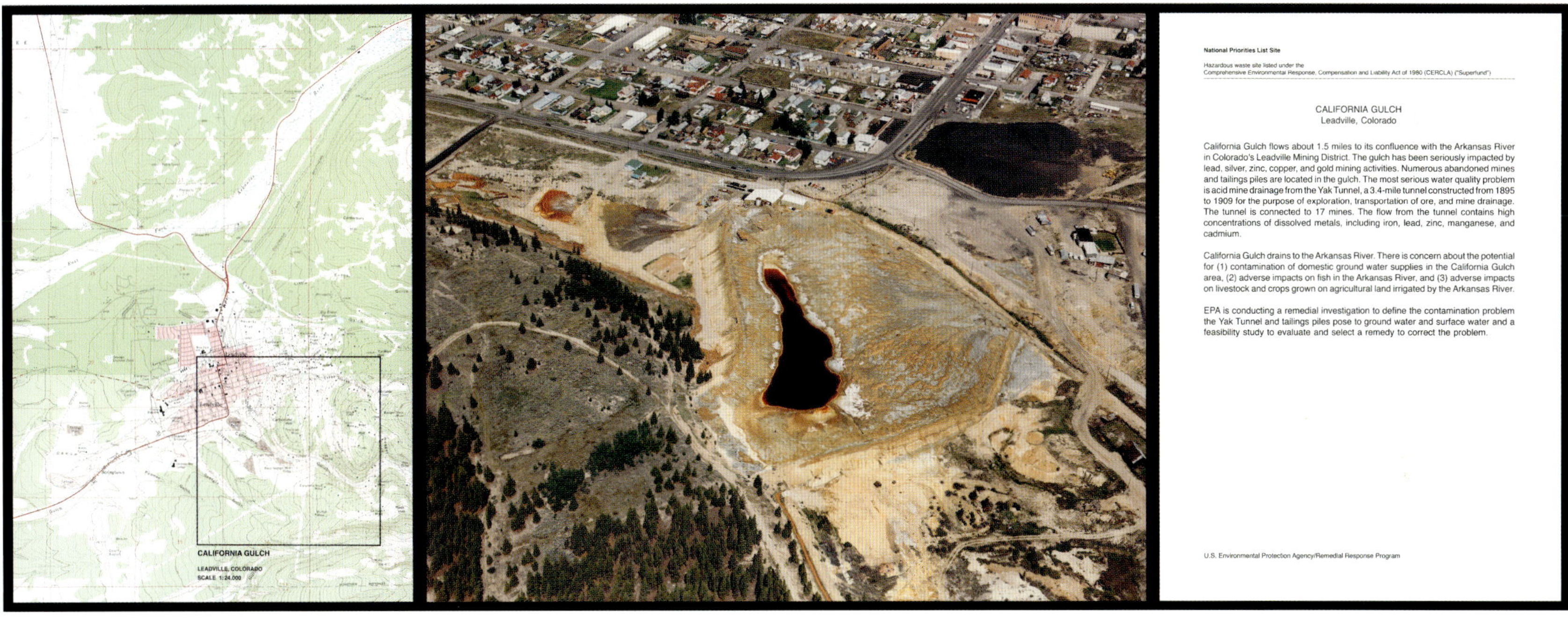

National Priorities List Site

Hazardous waste site listed under the
Comprehensive Environmental Response, Compensation and Liability Act of 1980 (CERCLA) ("Superfund")

CALIFORNIA GULCH
Leadville, Colorado

California Gulch flows about 1.5 miles to its confluence with the Arkansas River in Colorado's Leadville Mining District. The gulch has been seriously impacted by lead, silver, zinc, copper, and gold mining activities. Numerous abandoned mines and tailings piles are located in the gulch. The most serious water quality problem is acid mine drainage from the Yak Tunnel, a 3.4-mile tunnel constructed from 1895 to 1909 for the purpose of exploration, transportation of ore, and mine drainage. The tunnel is connected to 17 mines. The flow from the tunnel contains high concentrations of dissolved metals, including iron, lead, zinc, manganese, and cadmium.

California Gulch drains to the Arkansas River. There is concern about the potential for (1) contamination of domestic ground water supplies in the California Gulch area, (2) adverse impacts on fish in the Arkansas River, and (3) adverse impacts on livestock and crops grown on agricultural land irrigated by the Arkansas River.

EPA is conducting a remedial investigation to define the contamination problem the Yak Tunnel and tailings piles pose to ground water and surface water and a feasibility study to evaluate and select a remedy to correct the problem.

U.S. Environmental Protection Agency/Remedial Response Program

15. David T. Hanson, *California Gulch, Leadville, Colorado, 1985–1986* (From *Waste Land,* by David T. Hanson [Taverner Press, 2018], courtesy of David T. Hanson)

16. Sharon Stewart, *Entrance to Texas Low Level Radioactive Waste Disposal Authority Monitoring Station. Previous Day's Rainfall: 2.72 inches* (© 1990, Sharon Stewart)

Entrance to Texas Low Level Radioactive Waste Disposal Authority Monitoring Station
Previous Day's Rainfall: 2.72 Inches

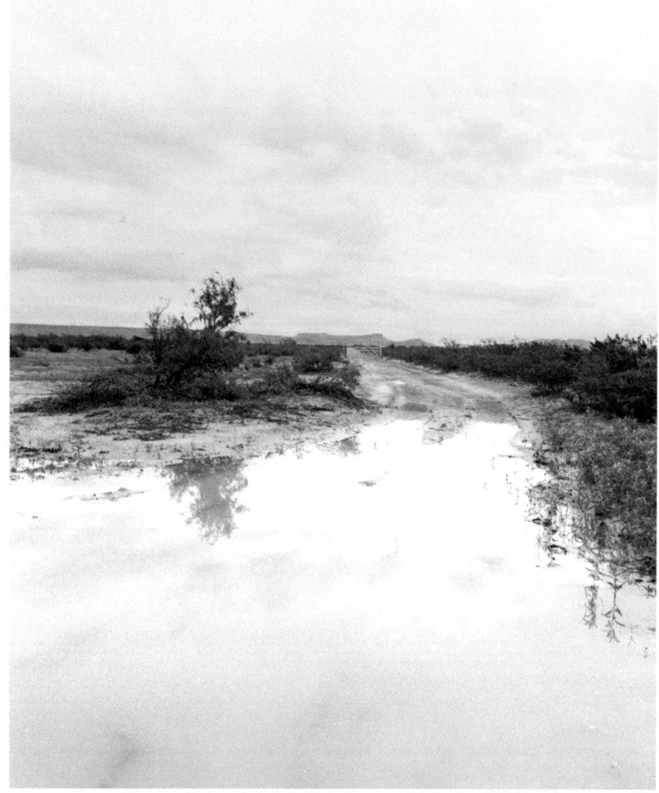

Between the two gates is the worst part of this whole road where the water collects. The water along here was two feet deep. You couldn't even see the bottom of the mesquites. I tried to pull out and got stuck here for two hours. This is by far the wettest, most runoff area: that's why I couldn't believe anyone would put the site here. They've (Texas Low Level Radioactive Waste Disposal Authority) had their brown Suburban stuck up to the rear window in mud over there.

Mary Alcorn, Resident
MacGuire Ranch

This court declares that the Fort Hancock site violates...the 100 Year Floodplain Exclusionary Zone; the Floodplain Standard...Minimalization of Upstream Drainage Standard...the Potential Disposal Site Protocol; the Statewide Site Selection Protocol; Determination of Area for Suitable Protocol...as set forth in the Plaintiff's Fourth Amended Original Petition for Declamatory Judgement, Mandamus Injunction.

Judgment Excerpt
El Paso County, et alia v. TLLRWDA, et alia
District Judge William Moody, Presiding

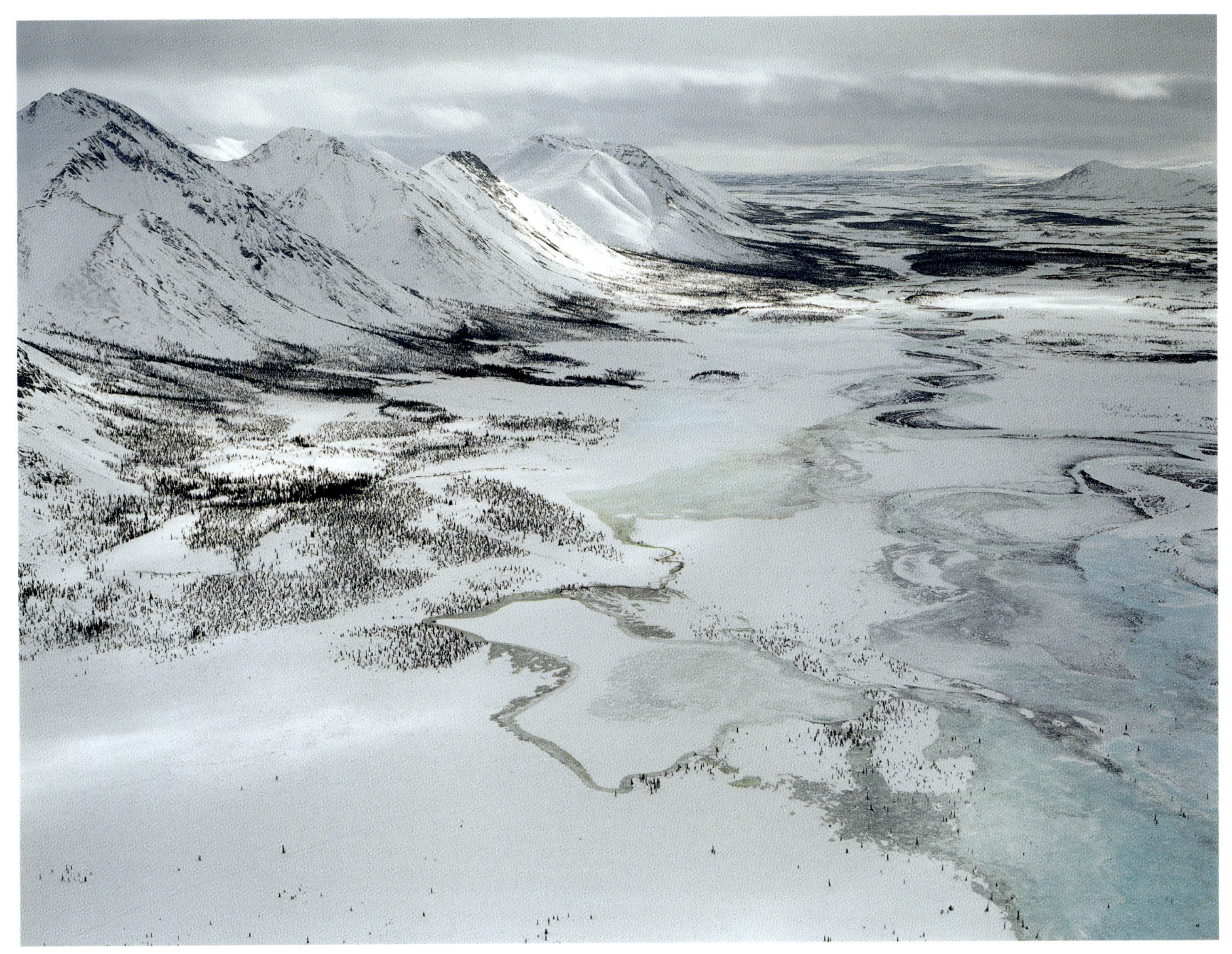

17. Subhankar Banerjee, *Sheenjek River II: A Gwich'in Homeland*, 2002

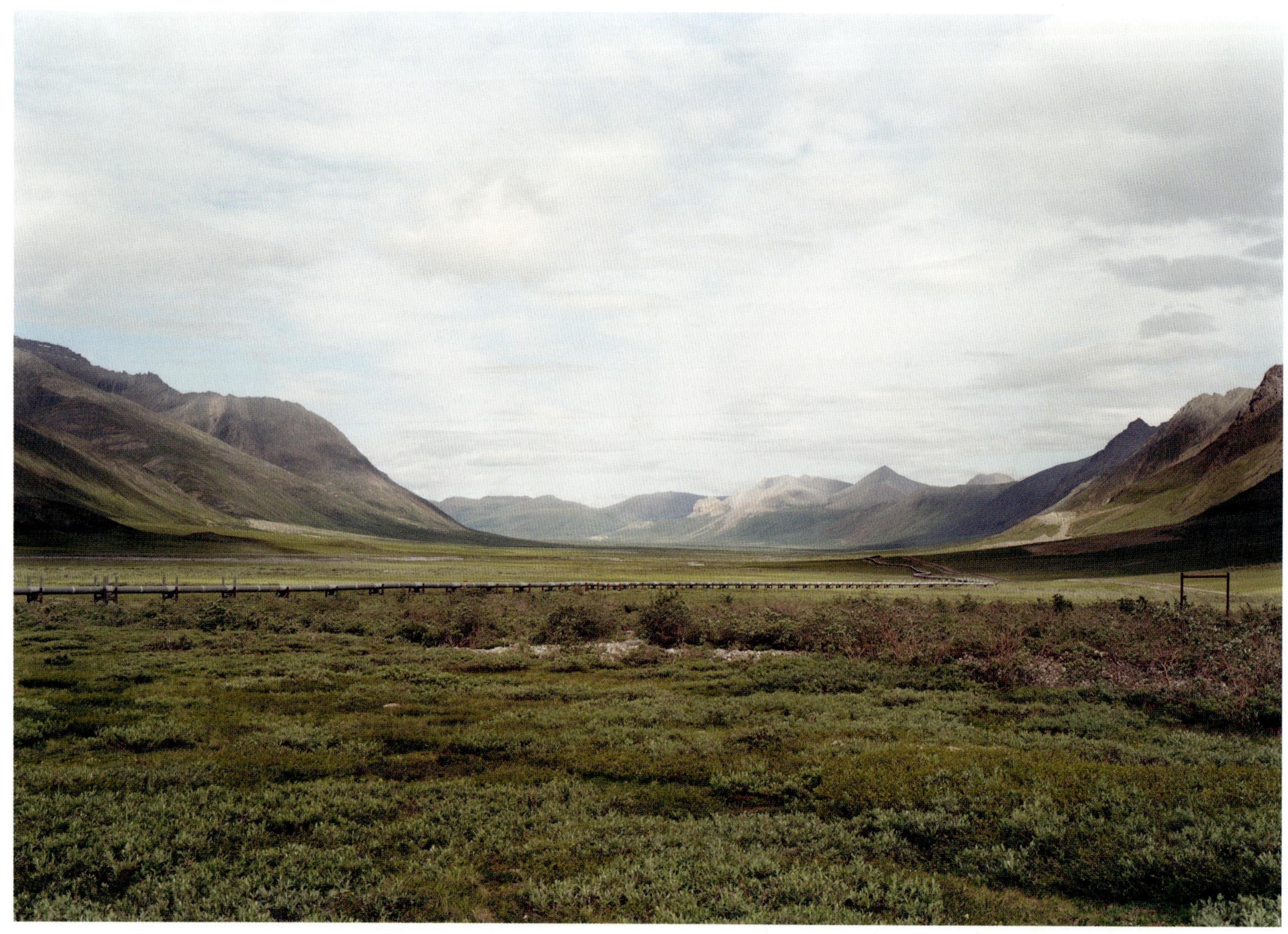

18. Victoria Sambunaris, *Untitled (Alaskan Pipeline at Antigun Pass), Brooks Range, Alaska,* 2003

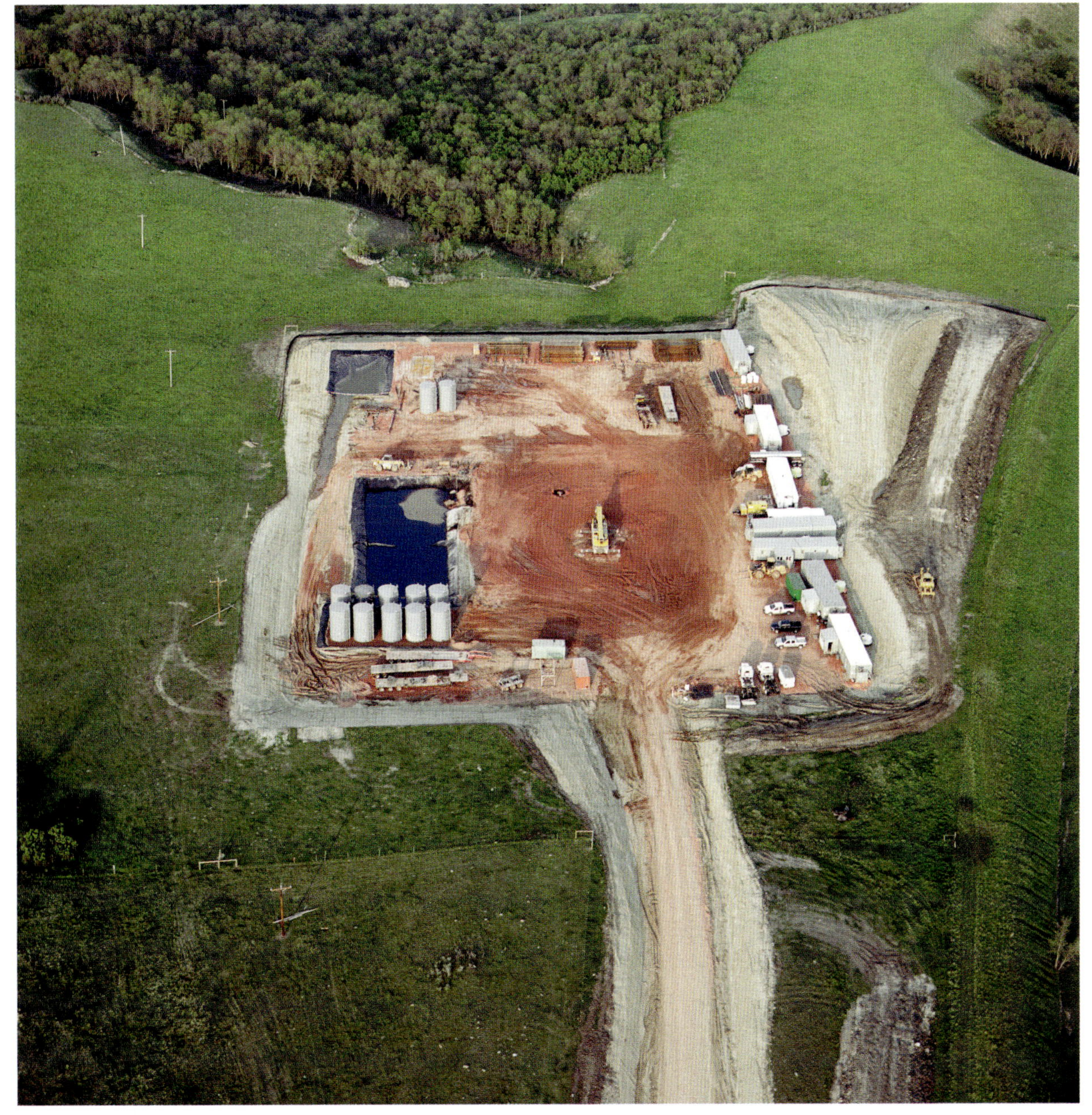

19. Terry Evans, *Davis Oil Pad, Near White Earth, North Dakota,* June 6, 2011

The Power of the Wild

At the end of August 1846, Henry David Thoreau set out for Mount Katahdin, the highest peak in Maine. Rugged, remote, and blanketed by the North Woods, at the time of Thoreau's trip it was little known outside of the region's Native American communities, including the Penobscot, who believed that an evil spirit summered on the top. The mountain wasn't even surveyed until 1804, more than a century after Mount Washington, its more popular New Hampshire cousin. Thoreau was beguiled by its off-the-beaten-path status, taking great delight in the fact that, as he put it, "it will be a long time before the tide of fashionable travel" makes its way to Katahdin.[1]

The essay that emerged from the trip, which appeared in his book *The Maine Woods* (1864), recounts the journey. It's stuffed with period detail as Thoreau journeys to the mountain, first on a train out of Portland, then via steamboat, wagon, ferry, and finally, by foot. Despite its place in the wilderness canon, the bulk of Thoreau's Katahdin essay is actually given over to describing what today we'd call a "working landscape," rather than a wild one: a region dotted with logging camps, sawmills, dams, and homesteads. It may be a wilderness story, but it's one firmly ensconced in a narrative of human activity and industry in northern New England in the mid-nineteenth century.

Thoreau's response to the wilderness when he made it to the mountain is complicated, and often misunderstood. In the most famous passage in his Katahdin essay he wrote how confronting nature in a more primitive state than the pastoral trappings of Walden Pond was both thrilling and deeply unsettling: "Here was no man's garden, but the unhandselled globe. . . . It was a place for heathenism and superstitious rites,—to be inhabited by men nearer of kin to the rocks and to wild animals than we."[2] It wasn't the rhapsody one might have expected from the author of the preservationist maxim "In wildness is the preservation of the world." But then again, wildness was more a condition than a place, a quality that clearly enjoyed some wiggle room in Thoreau's thinking. It was often an abstraction for him, as when

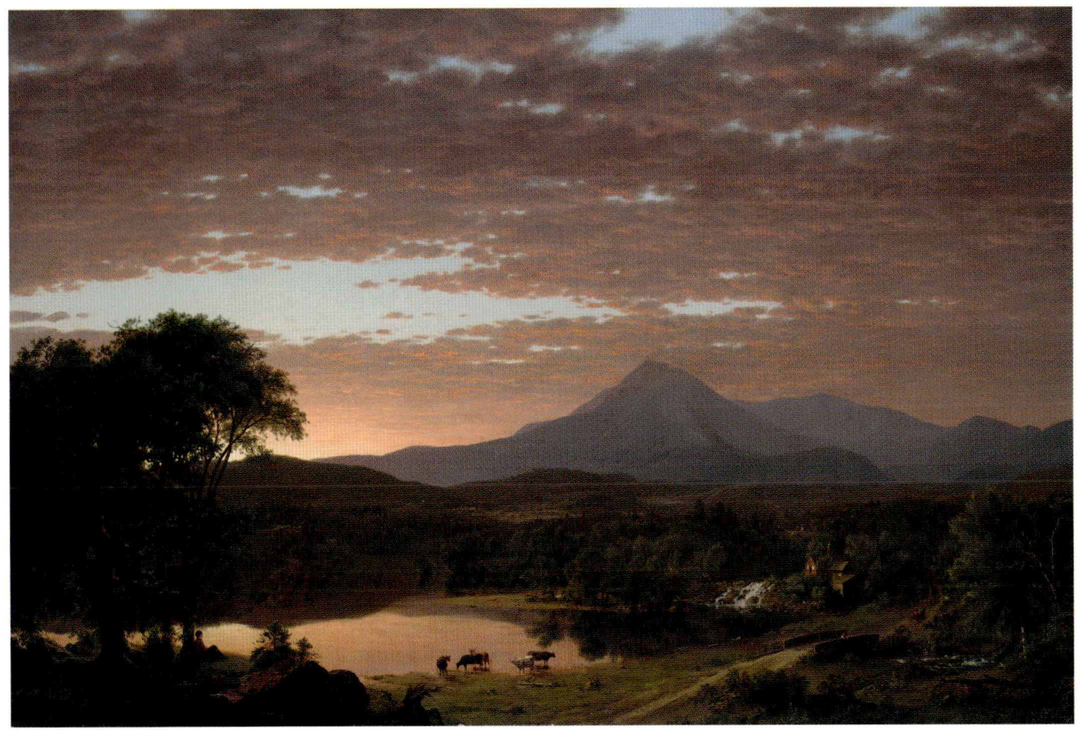

20. Frederic Edwin Church (1826–1900), *Mt. Ktaadn*, 1853 (Oil on canvas, 36¼ × 55¼ inches, Yale University Art Gallery, New Haven). Church visited northern Maine not long after the publication of Thoreau's essay in *The Maine Woods.* The scene is actually an imagined view of a more tamed and domesticated wild, with the boy in the lower left envisioning how settlement and industry will soon reshape the landscape. Interestingly, the mountain continues to defy human control. Its sublimity remains intact.

he needed a philosophical counterpoint in his critique of the corruptions of "civilized" society. Encountering the elemental harshness of a real, physical wilderness was a different story, and it elicited some darker notes.

And yet, even though a familiar take on the Katahdin episode has Thoreau becoming unglued in the face of the actual wilderness, his description of the experience was not the record of a metaphysical breakdown. It's better described as a complex emotional and psychological reaction to a place that seemed so indifferent to him, where he was in "the presence of a force not bound to be kind to man." Thoreau's response to Katahdin was couched squarely in the language of the *sublime,* a style that attempted to capture the terror and awe experienced in the face of nature's undiluted power. It was an aesthetic sensibility that landscape painters of his time, such as Thomas Cole and Frederic Church, mastered through their deft representations of what Thoreau dubbed "titanic" nature, laced with dramatic flourishes and religious atmospherics (plate 20).

The encounter with nature's rawness could surely be unnerving and alienating, even to a nature romantic like Thoreau.

Yet as Laura Dassow Walls writes (in one of the best biographies ever written about the philosopher-poet of Walden Pond), this experience seems to have only strengthened his bond with the land. If the wilderness at Katahdin struck Thoreau as "savage and awful," it was also beautiful; a "specimen of what God saw fit to make this world."[3] Even though he never made it to the summit—the weather and his unfamiliarity with the terrain saw to that—Thoreau's Maine experience would have a profound impact on his understanding of the landscape and become part of American wilderness lore.

The wild sublime found its most zealous literary champion, however, in the naturalist and wildland advocate John Muir. Enrapt with the High Sierras and the transcendent environs of Yosemite, Muir reveled in the otherworldly power of the wilderness. In December of 1874, while hiking along the Yuba River, Muir decided to make his way to a high stand of Douglas spruce, and he climbed a hundred feet to the top of one to take in the full force of an approaching winter storm. Buffeted by the strong winds, Muir swayed back and forth on his tree for hours in what seems to have been a state of total euphoria. When the storm passed, he looked on in awe at the newly burnished landscape. "As I gazed on the impressive scene, all the so-called ruin of the storm was forgotten, and never before did these noble woods appear so fresh, so joyous, so immortal."[4]

Muir's resolute biocentrism ("Why should man value himself as more than a small part of the one great unit of creation?" he once asked) and his penchant for deep immersion in the wild was eccentric at the time. Yet Muir's desire to immerse himself in the wild would become the taproot for an array of seekers of an authentic wilderness experience in the generations that followed. Some weren't as fortunate as Muir and succumbed to a hostile environment. The poet Everett Ruess went into the Utah desert in November 1934 and was never heard from again; Timothy Treadwell (the "Grizzly Man" of Werner Herzog's film) saw his luck with Alaskan brown bears finally run out after more than a dozen seasons in their midst; Christopher McCandless (of Jon Krakauer's *Into the Wild*) died of a combination of starvation and inadvertent poisoning in an abandoned bus near Denali National Park. The wilderness, as Thoreau might have warned them, was in the end not interested in their motives and passions.

Thoreau's and Muir's literary explorations of the sublime were not only of a piece with the American landscape painters of their time; they dovetail with the visual language of nineteenth-century survey photographers like Carleton Watkins and also later modernist photographers such as Ansel Adams. Adams's pictures of Yosemite and the national parks in the 1930s and 1940s captured the sense of power and beauty that Thoreau and Muir found so exhilarating. Viewing an Adams photo like *Clearing Winter Storm, Yosemite National Park,* or even a lesser-known image like his picture of Two Medicine Lake at Glacier National Park (plate 21), we can understand why he was often referred to as "John Muir with a Camera."

The photographic regard for nature's majesty and beauty may have crested with the work of Adams, Porter, and the other artists of the Sierra Club books in the 1960s, but like the tradition of photography-driven advocacy it certainly didn't vanish from magazines, galleries, and coffee tables. It was kept alive in the compositions of many of the photographers that followed, yet they found other means to depict the force and awe-inspiring qualities of the wilderness, pushing the image into new aesthetic and technical territory.

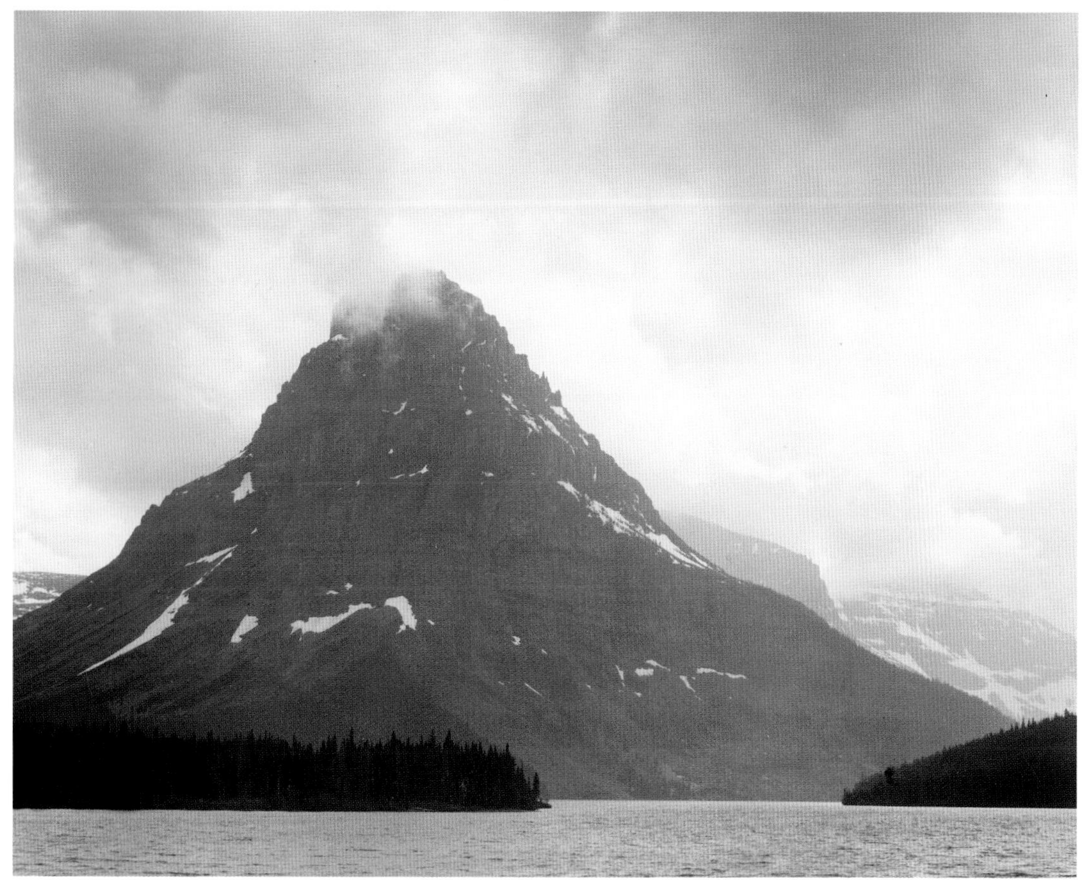

21. Ansel Adams, *Two Medicine Lake, Glacier National Park, Montana,* 1941–1942 (Ansel Adams Photographs of National Parks and Monuments, 1941–1942, National Archives and Records Administration, College Park, Maryland)

Their pictures often caught the landscape in moments of high drama, such as the devastation following volcanic eruptions, fires, blowdowns, and biblical-scale floods. Or they experimented with light and printing techniques to create an altered reality that heightened the mystery and uncanniness of a scene. Sometimes, the fearsomeness of the shot inspired wariness, keeping the viewer at a safe distance as in the traditional mode. Other times the pictures drew you into the frame by scaling nature's might in more poignant and personal ways, as in the blowing of the wind along a desert highway. Finding their own foothold on the transcendent features of the American landscape, these artists remind us of nature's singular power and beauty in a human-defined age.

BAM: As an aesthetic tradition, the sublime clearly played an outsize role in how artists and nature writers of an earlier era described and represented the American wilderness, a sensibility that hasn't exactly disappeared (as high-definition productions like the "Planet Earth" series demonstrate). And yet the experience of the sublime was always meant to be partly unsettling, provoking a twin sense of awe and terror when confronting the vastness of nature, such as Thoreau's unnerving experience on Mount Katahdin.

Mark, how have photographers working today like Buzzy Sullivan (plate 22) and Mitch Dobrowner (plate 25) brought this older idea and imagery into the modern period, particularly the depiction of nature's beauty alongside its destructive power? As a photographer, what do these images convey to you when thinking about the sublime and its expression in print and picture?

MK: As you say, the sublime was a real focus in the early days of western landscape photography, but that term isn't used much these days by photographers. Even so, one could argue that awe and terror are still motivating forces, though not always at the same time. I think most landscape photographers respond to their physical experiences in the field. That certainly seems the case with Sullivan and Dobrowner, who photographed powerful and dangerous natural phenomena. Laura McPhee shows us the aftermath of a forest fire that is both humbling in its raw power and beautiful to behold at the same time (plate 23). I'd argue that all the photographers in

this section acknowledge some kind of awe-inspiring event. Does terror of human-caused events like climate change evoke a modern-day kind of sublime response?

BAM: Well, I think it does (or should). Perhaps it's also a case where we as the audience bring that prior awareness to the viewing of the photo rather than having the art alone shake us down to our shoes.

And I get what you're saying about the empirical (or maybe experiential is a better word) aspect of this, that is, the photographer responding to what they see and feel in the field, in the moment. I can see that especially in the photos by Serge Levy, Debra Bloomfield, and Lilly McElroy (plate 24, plate 28, and plate 29). Bloomfield and McElroy in particular seem to evoke that older sense of natural awe.

MK: Michael Lundgren does so as well (plate 27). Though I would say that McElroy has a bit of fun with this notion of awe, and plays with the idea that one could control the power of nature, if only through one's perception.

SP: I wonder if something like this is at work: The sublime bonded to the monumental, and there was agreement about what that meant and looked like. The group making that judgment was small. Now we have lots of places that can strike awe and terror for lots of reasons and lots of perspectives about what they mean and no consensual elite to rank everything. The sensibility of the sublime has entered quotidian life. The mundane takes on the quality of the monumental, even if ironically. Art isn't just stuff in museums—as we'll discuss in a later essay, the New Topographics movement, despite its fine art compositions and presentation, ushered in an image of landscape as pop art. We have general sentiments but maybe not a consensus sensibility? Every place has its fifteen minutes of fame?

BAM: But of course the old attachment of the sublime to monumental scenery hasn't disappeared, as we can see in pictures like Adam Katseff's striking and mysterious image of Half Dome (plate 30).

MK: The thing I find fascinating about Katseff's photograph is how one of the great icons of Yosemite is barely visible: it comes out of the darkness and is at the edge of vision as night falls. It's so different from the way the land was seen either during the exploration era of the late nineteenth century, or by the mid-twentieth-century modernists. Yet it's also such a beautiful new way to see Half Dome. Maybe photographers are always looking to create a new way of seeing something, but I also think they're looking for a way to express what is felt at the moment they experience the scene before the camera, which is fleeting.

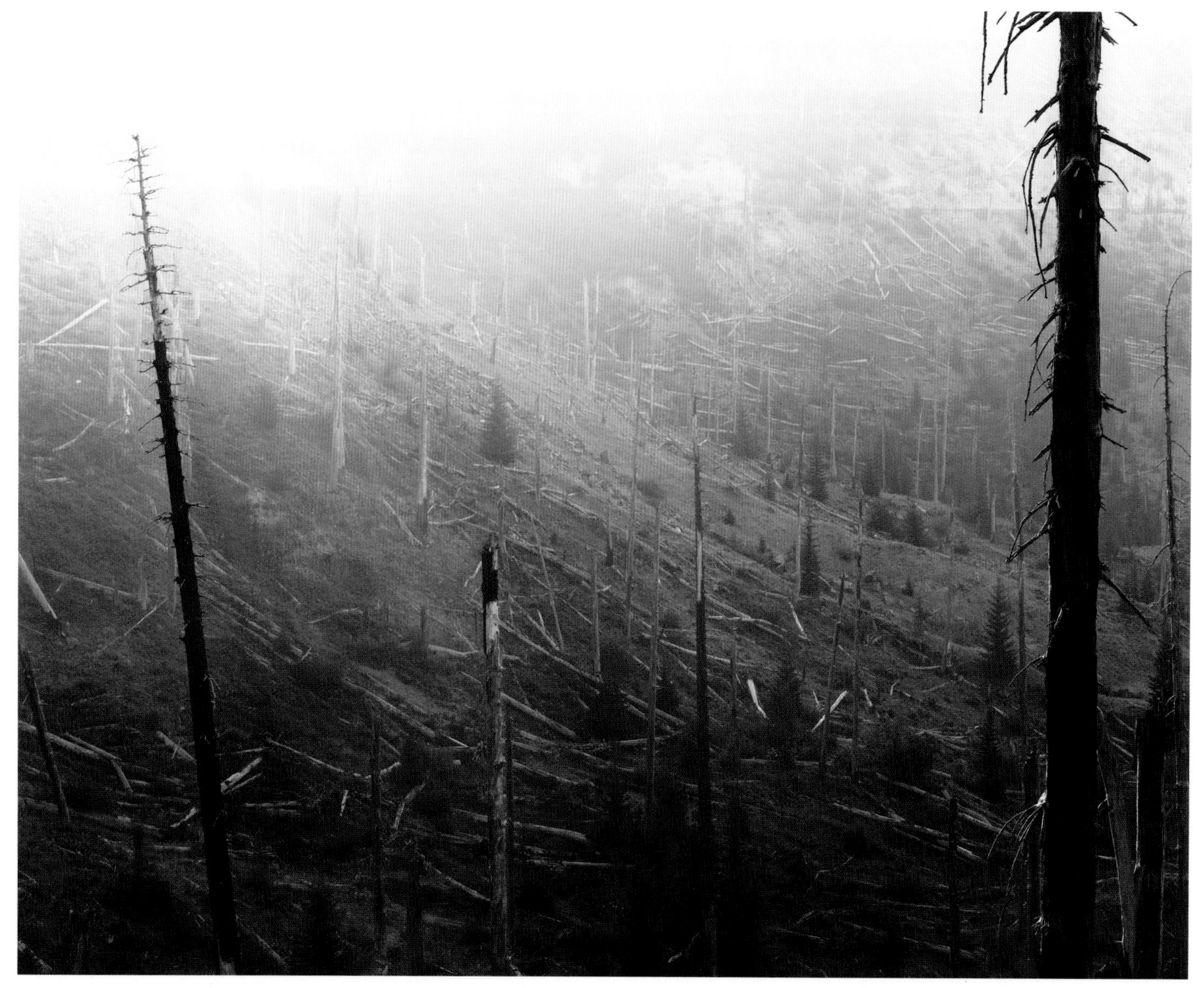

22. Buzzy Sullivan, *Standing Dead on the Boundary of the Blowdown Zone, Approximately Ten Miles Northeast of Mount St. Helens,* 2017

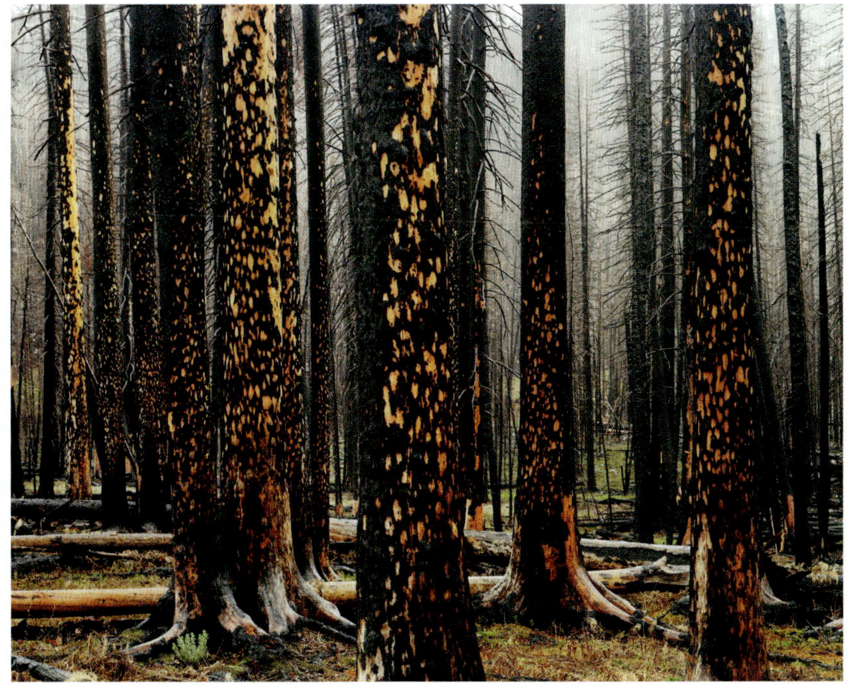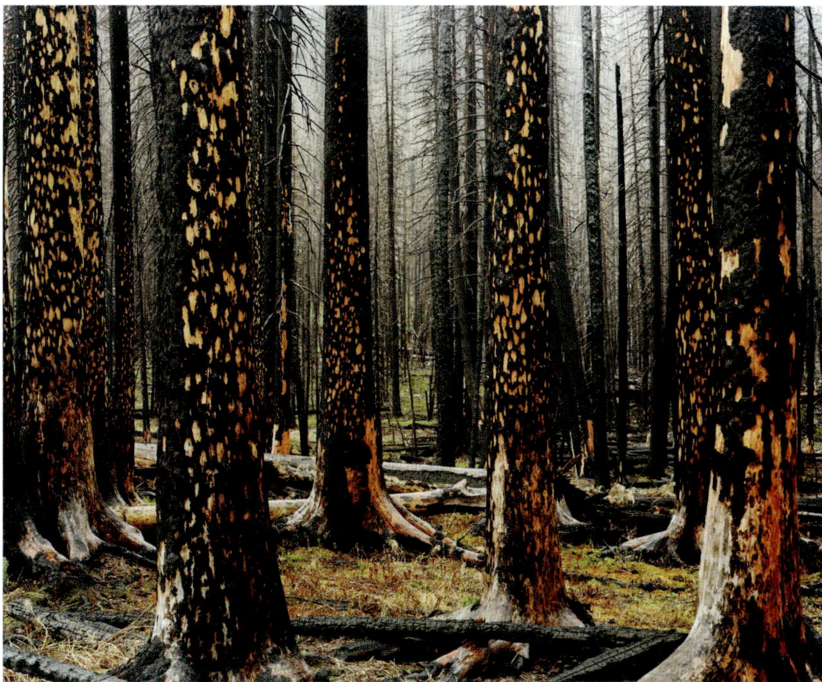

23. Laura McPhee, *Early Spring (Peeling Bark in Rain),* 2008 (From the series "Guardians of Solitude," courtesy of the artist)

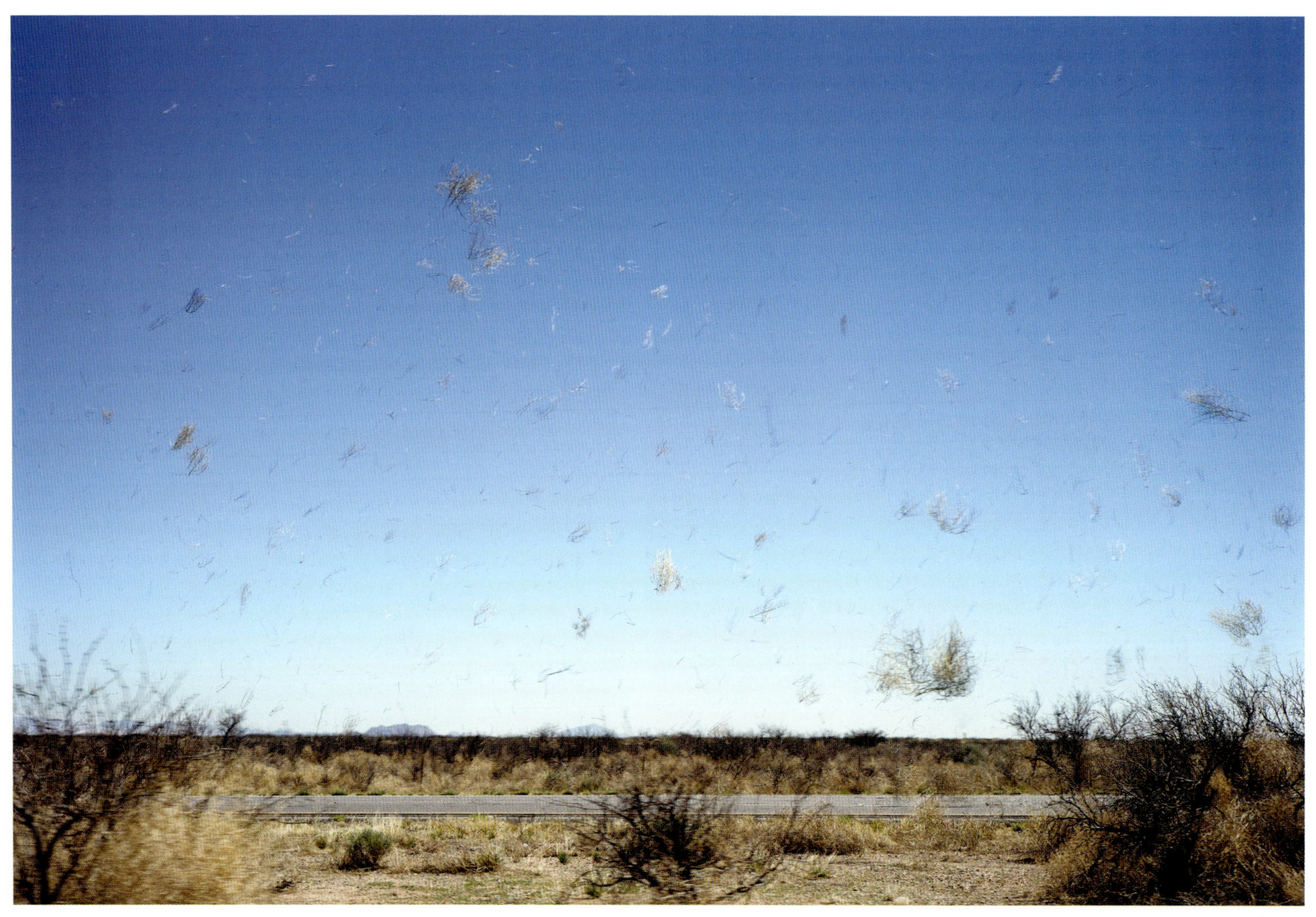

 24. Serge J-F. Levy, *I-10 East of Tucson, Arizona*, 2016

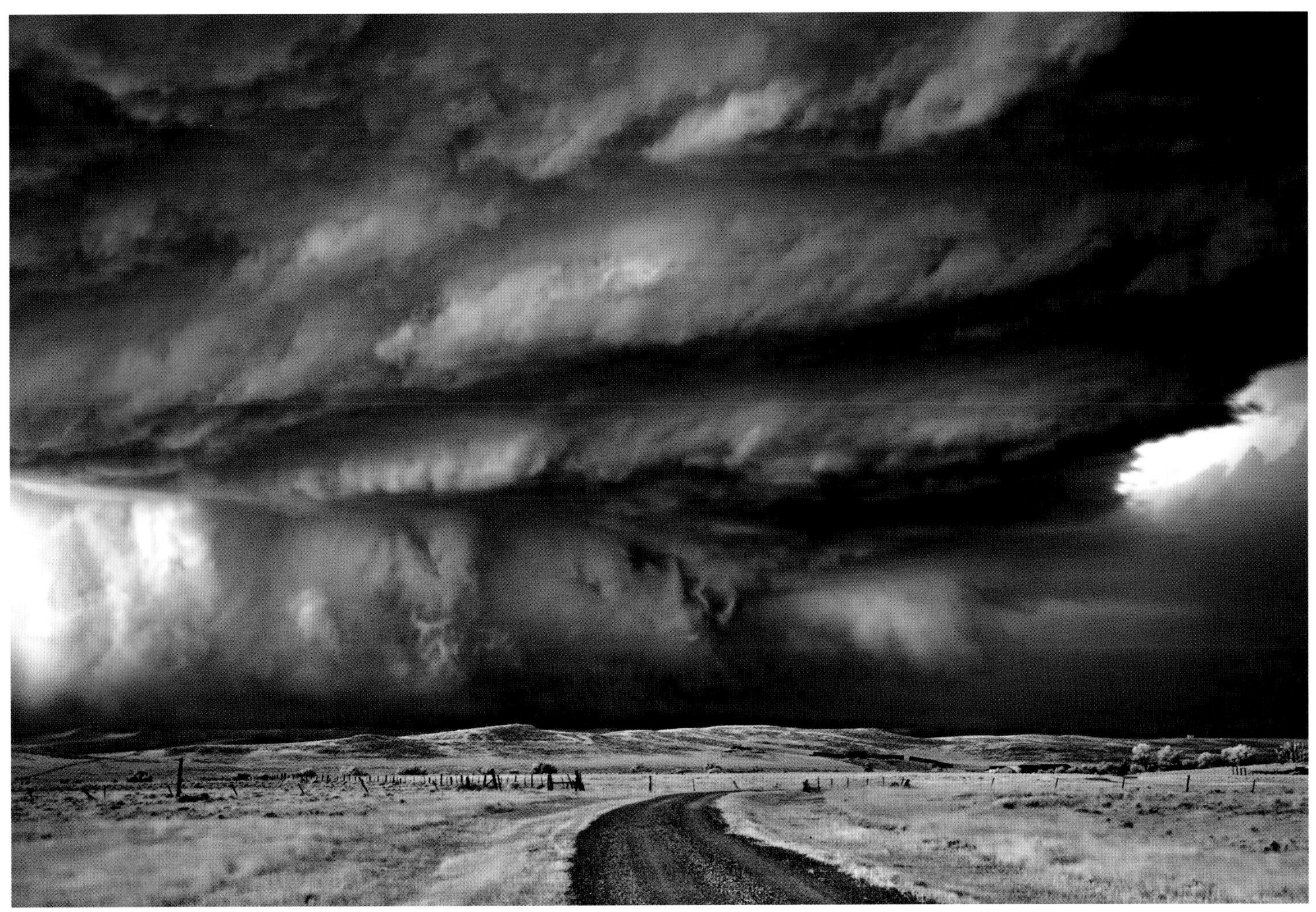

25. Mitch Dobrowner, *Bear's Claw*, Moorcroft, Wyoming, 2010

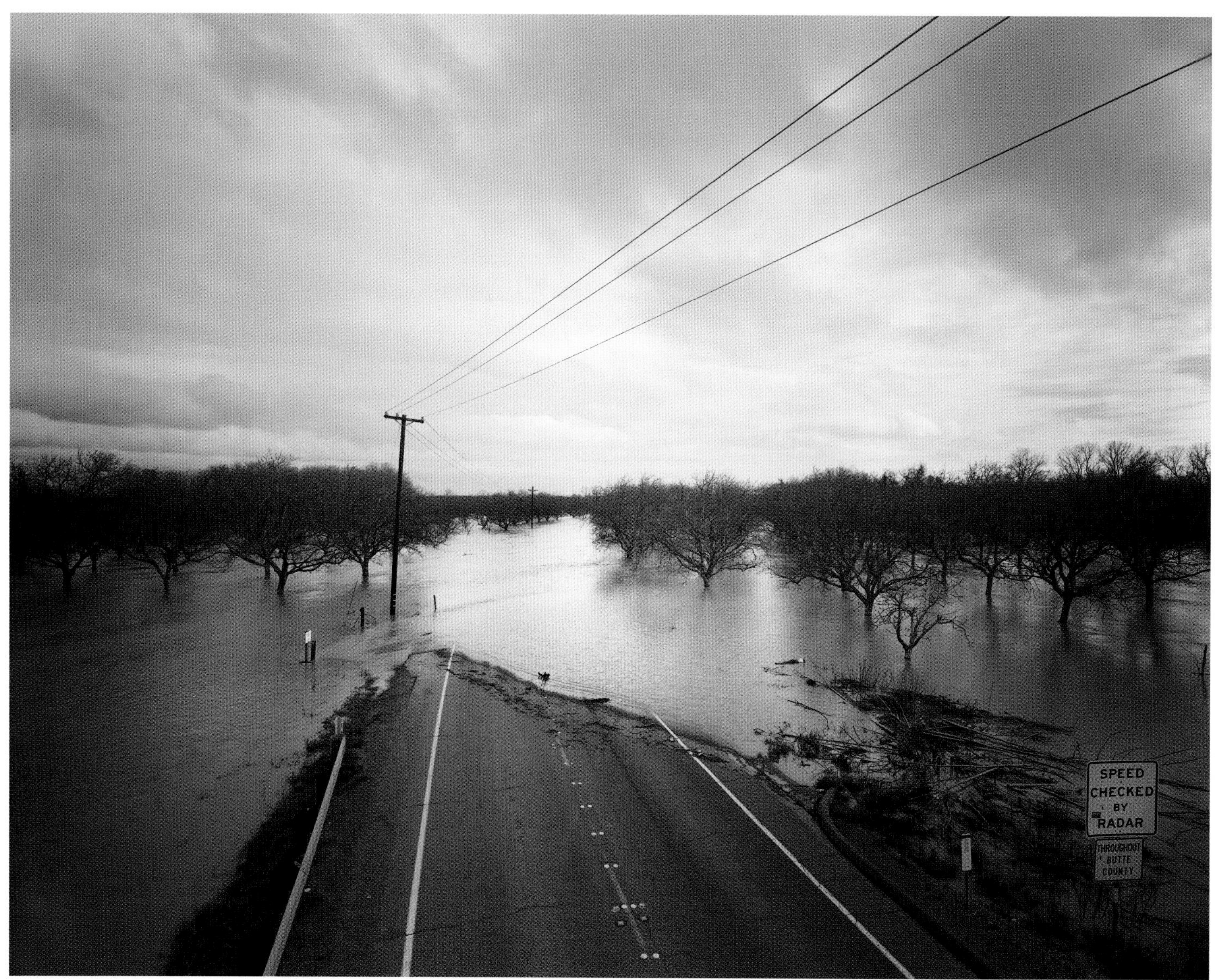

26. Geoff Fricker, *Speed Checked by Radar, Ord Bend,* 1997

27. Michael Lundgren, *River Valley*, 2003

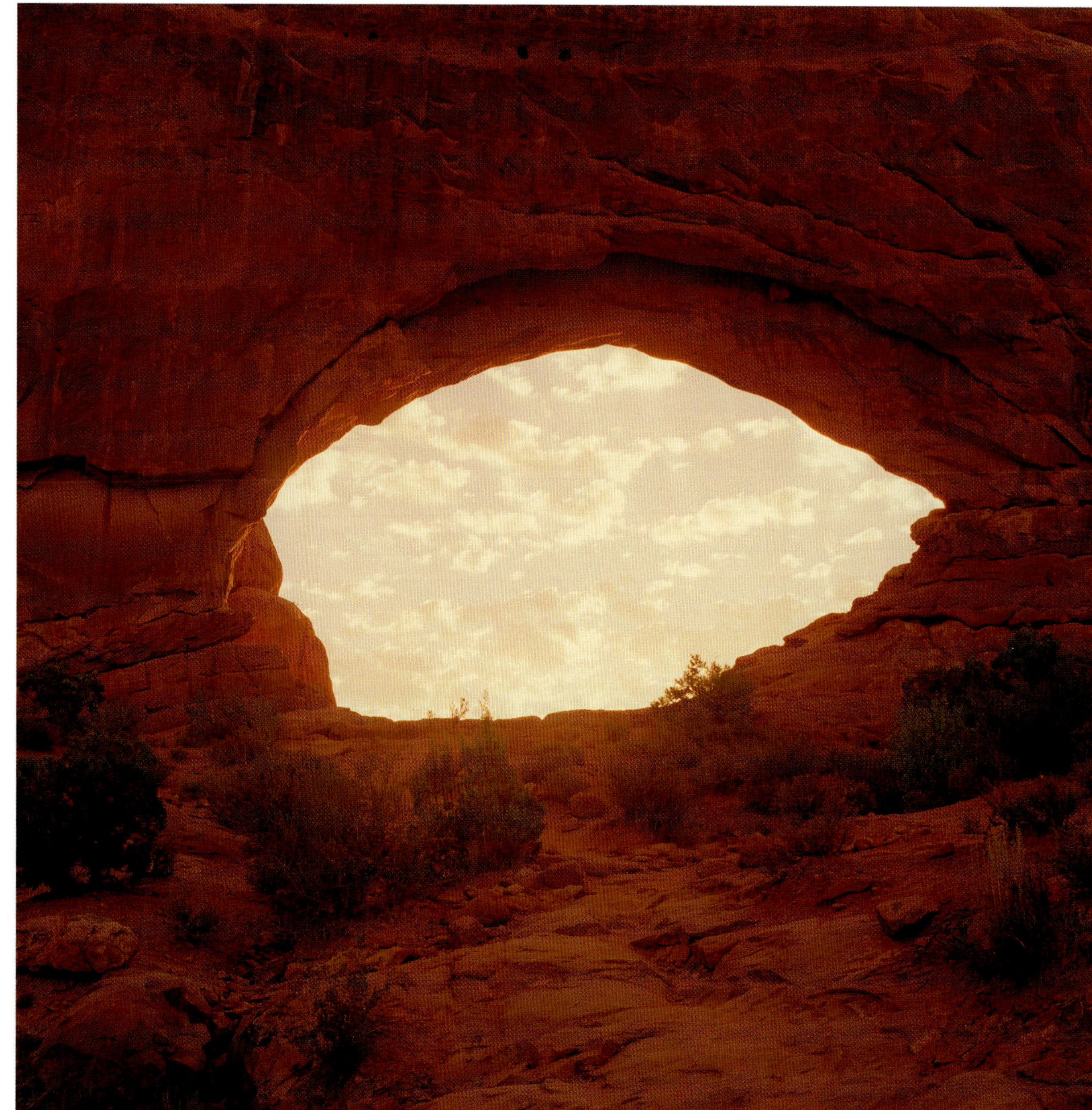

28. Debra Bloomfield,
Sunrise—Moab, Utah,
1995

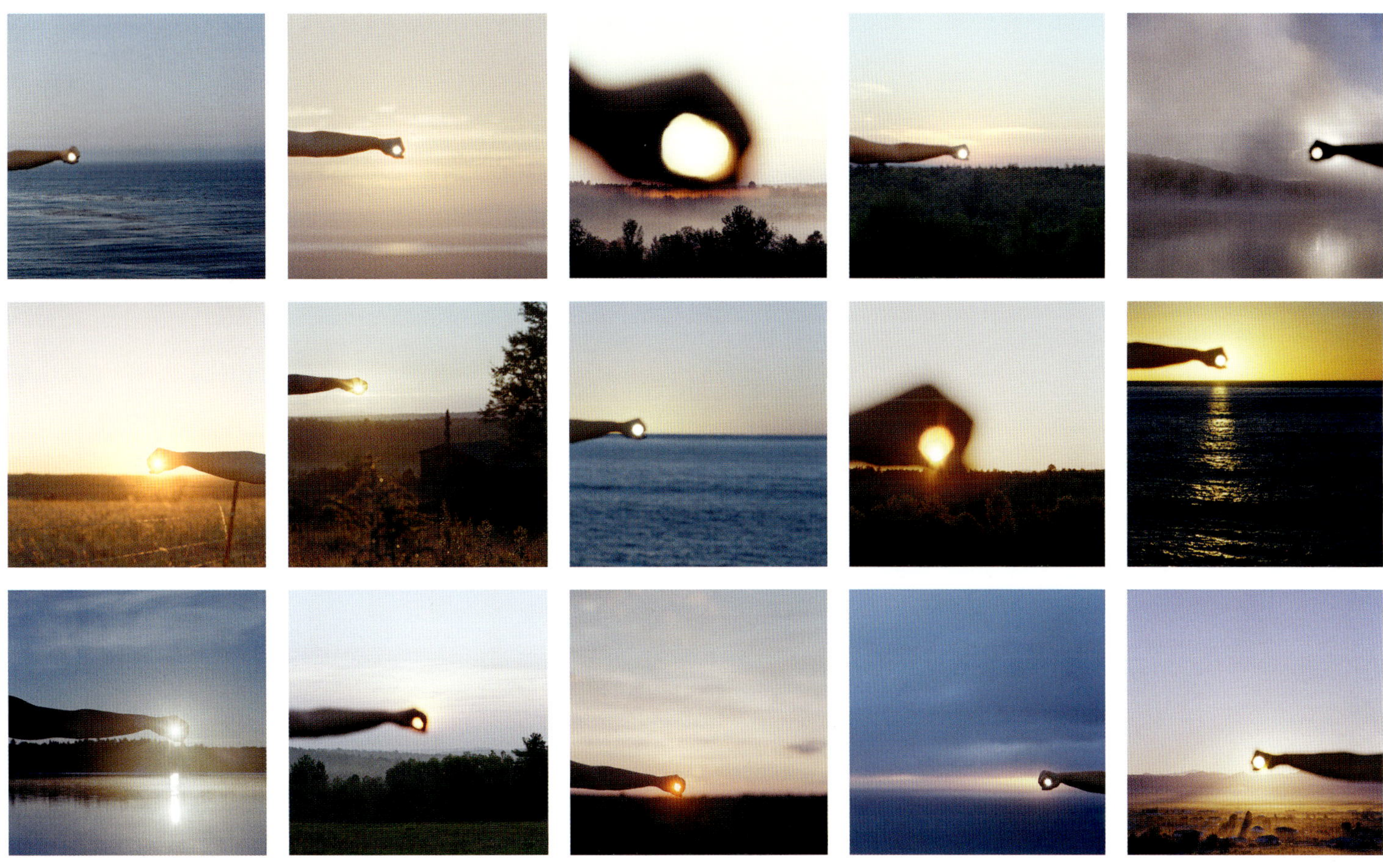

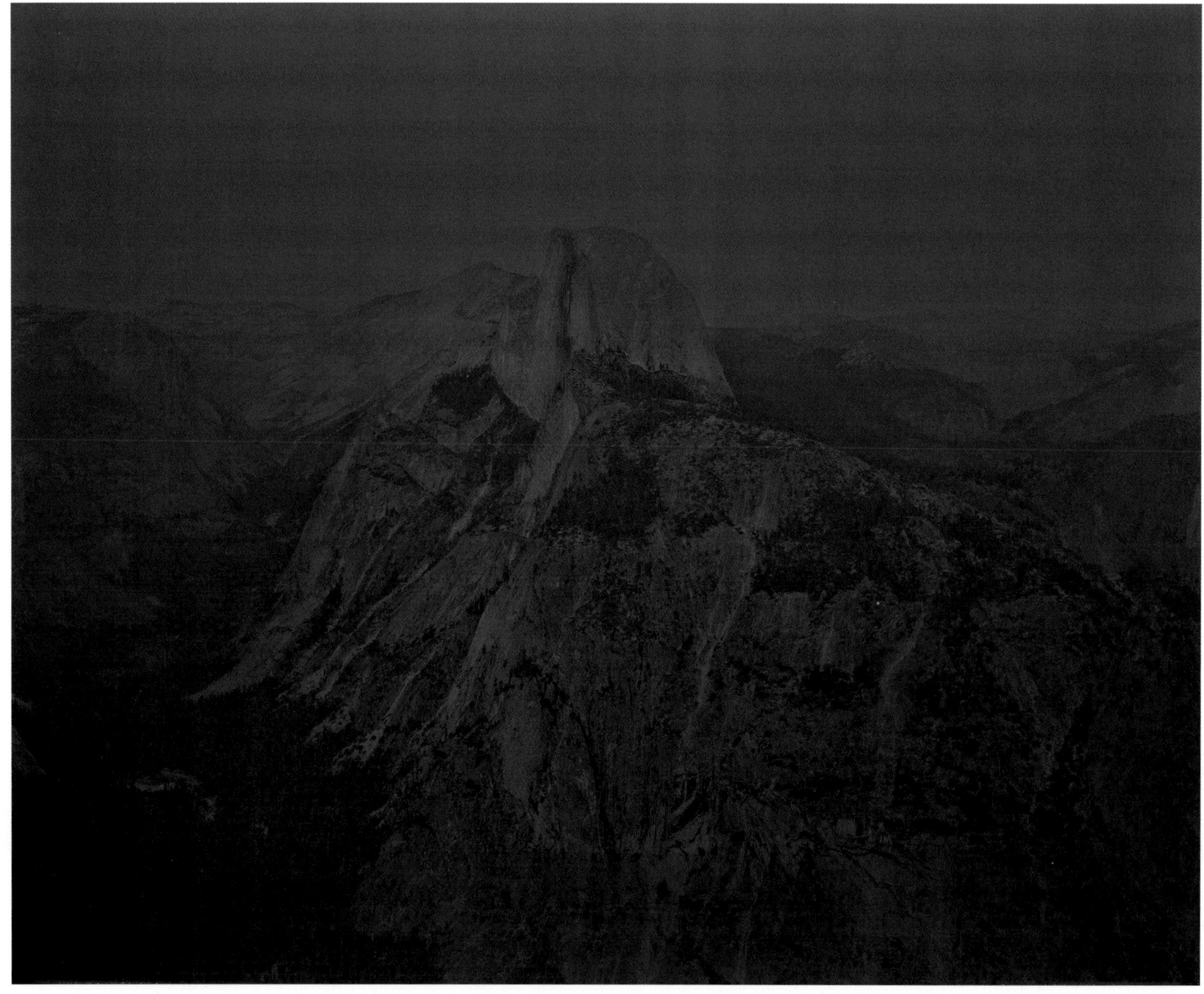

30. Adam Katseff, *Half Dome, Yosemite,* 2012 (Courtesy of Sasha Wolf Projects and Robert Koch Galley)

Cropping the Narrative

As scenes go, certainly for the wilderness movement, the image is legendary. Teddy Roosevelt, then president, and John Muir, the prophet of wilderness, stand atop Glacier Point with Yosemite Valley and the Range of Light behind them (plate 31). The accompanying caption, now a prologue to a national narrative, tells how Muir persuaded Roosevelt to commit the federal government to the protection of the nation's natural heritage. The origins of American environmentalism begin with that choice between the wild and the wrecked. The century that followed hewed to the resulting narrative arc and informed images to which it served as master caption.

The premise was that wilderness is the foundational state of nature, and the story of how America encountered, converted, and finally preserved vestiges of wilderness is the foundation of our national narrative. The story holds that wilderness is the highest possible use of the land; that the protection of the pristine has been the ultimate goal and highest achievement of American environmentalism. There are few examples in which image and story fuse so thoroughly. The legend, to invoke that line from an old John Ford film, has been printed.

But that trip in 1903 included a second moment, complete with an alternative image and caption. In it, Roosevelt and Muir stand side by side in front of Yosemite's Grizzly Giant, the oldest of the sequoias in the Mariposa Grove (plate 32). Only the trunk of the tree is visible, and unlike that Glacier Point image, the two men are part of a group that forces the scene to spread horizontally, against the upward thrust of the Giant.

Often the photo is cropped to repeat the simpler scene such that Roosevelt and Muir stand uprightly, aligning with the grain of the deeply furrowed Big Tree behind them. The inherited narrative remains the same, however. After all, the giant sequoia was the catalyst for three of America's first four national parks. What complicates that cropping is that another figure stands behind and between them. Typically, he is (figuratively) airbrushed out, but when cited is often mis-identified as Gifford Pinchot. Pinchot was, of course, another

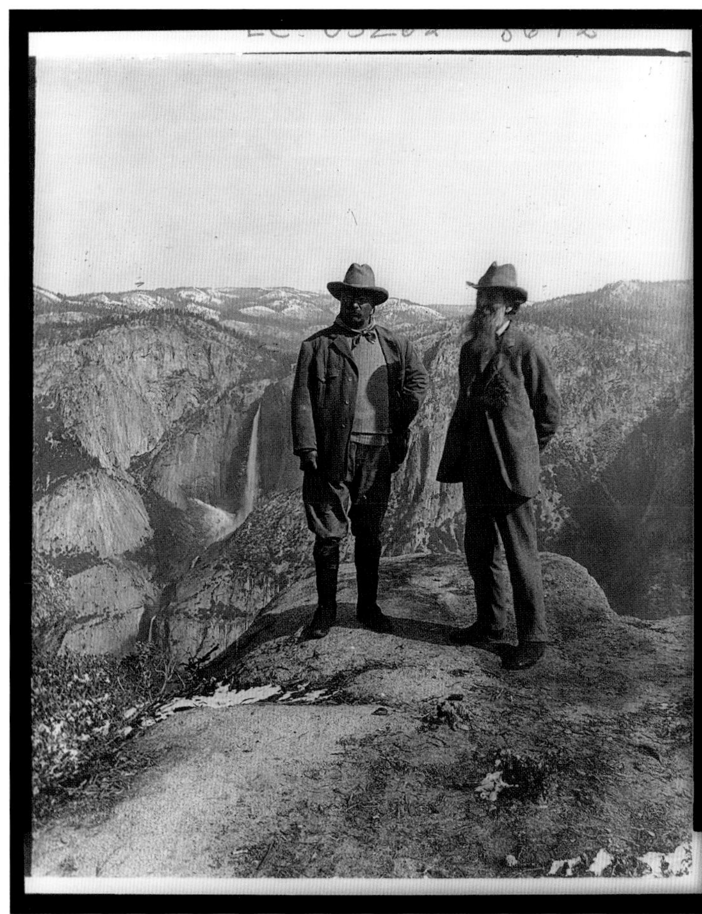

31. *Theodore Roosevelt and John Muir on Glacier Point, Yosemite Valley, California*, 1903

major player in this early environmental era and a rival for Roosevelt's attention. At the time of the photo, however, he headed the minor Bureau of Forestry. Two years later, Roosevelt transferred the forest reserves to that agency, which then became the Forest Service. In contrast to the nation's parks, which stood for the pristine and the preserved, the surrounding national forests argued for rational use under the aegis of conservation. In 1903, the two visions were broadly complementary as both contested against those who, in Roosevelt's striking phrase, "scalped" the land.

Within a handful of years, however, they became competitors over the question of whether to build a dam at Hetch Hetchy. Pinchot approved, and Muir protested. In 1913, the dam was authorized. That controversy established a conflict within the narrative of nature protection to match that between exploiters and preservers. It speaks of a rivalry between two seemingly incommensurate philosophies of public land use, of a quarrel between conservation and preservation, and of a hideous resolution leading to a dam and a martyred landscape. That observers might try to insert Pinchot into the image is historically inaccurate but psychologically (and historiographically) perceptive, for he did seek to interpose himself between the other two.

What makes the image into a narrative anchor point is that, as noted earlier, the controversy was reenacted forty years later when a dam was proposed for Dinosaur National Monument. This time the preservationists won. They won again in the 1960s when they successfully opposed two dams considered for Grand Canyon National Park. For many, the Echo Park and Grand Canyon dam controversies mark the start of the modern

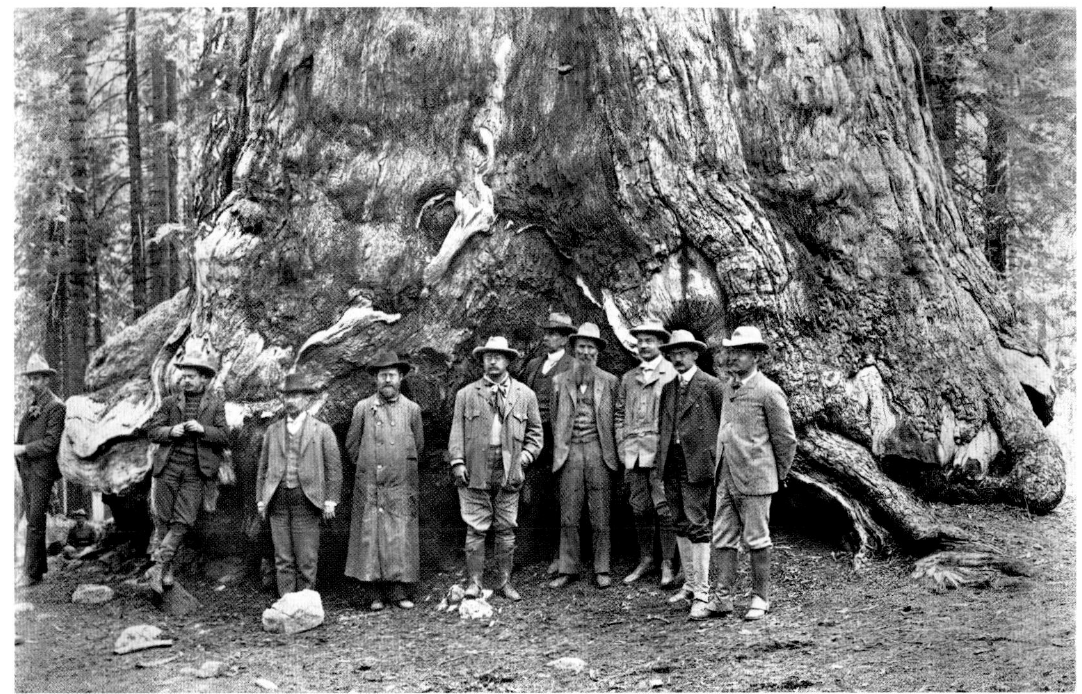

32. *John Muir and Theodore Roosevelt at the Grizzly Giant, Mariposa Big Tree Grove,* 1903, photograph by Joseph N. LeConte (Courtesy of the Yosemite National Park Museum, Archives and Library)

American wilderness movement that updated Muir, Pinchot, and the polities that decided between them. Revealingly, the Sierra Club (Muir served as its first president) was at the political barricades. Those crises correspond almost exactly with the emergence of U.S. environmental history and philosophy. It all syncs nicely—the photo, the personalized visions, the setting, and the story that links them. By cropping it is possible to make that second photo repeat the first, and in a real way that is what has happened to the narrative and philosophy of American environmentalism.

That cropping, however, does a disservice to the complexity of the event. The actual photo, taken by Joseph N. LeConte, centered on Teddy Roosevelt, and it included an entourage of which John Muir was but one member among ten. The man between TR and Muir was Dr. Presley Marion Rixey, surgeon general of the navy and Roosevelt's personal physician. To Muir's left stand Nicholas Murray Butler, president of Columbia University; William Loeb, Roosevelt's personal secretary; and Benjamin Ide Wheeler, president of the University of California. To Roosevelt's right are George C. Pardee, governor of

California; William Henry Moody, secretary of the navy; two Secret Service agents; and further hidden, two soldiers, unidentified but undoubtedly members of the U.S. Cavalry, which ran Yosemite and other parks until 1916.

In brief, the visit was a political event by a head of state. It was one act of many that Roosevelt as president performed to advance the cause of state-sponsored conservation. The same year he visited Yosemite (1903), he created the first wildlife refuge, on Florida's Pelican Island, and standing on the rim of the Grand Canyon he declared it the "one great sight every American should see." In 1905, he transferred the national forests to the Bureau of Forestry and began cleaning up the General Land Office. In 1906, he signed the Antiquities Act, which allowed for the creation of national monuments by presidential proclamation. In 1907, he doubled, at one stroke, the size of the national forest system. In 1908, he established a Country Life Commission, chaired by Liberty Hyde Bailey, and then convened the Governors Conference on Conservation, making that program his last hurrah and political testament; the project went continental the next year with a North American Conference.

But the politics of state-sponsored conservation was itself intertwined with political and economic reform, the enlargement of American nationalism, and the projection of the United States as a global power. As president, Roosevelt promoted a "New Nationalism." He attacked trusts and monopolies as he did despoilers of the land. The year he visited Muir he authorized the Panama Canal. The year of the Antiquities Act he received the Nobel Peace Prize for brokering an end to the Russo-Japanese War. The year he doubled the national forests, he launched the Great White Fleet. The meeting beneath the Grizzly Giant had a far wider context than an inspired campout with the charismatic John of the Mountains.

Not least, Roosevelt was a well-educated intellectual, a naturalist, a historian, and a man attuned to the grand issues of his day. The Yosemite party, after all, included two university presidents, and the photo was taken by a professor of mechanical engineering. This was an era of intellectual ferment as much as political reform. If the latter points to the Progressive Era, the former points to Pragmatism, that creative outburst that led to an American school of philosophy as distinctive as giant sequoias. The year before Muir explained his spiritual interest in nature to Roosevelt, the philosopher William James published *The Varieties of Religious Experience,* and as Roosevelt was enlarging the national forests and dispatching the Great White Fleet, James summarized his particularized formulation in the anthology *Pragmatism.* As the old saw goes, there are as many creeds of Pragmatism as there are pragmatists, but that pluralism is of a piece with the pluralism that was also coming to define the national estate. The American experiment would follow not from the logic of first principles but from adherence to fundamental processes of thought and politics that judged ideas and practices by their outcomes rather than by their ideological character. James's epigram, "By their fruit ye shall know them, not by their roots," suited a nation-in-the-making populated by immigrants and chock-a-block with ideas and creeds.

All this is lost in the Glacier Point image, and the omission matters because it changes the narrative. Begin, instead, with the Grizzly Giant photo, and the story is one of American innovations across the board, from institutions to ideas, and of environmental reform within a broader program of a bois-terous nationalism. Conservation had its origins in democratic politics as much as with intangible values. A commitment to patches of preservation does not lie outside of (or in defiance to) American experience any more than religion does. Instead, it thrives as part of American pluralism, as testimony to the abundance that made such practices possible, and as part of a national epic, the frontier, that threw the wild and the wrecked into stark confrontation. All the pieces did not mesh smoothly, any more than any other American experience did, but they were all part of what Roosevelt called a Square Deal.

Where the narrative begins matters because it defines where it ends. The cropped photo leads like the trajectory of a crossbow bolt to the dam controversies, and the triumph of parks, preservation, and a more formal philosophy of the wild, the deep, and the non-human. Arguably, the foundational works for both environmental history and ethics in the United States appeared in 1967. Behind both lay increasing attention to Aldo Leopold's posthumous classic from 1949, *A Sand County Almanac,* which really found its readership in the 1960s.

The historian Lynn White achieved the widest reach with a polemical essay in the magazine *Science* in 1967 that placed the blame for the emerging "ecological crisis" on the "anthro-pocentric" or human-centered Judeo-Christian worldview.[1] The charge that the root cause lay with flawed ideas about the world inspired a first generation of environmental philosophers to call for a nonanthropocentric ethics that elevated nature as a bearer of moral value. A field coalesced around a shared per-ception that humanity, or at least Western civilization, needed an alternative to its prevailing chauvinism toward wild species and landscapes, and its failure to respect the intrinsic value of nature. The obvious alternative was wilderness; a counter-ethos could align nicely with general enthusiasms that had led to passage of the Wilderness Act three years earlier. In 1973, the Norwegian philosopher Arne Naess expanded the realm with the first essay on deep ecology, perhaps the purest expression of the nature-centered worldview and a vision that would later shape wilderness and environmental activism in the United States, Australia, and Europe.[2] The rising appreciation of Native and Indigenous worldviews and spirituality was also part of this movement, especially the reissue of works such as *Black Elk Speaks* (1961) and the publication of N. Scott Momaday's novel *House Made of Dawn* (1968).

The parallel project was to invent a narrative, and histori-ans in the United States also acquired their origin story in 1967 with Roderick Nash's *Wilderness and the American Mind.* The book became a sensation, and it seemed natural that it placed the subject, one about ideas and spiritual values, within the realm of ideas. The history of American environmentalism became, by default, a history that traced the aftermath of that rendezvous atop Glacier Point.

Wilderness, deep ecology, intrinsic values, nonanthropo-centric philosophy, and a narrative to place them at the apex of environmental thought and ethics, all bonded with a strong nuclear force. They did not play well with others: it was axi-omatic, in fact, that the others were the problem, and that the whole enterprise had to be refounded on these newer ideolog-ical principles, much as ecological science looked to the pris-tine to furnish a baseline for natural processes, and as activists and philosophers turned to wilderness preserves as the purest and defining expression of environmental management. Even Leopold was enlisted in this emerging, unswerving biocentric vision of the wild, despite his innate pragmatism, his labors in restoring abused land (and sustaining "working" landscapes), and his acceptance of a continuum of human-environment relationships within his influential "land ethic."

As yet the American invention of wilderness, taken as an emblem of American exceptionalism, has not shown it can migrate successfully beyond the United States and has frequently led to charges of "green imperialism." More insidiously, the notion is increasingly troubled in its place of origin. The destabilizing begins with practice. Wilderness-as-norm is challenged by threats such as wildfires, beetle epidemics, and swarms of invasives many times larger than the preserves; by global-scale climate change; and by notions of working landscapes that may better advance ecological goods and services. The nation's largest park, Adirondack Park, contains both public and private land; perhaps the country's boldest experiment in staying the push of urban sprawl is the 1.1-million-acre New Jersey Pinelands National Preserve, which relies on stringent zoning over a mosaic of public and private holdings. Environmental reformers have discovered the vastly richer returns from a full-gamut spectrum of restoration projects and view the human problem less as original sin than as bad choices.

Or to restate the issue, the prevailing picture of U.S. environmental history has been cropped too closely. The reality is, environmental concerns have always been connected with everything else in society. A more useful narrative would accept such pluralism—would accommodate a democratic politics, the swirl of ideas, the proliferating ethical creeds, the racial, class, and gender identities, and the many places and meanings of environment. It would put the physicians, the bureaucrats, the politicians, the personal secretaries, the professors, the Secret Service agents, and even the dismounted cavalry into the narrative. To do so is, by default, to accept a pragmatic definition of environmental history. It says the Muir Moment was one event among many, and its narrative was one subplot among milling throngs that populate the prevailing story.

The cropped image also strips out a philosophical tradition of great value to conservation. Like wilderness, pragmatism was an American invention, and both were birthed out of a peculiar American experience. From the late nineteenth century the two had co-evolved. Both were messy in their application—how to cope with such applications, in truth, was at the core of Pragmatism. Yet in the postwar years broad-spectrum environmentalism where it wasn't narrowly focused on pollution tended to be distilled into wilderness, and Pragmatism was pushed to the sidelines, even as issues such as habitat restoration, active-measures intervention, and the outright re-creation of landscapes increasingly came to the fore of practice.

What created the wilderness narrative was its seamless melding of word with image. Surely the seductive aesthetic attractiveness of the images the wilderness movement spawned, so pure and radiant, helped give it pride of place, while pushing to the margins more complicated images of the messy landscapes that constituted most of America. Wilderness could be understood more easily than the compromised, endlessly negotiated places outside it. That inspired narrative into a comparable clarity and simplicity.

The needs of contemporary America require us to deal with those other places, to widen the field of our vision, to open the aperture of our appreciation. In recent decades, beginning roughly after the political exhaustion of the wilderness movement, such images have burst forth. The imagined landscape of America is today a scatter-diagram of recorded scenes, some pristine, most messy with signs of a human presence, or even wholly built. The wild and the unwild can interpenetrate, blur, and tint each other. An agricultural scene can seem sublime, and a wild one, tainted. Wildlands can be degraded, and farms and pastures, rehabilitated. Most of the country is neither wild nor urban. Collectively, they aptly depict the many environmental challenges before American society.[3] It remains for artists to give these activities an aesthetic frame and for wordsmiths to draw a regression line called a narrative through those scatter points.

Wilderness Movement as Historical Moment

In its classic formulation the wild is the transcendent. It stands outside culture, outside history, even outside place. America may have been the vehicle for granting the wild status as an idea and an institutional context as legal wilderness, but true wilderness lies outside any particular people or historical period, or for that matter humanity altogether. It stands as a Platonic ideal.

Yet context clings to the notion like lint. The movement that led to the Wilderness Act couldn't have happened fifty years earlier, or fifty years later. It occupied a historic moment in which the right minds, the right national politics, and the right kinds of lands came together. The arguments for wilderness were largely made on cultural grounds, and in Roderick Nash's timely formulation became a creation story in which a global-power America was the outcome of European civilization encountering American nature. As that series of frontiers evolved, it led to protected wilderness.

Culture mattered in that ideas of wilderness led to protection. There were arguments—Nash made them—that wilderness was as much a state of mind as a state of nature. But the prevailing concept was that the wilderness had been the foundation state, that American settlement had chipped away at it, and that now it was critical to save the remnants. We were preserving something that already existed—that's what preservation meant. That's what inspired people. That's what made wilderness transcendent.

Historians, however, have in turn chiseled away at the belief that those originating lands were wilderness in the original sense. Peoples lived on them for thousands of years; they had hunted, foraged, planted, and burned. Those contact landscapes were cultural places and homelands. They appeared empty, or lightly (and ineffectively) occupied, because the indigenes had left or been stripped of their tenure on the land through wars, diseases, and uprootings. What appeared as virgin land was, in reality, a widowed land. The wilderness scenes encountered by explorers and pioneers were mostly an artifact of contact and conquest. They were less wild than feral. The illusion of preserving wilderness came at the cost of removing both physically and historically the peoples who had lived on them.

So, too, the wilderness movement was a matter of cultural timing. Although early advocates such as John Muir beat the drum for the protection of his beloved Yosemite and other parks during the late nineteenth and early twentieth centuries, the more stringent protection of wilderness lands lagged behind. By the 1920s it was clear that the wilderness values coveted by Muir and others after him were in danger of being extinguished, not only by dams and grazing, but by road building, commerce, and the rise of mass tourism. A group of conservationists and resource managers, many of them affiliated with the U.S. Forest Service, including Leopold, Bob Marshall, and Arthur Carhart, pushed for reform, and a piecemeal wilderness policy in the national forests began to emerge.[1] Early arguments for wildland preservation often emphasized the special cultural and recreational importance of these areas. In his writings during this period, Leopold, for example, suggested that as long as we had wild country still big enough to absorb a two-week-long pack trip without getting "tangled up" in our own back track, the rugged virtues of the American frontier spirit (what he would later dub "split-rail values") could be kept alive.[2]

The first designated Primitive Area, the Gila, was established in New Mexico in 1924 (Leopold, then with the Forest Service in New Mexico, was a major force behind the proposal). That same year, a new and restrictive Immigration Act went into enforcement. The Wilderness Act, which created a national system of wilderness areas designated by Congress, passed in 1964, the year before a new Immigration Act opened the floodgates to the largest wave of migrants by number in American history. The years between were an era of assimilation, hardened by the Depression and World War II, and then burnished by the afterglow of American triumphalism after the war and the ideological rivalries of the Cold War. Here, along with national parks, was a benign and fulsome American contribution to the global commonwealth. Here was America—real America—at its shiniest. As a place apart from lived ties with a landscape, wilderness was the perfect embodiment of the American melting pot. It belonged to everyone because it belonged to no one. Or as Lauret Savoy puts it in *Trace,* her powerful reflection on the confluence of history, race, and the landscape, "The American land preceded hate."[3] Americans had to surrender historic ethnic ties and land-rootedness in favor of a shared ideal landscape much as they did ideals of governance. Wilderness was the antithesis of blood-and-soil nationalism.

Wilderness was the jeweled bearing on which the postwar pivot from old-style conservation turned to a newer-age preservation. Yet despite a growing sentiment that the protection of the wilderness was worth making certain sacrifices, its political purchase remained tenuous. The Bureau of Reclamation's damming of Utah's Glen Canyon, a project that began after the plans at Echo Park were scuttled, reminded preservationists that the campaign for the wild would likely never end. David Brower of the Sierra Club made a strategic concession not to fight the Glen Canyon dam as part of the political gambit to save Dinosaur National Monument in the mid-1950s. Once again, Brower shepherded a book celebrating a wild place in

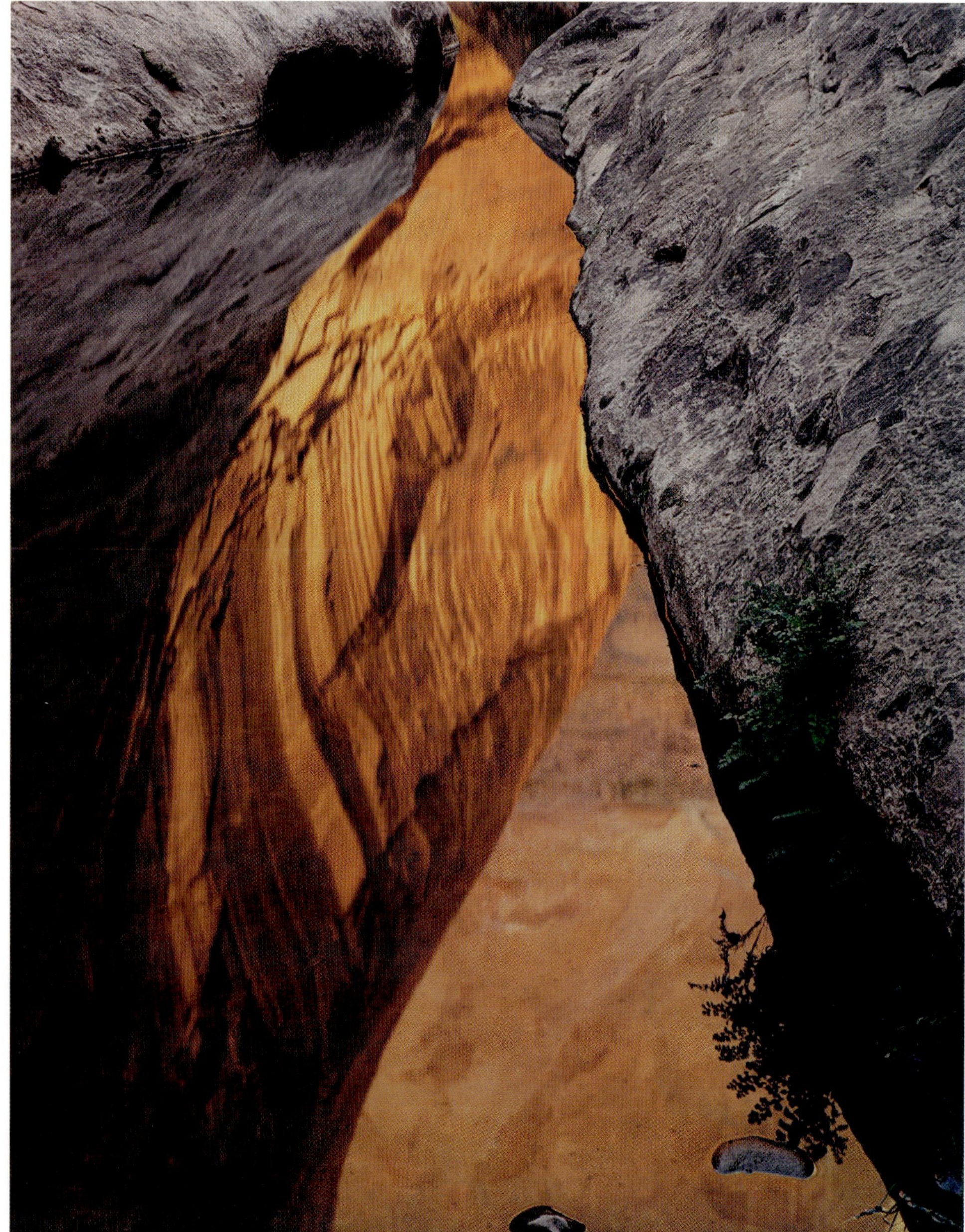

33. Eliot Porter, *Pool in Hidden Passage, Glen Canyon, Utah, August 27, 1961* (© 1990, Amon Carter Museum of American Art, Fort Worth, Texas; bequest of the artist)

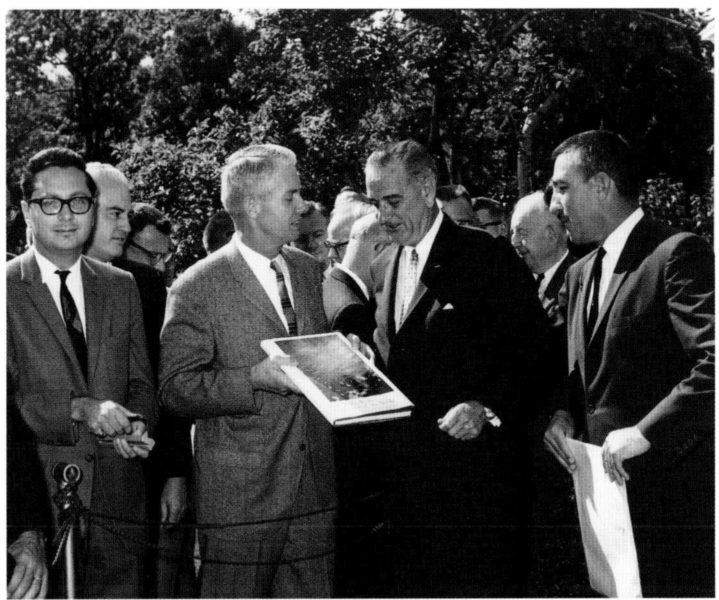

34. David Brower presents President Lyndon Johnson with a copy of Eliot Porter's *In Wildness Is the Preservation of the World,* 1964 (Photograph by Abbie Rowe, the White House, courtesy of Earth Island Institute)

peril, publishing the photographer Eliot Porter's *The Place No One Knew: Glen Canyon on the Colorado* in 1963 (plate 33). This time, however, the book functioned as a pictorial lament for a lost landscape. "Glen Canyon died in 1963 and I was partly responsible for its needless death," Brower wrote in the book's foreword. Yet he also wasn't going to take all of the blame. "So were you," he followed.

Glen Canyon may have been submerged, but the publishing program at the Sierra Club was on the rise. The spectacular color photographs of *The Place No One Knew* had set a new tech-

nical and aesthetic standard for Brower's Exhibit Format series, and the book's production values made it pop and crackle. Porter's previous Sierra Club volume, *In Wildness Is the Preservation of the World,* a collection of pictures of pastoral woodlands joined with texts by Henry Thoreau, had been a big hit only the year before, convincing Brower that a series of environmental fine art books could find an audience (plate 34).

Porter's experimentation with color printing and the intricate, close-up composition of his photographs distinguished them from the sweeping black-and-white vistas of Ansel Adams, his colleague and (mostly) friendly rival in the Sierra Club photography space. Porter joined Adams on the Sierra Club board in the mid-1960s, and *The Place No One Knew,* despite or perhaps because of its elegiac character, served as the high-water mark for Brower's book program.[4]

Despite its cultural florescence in the 1960s and early 1970s, it is striking how poorly wilderness has translated outside the U.S. context, and even within American experience, outside its formative years and western landscapes. Other countries are not willing to deny homelands for the sake of a deracinated, decultured place. They protect nature for particular purposes, not simply as monumental sacred groves. National parks were a more flexible concept that could be adapted to local conditions; even better were UNESCO's Biosphere Reserves, which could juggle core and peripheral areas, places where humans were transients with places where they resided. The very purity of wilderness meant it was less, not more, transportable.

Preserving wilderness was the emblem of an era between a doctrine of conservation and a doctrine of sustainability, between the need to halt the wreckage wrought by settlement and the disruptions of that broader frontier now labeled the Anthropocene. What Persepolis was to Persia, what the Acropolis was to ancient Greece, what Chartres Cathedral was to medieval Christendom, its wilderness system was to twentieth-century America. It now seems a unique portrait of a time and place, but an idea not likely to be exported or repeated.

In fact, it is hard to imagine the America of today creating a national wilderness preservation system. The American melting pot has become a salad of seemingly incommensurable peoples sorted by race, gender, ethnicity, and class; the country obsesses over how to find a common narrative among its cacophony of voices, with many newcomers no longer from a Western civilization that had written the intellectual score behind the idea of the wild. Wilderness preservation, and the environmental movement more generally, have become just a part of this wider conflict. Between the publication of *Sand County Almanac* and the election of Donald Trump as president, the country's population had more than doubled. The contest between peoples, not between people and land, dominated the national discourse. Often globalism was cast as a contest between people from somewhere and people from nowhere. The resurgence of blood-and-soil nationalism and its literary celebration of place and homeland undercut the transcendent unity proposed by wilderness, which could appear as suited only for people of nowhere.

Yet the achievement was real. For a historic moment, over roughly two decades, a constantly evolving state of nature had bonded with a continually changing state of mind to create an idea that became a law that fashioned a special landscape.

Inevitably, its meaning would change. Its essence, "wilderness character," was a cultural creation that had—could have—no permanent definition. Its most distinctive property was a call for restraint. If not a true *terra nullius,* it could show properties of a *tabula rasa*—a screen on which people could project their own sensibilities. What it preserved, in the end, was less a particular vision of a place or a plexus of processes than an ethic, that we could choose to leave nature alone as best we could.

About the Gallery

BAM: There are only two photos in this gallery, Mark, but one of them is yours (plate 36, with Byron Wolfe). So, let me ask you (while borrowing the title of your own book on Glen Canyon), is there still beauty to be had in a "drowned river"?

MK: Ben, as you know, even Edward Abbey had to admit that floating in the waters of Lake Powell had its pleasures.

BAM: Fair enough. But what I'm interested in probing a little here is your thoughts about how photography has shaped our understanding of places like Glen Canyon, which figured so prominently in historical campaigns for wilderness preservation and in landmark Sierra Club books like Eliot Porter's *The Place No One Knew* (1963). As we mention in the essay, Porter's book was an elegy for a lost world and also an apologia from the Sierra Club's David Brower, who lamented not doing more to save it. But for you and Byron I imagine it's a little more complicated than that, as it is for Adam Thorman in his photo of Hetch Hetchy, another "martyred wilderness" (plate 35).

MK: For better or worse, I tend to take the long view about places like these. I don't know how long it will take, and we may not be around to see it, but someday the water behind those dams will flow again. It's almost a geological certainty.

BAM: Well, I think you're better at taking the long view than I am! And the fact that you can do that in a place like Lake Powell, which you've immersed yourself in over the years, is heartening. Still, I have to admit that knowing something about these places and their history I can't help but feel an undercurrent of loss. It's not always easy to "think like a canyon" (to paraphrase Aldo Leopold) and take the geological view on these choices. But I want to.

MK: You're right, being able to think in the long term offers little consolation. When I see these pictures there's this conflicting feeling of loss while at the same time they acknowledge the complexity of modern society and implicate us in the trade-offs that have made our lives in the West possible. But if we can see these as being single frames in a gigantic time-lapse film it also says something hopeful about visualizing a future. That may help us come to lessons that need to be learned about playing with nature—and drowning a river.

SP: And maybe about imagining a future for the art of those places. The old style looked into gorges and saw what was lost. The new style has to contend with surfaces and see what exists. The contrasts are not merely changes in topography but in sensibility—bound to result in a little cultural wind-shear. The aesthetic style of the photos may look similar, but for me their effects differ.

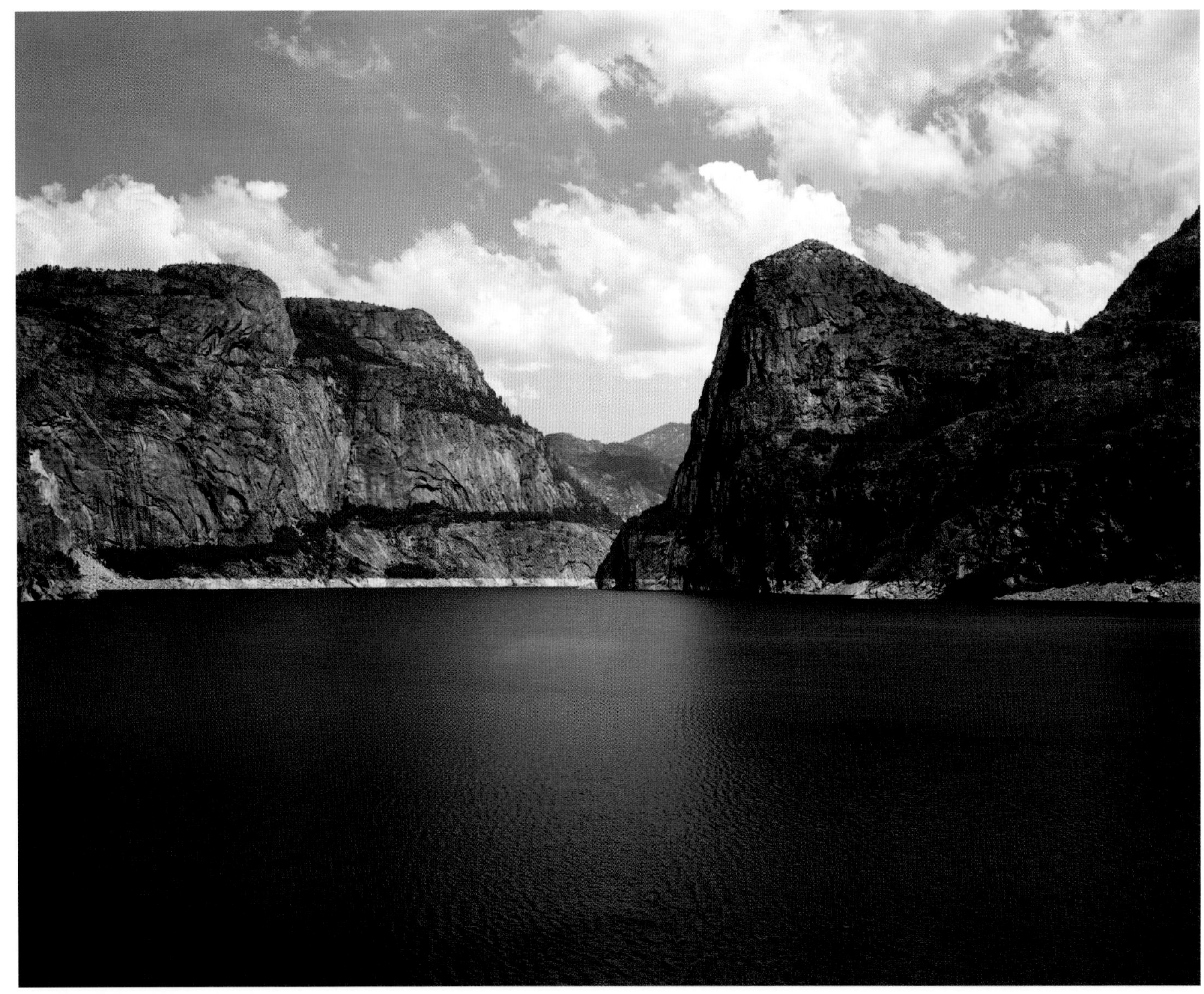

  35. Adam Thorman, *Hetch Hetchy Water System from California Water*, 2016

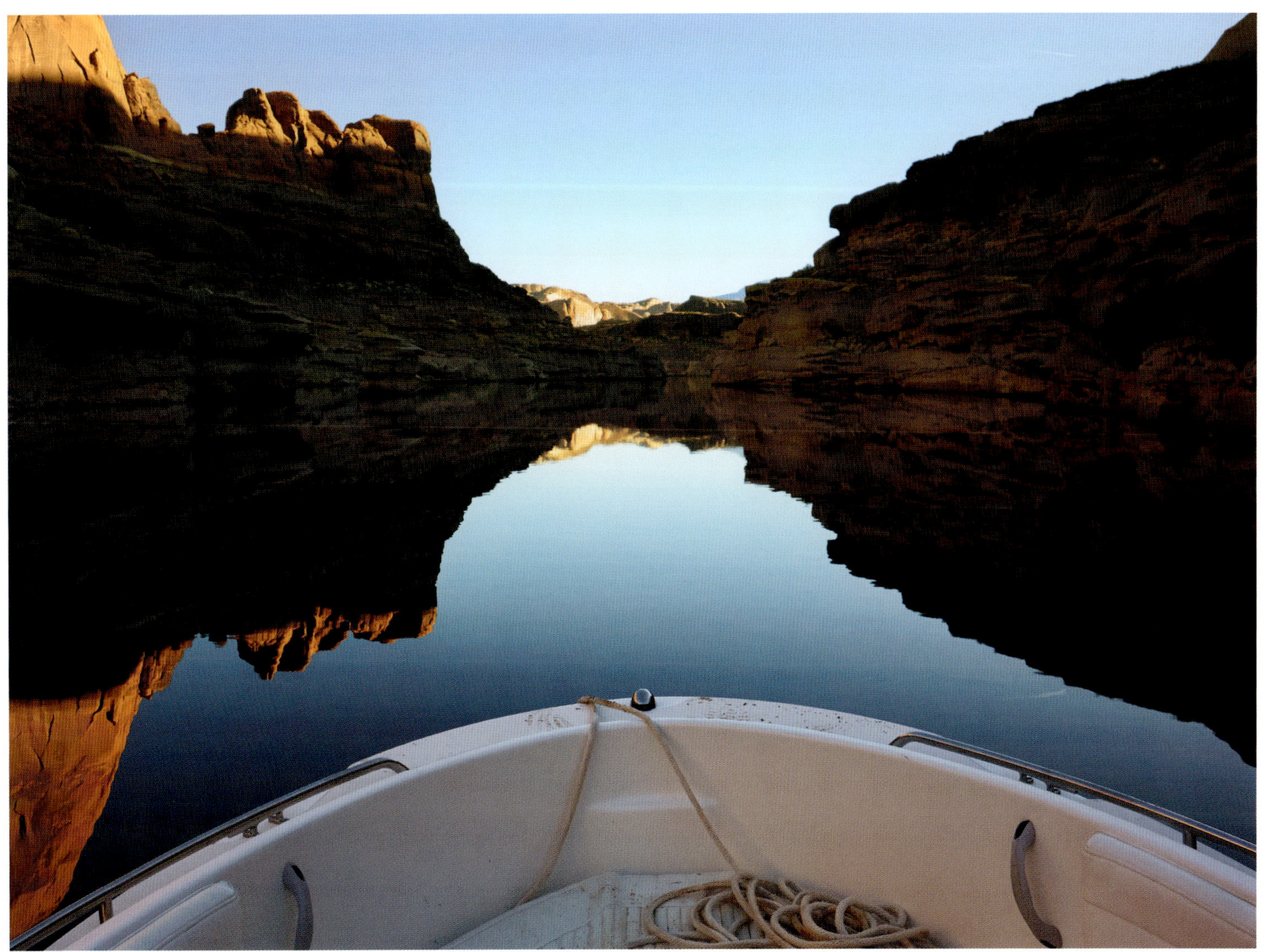

36. Mark Klett and Byron Wolfe, *The Bow of Our Boat Near the End of a Narrow Canyon, Lake Powell*, 2011

Effect on Federal Lands

With the Wilderness Act, the ideal became real. Wilderness had boundaries drawn on maps and protocols written for their administration. They became bureaucratic categories. They had to be managed. In the past, new categories of land had come with an agency designated to administer them. Often, in the early years, there was some shuffling among bureaus before one became the designated driver—not always by choice. The General Land Office administered the forest reserves before the Forest Service assumed control in 1905 and renamed them national forests. The Biological Survey had responsibility for the archipelago of wildlife refuges for decades until a newly constituted Fish and Wildlife Service in the early 1940s oversaw the national wildlife refuge system. For thirty years the national parks were administered by the U.S. Cavalry until, in 1916, the National Park Service (NPS) was created; it subsequently took over most historic sites and monuments.

But there was no National Wilderness Service founded to administer the National Wilderness Preservation System. Instead, each agency had to absorb wilderness within its own apparatus. That arrangement reduced somewhat agency resistance to wilderness since it would not "lose" those lands, as the Forest Service had lost the scenic Olympic Mountains to the NPS. But holding those lands under a special-use category significantly reduced agency discretion. The Wilderness Act laid down fairly stringent guidelines about what could and could not be done. No roads. No vehicles, no chain saws, no bulldozers. No permanent structures, not even fire lookouts. Bureaus that had evolved around founding charters now had their traditions and established procedures for decisions challenged.

That of course was the issue for many wilderness advocates. The old ways inevitably eroded wilderness to vanishing points. The greatest threat to remaining roadless areas seemed to be the Forest Service. It had the most public lands outside Alaska; most of the potential wilderness sites that might be compromised by logging, grazing, roadbuilding, and recreational developments; and the most malleable doctrine, codified into the Multiple Use–Sustained Yield Act in 1960. If wilderness remained only an administrative choice, one of many competing options, then a designated site could easily be converted by a change in administration, and once broken, the character of the wild might be irrevocably lost. The point of the Wilderness Act was to remove that discretion. The agency had to learn to actively do nothing, or more accurately, to aggressively keep its hands to itself.

So the Forest Service bore most of the criticisms. It suffered from within as well as without. It had to absorb the tensions between foresters and wilderness enthusiasts in its own workforce. The cost of retaining administrative control was to cope with the kind of national tensions over environmental issues inside its own house. The old multiple-use doctrine stumbled in an era that favored special-use lands: the public domain went from a kind of multiple-use melting pot to a special-use mosaic. Practices that once spanned all the forests throughout the National Forest System now broke down into more local particulars (fire management is a good example). It was no longer the case that one agency promoted one philosophy and practice and other agencies did others, but that each agency became a sometime quarreling multitude in itself. Legal enclosure started to fracture what had been a kind of public-domain commons.

The wilderness movement then turned to the other agencies. The National Park Service was mostly spared because the Leopold Report in 1963 had endorsed a redefinition of the parks as "vignettes of primitive America"—to most observers, a good-enough approximation of the wild. It's easy to forget what a radical proposition that was at a time when the NPS was still bustling with Mission 66, a ten-year program to overhaul its

infrastructure. The Fish and Wildlife Service had some maneuvering room since it was already committed to habitat and was the agent for the Endangered Species Act. The Bureau of Land Management received an organic act only in 1976 (that is, a law establishing territory and terms for governance); most of its lands were those that had never been settled during the frontier era. Its attraction for wilderness advocates lay mostly in Alaska, and its internal tensions were resolved with the Alaska National Interest Lands Conservation Act of 1980.

By then, however, the Wilderness Act was only one of a menagerie of environmental legislation that sought to limit agency discretion. The Clean Air Act, the Clean Water Act, the Endangered Species Act, the National Environmental Policy Act—the list rushes on. Wilderness was often the most prominent because it was the least negotiable, but land managers on the public domain found they could do less and less. There was a lawsuit waiting behind every stump, a court injunction around every stock tank, a public relations brouhaha over every species with an advocate able to afford the cost of a first-class stamp. More and more the public lands looked like one another regardless of the agency administering them. From an agency standpoint legal wilderness was domesticated into one of many administrative considerations.

Still, it aroused powerful passions among partisans for and against. The call for untrammeled places collided with the call for unfettered access. The polarization seems not to be whether to protect or exploit nature, but the nature of the protection. The Fish and Wildlife Service and Nature Conservancy can do aggressive conservation and restoration treatments on the land and not be pilloried. What seems to rankle is the pure preservationist approach, especially where forms of land use such as hunting are regarded as part of cultural heritage. How wilderness will cope with the mounting insults of the Anthropocene and the attendant pressures to act will likely define the movement in the coming decades.

As we've seen time and again, from the Arctic National Wildlife Refuge to Utah's Grand Staircase–Escalante, most of those conflicts will play out on federal lands. In recent times America's political climate, like nature's, seems prone to more violent swings between extremes. The Trump administration stripped away most of Bears Ears National Monument; the Biden administration appointed a Native American as secretary of the interior. The increasingly feral floods and fires of Congress will express themselves in the nation's public domain. Those lands made a National Wilderness Preservation System possible. The future of the system cannot be segregated from the future of the public domain that contains them.

Rupture
Reconfiguration

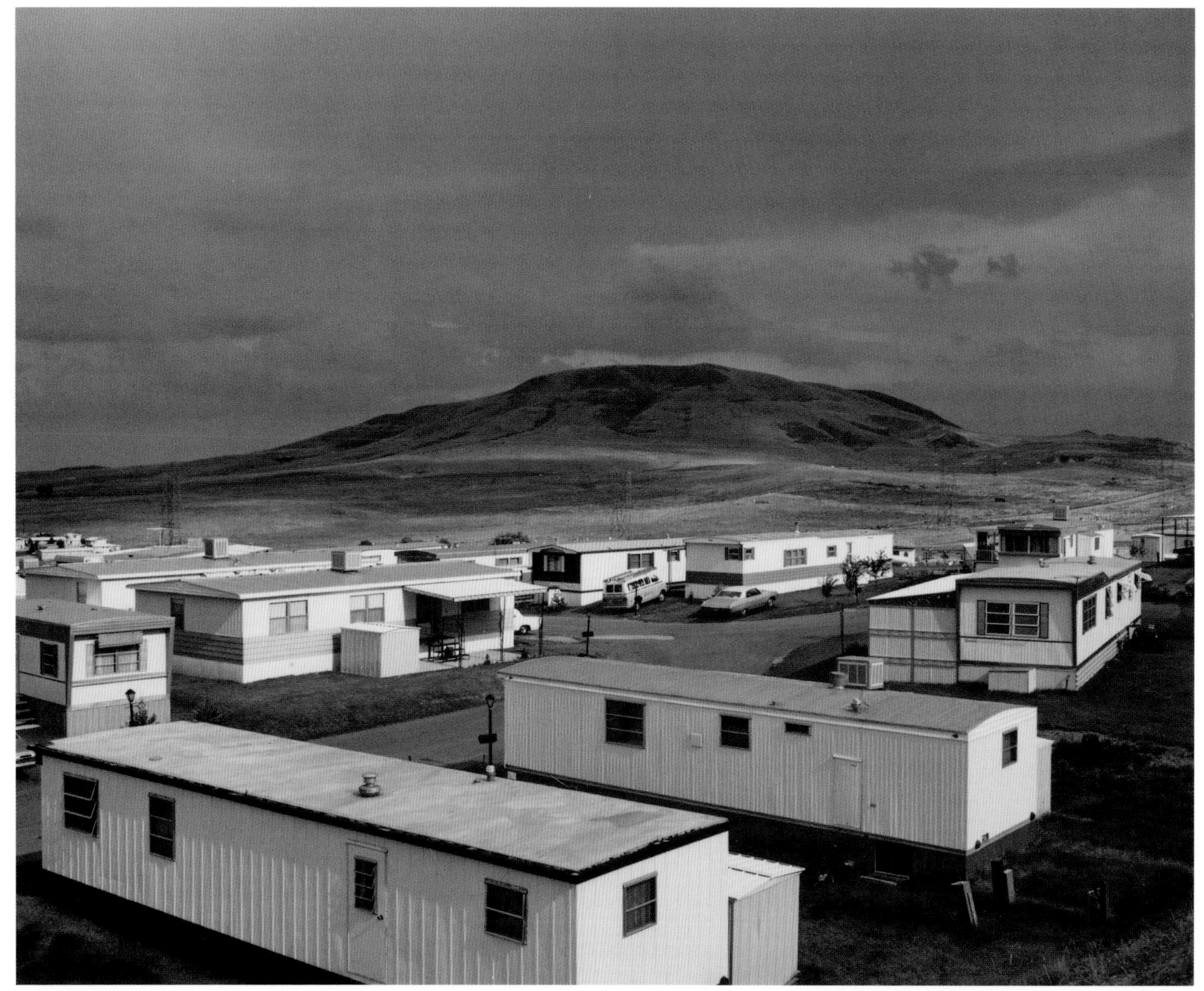

37. Robert Adams, *Mobile Homes, Jefferson County, Colorado, 1973* (© Robert Adams, courtesy of the Fraenkel Gallery, San Francisco)

Wrecked Wild? Considering the "Man-Altered" Landscape

The sky is still big, still a western sky. But instead of framing towering peaks and deep canyons it hovers over a bleak landscape foregrounded with mobile homes. Nature here isn't beautiful, at least in the traditional sense. And it no longer dominates the frame. Despite the compositional refinement of the picture, we're clearly a world away from Ansel Adams.

The photo, taken by the photographer Robert Adams outside of Denver in the early 1970s, was a picture of the changing American West of the late twentieth century, a landscape fast becoming overrun with tract houses, billboards, and parking lots (plate 37). Adams's work helped define a new movement in landscape photography in the 1970s that found photographers self-consciously turning away from the romanticism, overt emotionality, and wilderness-centric vision of Ansel Adams, Eliot Porter, and the familiar environmental aesthetic of the Sierra Club books. In Robert Adams's pictures, as well as those of a group of sympathetic photographers including Lewis Baltz, Joe Deal, and Frank Gohlke, Half Dome and Canyon de Chelly were replaced by gas stations and strip malls as photographic subjects. The vernacular shoved aside the spectacular; the sublime traded for the banal.[1]

This was the landscape counterpart to punk rock, literary deconstructionism, and the let-a-hundred-flowers-bloom of postmodernist art, when galleries filled with Campbell soup cans, comic book stills, and sculptures of hamburgers, when pop art, op art, conceptual art, and a vibrant palette of ephemeral schools splashed across the era. They challenged the high seriousness of the reigning titans of modernism with satire, and confronted art with mocking artifacts of everyday life. Landscape photography joined the cavalcade.

Branded the "New Topographics," a moniker that conveyed a quasi-scientific, documentary mode of picture making, photographers working in this style captured the human transformation of nature, eschewing depictions of pristine park and wilderness vistas for a more altered, "peopled" environment.[2] They joined the annals of photographic history in 1975, when the curator William Jenkins organized an exhibition of their work at the George Eastman House in Rochester, New York. Intriguingly, the New Topographic photographers presented a somewhat ambivalent take on the development of the American West. Although billed as a dispassionate and value-free recording of the landscape, as the art historian Deborah Bright notes, it was hard not to see the work of the New Topographic photographers as a critical response to the development and exploitation of the natural world, especially in the 1970s, when an awareness of environmental degradation and decline had become part of the mainstream. Or more dramatically, "the end of romantic nature and the blurring of the boundaries between the human and the natural on which that old myth depended."[3]

That last bit may have been too much; Robert Adams, probably the most influential among the New Topographic photographers, was at pains to express his regard for the form and environmental philosophy of Ansel Adams's wilderness compositions. The older Adams's work remained important, he wrote, because it revealed the "absolute purity of wilderness, a purity we need to know."[4] But it's clear that he and his fellow New Topographic photographers were turning viewers' heads in a different direction, toward a view of landscape and nature that carried with it a more anthropocentric outlook than their Sierra Club forebears. While the closed and covered landscapes of the East could often mask development and unsavory flotsam and jetsam in forested valleys and rolling hills, in the wide-open vistas of the West there were fewer places to hide, which no doubt magnified the visual disruption of the scene.

In hindsight, the New Topographic aesthetic anticipated the broader revisionism toward the American West (and eventually the wilderness) that developed in the 1980s, including the rise of the "New Western History." Like the New Topographic photographers, New Western historians dismissed triumphalist notions of the American West and sought to present a more nuanced portrait, highlighting the roles of social conflict, development, and environmental decline in shaping the region's history. Myth-making about an "end of frontier" in the late nineteenth century was rejected in favor of a more complicated narrative propelled by intricate and ongoing cultural, economic, and environmental processes.[5] The wilderness became another element in this larger struggle, a contest that, in historian Donald Worster's words, "left behind it much death, depletion, and ruin."[6] The old aesthetics of wilderness photography were transferred to the landscapes that actually characterized the West, with plenty of irony, dissonance, and dismay.

As a more historiographically sharpened perspective on the American West took hold, it became harder to keep alive the ideal of wilderness as Eden, a place outside this complex and messy history. By the early 1990s, the implicit photographic critique of the wild by the New Topographic photographers and the revisionism of the New Western historians was complemented by the writing of scholars eager to break the grip of the wilderness myth on American environmentalism.

One of the more influential and interesting voices in the mix was the cultural geographer J. B. Jackson, who saw a troubling ethos in traditional American wilderness imagery, one ruinous for striking a more sustainable relationship to the environment. Singling out the writing of Edward Abbey and the Sierra Club Exhibit Format books, which he faulted for an "anti-urban, antitechnological, antipeople, antihistory and anthrophobic" vision urging us to "worship nature," Jackson argued for a more humanist environmentalism, one more appropriate for a rapidly urbanizing and crowded planet.[7] In what must have seemed like heresy to preservationists, he extolled the value of roads and highways, which had been depicted by generations of writers and activists as an existential threat to the wild. Yet the highway was, Jackson pointed out, a vital mechanism for getting people out to the countryside (much as the railroad had been for the national parks in an earlier era). It was the quintessential public good, offering the opportunity for individuals and families to briefly connect with nature before heading back to their sprawling suburbs and the concrete canyons of the city. Besides, from Walt Whitman to Jack Kerouac the Open Road had been celebrated as a great American place. Roads might belong as much as cliff-dwelling ruins in Grand Gulch.[8]

Although his critique was often compelling, Jackson undersold the role of wilderness imagery and texts in building a wider public appreciation of wild country and its vulnerabilities in the second half of the twentieth century. Before the passage of the Wilderness Act in 1964 it wasn't guaranteed that we would have an effective legal mechanism for protecting wildlands from development. Nor was it certain that there would be a public that cared enough about wilderness to make its destruction a political liability. The Sierra Club Exhibit Format series, and books like Abbey's *Desert Solitaire,* despite Jackson's misgivings, played a role in both cases.

Still, he had a point. Viewing wilderness as a sacred, inviolable place, one at the moral and aesthetic pinnacle of environmentalist concern, often encouraged a blinkered view of the rest of the landscape. It was a message that became amplified by a number of scholars in the early and mid-1990s, most notably William Cronon, whose historicizing of the wilderness idea in his essay "The Trouble with Wilderness" in 1995 suggested the cultural, philosophical, and strategic limitations of the wilderness-centered mindset.[9] Like Jackson and the New Topographic photographers, Cronon's wilderness critique found him promoting a more geographically and aesthetically ecumenical environmental ethics, one reconciled to the altered and built environments in which most people lived, worked, and played. "We need," Cronon urged, "to embrace the full continuum of a natural landscape that is also cultural, in which the city, the suburb, the pastoral, and the wild each has its proper place, which we permit ourselves to celebrate without needlessly denigrating the others."[10]

If a growing number of writers in the 1980s and 1990s worried that a century of myth-making about the wild and the American West led many to think of the region as a timeless and untouched Eden, a place "without industry or cities," as Worster put it, the New Topographic photographs of the 1970s therefore offered a kind of early aesthetic corrective.[11] Yet the ambiguity remains: were the pictures intended to legitimize the trailer parks, malls, and tract houses snaking across the western landscape, or were they sounding a kind of photographic alarm? For many observers, the images did more than teeter on the brink of despair. One of them is the writer Rebecca Solnit, who feels that Robert Adams's photographs, especially in the 1980s, conveyed a deep state of melancholy and pessimism about our ability to pull back from the environmental abyss.[12]

No doubt there is a profound sense of concern about the

development of the West and even a kind of quasi-metaphysical alienation from nature in Robert Adams's work, including in his early photographs in the 1970s. Yet it is interesting that Adams would eventually strike a more hopeful tone in his writings about photography in the 1990s, conveying a far more pragmatic environmental philosophy than might be expected. "Areas of the American West are not wholly irredeemable," he declared, suggesting that "half-damaged" as the land is, there was still the possibility of recovery. And it was this hope of renewal, he suggested, that made the photographs of Carleton Watkins and Ansel Adams still vital. As he wrote, "To love the old views is not entirely pointless nostalgia, but rather an understandable and fitting passion for what could in some measure be ours again."[13] In that sense, the enthusiasm for rephotography (returning to the sites where Watkins and other early photographers of the American West made their marks to capture both permanance and change) might be considered in the same genre as Civil War reenactors, but it also aligned with enthusiasms for prairie restoration and for understanding historical ecological change more generally.[14] It could be penance for past sins and promise for what might be.

Photographers working in the shadow of the New Topographics movement would continue to document the tangled ways of mixing nature and culture in these altered lands, grappling with earlier aesthetic traditions while finding new forms and meanings. If their photographs offer no simple answers to the collision course of people and nature on the western landscape, they help us understand the choices we make when we write our signature on the land, as Aldo Leopold put it. In the process, they take visual measure of the shifting distance between the wild and the wrecked.

About the Gallery

BAM: The New Topographics exhibition discussed in this chapter clearly cast a long shadow. For some it informed a new aesthetic of the landscape, one that had room for billboards, tract houses, gas stations, and other markers of the human enterprise. For others, it was a dreary documentation of the decline of the American West. And for still others (OK, sometimes the very same observers) it punctured the long-running myth of the wild and of the American frontier. Like other single events that later become credited with ushering in a new way of thinking (and in this case, seeing), there's a danger of projecting too much historical influence on what happened in Rochester back in 1975. Yet the impact of these photographs gathered in one place—and at that time—seems indisputable.

Mark, what do you see as the lasting significance of the work of Robert Adams (plate 37), Lewis Baltz (plate 38), Joe Deal (plate 39), and the other NT photographers in that exhibition at the Eastman House all those years ago for how we see and value the landscape, especially in its wilder varieties?

MK: The New Topographics exhibition did open a door for photographers to move past established conventions. The timing is interesting in that it took place roughly forty years after some of the most influential work was made by Ansel Adams, Edward Weston and other modernist photographers. At the time, NT didn't look like a movement, and in fact very few people even saw the exhibition in Rochester.

SP: Couldn't the same could be said of the 1913 Armory Show that introduced modernism to America? The Rochester exhibit was the shock of the new for landscape photography. It forced a new aesthetic, one that had to be cultivated, and had an impact better recognized in historical hindsight than at the moment.

MK: Right, you might think of that event as a place marker in time, that observations of human interaction with the land had risen to the level of critical awareness. The work included in NT may have seemed to contradict the notion of beauty and the wild established by earlier photographers, especially in the American West. But the concept had broad, even international, appeal because it related to the landscapes of everyday experience (as someone once told me in the Netherlands, there wasn't a square meter of that country that hadn't been touched by human hands). That helps explain why the concept of the man-altered landscape had real staying power, and it meant that photographers found subject matter outside of the wilder places, and closer to home.

BAM: OK, but let me push you on this point a little and inject a little pessimism (or maybe just realism) into this notion of the ubiquity of the "man-altered" landscape. When you look at the more contemporary images in this gallery it can certainly seem like a visual narrative of intensifying degradation—for example, Bryan Schutmaat's Nevada wasteland (plate 41); Michael Light's upscale mountain development (plate 42), and so on. Eventually, we appear to be left with Kwasi Boyd-Bouldin's world, where nature and wildness are diminished to only those elements able to sprout up through cracks in the concrete (plate 44).

SP: I confess it's not my natural taste. But some things speak to the mind better than the heart. I can appreciate what these photos are saying and value them intellectually. There is a lot of ugliness to the Anthropocene, and these images present that ugliness in an artful way. But I find I need the caption—what Tom Wolfe termed "the painted word"—to engage fully with them.

BAM: I certainly find it hard to get past a knee-jerk aesthetic response to the "junk" (for lack of a better word) in many of these scenes, Steve. So no doubt these are difficult photos, at least in the wilderness context. Still, it's also true that pictures like the one by Edgar Cardenas seem to pull us out of the fire, offering something more positive—and maybe even a reconciliation of the built (sometimes, though not always wrecked?) and the wild (plate 45). It's the hope emerging from the ecological Pandora's box we've opened in the "Age of Humans."

Mark, is this how you view this particular sequence? And are these contemporary photographers working in the shadow of the NT forebears, or are they doing something different?

MK: I get what you're saying. It's true that in the decades since the NT exhibition, the concept of a man-altered landscape has become the new normal for many landscape photographers. And quite a bit of that focus has been on the negative impact human activity has had on the land. It's still quite shocking to see how careless that relationship has been in some places. Or in other places, how widespread our human footprint has become. That's what we see in the photos you mention.

SP: Our handprint is everywhere. For some the Anthropocene means not just the end of wilderness but the end of nature. The wild is the chaos we've created.

MK: Yes, in the face of such human omnipresence the notion of wild places can seem almost quaint, or irrelevant. But I'm reminded of something Phillip Hyde (one of the photographers of the classic Sierra Club book series) once said after seeing a map of the remaining wilderness areas left in the United States [Full disclosure: I was showing the map in a lecture, and that map rather depressingly revealed that there wasn't much "wilderness" left]. He said defiantly: "I think you can find wilderness by the side of the road."

BAM: Those are likely fighting words for wilderness purists! But his remark makes me think of Aldo Leopold, who wrote nearly a century ago that "Wilderness exists in all degrees, from the little accidental wild spot at the head of a ravine in a corn belt woodlot to vast expanses of virgin country." It's a more qualified and relative take on the wild that Gavin Van Horn articulates so powerfully in a later chapter, and that we can see in several of Ed Ranney's striking images that accompany his essay. So Hyde's view actually enjoys quite a pedigree in the annals of American wilderness thought.

MK: Yes. He's not alone, and one of the things I like about Kwasi and Edgar's photographs is that they show that the natural world and its processes are still at work and accessible, even in urban areas.

So I think you're right that the image sequence in this section does reflect a bit of hope emerging from our Pandora's box. It's also a reminder, now long after NT brought the man-altered land to the front and center of the medium, that photographers have for some time been busy at work expressing complex rela-tionships to the land. Their work doesn't avoid the evidence of human occupation, rather it poses alternatives to how to live in spite of it.

BAM: Actually, this reminds me of a conversation we had many years ago, one that planted some of the seeds that sprouted into this book. You and I are both originally from the East and I remember you saying that when you first came to the West you understood the sense of decline that photographers like Robert Adams (and writers like Sam Shepard) seemed to be document-ing in the 1970s. But you also confessed that you appreciated the West as you found it, valuing what was here rather than mourning what was lost.

I thought that was an interesting way to put it. It brings to mind the idea of shifting baselines, which is a concept borrowed from fisheries biology, I think. We end up not seeing the land-scape as degraded or blighted because we experience it as it is, not as it was. Usually that's seen as a kind of race to the bottom, where we keep accepting decreasing environmental quality as the norm. But you're describing something more nuanced and maybe even hopeful. The West is still beautiful and compelling, not just in spite of the human presence but often because of it.

SP: Bertrand Russell once observed that when you trace what someone means by "state of nature," it usually refers to the world the writer knew as a child. What was in that world is nat-ural, what has come since is not. The world we first saw, even if we saw it later in life, remains the point of reference. For me suburbs seem natural, though in the same way a bark beetle infestation can seem natural. Casinos don't.

BAM: Still, there's no getting around the jarring nature of some of these images, Mark. It can take some work to appreciate the landscapes they reveal to us.

MK: Ben, in the essay you mention the cultural geographer John Brinckerhoff Jackson, who was one of the writers who influenced many photographers in the 1980s (myself included). I think he had a kind of cascading effect on later photographers. Jackson wrote about how contemporary landscapes influence us, focusing on things like strip malls and four-leaf clover interchanges on interstate highways, typically not thought of as beautiful stuff, exploring what makes them worthy of our attention, and even compelling.

In other words, photographers are heavily influenced by the land they see and that's not always beautiful these days. But many also strive for what photographer Robert Frank once described as "transforming destiny into awareness." We now have a human presence on the land that isn't going away, so they envision how we are living with that.

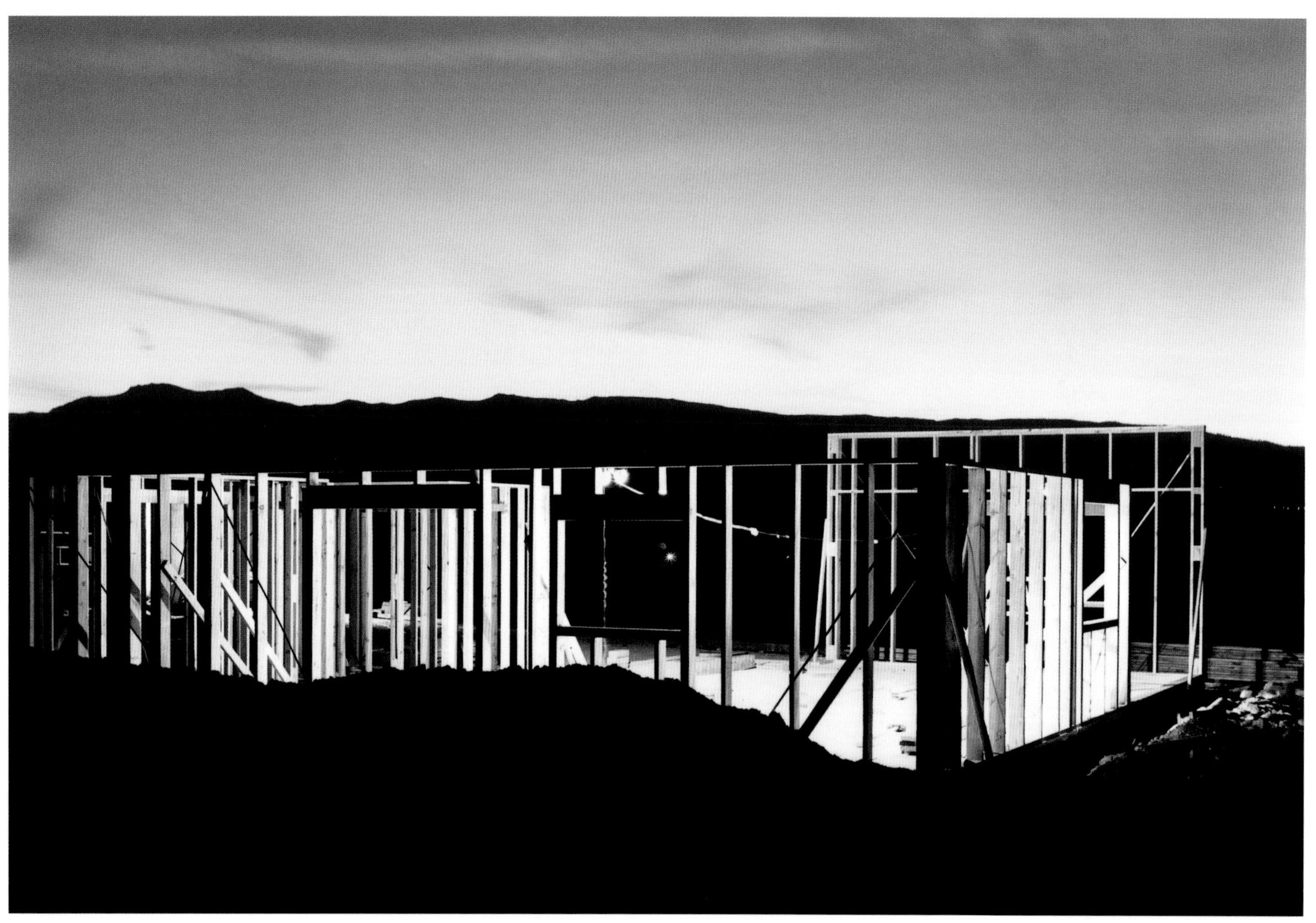

38. Lewis Baltz, *Night Construction, Reno,* 1977 (© Estate of Lewis Baltz; used by permission)

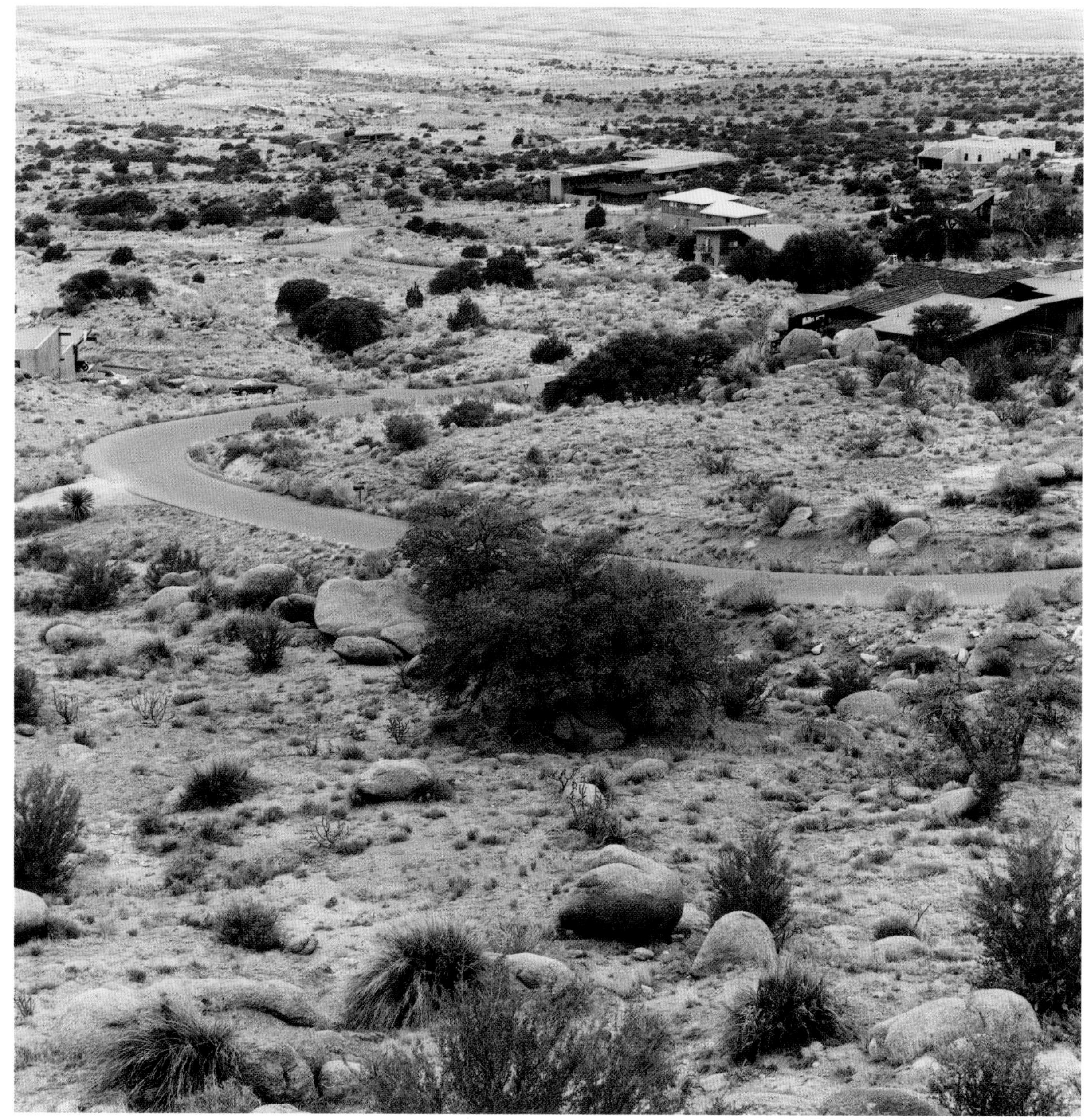

39. Joe Deal, *Untitled View (Albuquerque), 1974* (© The estate of Joe Deal, courtesy of the Robert Mann Gallery)

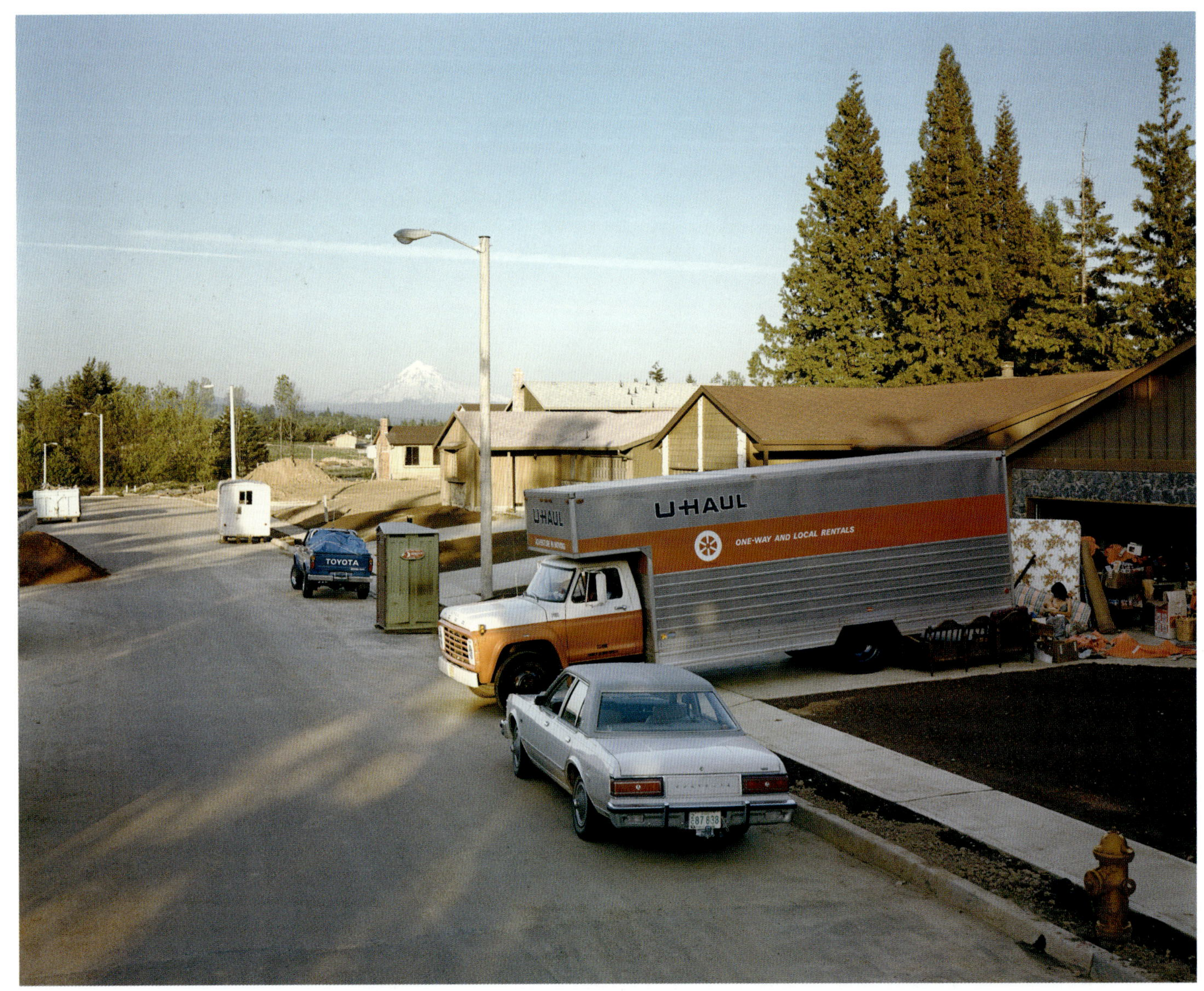

40. Joel Sternfeld, *Gresham, Oregon, June, 1979* (© 2021, Joel Sternfeld)

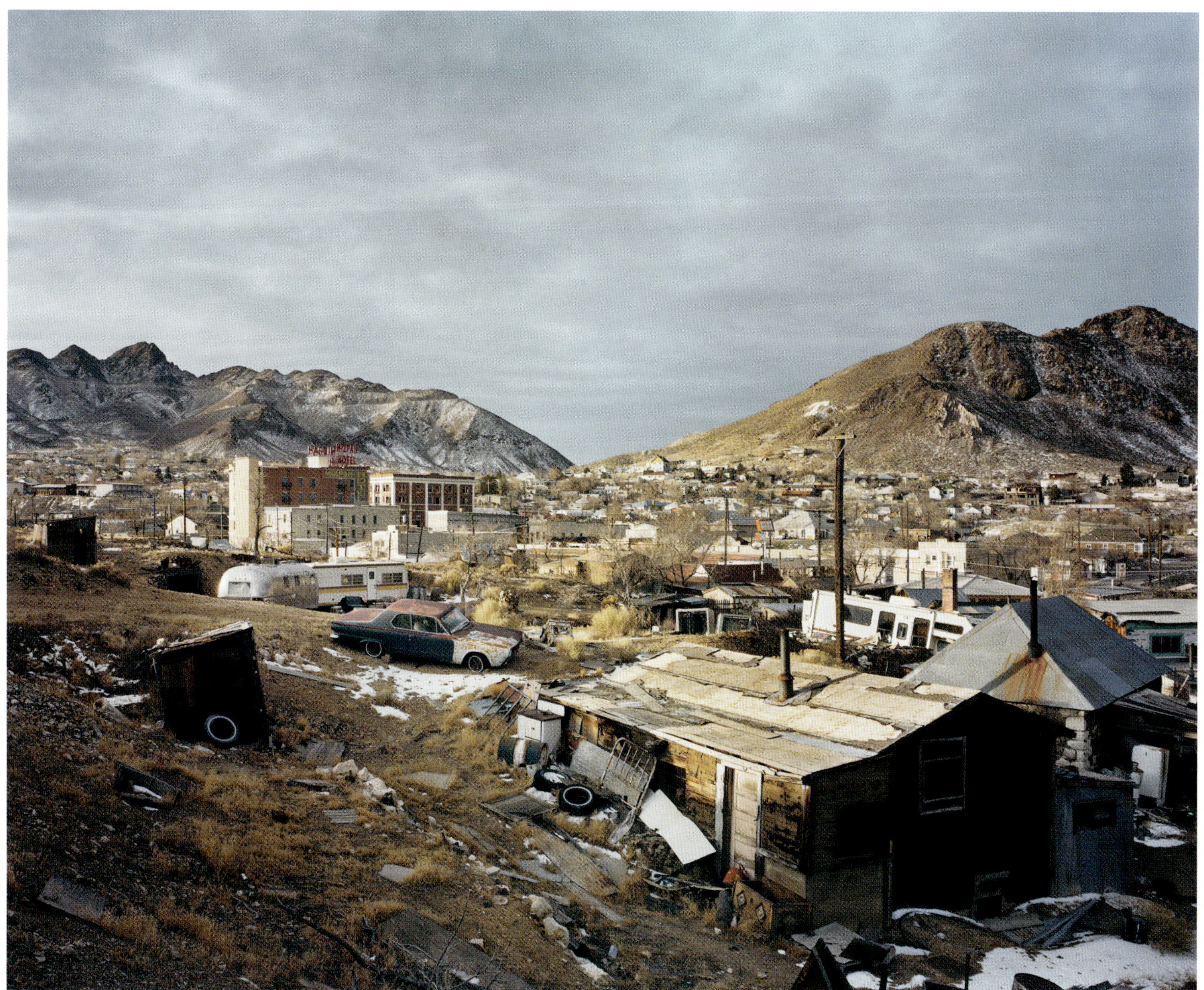

41. Bryan Schutmaat, *Tonopah, Nevada*, 2012

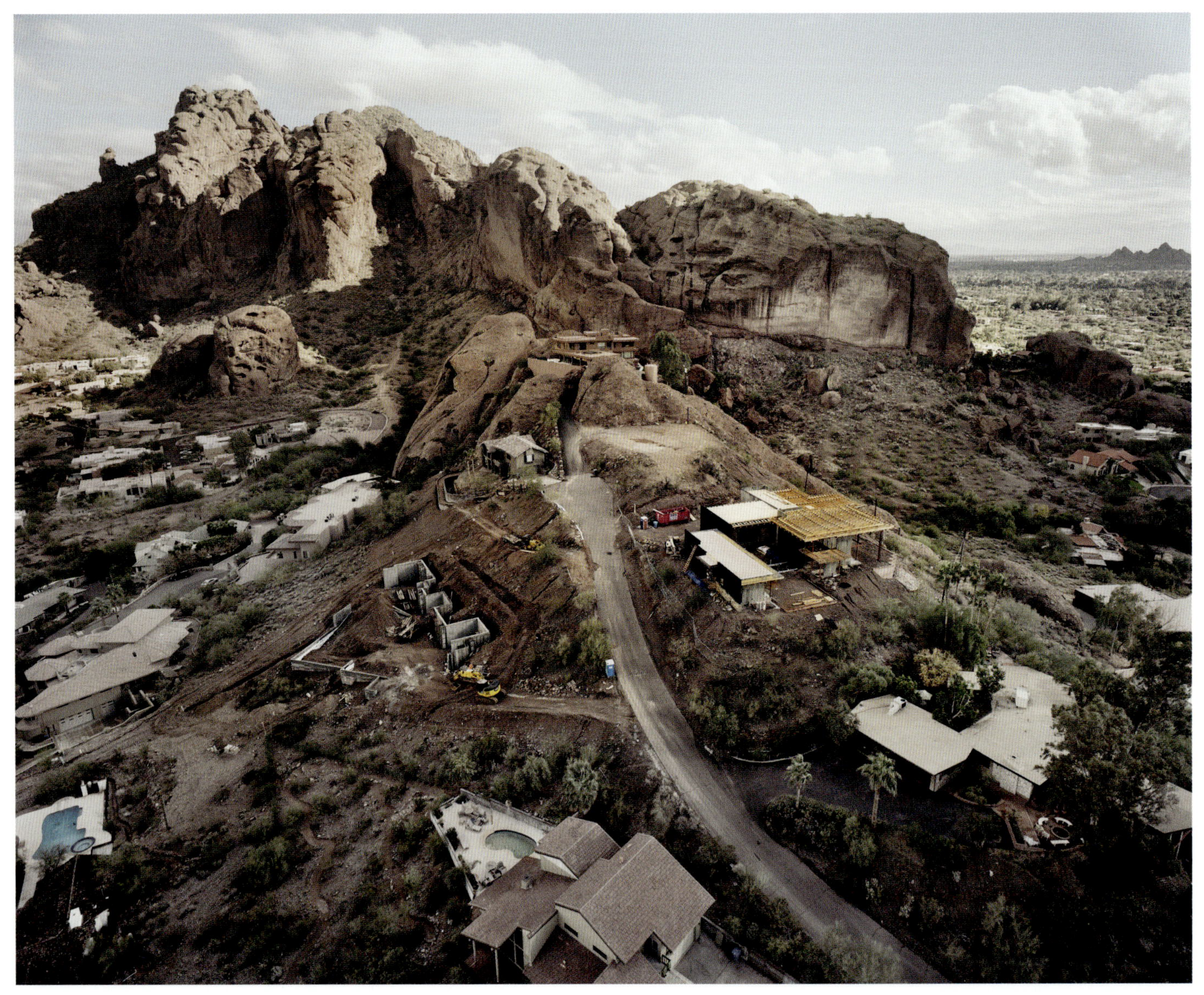

42. Michael Light, *New Construction on East Porter Drive, Camelback Mountain Beyond, Scottsdale, Arizona*, 2007 (© 2007, Michael Light)

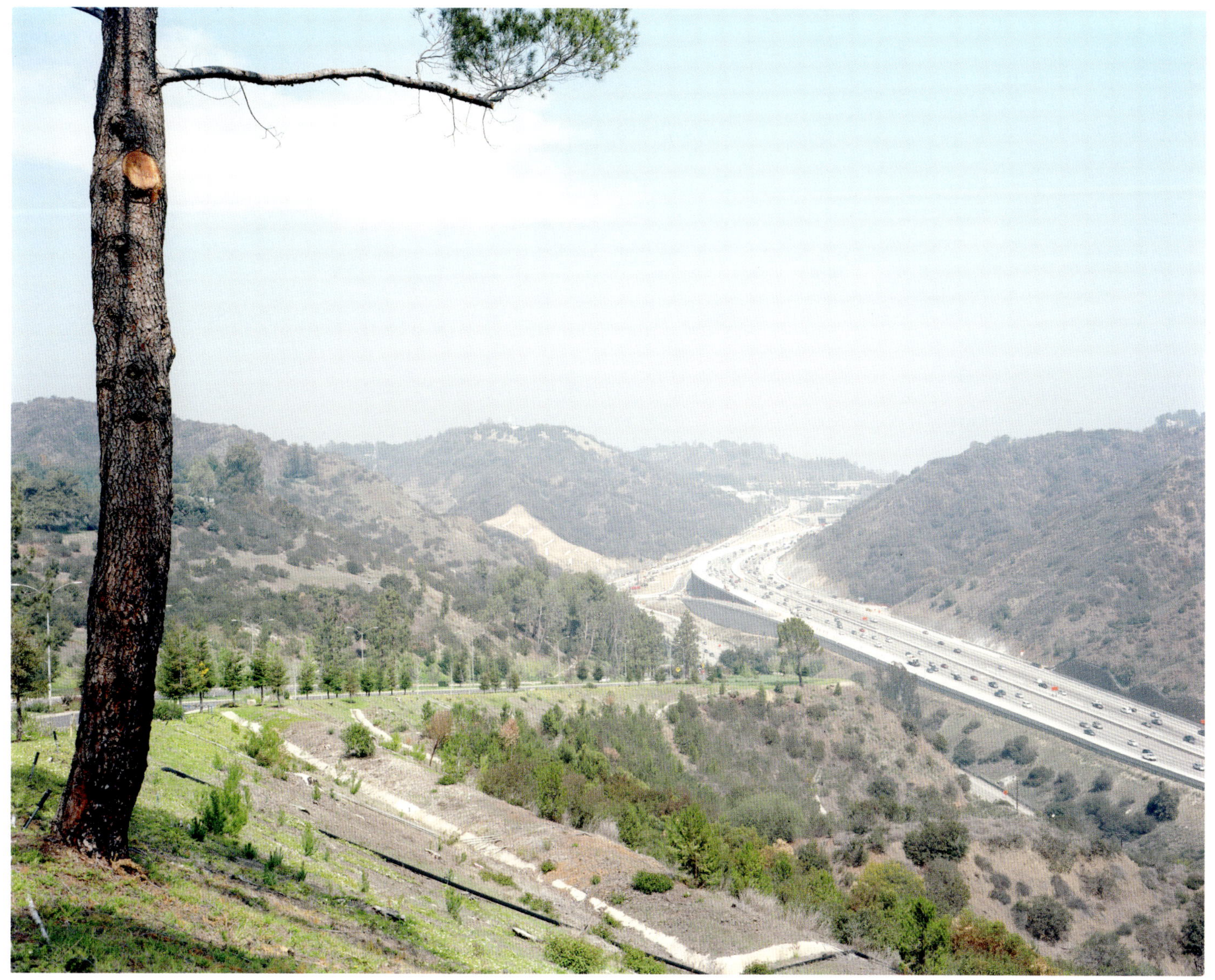

43. Daniel Leivick, *Freeway*, 2014

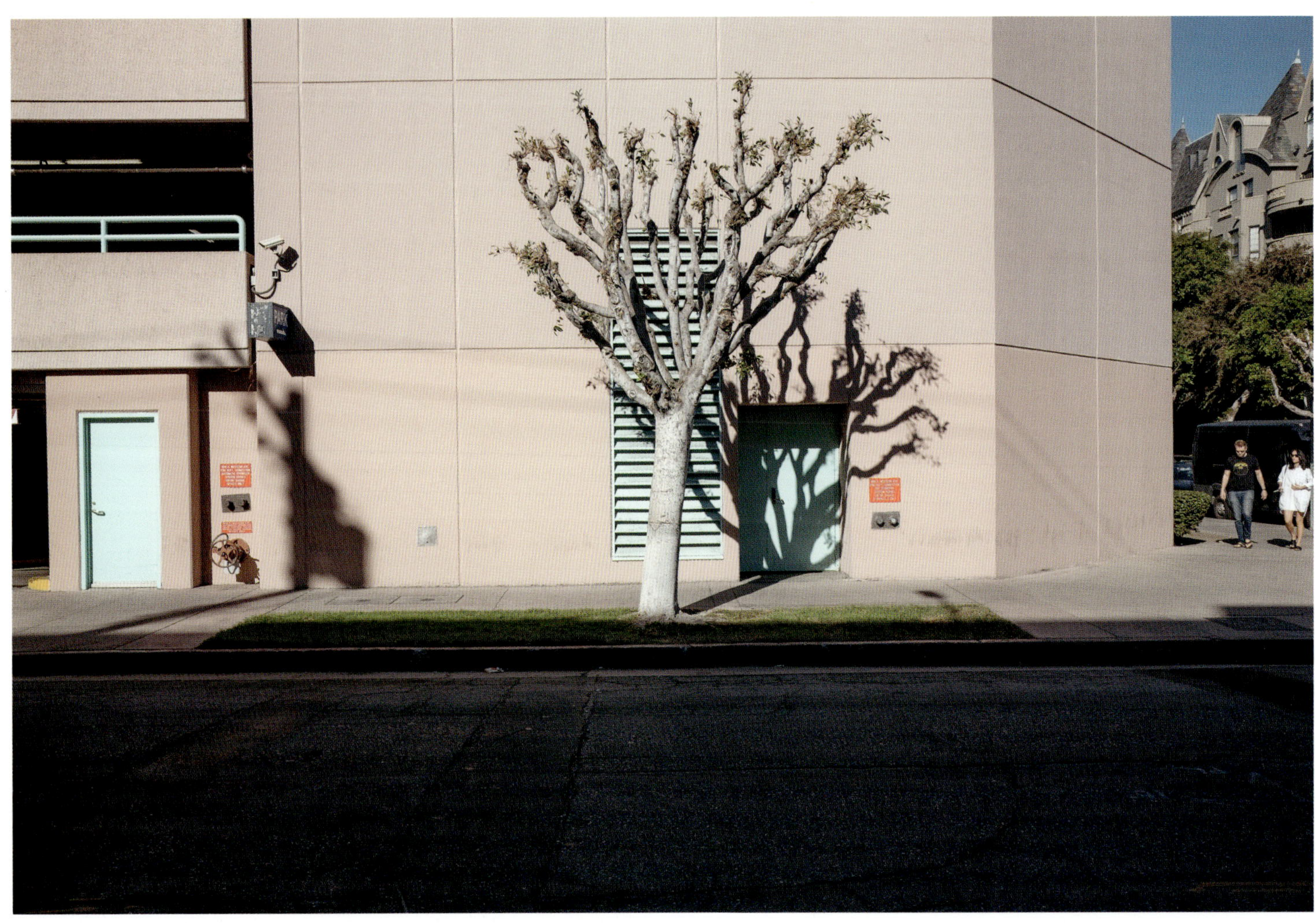

 44. Kwasi Boyd-Bouldin, *San Marino Street, Koreatown Los Angeles*, 2017

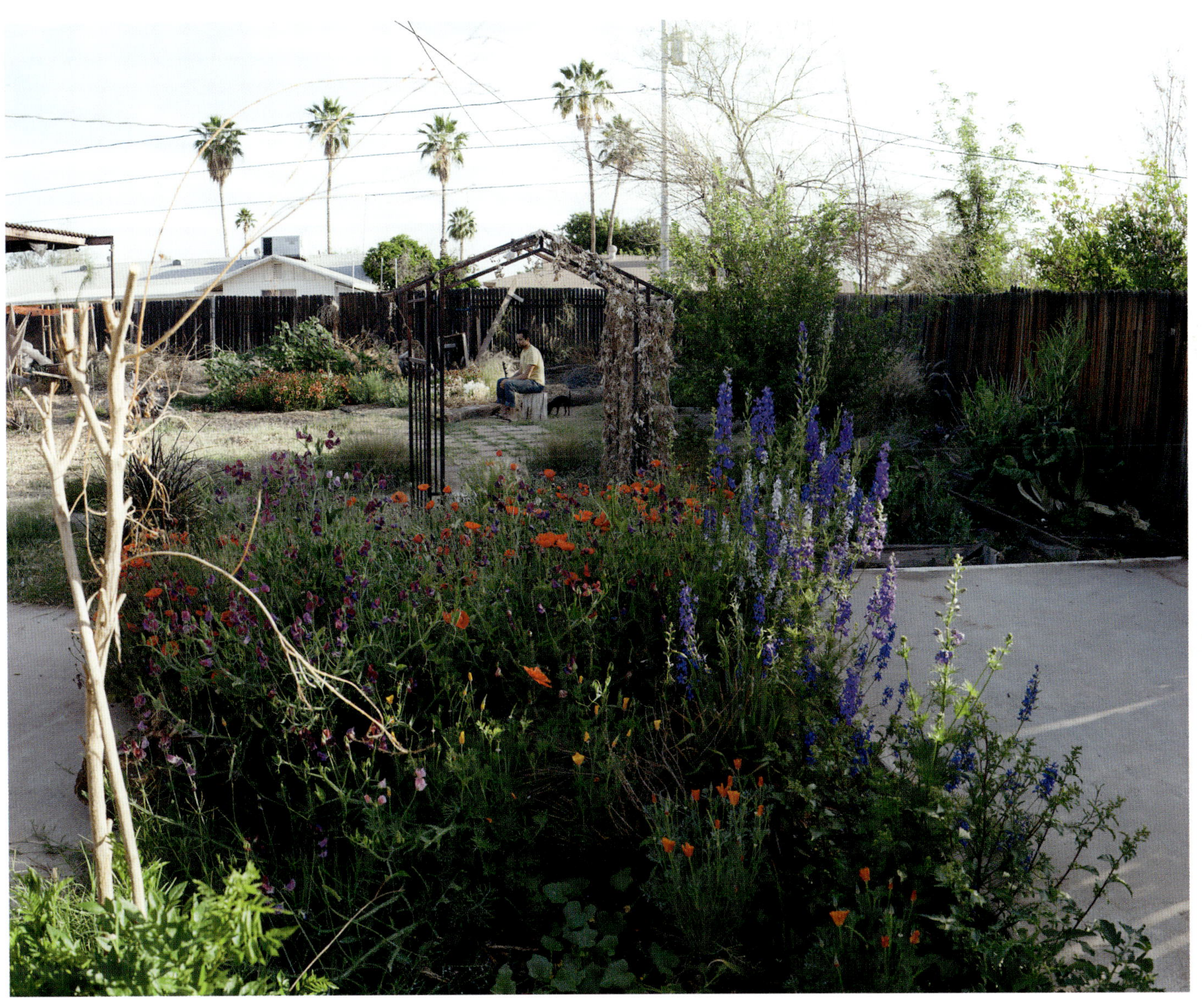

45. Edgar Cardenas, *Untitled (Final Image Before Moving to a New Home),* 2013. From a series that depicts the transformation of a neglected backyard into a sustainable desert landscape.

Edward Abbey's Wild Visions

BEN A. MINTEER

As the wilderness idea began to gain purchase on the public domain it was quickly sucked into the maelstrom of environmental activism and policy advocacy that defined the late 1960s and 1970s. New worries began to emerge about whether Americans were prepared to go the distance for wilderness protection when and where it counted. To the usual insults of bulldozers and chainsaws a new wave of wilderness defenders raised fears about more insidious and sweeping threats: the explosion of car-based tourism on the public lands, worsening air and water quality, overpopulation, and, in a more aesthetic register, the erosion of "true" wilderness values and experience—especially an authentic sense of solitude and freedom—in an increasingly crowded, technologically mediated, and commercial age.

Among the fiercest critics of these trends, and one of the most articulate and passionate defenders of the American wilderness idea, was the writer and naturalist Edward Abbey (1927–1989). Abbey's 1968 classic, *Desert Solitaire*, remains a winning mix of nature writing, environmentalist polemics, and autobiographical musings. Although it received attention upon

publication, Ballantine put out an inexpensive paperback edition shortly after the first Earth Day in 1970 and the book took off—a timely confluence of theme and audience at the dawn of the American environmental movement. The 1975 publication of Abbey's raucous novel *The Monkey Wrench Gang,* a woozy, comic tale of a group of environmental merry pranksters and saboteurs running wild in the Southwest, further cemented his reputation, for better or worse.

Although Abbey is often read as one of the environmental movement's most belligerent misanthropes, a shrill luddite preaching pure and total allegiance to the wild, the truth, as it often is, is more complicated. It's also more interesting. As with a photograph, sometimes it requires a sidelong view to see a familiar subject with fresh eyes, including, maybe, what's been hiding in plain sight all along.

In May 1988, Abbey went into southeastern Utah for a four-day horseback trip with a small "expedition" party. Accompanying him was his friend, outfitter, and guide Ken Sleight (according to Abbey lore, Sleight was the model for the character "Seldom Seen Smith" in *The Monkey Wrench Gang*); Sleight's assistant, a young packer named Grant Johnson; and two others.

The journey was into the craggy backcountry of Grand Gulch, a winding series of slickrock canyons worn into the sandstone plateau of Cedar Mesa in Utah's San Juan County. It is, by all accounts, an extraordinary place, its arresting red rock beauty embroidered by bursts of archaeological richness. The Grand Gulch canyons contain a remarkable collection of Ancestral Pueblo cliff ruins and rock art, some of it long since rendered inaccessible by the erosive force of the desert wind.

Despite the company of his friend Sleight, despite the appealing remoteness of the place, and despite it being the desert Southwest (a place that was for Abbey "love at first sight"), it was in many ways just another job. Abbey was there on assignment for *Condé Nast Traveler,* which had commissioned him to write an essay for a special issue of the magazine on "The Glory of the West." The essay that emerged from Abbey's Grand Gulch trip carried an alluring air of mystery in its title: "The Secret of the Green Mask." Reading it today a couple of things stand out.

One is the photographs: two large black-and-white photos from the trip accompany the essay. Abbey appears in both.

In the first, he's taking an afternoon siesta, lying on the valley floor on his back with arms outstretched, his straw hat strategically placed over his face to provide some shade (plate 46). He's framed in the lower right of the photo, reclining to the right of a round cottonwood tree. Two packhorses stand at the left of the tree, one of them with its head partly in the branches, perhaps seeking shade or looking for something more interesting. The canyon walls fan upward in the background appearing to move away from the tree at the center of the photograph,

ending in a puff of white cloud and sky at the top of the photo. It's a nicely composed image, conveying at once the power of the personality—even at rest—and the beauty and resonance of place.

The next photo is even more striking (plate 47). In this one, Abbey is positioned on the left side of the image, sitting on a small rock bench and taking notes, with his back nearly pressed against the curved wall. The place is Turkey Pen Ruins, a sandstone alcove that curves upward to the top of the image and appears as an amphitheater of stone, framing a view of the canyon to the right of the photograph. Abbey's here a solitary figure looking out into the distance, into the vastness of the desert landscape.

The photos were the work of Mark Klett. Mark was a member of that Grand Gulch party in May of 1988 and also there on assignment for Condé Nast. The editor of *Traveler* had in fact paired the two men, thinking that it would be interesting to couple prominent writers and landscape photographers for the special issue on the West. Interested in the story behind the story, I invited Mark to sit down with me to discuss his time spent with Abbey all those years ago, and to talk a little more about those indelible photos.

Already by then an accomplished fine arts photographer known for his innovative "rephotography" of the western landscape, at the time of the trip Mark had read and admired *Desert Solitaire* and some of Abbey's other essays. But he had little sense of Abbey the person other than the familiar stories of the writer's outrageousness (often told by Abbey himself). He thought that the author's persona was a bit over the top, so when Condé Nast called and asked him if he "wanted to go on horseback trip into southern Utah with Edward Abbey," he agreed, but with slight trepidation. Abbey chose the location for the Condé Nast

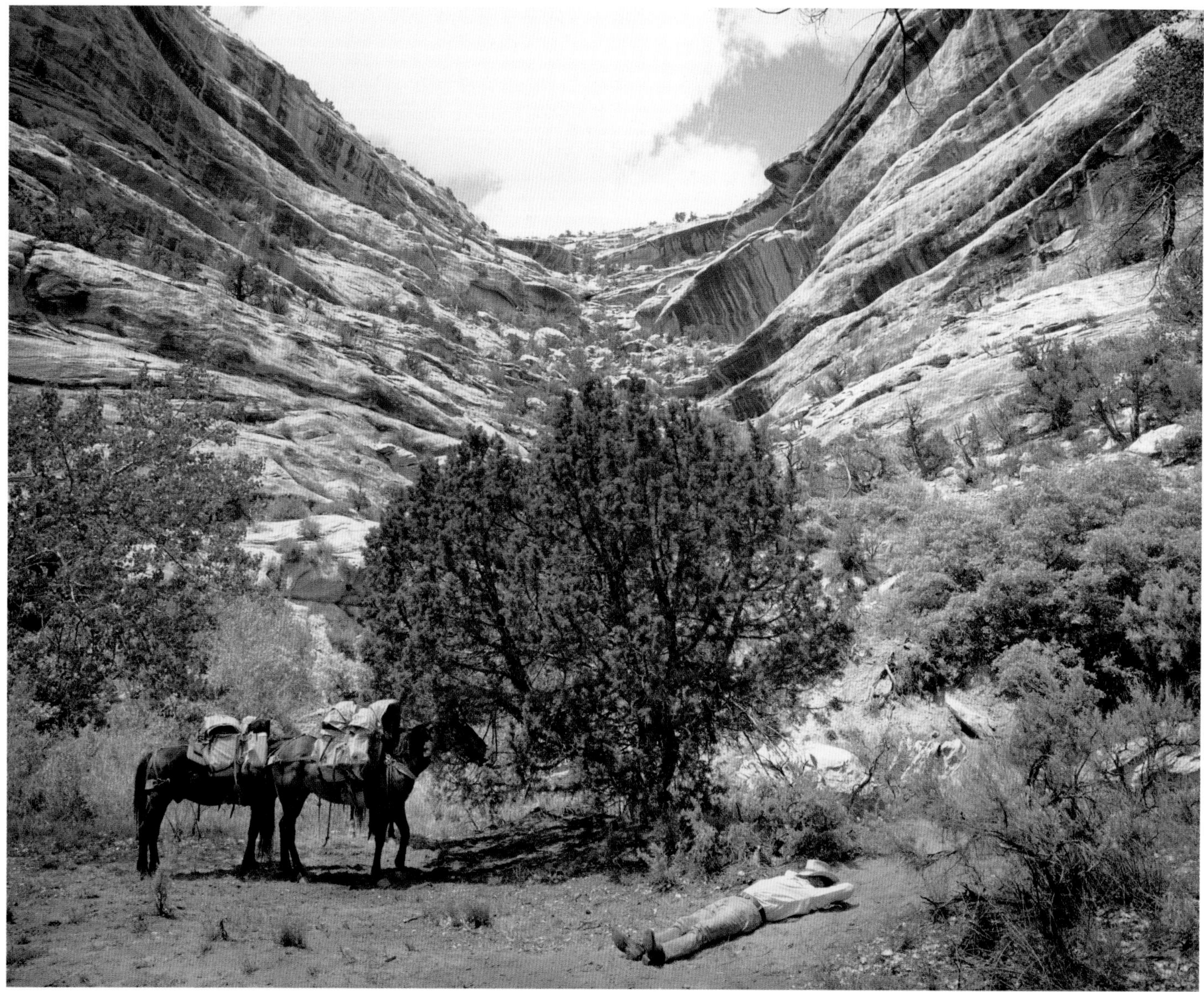

  46. Mark Klett, *Ed Abbey in Grand Gulch, Utah,* 1988

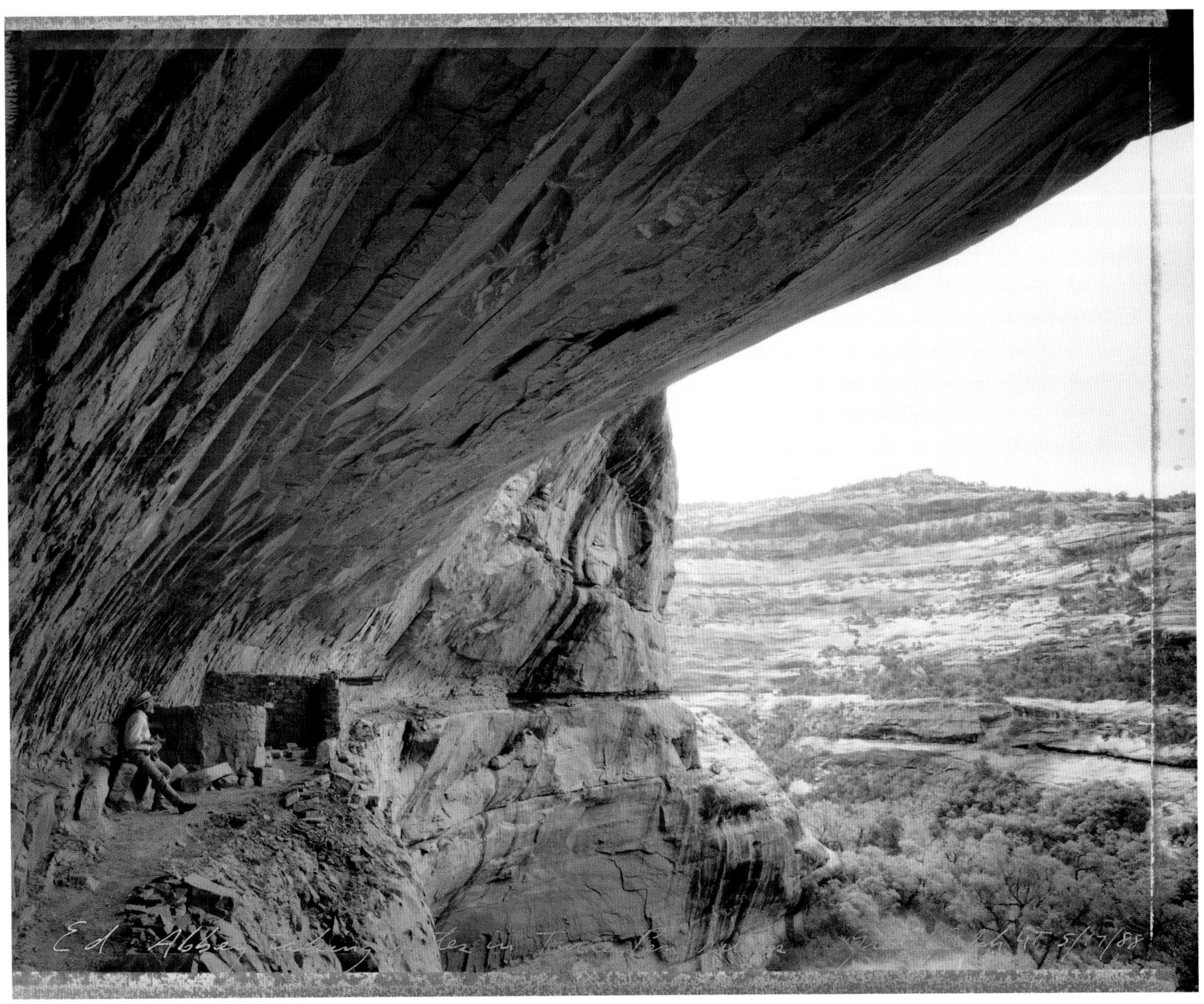

47. Mark Klett, *Ed Abbey Taking Notes in Turkey Pen Ruins, Grand Gulch, Utah*, 1988

expedition; he hadn't been to the Grand Gulch area since the early 1970s so he was ready for and curious about the return.

The author's arrival at the Grand Gulch trailhead did little to dispel his over-the-top reputation. Mark described the author's showy entrance in his red Eldorado convertible, a Cadillac cowboy riding high on the seatback, whooping loudly and wildly waving his hat. But Abbey soon set him at ease, and today the photographer has very fond memories of the trip.

Mark shot more than a hundred photographs on the Grand Gulch assignment, although only two ended up in the published article. I asked him about that Turkey Pen Ruins image, which Mark has put on exhibition at various venues over the years. A slight smile crossed his face. "It's my favorite photograph from the trip and from that period in my work. It really captures how I saw Abbey experiencing the place on that trip, gauging that experience, recording it."

Abbey's *Traveler* essay is a light piece, but a lively one (he may have been writing for Condé Nast but he was still Ed Abbey). For the most part he stays within the sunny conventions of the travel essay, though he can't resist taking a few jabs at old foes. Noting that cattle were banned from the canyon decades earlier, Abbey delights in the signs of a recovering landscape: the reappearance of wild plants, the stabilization of the stream banks, the return of deer to the canyons. And he expresses the hope that someday all of the public lands of the American West will be similarly regenerated once they, too, are no longer "infested with domestic livestock." It's a vintage Abbey riff, though his punches were pulled more than usual (he was clearly on his best behavior for the Condé Nast crowd).

And then there is that mystery alluded to in the essay's title. It's one that Abbey the dramatist takes his sweet time in unveil-ing. But he eventually describes a haunting image encountered in the rocks, the Ancestral Pueblo "Green Mask" pictograph high up on the wall of Grand Gulch's Sheik's Canyon. Abbey's depiction of it is one of the essay's best passages:

Most unusual, however, is the life-size floating head at the far end of the gallery, a yellow face with red hair (or headdress) and a green mask painted across the eyes. A troubling apparition, centuries old, spooky, queer, sinister—if I were the superstitious type I'd flee this place at once. But as comfortable modern rationalists, we simply turn our backs on the Green Mask, eat our lunches, and stare with pleasure at a scrim of light rain falling beyond the shelter of our amphitheater.

At the end of the essay Abbey struggles to capture the essence of "this quiet, secret, and secretive canyon." He quickly throws in the towel, however, and acknowledges that a four-day pack trip is nowhere near enough time to understand the place. To really understand it, Abbey writes, he'd have to come back and live in the canyons for a while, "perhaps a century or two, through all the transformations of the seasons and the years." Until then, he'd rather not discuss something he can't even name. If we really want to know more about the elusive essence of the canyon, Abbey suggests that we should "Ask that head on the wall, the creature behind the Green Mask."

It's a circumspect and meditative Abbey, playing a game of metaphysical hide-and-seek that he started decades before in *Desert Solitaire*. An unsettling cipher, the green mask seems to signify to him the irreducible mystery and power of place, a sublime marker both of our presence and our evanescence. The true meaning of the desert landscape is in the end unknowable, beyond the measure of science, beyond the comprehension of even Abbey's vast poetic faculties.

Abbey's ideal of wilderness as a realm beyond the human was the bedrock of his philosophical approach to the wild. It's a vision in which the wilderness provides an alternative set of values, an ethos counter to the uniformity, artificiality, and technological control of modern life. The wild provided an opportunity for a type of freedom and experience, he believed, that just wasn't available in more overtly humanized and technological environments. But appreciation of the wilderness was for Abbey also a deeply moral act, an expression, he writes in *Desert Solitaire,* of "loyalty to the earth, the earth which bore us and sustains us, the only home we shall ever know, the only paradise we ever need—if only we had the eyes to see."[1]

Beyond the human. It was a foundational belief for Abbey, but many scientists and environmentalists today would argue that it reflects an outmoded, even reactionary image of the wild as we push deeper into the twenty-first century. Abbey's celebration of wilderness as a place apart seems to have become eclipsed by our growing understanding of the power and reach of the human enterprise—and the resulting imprint of this insight on our environmental imagination. There is a danger, these revisionist voices warn, in thinking our ideals of nature and especially the wild are solid and real.

Abbey, for what it's worth, recognized the partly invented nature of the places we call (and manage) as wild on the landscape. "The boundary around a wilderness area may well be an artificial, self-imposed, sophisticated construction," he wrote in *The Journey Home,* "but once inside that line you discover the artificiality beginning to drop away; and the deeper you go, the longer you stay, the more interesting things get … "[2]

But he clearly also took a much different lesson from the evidence of human influence on the landscape, a conclusion that was evident to him decades before any fancy scientific talk about the Anthropocene. In a letter to *Wilderness* magazine in 1987, Abbey made it clear that our ability to change and manipulate the wild wherever it existed wasn't justification for taking these actions. "Simply because humankind have the power now to meddle or 'manage' or 'exercise stewardship' in every nook and cranny of the world," he wrote, "does not mean that we have a right to do so. Even less, the obligation."[3]

Not surprisingly, this sort of attitude has made Abbey a polarizing figure to a new breed of environmentalists promoting a more intensively humanized and managed landscape. A case in point is the prominent ecologist Peter Kareiva, former chief scientist at the Nature Conservancy and one of the most high-profile critics of the traditional preservationist mission in conservation today. In a series of publications, talks, and videos, Kareiva has called out Abbey's vision as misguided, even destructive for today's environmentalism. He's gone so far as to brand Abbey a hypocrite and a liar for waxing poetically about solitude in the desert Southwest while at the same time expressing (in his journals) profound feelings of loneliness. Kareiva makes much of the fact that Abbey wasn't really alone during the time he spent as a ranger at Arches National Park in the late 1950s (the experiences that inform *Desert Solitaire*); he had his wife with him.[4]

What Kareiva and similarly minded critics don't seem to understand is that the Abbey of *Desert Solitaire* was in many respects a persona, a literary character, a rascally invention. Although based in fact, the narrator of *Desert Solitaire* was in an important sense a product of Abbey's aesthetic imagination. As a fiction writer, you might say that Abbey's most famous character is his public self.[5]

In other words, *Desert Solitaire* shouldn't be read as a work of science journalism. Like *Walden,* the book artfully compresses the experiences of two-plus years into a single "season in the wilderness." As Abbey's biographer James Cahalan writes, the author's family is left out of the picture for both personal reasons (Abbey's marriage was on the rocks during the time; he'd soon divorce) and also aesthetic ones.[6] Even Abbey's journals—the evidence Kareiva put forward to "out" Abbey as something other than a desert solitaire—were partly works of the author's imagination. "I never wanted to be an environmental crusader, an environmental journalist," he told interviewer James Hepworth in 1977. "I wanted to be a fiction writer, a novelist."[7]

Desert Solitaire is what today would be called creative nonfiction or perhaps more aptly, memoir. It blurs genres; it puts facts to the purposes of a larger vision; it's a composite life of a persona who happens to share the name Edward Abbey. This is what artists do: it's what most wilderness photographers do, for example, when they elide evidence of a human presence. Abbey's book becomes problematic if it is presented as strictly nonfiction. As a text based on personal experience, remade by an artist's mind, it has resonated with a large audience who share his sentiments and are happy to have someone express their vision, even if it passes through a cracked prism.

But a blinkered reading of Abbey simply as the anti-modern, misanthropic environmentalist misses both the literary nature of the work and his more tempered thinking and writing, with the effect of rendering the latter all but forgotten. Yet recall the philosophical punch line of *Desert Solitaire:* "Balance, that's the secret. Moderate extremism. The best of both worlds."[8] Hardly the words of a radical primitivist. Or how Abbey similarly commends (in *Abbey's Road*) "a wholesome and reasonable balance between industrialism and agrarianism, between cities and small towns, between private property and public property."[9]

Or, more pointedly, how about when he writes in *The Journey Home* that the "sweet aching loneliness" of the desert is ultimately not enough, and that "we must save the city" because it's "the essence and substance of us all—we cannot lose it without diminishing our stature as a nation, without a fatal wound."[10] It's a sentiment that very well might have been voiced by the urbanist and architectural critic Lewis Mumford. Mumford, it should be noted, was one of Abbey's literary heroes—and one of two American writers he felt was deserving of the Nobel Prize (the other being his former teacher Wallace Stegner). The desire to balance wild and civilized animates some of Abbey's best and most mature work. Not surprisingly, it's also his most careful and restrained.

But there's a further problem with calling Abbey a charlatan for rhapsodizing about being alone in the wilderness while at the same time feeling isolated, even lonely. It reveals a naive understanding of the psychological complexity of the human experience of solitude and belonging in the wild in the modern age.

As historian Patty Limerick points out, Abbey, like many of us, wanted isolation and he wanted kinship; it was part of a series of paradoxes that he wrestled with throughout his work—and, we might say, throughout his life.[11] For him, there was no contradiction between loving solitude and craving companionship, between recognizing the partly constructed nature of the wild while cherishing its authenticity, between passionately defending wild country and throwing empty beer cans out of a gas guzzler on the highway.

That last one may have been one paradox too many.

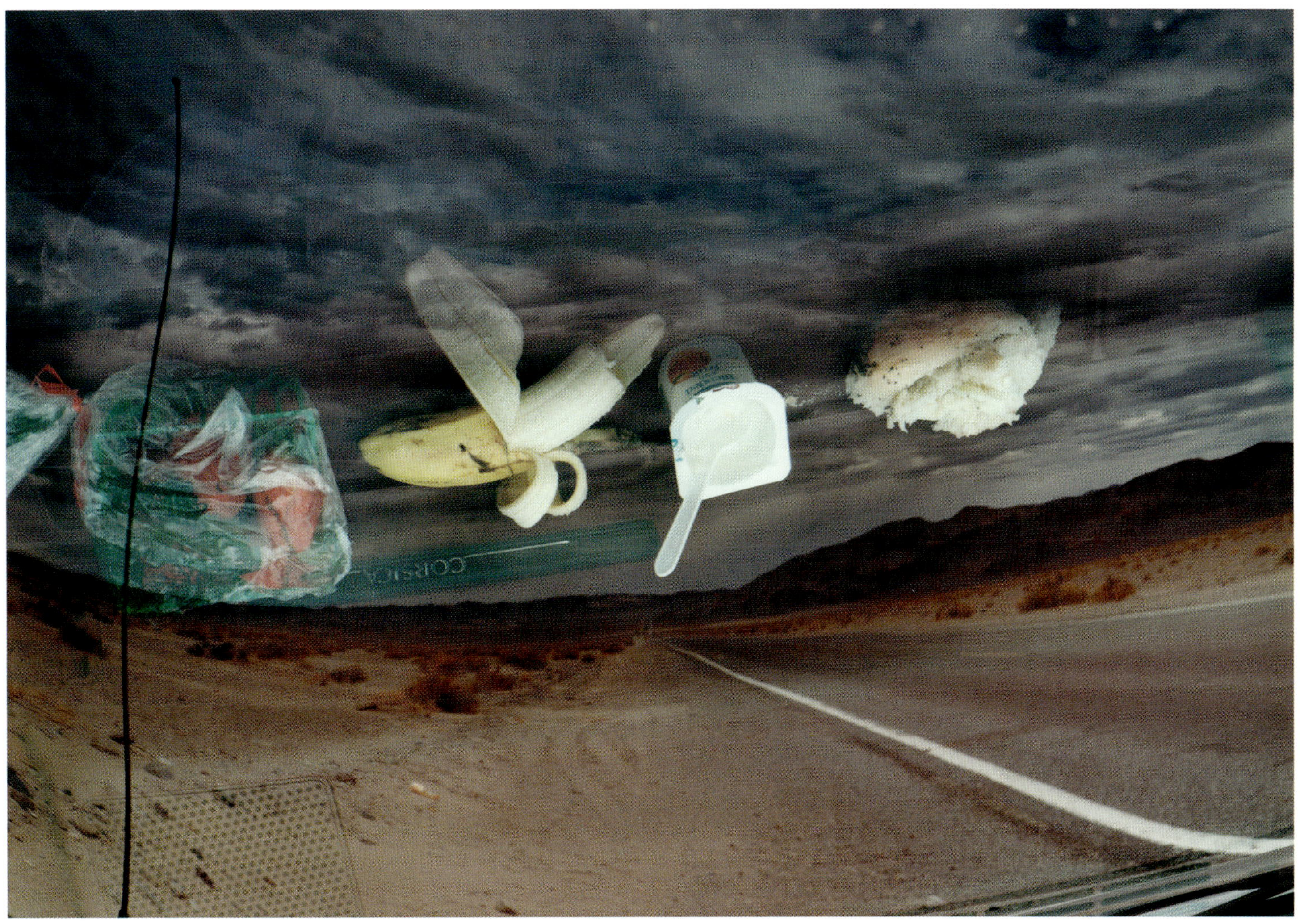

48. Len Jenshel, *Rt 127, near Death Valley National Monument, California*, 1990

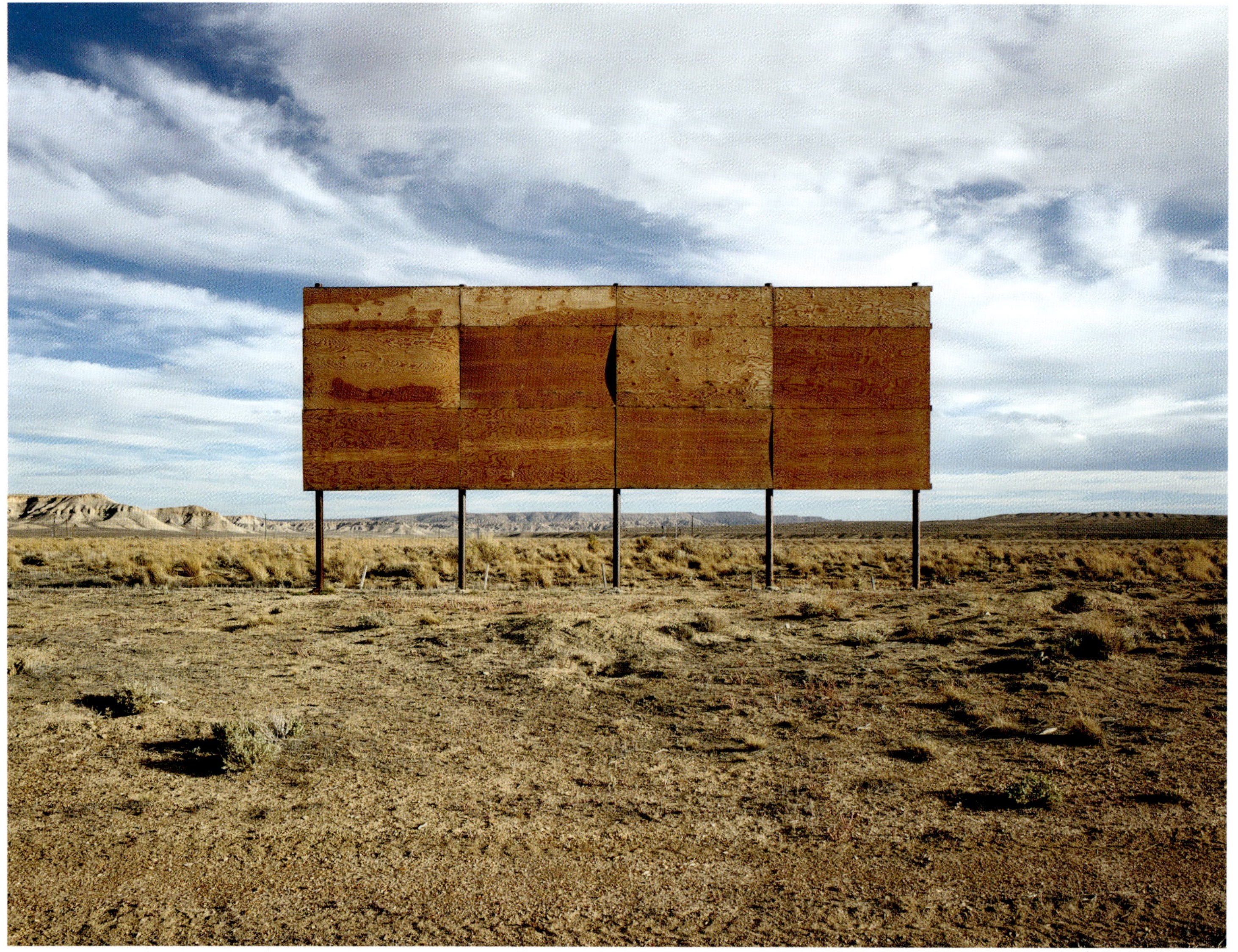

  49. Joshua Haunschild, *Rock Springs, Wyoming*, 2015

In *Desert Cabal: A New Season in the Wilderness,* author and public lands activist Amy Irvine writes (with clear ambivalence), "*Desert Solitaire* framed the American West" through Abbey's lens, creating a set of aesthetic and experiential expectations about the "red raw desert" that would exert considerable power over generations of readers.[12] Yet despite the highly visual character of Abbey's writing, he apparently didn't think much of landscape photography as a catalyst for environmental ethics. "As I say to my friends Eliot Porter, Ansel Adams, and Philip Hyde, one word is worth a thousand pictures," Abbey snickered. But he offered an immediate qualification: "If it's the right word."[13] This being Abbey, though, his relationship to photography was a little more complex than that.

In fact, Abbey published a series of major photographic books in the 1970s following the success of *Desert Solitaire,* both for the Time Life American Wilderness Series and the Sierra Club, working with photographer heavyweights like Porter and Hyde. But he was apparently somewhat bitter about the books' failure to generate the response of some of his other work. Abbey felt that the pictures tended to overshadow his prose and would later refer to them as his "trashy little picture books." (For the record, they're actually quite appealing publications. Some of this has to do with Abbey's tone, which is generally more tempered than in many of the essays he wrote after *The Monkey Wrench Gang*—and when the Cactus Ed persona was in full bloom.)

Abbey understood that the aesthetics of wilderness preservation often rested on romanticized, and thus partial, images: the photographic iconography of the wild sublime. But he also knew that these images were at the same time idealizations, artistic inventions.

We can see evidence of Abbey's more nuanced view on this question in an essay he wrote describing a return visit to Yosemite National Park in 1970 (collected in his book *The Journey Home*). During his trip, Abbey ends up at the park's most iconic vantage point. "Somewhere near Cascade Creek," he writes, "we stopped at a turnout for the classic view of Yosemite Valley, as *invented by Ansel Adams* [emphasis added]. There was El Capitan, Half Dome, Sentinel Dome, Bridalveil Falls."[14]

But he also noticed something else, something that altered the classic Adams image. There was, he observed, "a blue haze above the valley floor."

Was it woodsmoke, he wondered? Or was it exhaust fumes?

"The Secret of the Green Mask" appeared in print in March 1989, the month and year of Abbey's death. It remains a little-known piece and hasn't to my knowledge been reprinted. Still, it's a nice example of the author's easy hand with the immersive travel essay and a reminder that Abbey didn't always carry a rhetorical blowtorch when he wrote passionately about a wild place that meant something to him.

And it turns out there's one more secret buried in Abbey's Grand Gulch piece, one that also hinges on a key image from the trip. It's a small secret, but knowing it has the effect of knowing all good secrets. It makes you feel like you understand something a little more fully, maybe even that you've become privy to some deeper truth.

As Mark and I were talking about the Turkey Pen Ruins photo, he shared a surprising detail. "You can't tell, but he's not alone in that photo." Abbey was, in fact, sitting next to someone in the scene, the fourth member of the trip, a woman named Carole who is mentioned only in passing in the piece

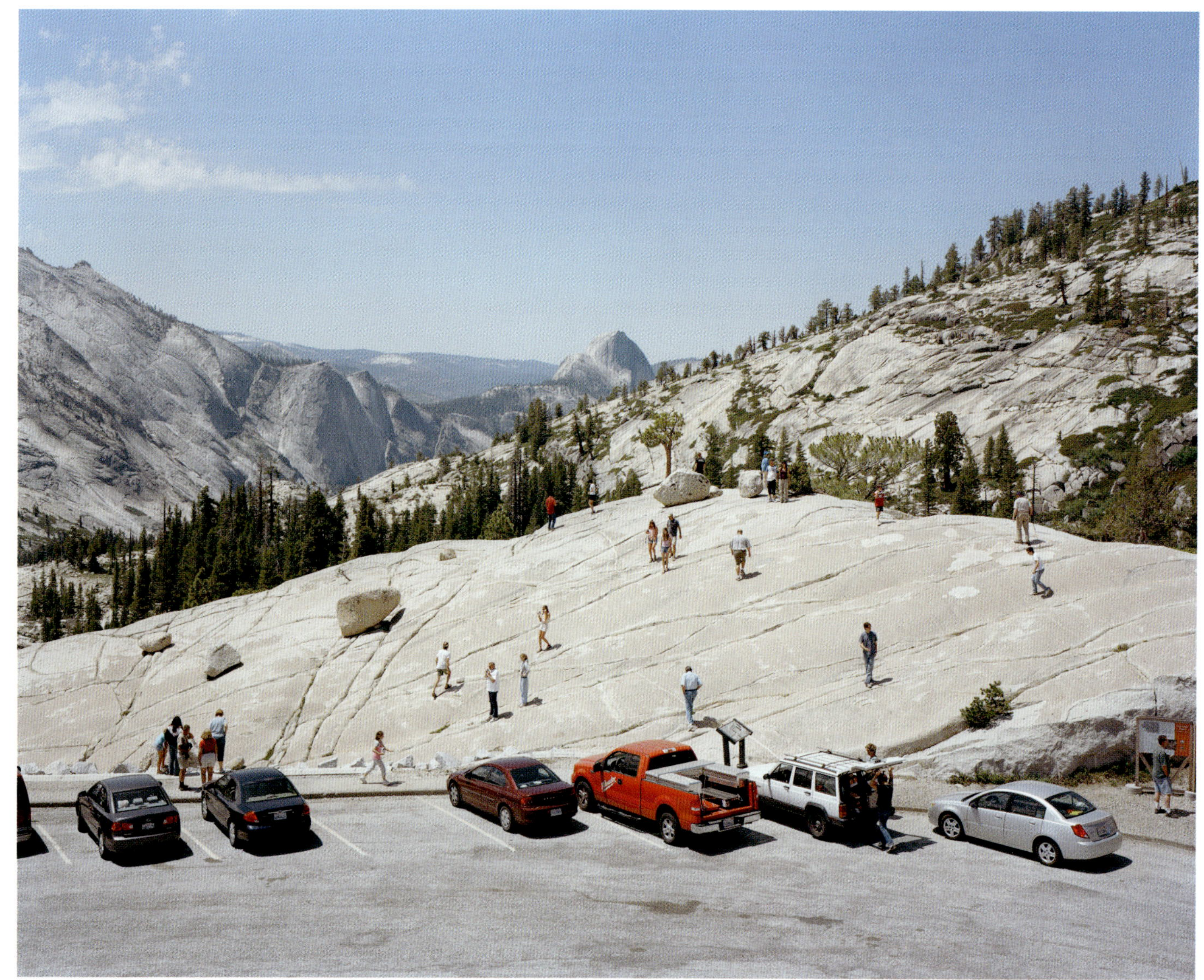

   50. Robert Voit, *Drive in, Yosemite, United States of America,* 2006

(she was apparently a friend of Sleight's, though that isn't entirely clear from the record of the trip). Mark didn't think the magazine would be interested in a duo in the photograph, and he didn't want to move them to get a solo shot of the author, so he found the perfect vantage point in which only Abbey is visible.

I looked even closer at the eight-by-ten print of the Turkey Pen shot that Mark showed me. I tried to see the other figure in the picture, looking for some sort of visual tell—perhaps a slight shadow, maybe something in Abbey's body language— suggesting that he was not really alone in the scene. Nothing. I still saw only Abbey.

Knowing this little secret about the photo, though, made me think differently about the image. And it reminded me that so much of the reception of the writer and his work has been swamped by the Abbey myth; the image of "Cactus Ed," the solitary, self-styled desert anarchist, zealous defender of the wilderness, someone who'd "rather kill a man than a snake." The power and beauty of Mark's photo of Abbey in the Grand Gulch ruins can reinforce this image (although it's far too tranquil a scene to evoke homicide): Abbey as the "lone voice crying in the wilderness." But of course, that's only on the surface.

Both the photo and Abbey's persona are careful and deliberate aesthetic creations (another kind of "mask"). If we forget that, we risk taking both images of Abbey as the truth.

When that happens, Abbey's voice, his work, his environmental vision—all get hollowed out and distorted. He becomes the one-trick pony: the radical wilderness preservationist with little appetite for modern society but a definite taste for writing screeds against cattle ranching, immigration, and urban sprawl. ("Phoenix should never have been allowed to happen.") Abbey, it must be said, brought much of this on himself, especially when he let it rip (which he did often). But those who knew him—and those who read him more carefully— know that this Abbey was mostly a fiction, a mischievous persona, the Merry Prankster driving his bus backwards through the conventions of the day.

In Grand Gulch, Mark got to know this more moderate, three-dimensional man behind the brash rhetoric and the Cactus Ed caricature. The photographer fittingly saw the fuller picture: "Here's a human guy, living a life, not taking himself too seriously. I liked that about him. If he'd really been a raging ideologue, an environmental extremist, well, it probably wouldn't have been a very good trip."

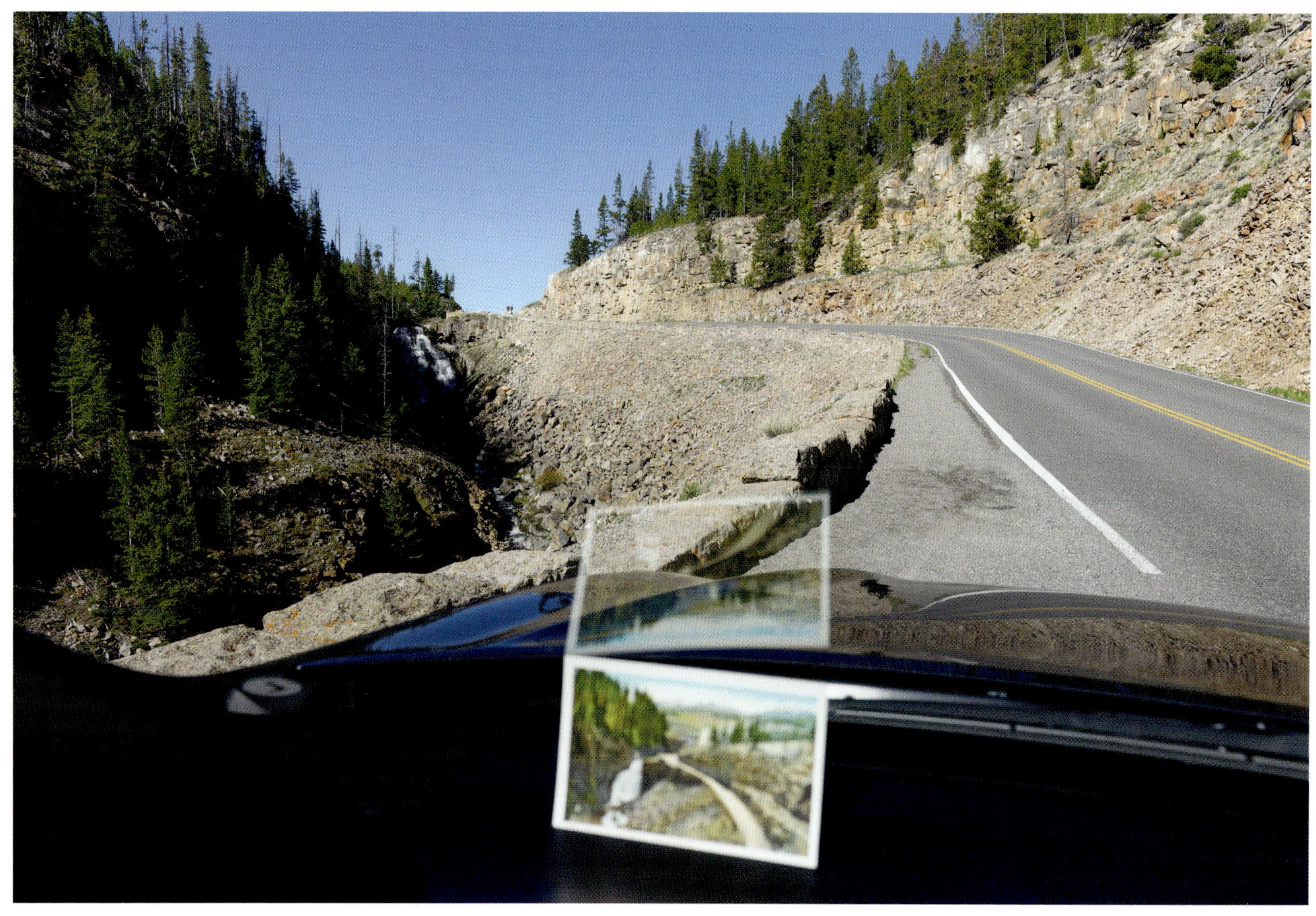

51. Janet L. Pritchard, *Vintage Haynes Postcard, Rustic Falls* (2010), from the series "More than Scenery: Yellowstone, an American Love Story"

Wilderness as Paradox

The purity, the absolutism, of the wilderness idea made for paradoxes. In itself such paradoxes were nothing novel. The twentieth century had overflowed with ideas that ended in logical paradoxes, such as Bertrand Russell's about how self and system related in mathematical set theory. Some spilled over into operational concepts like Werner Heisenberg's principle of indeterminacy, in which the act of measuring altered what was measured. The Antarctic Treaty codified into international law a concept of sovereignty that both did and did not reside in territorial claims. That wilderness should offer another variant in which people could be both present and absent might be unexpected but merely placed the idea into the wider philosophical landscape of modernism and its postmodern progeny.

Paradox became a problem when it had to be operationalized. A notion that defied definition had to be assigned to bureaucratic and legal boxes; a place that precluded people other than as transients had to be constantly administered. Wilderness was not simply a state of mind, but also a bundle of species, geological and ecological processes, and aesthetic, even ethical, choices.

The management calculus became more complicated. In 1901, John Muir wrote that "None of Nature's landscapes are ugly so long as they are wild." Back then, Muir could take comfort in imagining that there were parts of the earth that he assumed would always have to be wild, forever impervious to the human footprint: the seas, the sky, the granite domes of Yosemite. We can breathe easy, he wrote, because we can "change and mar them hardly more than can the butterflies that hover above them." He was obviously wrong about that one.

Today we recognize (though not always without argument) the degree to which we've influenced and changed Muir's wild world. It's an impressive but fearsome litany of global impacts: human-caused climate change, intensive urbanization, the disruption of biogeochemical cycles, ocean acidification, pollution, overharvesting of resources. Increasingly, human-dominated rather than nature-dominated systems are the norm. As the human presence expanded to define a geologic epoch, the Anthropocene, it was impossible to deny humanity's effect on even the largest wild landscape.[1]

It was no longer a case of keeping out a direct human residence: it was humanity's indirect influences that were reshaping wild lands, and the smaller and more fragmented those lands, the greater the impact. Through climate change, invasive species, lost species, the whole suite of consequences that marked the colonial conquest of North America, wilderness could no longer be segregated from an Age of Humans. Should threatened species be relocated? Should invasive species be extirpated? Should protective fires be lit? With mounting stresses came mounting cries for a more interventionist program of management.

Critics could thus point toward the whole notion as a contradiction, or as another in humanity's endless travail of ironies, or as simple hypocrisy. In reply, some advocates argued to shift the purpose of wilderness from the bundle of ecological and scenic pieces that had inspired early advocates and move toward a conception of the wild (or perhaps the quality of *wildness,* as we will see in the following chapter) in itself. True wilderness was whatever nature, untrammeled by human finagling, created. Its essence was what lay beyond the human grasp. It was simply the Wild.

But another response might be to accept the contradictions as only apparent, which is the definition of a paradox. Wilderness was a paradox and would be managed as such. Older notions of logic like the excluded middle were the problem, not paradoxes, which were a condition of the world. They might even serve as an operational definition of the wild.

If so, images of contemporary wilderness would be more qualified and radiate with seeming contradictions—wild

scenes with powerlines, roads, and fences running through them, or urban and industrial forms that evoked a sense of menace in which the wild lay not in pristine landscapes but in perverted ones. Rather than totems of nature's independence, they would reflect aspects of humanity's presence, including the passages, boundaries, and environmental negotiations and compromises of a species attempting to sort it all out. Again, it may be that the images are leading, the artists sensing a different reality than what prevailing or popular culture addressed. Captions would follow, and perhaps from them, new texts and novel concepts. The paradoxical wild could not be logically or even rationally resolved. It may be it just is.

About the Gallery

BAM: The photographs in this gallery have been made by a wide variety of artists of different generations, working at different times, with distinctive experiences and styles. And yet they seem to hang together in how they explore the sense of contradiction described in the chapter—or at least the tension and discord in our visualization of nature and the wild and the things we're doing within (and to) it. We see this at work in many of the images collected here, from John Pfahl's picture of a nuclear power plant nestled behind a pastoral foreground (plate 60) to Robert Voit's cheekily camouflaged telephone pole (plate 64).

Mark, how do you see these photographs relating to each other and to what we might call the "paradoxical wild"?

MK: These photographers have a very sophisticated and complex relationship with the paradox you describe. As a group

I'd say they all look like they follow common threads, and you could say these go back in history to New Topographics, which we've discussed. And as a field, it's probably true that we all influence each other in the creation of a shared dialogue. I'd imagine that happens in your field, too! But I'd also say that each photographer retains an individual approach. Unfortunately, what we can't see here in this book's edit are the nuances that would better define these individuals' works. We'd need to see a lot more pictures for that, so I'm hoping that readers will be enticed enough to explore the work of these photographers more. This is the reason we've included the resource page for more information about their work.

BAM: A good point, and I want to pick up on something from our previous conversation about photographers making aesthetically pleasing photos from, well, "bad places" (compared with the traditional beauty shots of nature and wilderness photography, that is). Most of the photos in this section seem not to want to document the degradation of the wild so much as they play with the idea that the wild is everywhere shot through with human design, technology, and activity. Again, on the purist account of the wilderness this is an act of aesthetic violation, akin to taking a Sharpie to the Mona Lisa. Yet I think we can also see a kind of beauty in the visual cleanness of some of these inscriptions, the anthropogenic geometry of the view.

I wonder if this is a case where the photographer is pulled between artistic vision (an appreciation of the scene as a visual composition) and a more critical wilderness ethic? Or is that assuming too much of a disjunction between wilderness and human activity in these images?

MK: I think you've hit upon an important dialogue that's been happening in contemporary photography, the tension between aesthetic practices and contradictory valuations. It comes across in images that are often beautiful in the way they look—the overall crafting of the photograph including the framing, the use of color, lighting, et cetera, to make a pleasing image. This is contrasted with the subject matter chosen, which is not something that one would usually want to aestheticize—polluted rivers, toxic waste dumps, severely abused lands, radioactivity, et cetera.

BAM: Or Sant Khalsa's photo, where nature's purity is reduced to "good" bottled water (plate 59).

MK: Yes, Khalsa's composite of "water stores" is pure conceptual irony, and a different approach entirely. Water has been turned into the ultimate natural commodity and isn't even visible in the photographs. As a series (from which this group is a selection), it does an end run around the issue of beautifying water.

BAM: Interesting. I imagine photographers are themselves divided on how they try to square beauty and utility (or more fitfully, degradation) in their work.

MK: That's right. There's been a mountain of critical discussion related to aesthetic practice over the years, and photographers are split in their methods. Some believe making a pleasing, even beautiful image of a "bad place" (as you say) is a useful tool because it gets people to look at the picture, that the experience of this dichotomy is a useful way to understand what has happened to the subject or in terms of advocacy, that it can spur people toward taking action.

Others feel that this kind of approach doesn't work, or crosses a line, and can't bring themselves to glorify a scene or situation they are intending to criticize. Some also straddle a little bit of both camps, employing tools like irony to temper the beauty of the image, and calling out the contradictions in a way that's hard to miss.

SP: I know what you are saying, Mark. But I prefer "paradox" to "contradiction" because it leaves some wiggle room. And as someone weary of casual irony, or irony as an end point of narrative, I welcome post-ironic sensibilities, which I think the best of these images have. There is a literary tradition of good people in flawed causes, and flawed people in good causes—maybe this is photography's version with lovely images of awful scenes. (We'll skip the awful images of lovely scenes.)

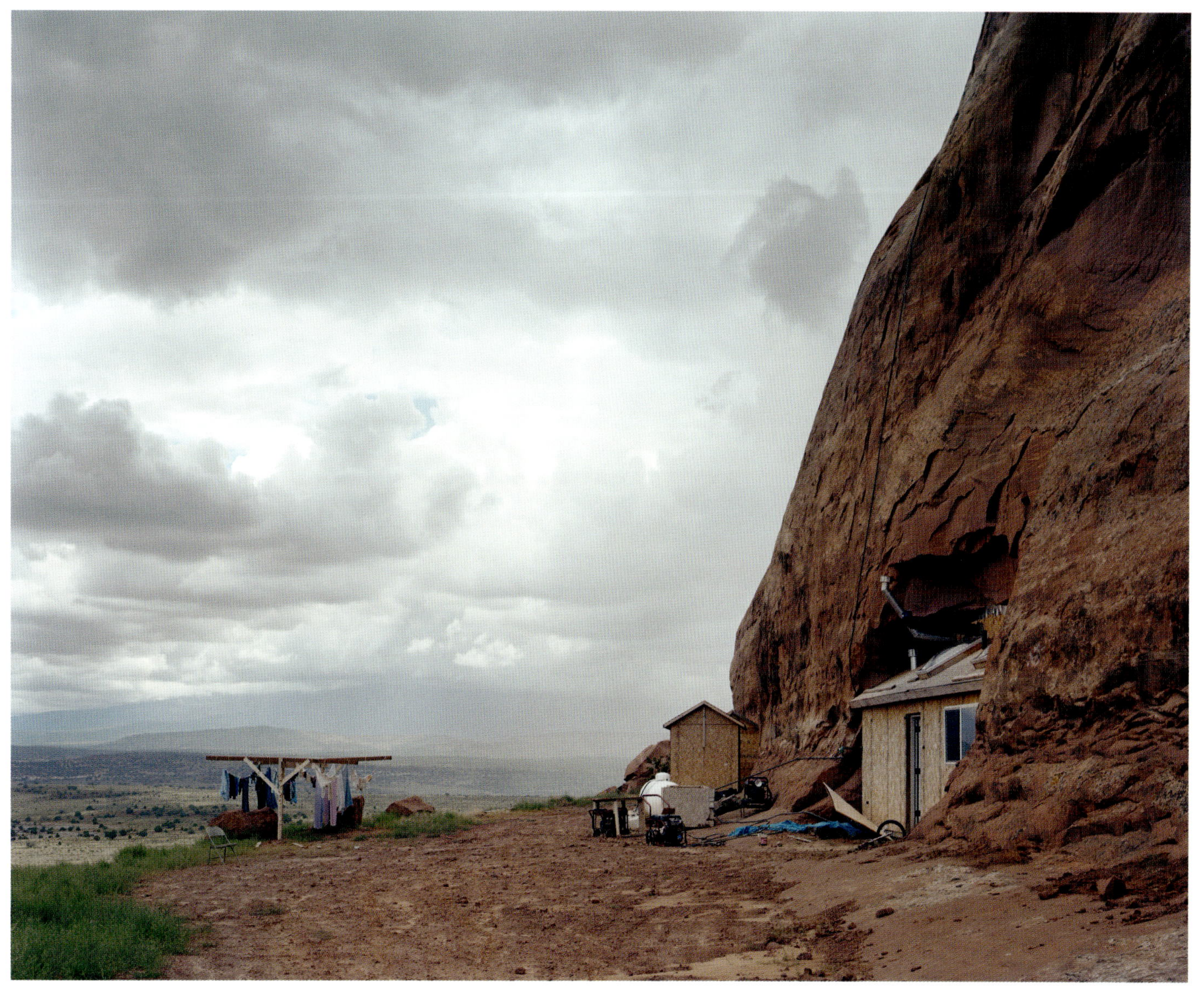

52. Alec Soth, *Utah,* 2008

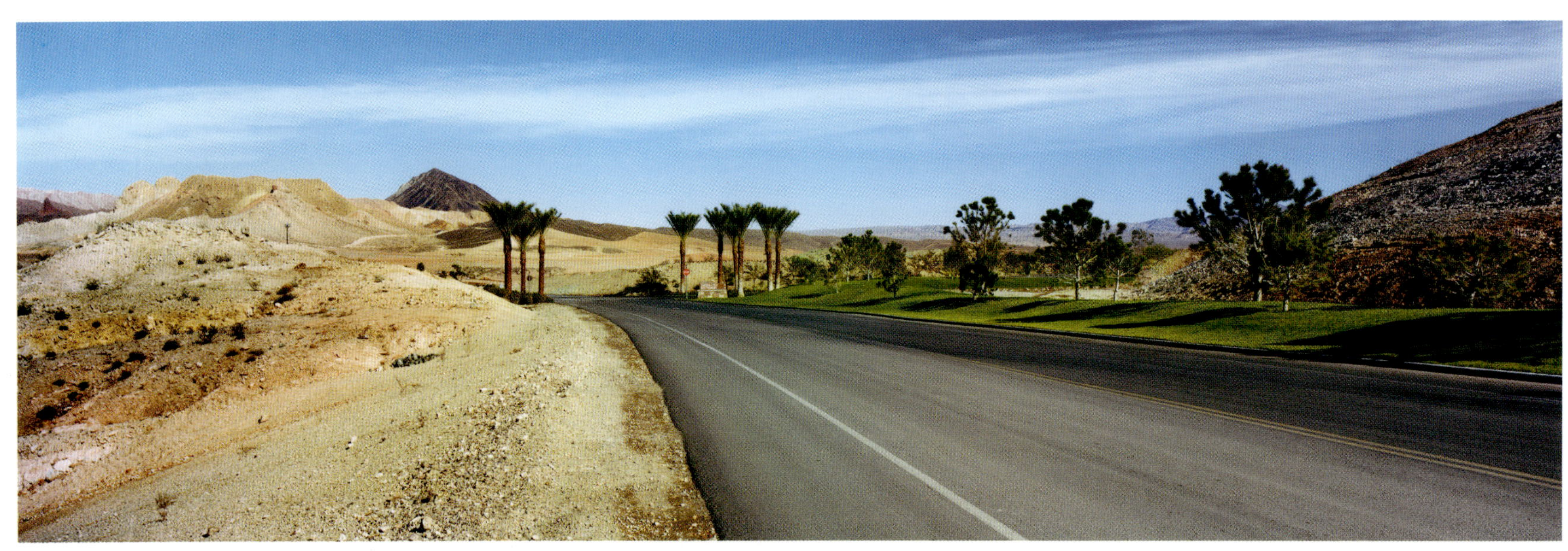

  53. Laurie Brown, *Entrance Road to Lake Las Vegas,* 1996

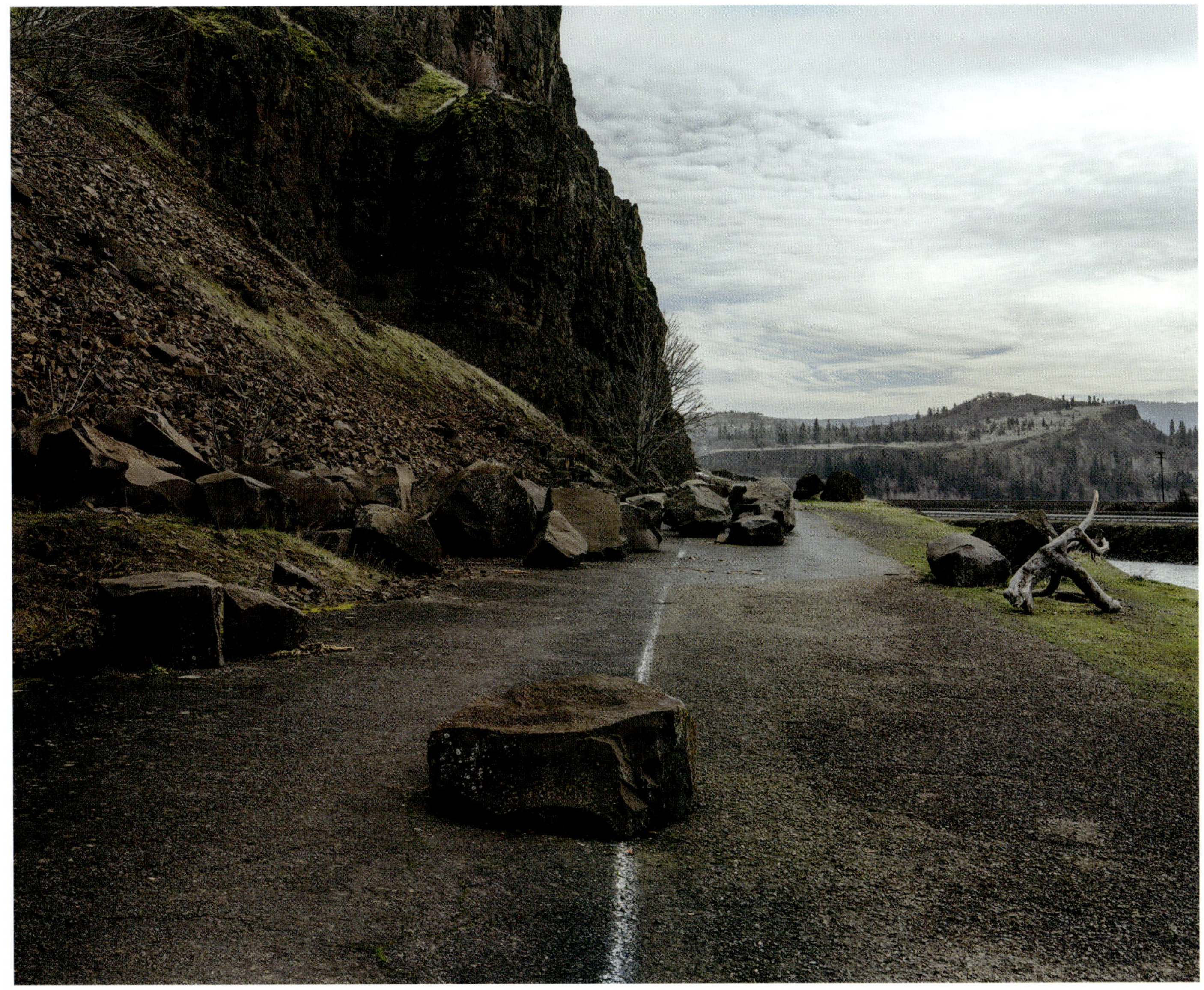

54. Buzzy Sullivan, *Coyote Wall, Washington*, 2017

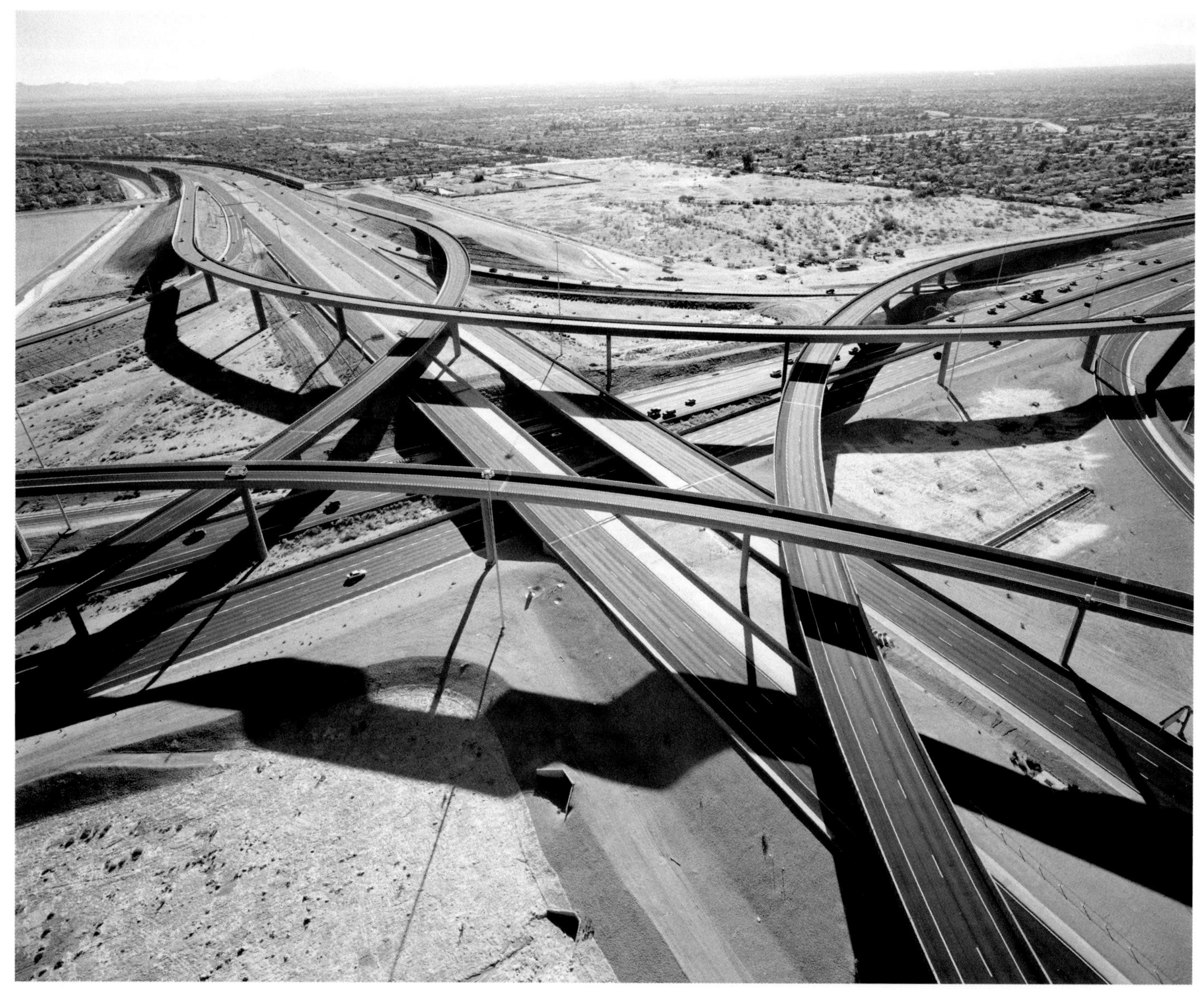

  55. Michael Light, *Interchange of Highway 60 and 202 Looking West, Mesa, Arizona* (© 2007, Michael Light)

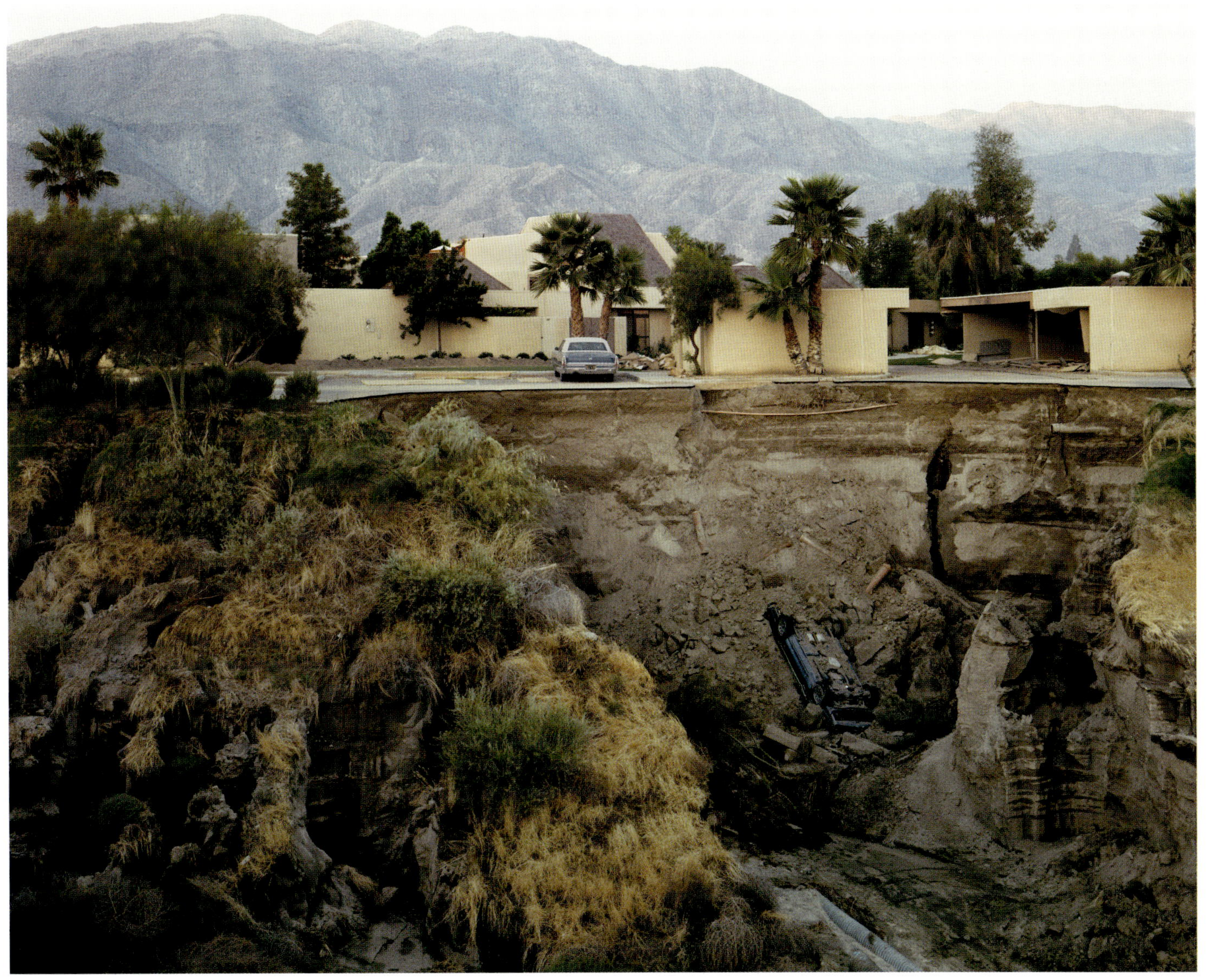

56. Joel Sternfeld, *After a Flash Flood, Rancho Mirage, California, July, 1979* (© 2021, Joel Sternfeld)

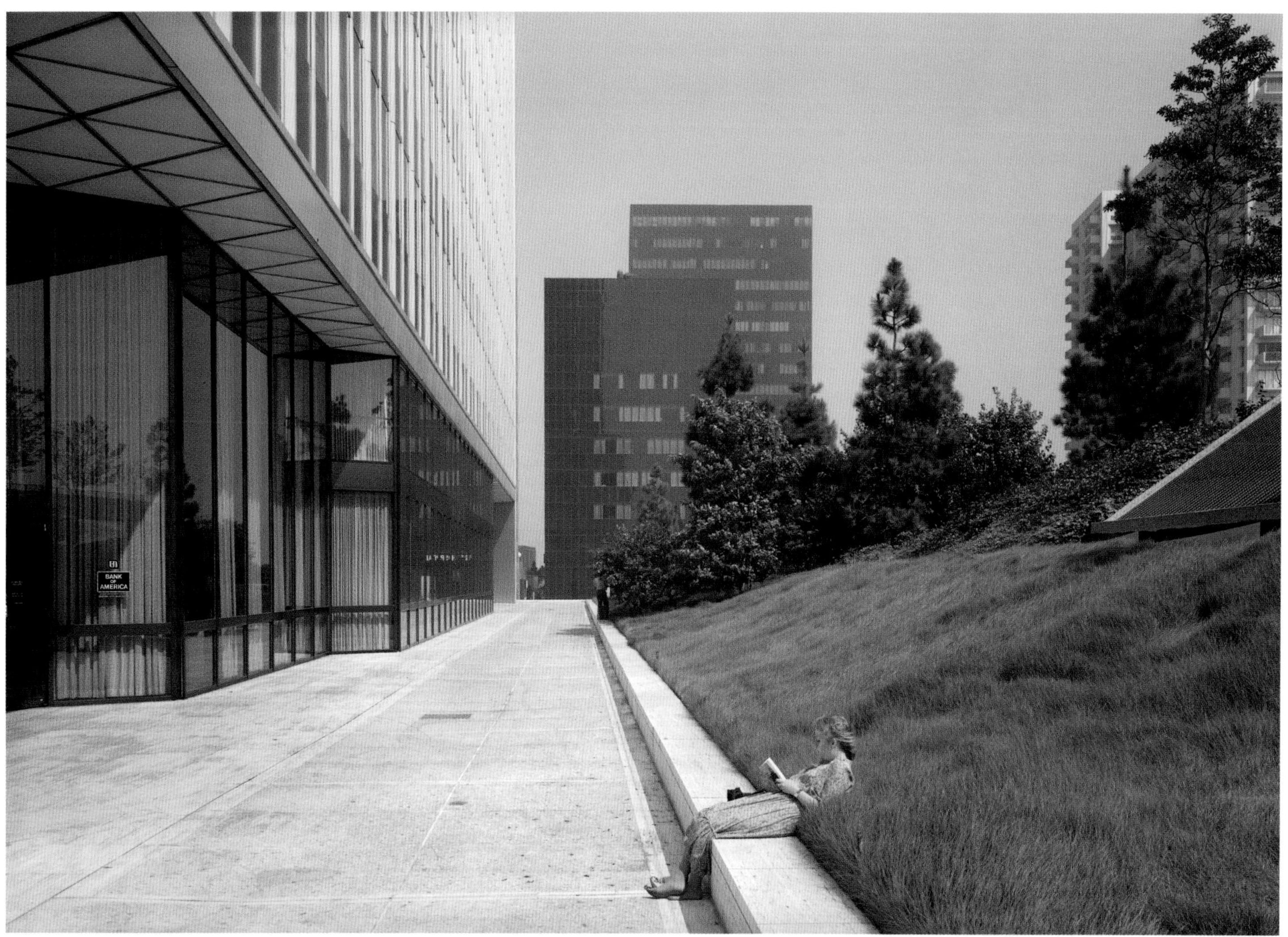

 57. Anthony Hernandez, *Public Use Areas #25*, 1980

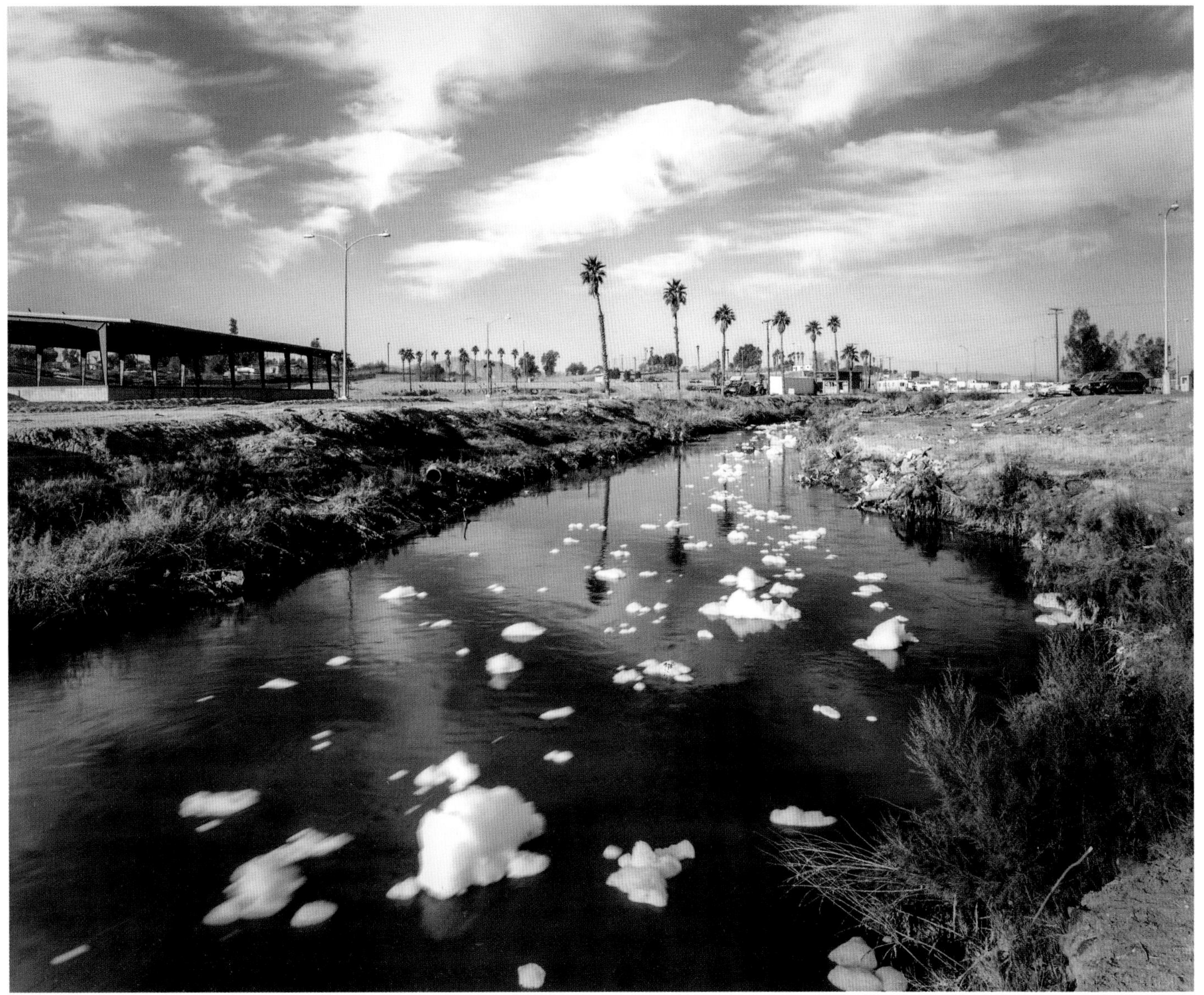

58. Robert Dawson, *Polluted New River, Calexico, California, from the California Toxics Project,* 1989

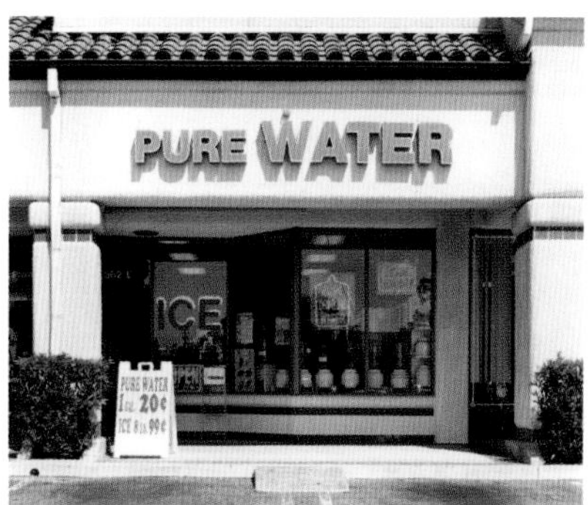

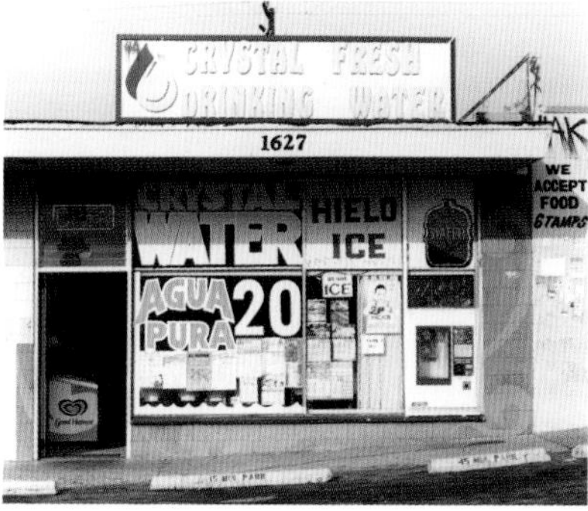

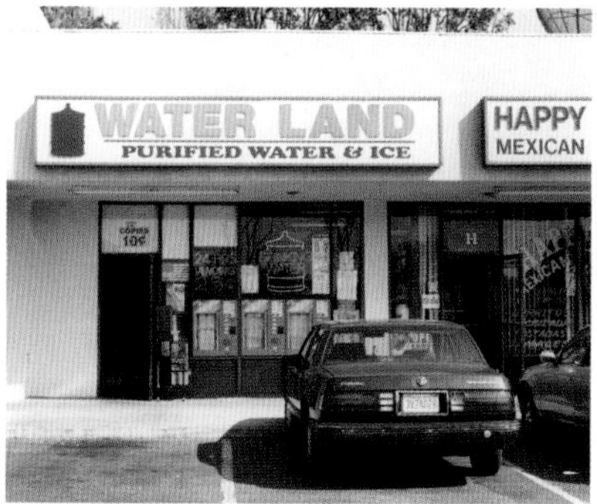

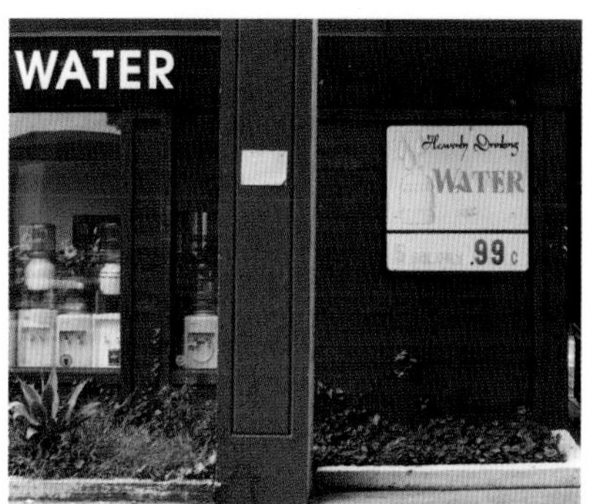

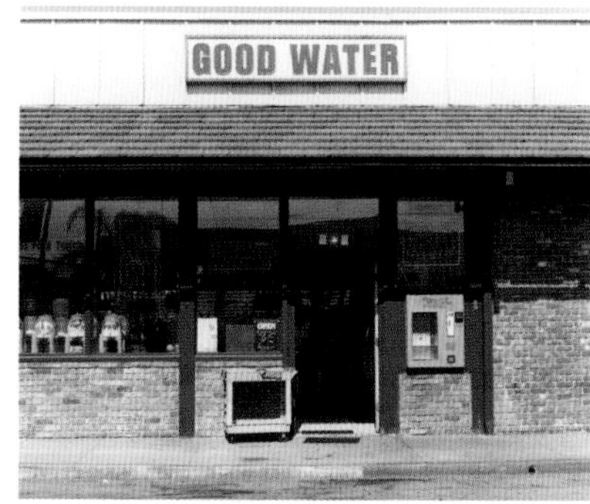

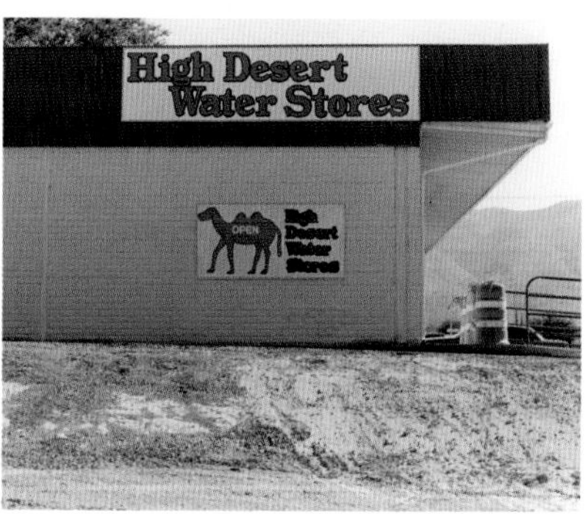

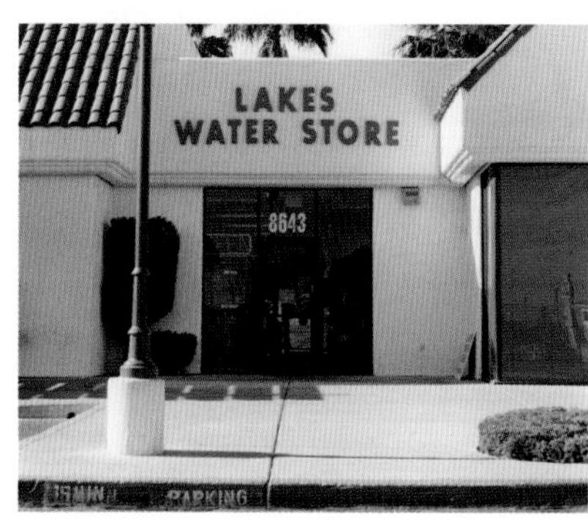

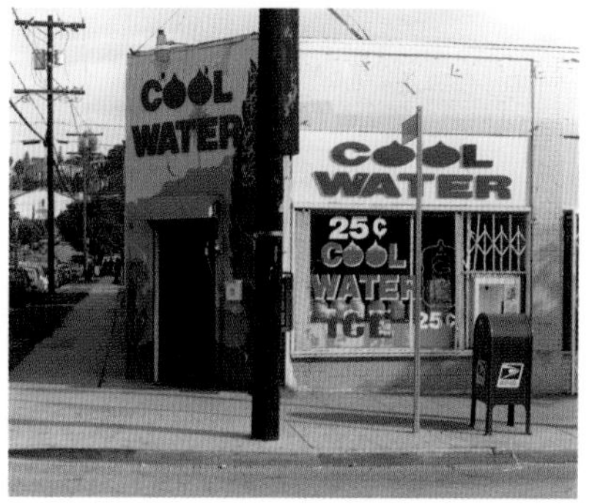

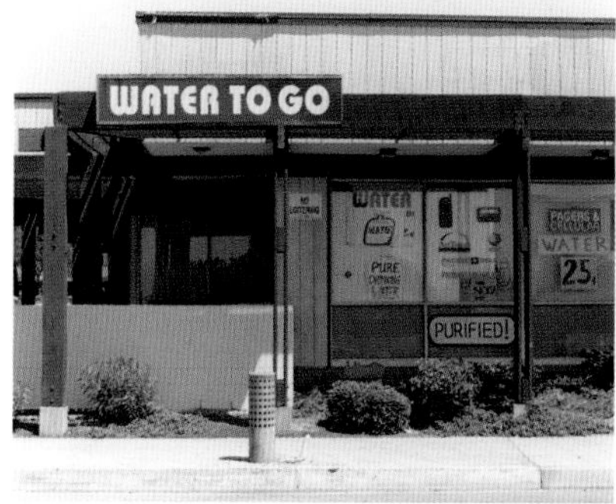

59. Sant Khalsa, *Western Waters* (*Pure Water, Ontario, California; Crystal Fresh Water, Pomona, California; Water Land, Santa Ana, California; Heavenly Water, Glendale, California; Good Water, Montebello, California; High Desert Water, Alamogordo, New Mexico; Lakes Water, Las Vegas, Nevada; Cool Water, Los Angeles, California; Water to Go, West Covina, California*), 2000–2002, Gelatin silver prints, 6 × 7 inches each (Courtesy of the artist)

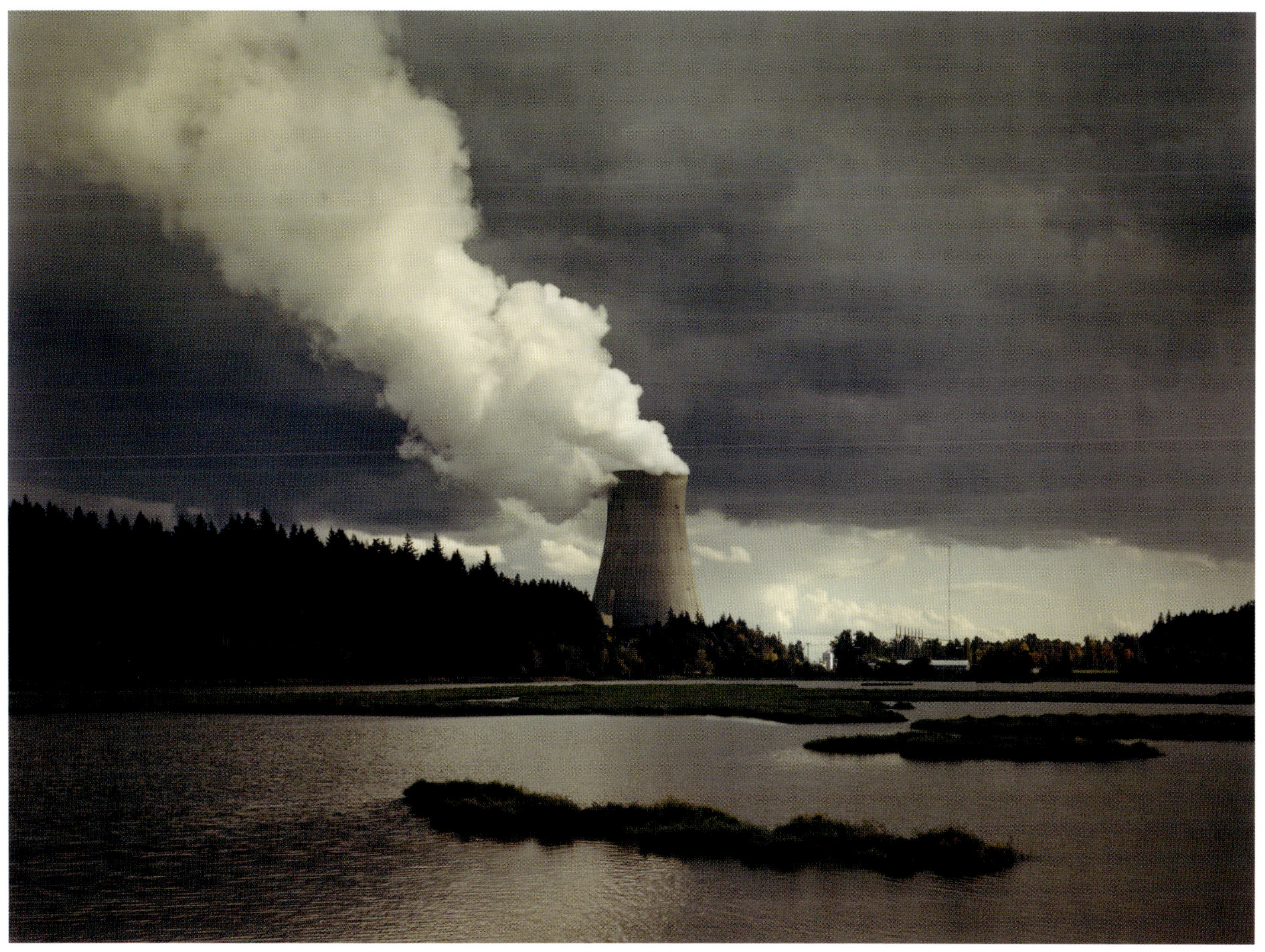

60. John Pfahl, *Trojan Nuclear Power Plant, Columbia River, Oregon, October, 1982* (Courtesy of the John Pfahl Trust)

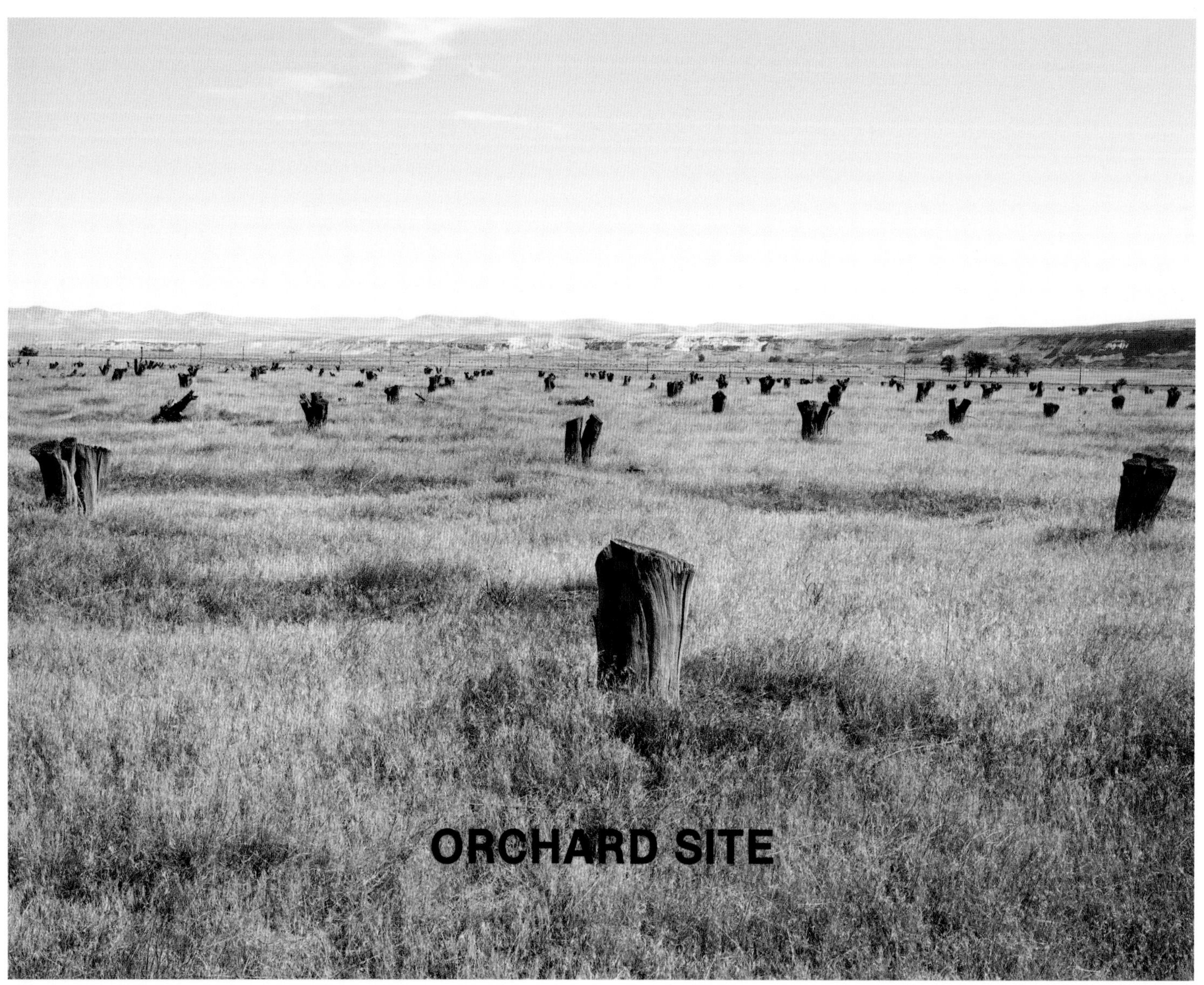

61. Peter Goin, *Orchard Site, Hanford Nuclear Reservation*, negative, 1988, digital pigment print, 2011 (From *Nuclear Landscapes*, by Peter Goin [Johns Hopkins University Press, 1991], courtesy of Peter Goin, © 1988)

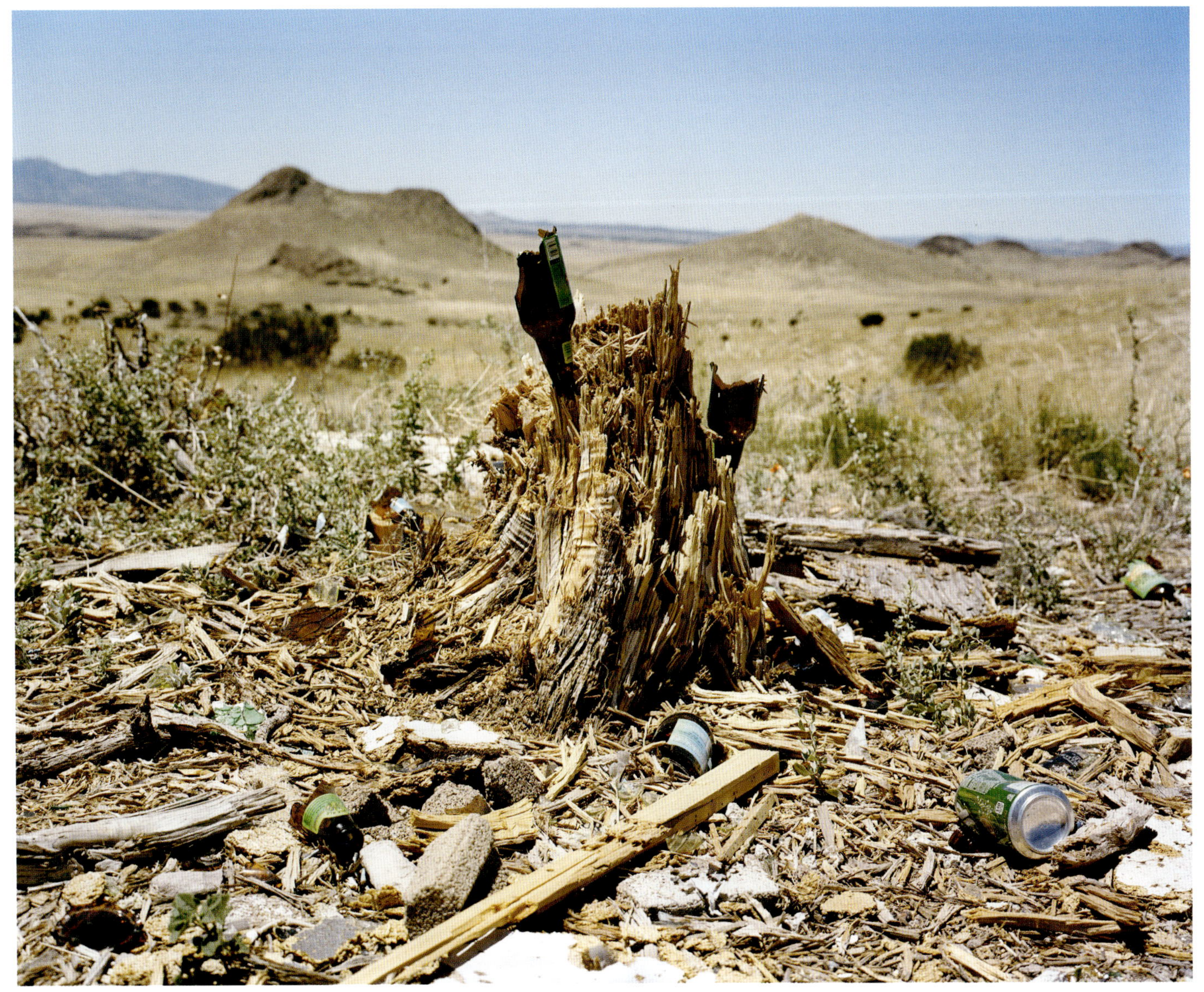

62. Serge J-F. Levy, *Chino Valley, Arizona*, 2013

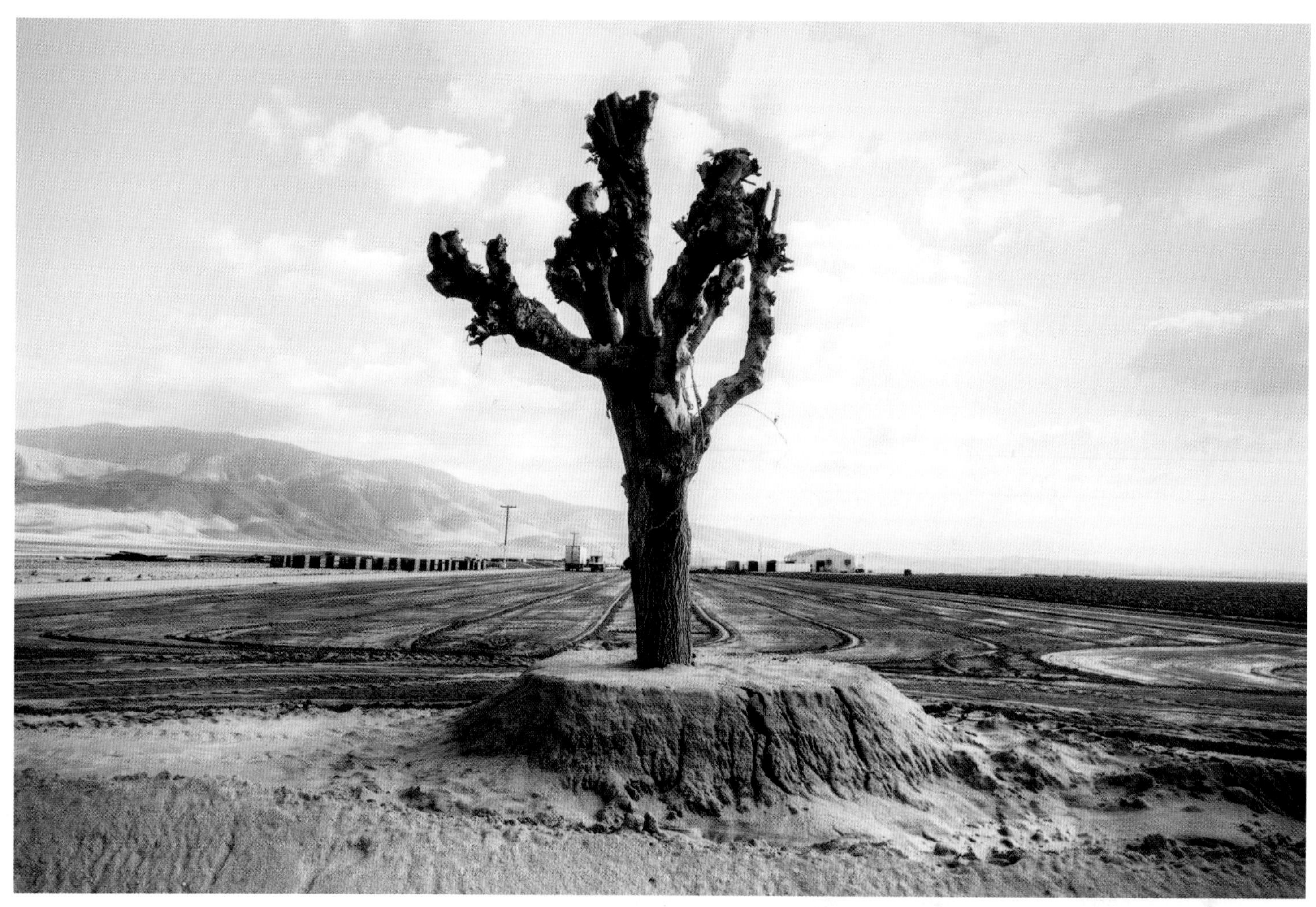

  63. Robert Dawson, *Large Corporate Farm near Bakersfield, California*, 1985

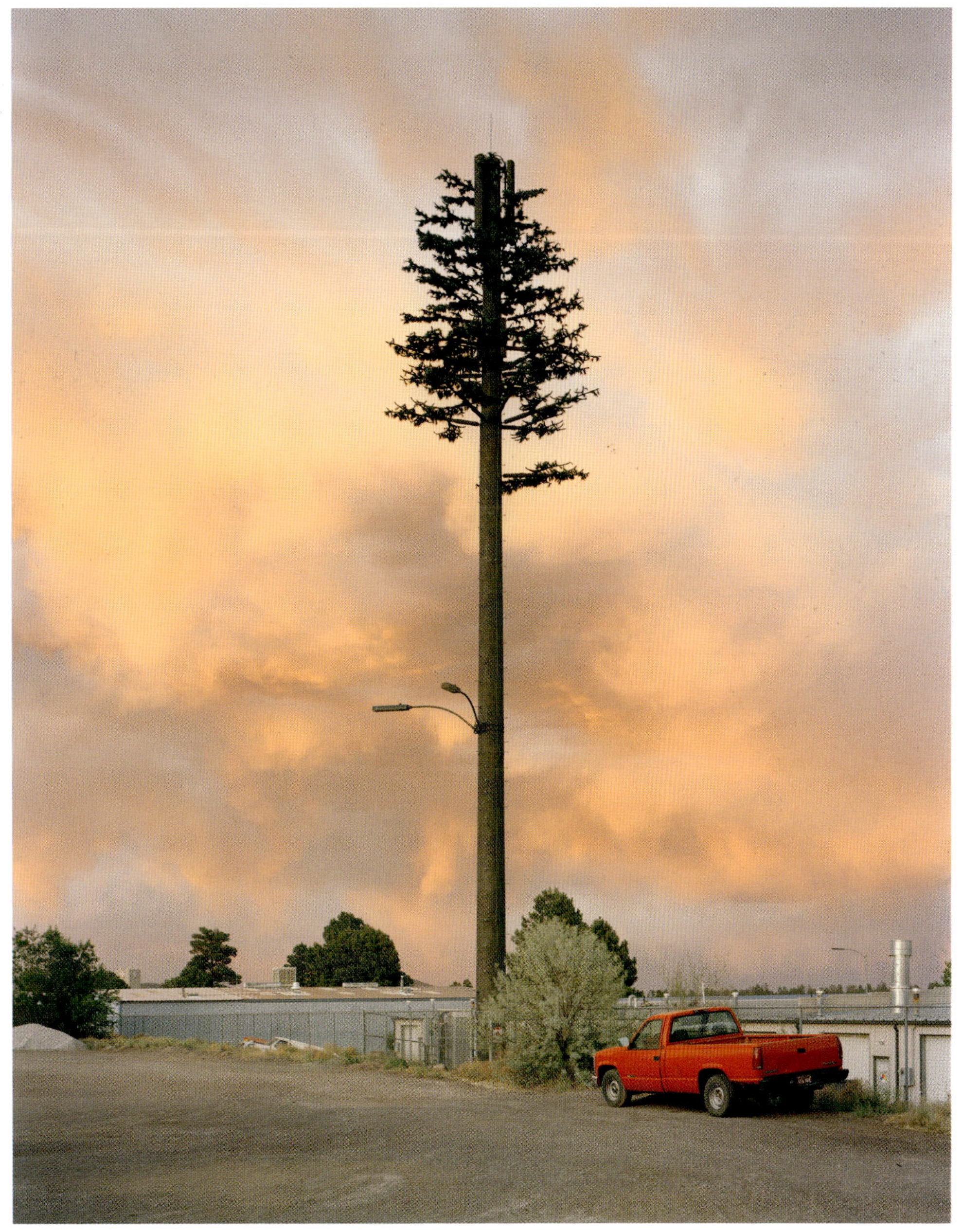

64. Robert Voit, *Industrial Drive, Flagstaff, Arizona, USA*, 2006

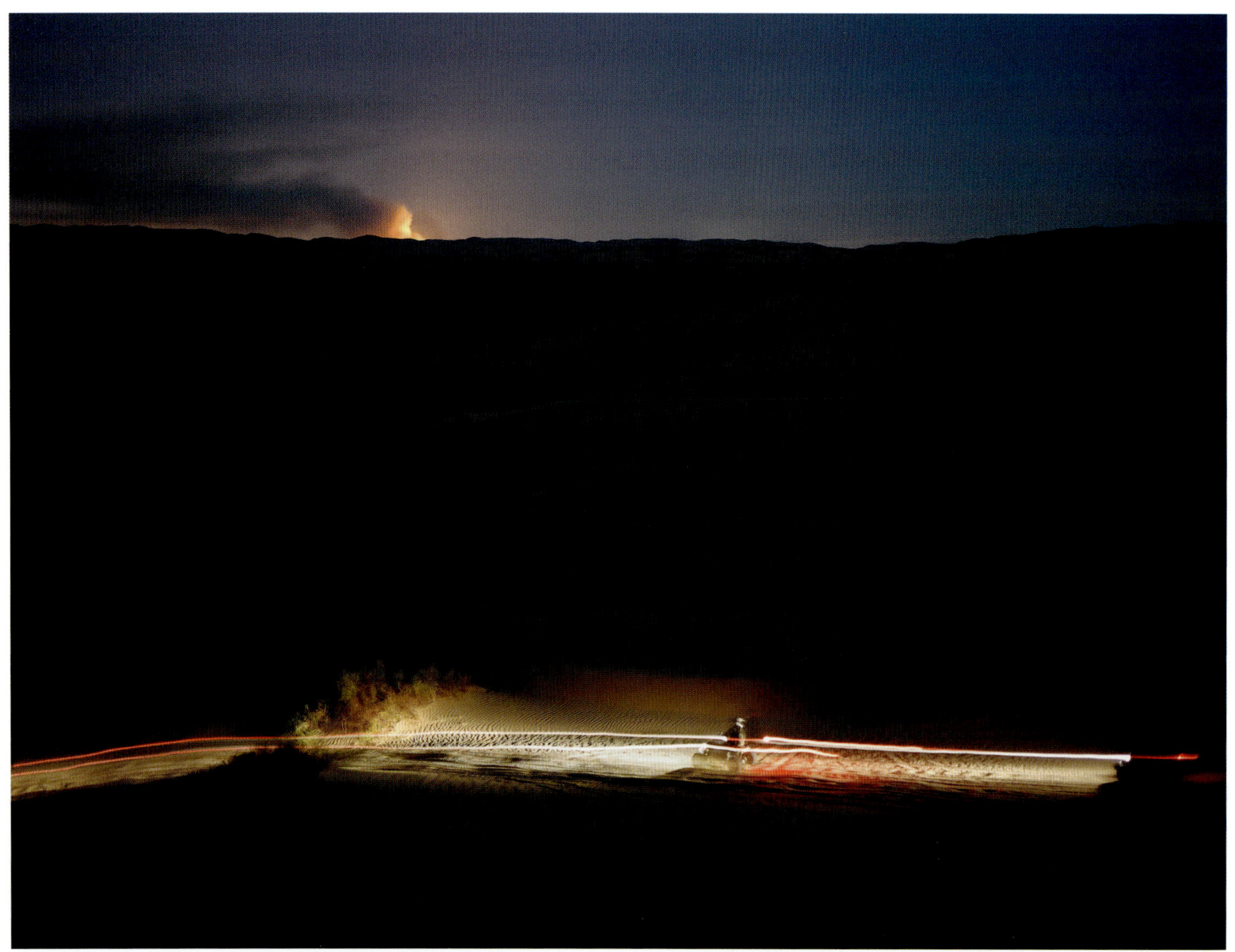

   65. David Taylor, *ATV Sign Cutting, California,* 2009 (Courtesy of the artist)

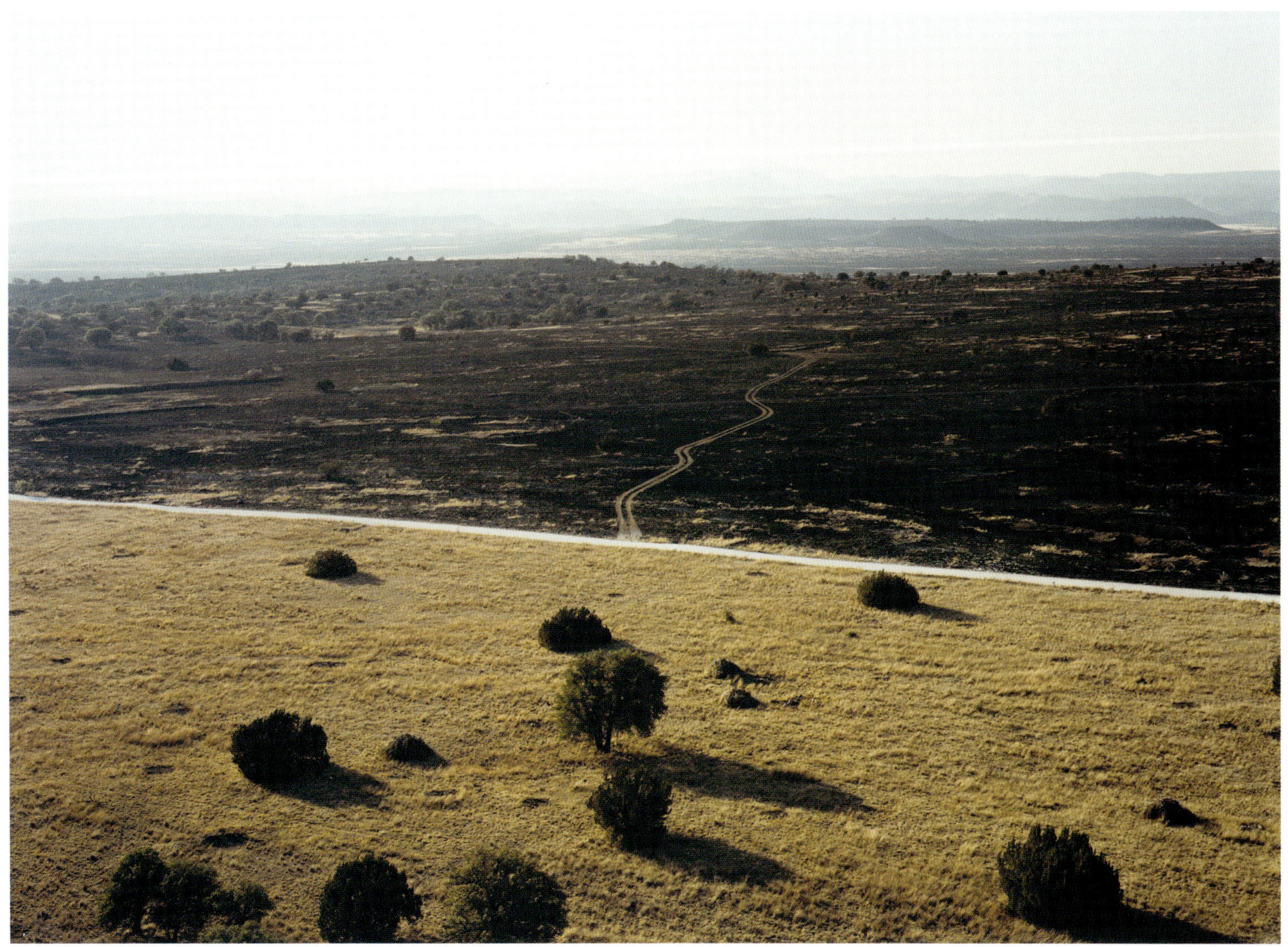

66. Victoria Sambunaris, *Untitled (Road), Fort Davis, Texas*, 2011

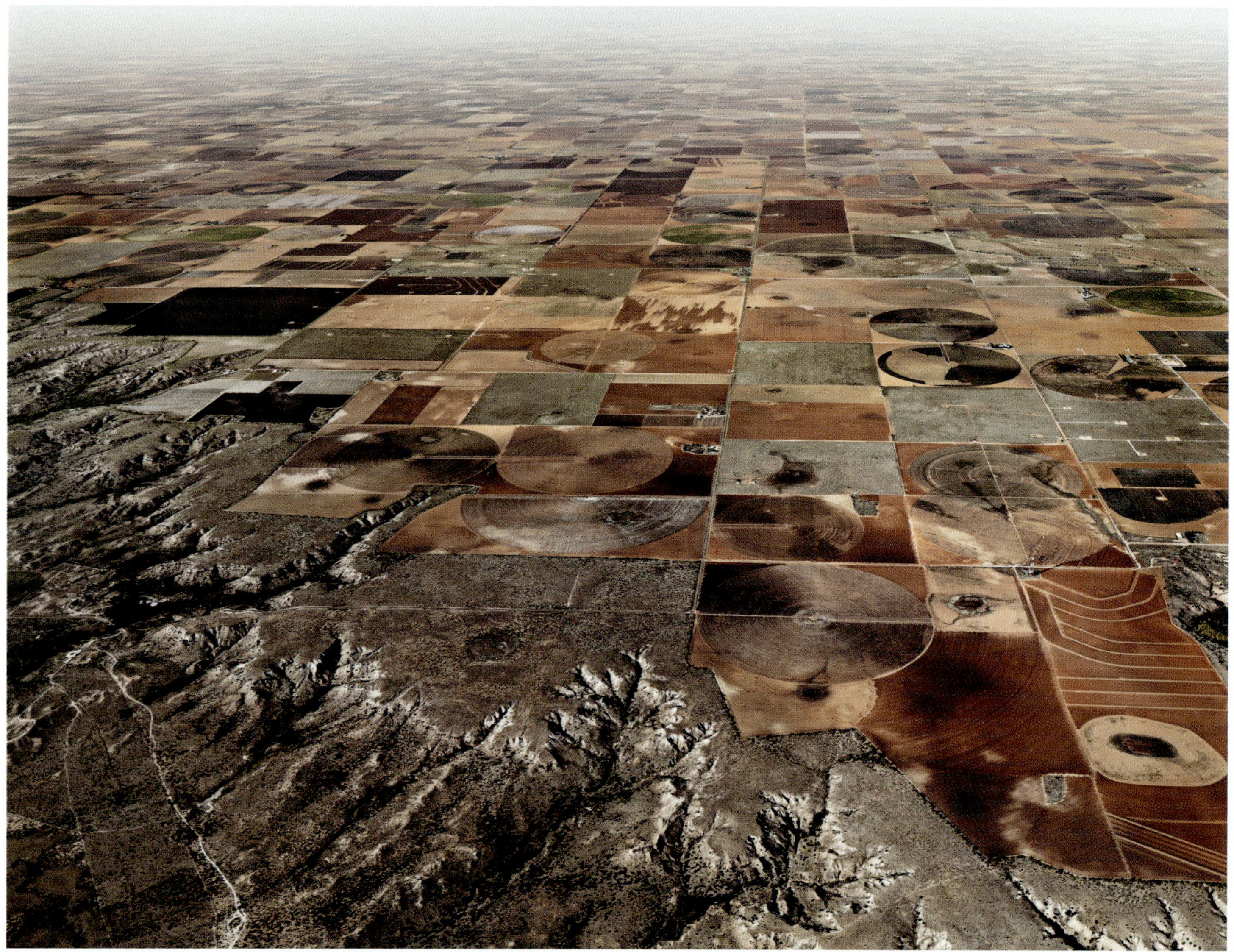

67. Edward Burtynsky, *Pivot Irrigation #11*, 2011 (© Edward Burtynsky, courtesy Nicholas Metivier Gallery, Toronto)

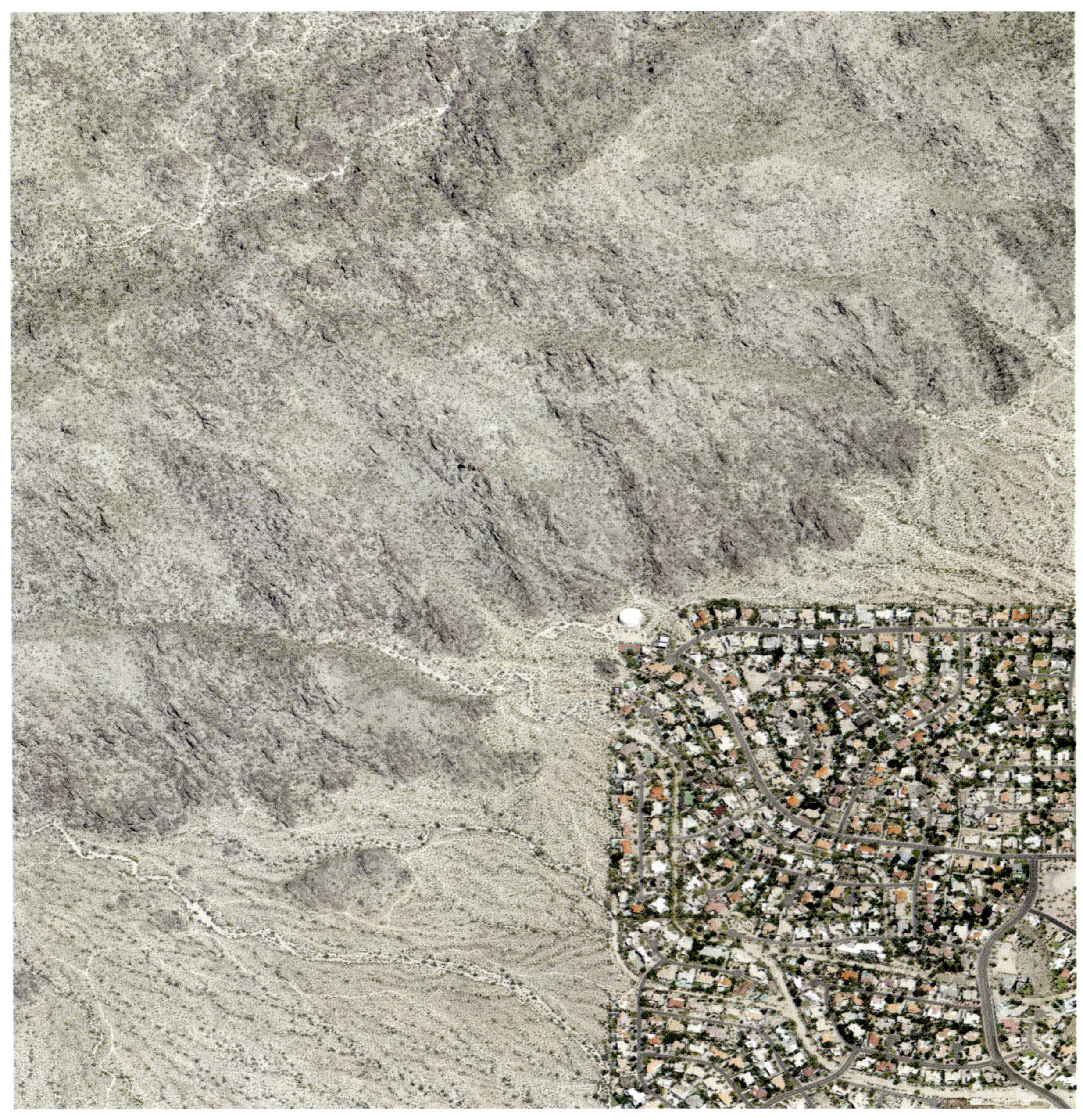

68. Daniel Leivick,
Encroachment #3, 2014

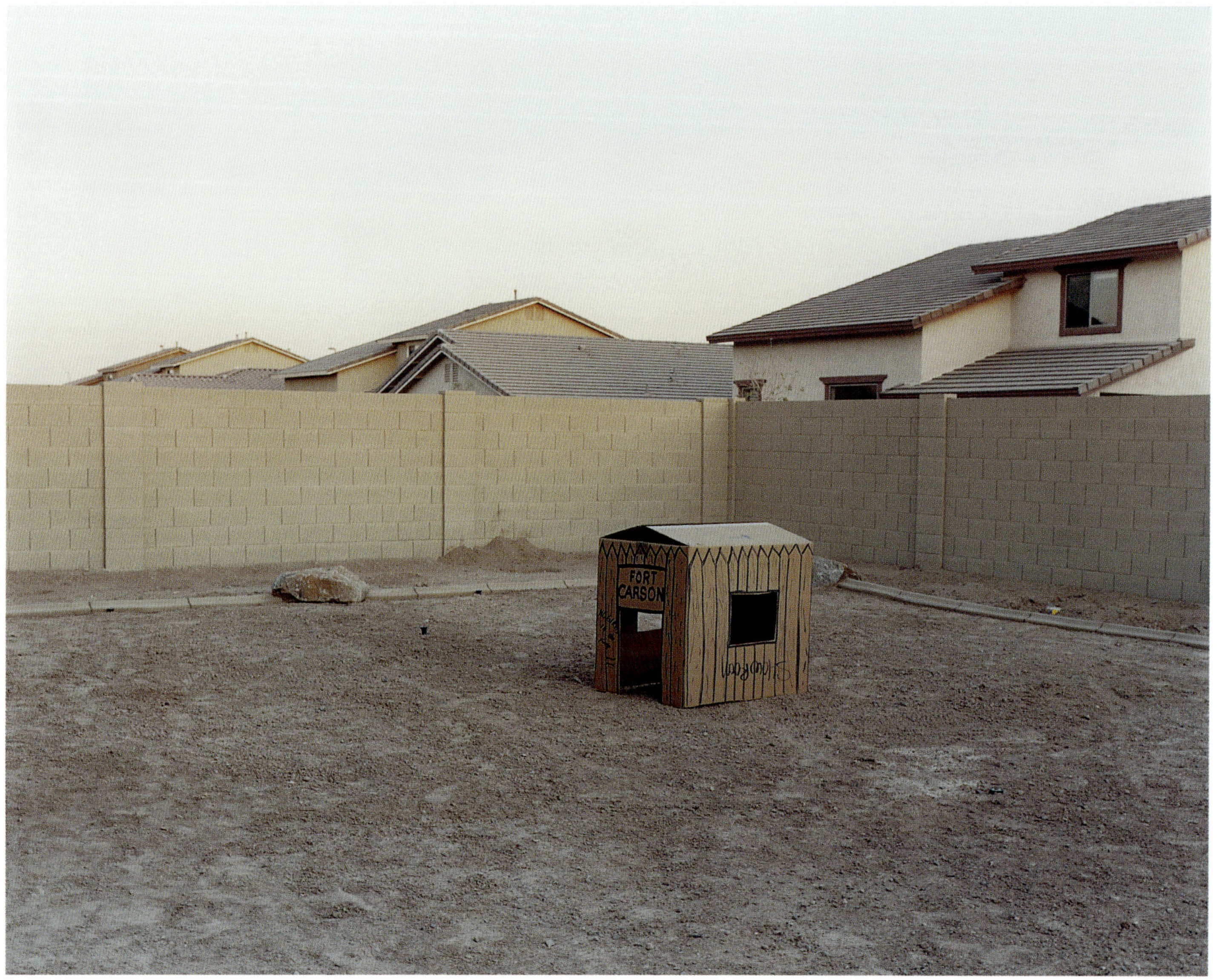

   69. Andrew Phelps, *Fort Carson,* 2007

Cultivating Wildness

GAVIN VAN HORN

As we've seen, the compass of the American wilderness tradition, both in text and image, points West, toward the sublime and spectacular landscapes of Yosemite and Yellowstone and the deep canyons and elongated mesas of the Colorado Plateau. Yet wildness can and of course does exist elsewhere, including settings far removed from the places celebrated by John Muir, Ansel Adams, and Edward Abbey. It's a quality and a wild vision that can be nurtured in seemingly unlikely environs.

I woke to pre-dawn darkness on Easter morning. Before my eyes fluttered open, the trace of an idea shimmered through my mind: see the sunrise. Where I lived in Chicago, the shoreline of Lake Michigan offers a prime spot to witness the sun's appearance. I rose and biked to the lakeshore. As expected, I had the beach to myself. Or so I thought. After nestling my shoulders into a clump of dune grass and tugging my jacket tighter, I waited for the earth to roll into the light. That's when a surprise came trotting into view—two coyotes, mere feet

away, silently padding along a sandy path. They caught my eyes with theirs, pausing to ponder why anyone would be up this early besides them. A cautious moment passed between us; then they circled back and out of sight.

This sunrise coyote encounter was brief and, if you know Chicago, not necessarily exceptional. There are a few thousand resident coyotes in the greater Chicago area—up from zero a couple of decades ago. By all accounts, their numbers seem to be growing. If the increasing coyote presence serves as an indicator of wildness, Chicago would appear to be rewilding. It certainly felt that way—the gaze of coyotes fresh in my mind, prickles still on my skin—as I watched the sun spread gauzy orange upon the lake water that morning.

There are other indicators of the expansion of urban wildness—some accidental, some intentional. As an urban transplant, I've spent some time thinking about what constitutes wildness; or, rather, rethinking this. I used to associate wildness almost exclusively with wilderness. The city, from this perspective, had little to do with nature's bountiful and hard-edged sublimity. My experiences inhabiting a city have undermined this wilderness-only view of wildness, causing me to parse my words with more care and to expand my wild lexicon. I now regard wildness as the sustaining *processes* that animate a landscape—not a bounded area so much as the *relational qualities* that can enliven any place. And, here's a critical piece of this relational understanding: humans can contribute to this wild flourishing. I've seen it happening.

From urban areas to remote unpeopled deserts and mountain summits, wildness exists in degrees. To borrow a phrase from the ecologist Aldo Leopold, "wilderness is a relative condition."[1] I appreciate the phrase *relative condition* because it underscores that wildness is not an all-or-nothing prospect. There are degrees of wildness—just as an individual or a community can be more or less healthy, more or less whole, more or less cohesive, more or less resilient. But there is an even stronger reason for my affection for the phrase: wildness is a *relative* condition—as in, we are related, kin to other species, genetically linked in unfolding epochs by our very DNA, bound together in our shared vulnerability and future prospects as fellow earthlings. The task of our time, perhaps, is to become better relatives than we have been to the nonhuman others who share portions of our genetic code, our bodies, and especially our landscapes.

In the context of our treatment of and care for urban landscapes, I want to suggest a form of relative wildness that may seem like a paradox: a cultivated wild. On first blush, and by dictionary definitions, cultivation appears to be the opposite of wildness. One of the more common uses for the word is the preparation of land for domesticated crop production. Culti-

vation may also be associated with someone well-groomed and sophisticated, the so-called civilized man, pinky raised in the air as he takes his tea. Whatever that is, it's not wild. But I'd like to reclaim a different sense of the word: that with proper attention and intention, we can *become more skilled* at aligning ourselves with the life-giving processes of the land community. Cultivation, in this formulation, creates a productive paradox. We can *cultivate* wildness.

To get a sense of what cultivated wildness might look like, let's begin sixty miles from Chicago and work our way toward the city proper. Midewin National Tallgrass Prairie is about as close as one can come within Chicago's reach to a sizable and thriving tallgrass prairie ecosystem. Midewin contains some twenty thousand acres of tallgrass prairie and woodland savanna in various stages of restoration. Roam the trails and dirt roads, however, and you'll see additional histories embedded in the land that make this accomplishment all the more remarkable.

In certain portions of Midewin, rising above the waving copper of little bluestem grass and the sunbursts of purple coneflower, concrete bunkers dot the landscape at orderly intervals. Viewed from certain angles, the bunkers resemble burial mounds, like the mortuary ruins of a vanished civilization. A few hundred of these "igloos" (as some of the locals call them) dot portions of Midewin, a visual cue that this land served different purposes than it does in its current incarnation (plate 70).

Before Midewin, this sizable government property was known as the Joliet Army Ammunition Plant (JOAAP). Commissioned during World War II, the JOAAP became a robust production facility for wartime munitions, including mass quantities of TNT. Now largely empty, the bunkers once provided on-site

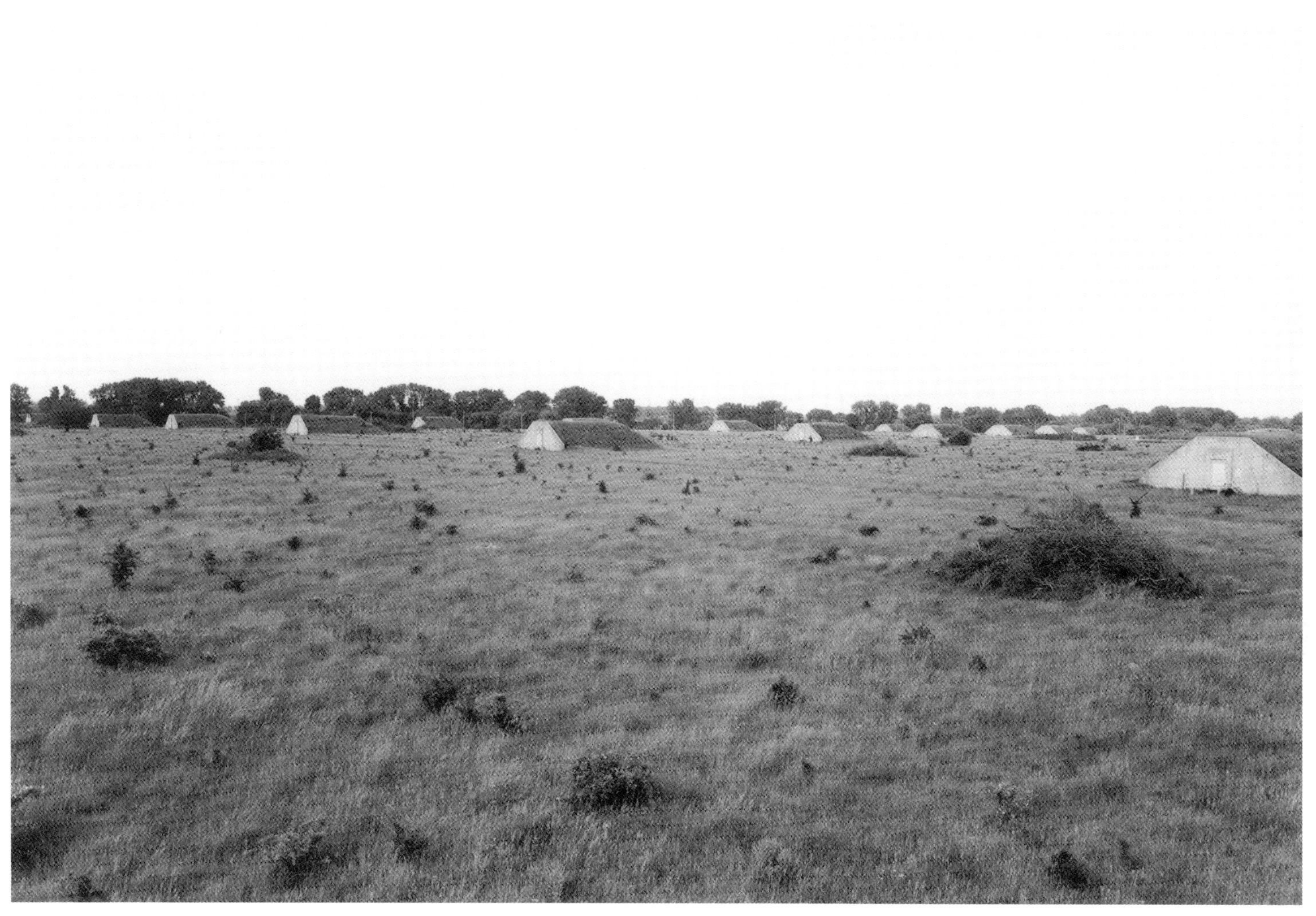

70. Edward Ranney, *Ammunition Bunkers, former Joliet Army Arsenal, Joliet, Illinois*, 1993

storage space and containment for this TNT as well as explosives of all sorts of deadly varieties. Arms production ceased at JOAAP by the late 1970s. Due to the advocacy efforts of a broad coalition of over twenty conservation groups and partners, the property was transferred to the U.S. Forest Service in 1996, and the country's first national tallgrass prairie was born.

I'm grateful many of the bunkers remain (removing them is a costly process), if for no other reason than their symbolic potency. A place that once dealt in destruction, or at least its threatened possibility, has become a place that now deals in resurrection—of a wild prairie ecosystem. Some have suggested the bunkers—cool, dry, solidly built—be used for seed storage.

Which brings us to an odd juxtaposition that exists at Midewin. In one section of the property, acres of prairie plants grow in tidy rows. If you didn't know what was being grown, you could be forgiven for thinking this was yet another Illinois plot of soybeans. And that expectation tells of the trouble: the state of Illinois's motto is "the Prairie State," but large-scale agriculture and development have left very little prairie standing—.01 percent, to be precise. And, so, as a large-scale effort in prairie restoration, the needed seeds must be cultivated at Midewin. In other words, the paucity of available wild prairie seeds prompted a DIY-prairie-farming operation.

A cultivated wild. Cultivation suggests domestication, diverting a plant away from its wild origins, favoring certain characteristics that favor us. Cultivating prairie thus brims with ironic and resurrective possibility. Cultivating a diverse prairie polyculture turns the trajectory of the land: from tame *thing* to wild *being*. These acts of prairie cultivation strike me as radical, literally reaching to the roots of our relationship to the land. It was once believed that prairie needed to be brought under control, civilized by the farmer's hand. Sewell Newhouse, who designed a steel trap in the late 1800s that was used widely by western forest rangers to capture wolves, provided a summation of this cultural perspective when he commented that such traps were "the prow with which iron clad civilization is pushing back barbaric solitude, and is replacing the wolf with the wheat field, the library, and the piano." Like the wolves in Illinois, the prairie's "barbaric solitude" threatened the pioneer's sense of good economic order, which amounted to a landscape in the firm grip of human dominion. Cultivating prairie, in contrast, unearths the will of the land. The power of prairie restoration derives not from denaturing in favor of so-called civilization but in unleashing care for the land's will, an active acknowledgment that there may be desires greater than our own that spring from the soil.

An indication of the quality of the area, in October 2015 Midewin welcomed a small herd of bison to the landscape. The bison don't yet have the run of the place (they currently roam inside twelve hundred double-fenced acres), but they are part of a grand experiment to show the ways that prairie and bison mutually shape one another. Another degree of wildness infused into this place, and, perhaps, if the excitement generated by their presence is an indication, a degree of wildness opened in the human imagination.

It may be worth noting that the Potawatomi root of the word *midewin* refers to something "mystically powerful," a reference to the ritual curing societies that once played an important role in Ojibwe, Ottawa, and Potawatomi cultures. For a landscape that's experienced so much abuse, prairie restoration—the return of wild plants and animals

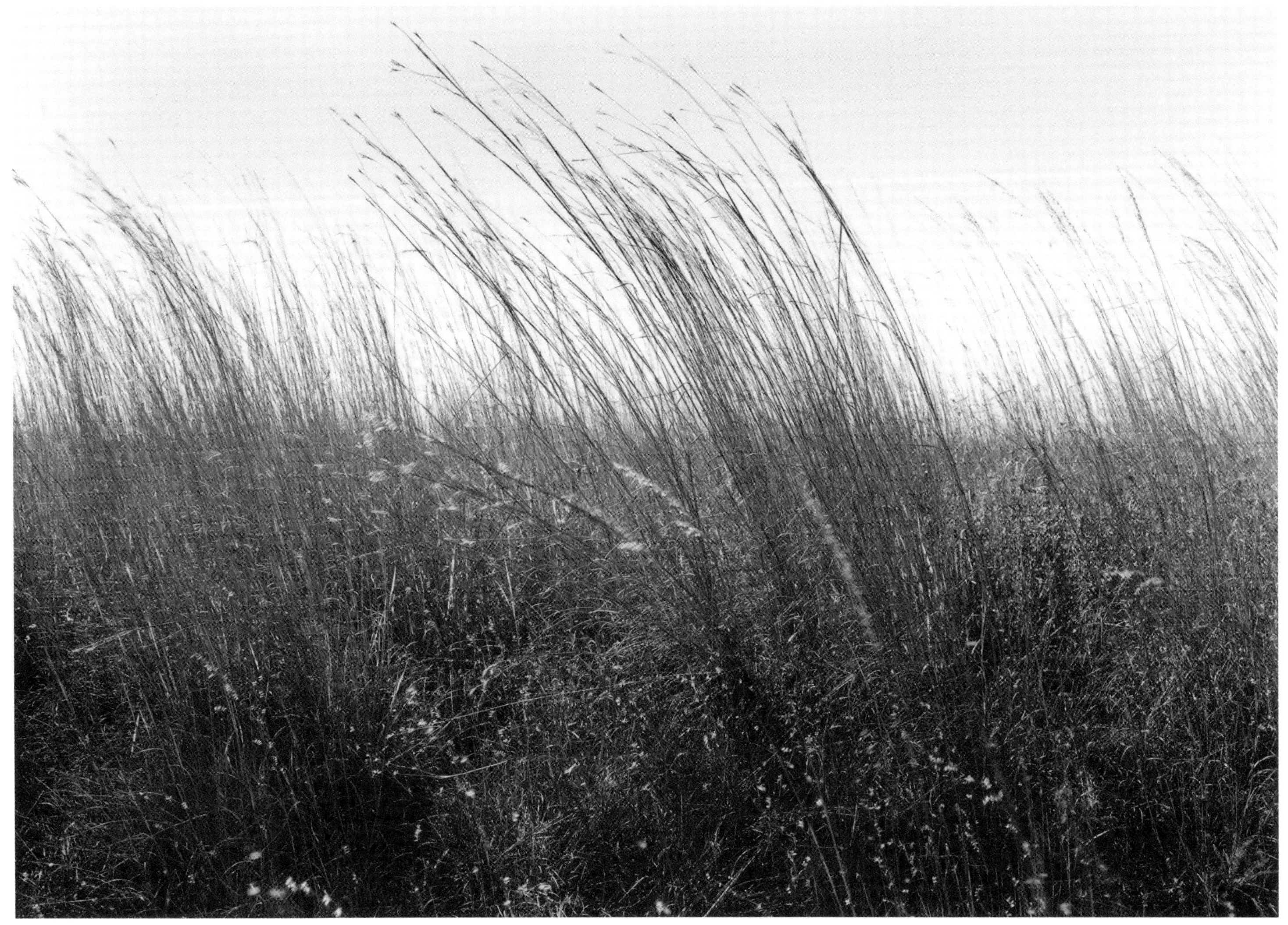

71. Edward Ranney, *Goose Lake Prairie State Park, near Morris, Illinois,* 1992

and those human prairie stewards who care about their well-being—does feel mystically powerful. Gary Nabhan's notion of "biocultural restoration" powerfully captures this idea.[2] Long-lost relationships are blooming in the sun again, a cultivated wildness brushing against the bellies of bison.

On a summer afternoon, my toes hanging from the aluminum edge of a small pleasure boat, I gaze into murky green waters and wait for my moment. I look behind me: a woman dressed in purple leggings with a few extra appendages (a nod to the octopus-witch Ursula, from the Disney movie *The Little Mermaid*) lets out a whoop and raises her red plastic cup in the air. In front of me, several people are already splashing around, in various approximations of backstrokes and dog paddles. A twenty-something-year-old swims with his batman cape trailing behind him in the water, while another man, dressed in a full suit-and-tie, hollers encouragement from behind a Donald Trump mask (in retrospect, much funnier pre-election), waving orange-painted hands at the crowd. I hesitate for a final moment, wondering how much I trust this group of relative strangers—city officials, nonprofit leaders, local volunteers. I'd made a commitment, though, and I intended to follow through. I turn around, facing away from the water, and dive backward into the Cal-Sag Channel. When I surface, the next person in line follows with a cannonball, clutching knees to chest, plunging into a human-cut canal where human contact with the water had been prohibited for as long as anyone could recall.

This little stunt was a small act of awareness-raising for a long-beleaguered stretch of the greater Chicago River system, a system that has been engineered—channeled, straightened,

dredged, reversed—to suit the purposes of heavy industry and sewage diversion. Since the arrival of Euro-American settlers and through its bustling industrial boom, the Chicago River and its tributaries were valued largely in terms of their ability to move toxic substances *away* from the city. Out of sight, out of mind.

Attitudes about the river began shifting only in recent decades. Friends of the Chicago River—an organization that took the inspiration for its name from a 1979 *Chicago Magazine* article title, which proclaimed the Chicago River "friendless"—has been at the forefront of many of these efforts. Riverbank stabilization and habitat creation, restoration of native species, volunteer cleanups, and lobbying for higher water-quality standards have become their stock and trade.

In certain places throughout the river system, sewage treatment has improved dramatically in the last few years, and longer-term plans for stormwater management are receiving increasing attention. The river has healed slowly as a result, and though many scars remain, it is healing. As riverside trails, amenities, parks, and kayak and canoe rentals proliferate, more people are lured to the river, creating a feedback loop of expectation for a clean and inviting waterway. Wildlife benefits from this attention. As one example among many, aquatic biologists from the Metropolitan Water Reclamation District (an independent government entity that manages water quality in Cook County) documented a dramatic increase in fish species in the river, from ten known species in 1974 to a present count of seventy-six total species, including fifty-nine that have been found in Chicago waterways since 2000.

I've kayaked various parts of the Chicago River, from canals to shallow creeks to the heart of downtown Chicago. Not yet highly trafficked, especially in comparison to the interstates and city streets that cross above, the gentle-flowing river has privileged me with many wild moments of paddling alongside early adopters and celebrants of the river's recovery. Kingfishers, herons, beavers, turtles, muskrats, damselflies, and a varied assortment of other wild beings hug the banks and hunt the shallows on this ribbon of urban water. One afternoon, from the vantage point of my kayak, I witnessed a mink—making a tentative comeback after being absent for many years—wind her sinuous, playful body between a gnarled maze of tree roots that line the riverbank. The creature carried something in her mouth nearly the size of her small ermine head, reminding me of a golden retriever with an oversized chew toy. I followed carefully, drifting closer and closer, until the mink paused and began expertly dismembering a crayfish between her pointed teeth. The crunching sounded like a muffled firecracker. *Kak-kak. Pop-pop-pop. Kaaak.* When her gnawing was complete, she danced away, down the bank and out of sight.

The encounter with the mink reminded me that water, even constrained water, offers a measure of wildness (or at least the hope of it). The Chicago River attests to this. When I pore over Ed Ranney's photographs, my eye gravitates to the line—the steel cable, the iron mesh of bridge, the hard edge of an old grain silo, battered train tracks, the channelized river (plate 72). The photographs trace long horizons retreating, pulling and tugging our vision, never quite letting us rest. Incompletion builds as a theme, on display in the bones and ribs of bridges, seemingly forgotten machinery, and aging storage tanks. I gaze upon these forms and see them as edifices and infrastructure of a *nonrenewable worldview,* one that testifies to the value of obtaining quickly, isn't concerned with residence, and shows little discernable alignment or reciprocity with a wild world. It represents a gutted logic of extraction, an ideology of forced submission, and a faith in quarterly profits over earthen time scales.

And yet I also see traces and bits of something else: the self-renewal of the land, weedy wildness spiraling up rusted metal and trees, vegetation encroaching from the borders. Give it time.

But what of our time? What if, instead of imposing our will upon other creatures, we sought alignment with the urban landscape and its river? Exploring such a question guides us toward a renewable worldview, one that is adaptive, acting within cycles and time scales more in keeping with wildness, and therefore, more in keeping with a culture geared for the long run.

When I'm on the river, the city is simultaneously up close and far away. To find clarity for a wild vision, I've found there are few better places to begin than thinking with water. A renewable worldview necessarily honors water. The river survives—bent and impounded, reversed and polluted—waiting, and in some cases receiving, release from Chicago's industrial grip. A river still knows how to be a river when given the chance.

At Midewin and on the recovering Chicago River, a powerful lesson is becoming more and more visible: wildness isn't about absenting ourselves from place; it's about learning how to live within that place, to be in better conversation with that place. The river has been partially released from the stranglehold of industrial reduction (transport and disposal of waste) and Midewin fully discharged from the task of industrial production (factory for war). In both cases, an attitude of dominion, a nonrenewable worldview, with nature as a stage solely for human actors, has given way to a larger imaginary. Lands and waters that once were regarded solely as human commodities

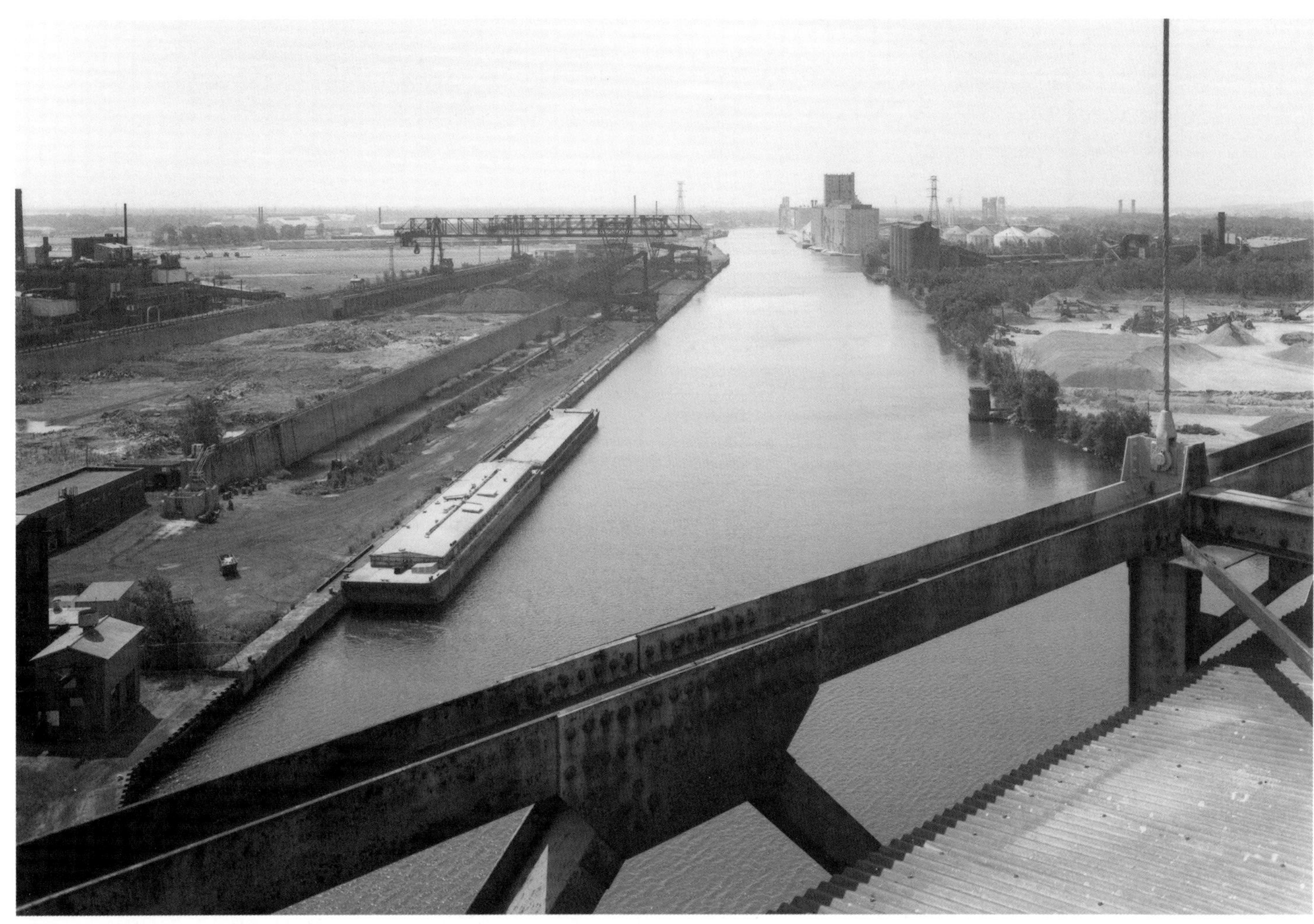

 72. Edward Ranney, *Calumet River, South Chicago,* 1993

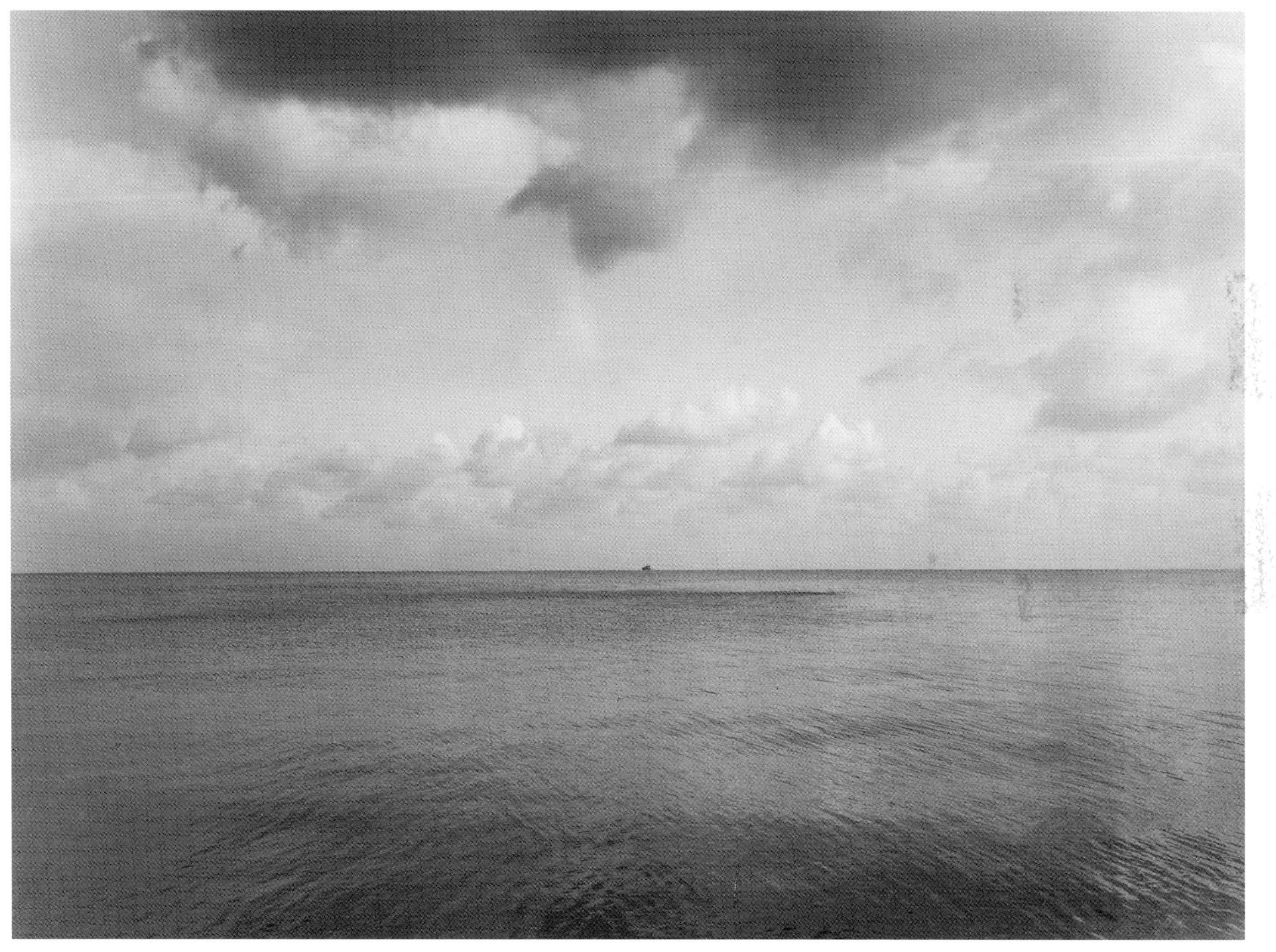

73. Edward Ranney, *Lake Michigan, Chicago*, 1993

are increasingly being recognized as more-than-human communities. As they are, further degrees of wildness, to be cultivated in spirit and landscape, can flourish.

If there were a sure-fire way to quantify wildness, would a statistician be tempted to proclaim a place like Midewin as wild as the pre-European landscape that flourished here a thousand years ago? Probably not. The Chicago River? Never. But the greater the attention, the deeper the emotional and physical involvement with our urban landscapes, the more opportunities are created to cultivate wildness in our shared habitats and in ourselves. The more we allow such wild, more-than-human forces the freedom to flow once again, the more the potential ecological and cultural self-renewal is actualized. That's a wild vision worth holding as an aspirational horizon. An actual horizon to appreciate such aspirations might include a Lake Michigan sunrise—with coyotes sharing the moment.

Rethinking
Remaking

From the Wilderness to the Wild

Like national parks, wilderness seemed something that belonged in remote settings, which meant out West, or in Alaska. After all, that's where the big-sky public domain lay. Studies repeatedly showed that the farther people were from wild lands, the more they valued them as wilderness. The highwater mark surely came with the Alaska National Interest Lands Conservation Act of 1980, which hugely expanded—tripled—the acreage in the National Wilderness Preservation System. The Alaska showdown marked the final frontier of argument over the unroaded national estate.

Yet the wilderness idea tapped into deep roots of American culture. There were good arguments, both on cultural and especially political grounds, to accept a more elastic definition of wilderness that would allow wilderness to come closer to where the people were. Much as the National Park Service in the 1970s sought to connect more fully with the citizenry by creating urban parks (and historic sites in urban areas) that would

place the agency closer to clusters of population, so wilderness advocates sought to expand its range and perhaps rally wider enthusiasm. In 1975 the Eastern Wilderness Act carried legal wilderness into the eastern United States. It was openly admitted that the traditional vision of the wild as untouched could not apply to such lands, many of which had been mauled in the early years of settlement. Even in Alaska, provisions allowed for traditional subsistence harvesting by Native Alaskans.

Where the land was feral rather than originally wild, it could be rewilded, and that nudged partisans into a sense that the wild as *wild,* not historic pedigree, or an unbroken chain of custody as pristine landscape, was the essence of wilderness. For example, the Apostle Islands National Lakeshore in northern Wisconsin is an archipelago of more than twenty islands and mainland territory on the western edge of Lake Superior. It certainly looks like what we think a wilderness should be: sea caves and sandscapes adorn the coastal areas providing habitat for the area's abundant waterfowl, while stretches of thick boreal forest on the islands are enlivened by an assortment of black bears, foxes, coyotes, and whitetail deer. A harbor of biodiversity, the lakeshore also contains critical nesting habitat for the bald eagle (federally threatened) and piping plover (federally endangered).

Although they comply with the familiar wilderness phenotype, the Apostles have in fact been shaped over the centuries by a wide array of human activities. Paleo-Indian presence dates back ten millennia in the region. For centuries, the Apostle Islands have been home to several bands of Lake Superior Chippewa (Ojibwe). Madeleine Island, the largest of the islands—though not included within the national lakeshore—was and is the spiritual center for the Ojibwe communities of western Lake Superior.[1] Most of those thick forests, it turns out, are actually secondary growth, for the islands have a deep history of logging and fire, as well as fishing, farming, quarrying, and tourism. The wilderness character of the place, in other words, is a relatively recent condition that has manifested itself after a long period of extensive human presence, exploitation, management, and change. Yet this partly anthropogenic dimension did not disqualify it as wilderness in the eyes of the public and policy makers. In 2004, the National Park Service established the Gaylord Nelson Wilderness Area on the islands, a legal affirmation of the area's wilderness values and a land management designation that covers roughly 80 percent of the islands. It was recognition of just how wild the landscape had become as many of the most visible aspects of the human footprint (save for the lighthouses) were slowly erased by the combination of new growth and stringent environmental management.[2]

Despite such humanistic nuances, it's clear that wilderness became an intellectual portal for general philosophies of biocentrism, intrinsic values, and deep ecology. The cultural heritage of a place mattered less than the contemporary willingness to withdraw a human presence from it, especially if its human history was easily naturalized and its aesthetic values were in sync with the traditional views and wilderness ethic.

The career of Roderick Nash tracks the transformation nicely. Nash completed his doctoral dissertation on wilderness in 1964, impeccably timed with passage of the Wilderness Act. The thesis morphed into a book in 1967, *Wilderness and the American Mind,* then went through four editions as the saga of the National Wilderness Preservation System continued. In 1989, however, he wrote a complementary work, *The Rights of Nature: A History of Environmental Ethics.* In the earlier book the idea had grown that Americans preserved patches of nature out of noblesse oblige. It was an act of generosity that showed a nobility of spirit beyond money-grubbing. In the later work, wilderness, and nature more broadly, had rights of their own, and pioneering thinkers, much on the model of civil rights, worked to widen ethical sensibilities to embrace them. The campaign to grant rights to nature had, in Nash's rendition, a comparable moral standing to abolitionism in the nineteenth century. In its pursuit violence was likely, maybe requisite.

The traits—and correspondingly, the moral energies—that had traditionally been invested into purely wild lands now ranged into all aspects of nature. Increasingly, the Endangered Species Act, not the Wilderness Act, was the Archimedean lever to move environmental reform. The ESA did not merely tolerate active measures but required them.

This more interventionist approach to managing wild-lands was said to be far more suitable for conservation in a time of uncertain ecological change and expanding human presence. Manipulation of landscapes to restore and improve their habitat value for both native and non-native species (via species introductions, plantings, and so on) became increasingly normalized. Yet even though wilderness areas were managed carefully for low-impact recreation and for ecological values, sometimes maintaining the full sweep of ecological goods on a landscape, including the protection of biodiversity in a rapidly transforming environment, required managers to consider interventions that challenged the conventional wisdom of "hands off" wilderness management.

It wasn't always easy. In Arizona, the U.S. Fish and Wildlife Service was sued by a wilderness advocacy group for building water tanks in designated wilderness to provide reserves for endangered bighorn sheep, a population stressed by drought magnified by human climate change. The preservationists argued successfully that the Wilderness Act prohibited building installations that disturb wilderness character.[3] At the same time, the ESA could be brought to bear to spare an invasive tree, the tamarisk, that had become a nesting habitat for the southwestern willow flycatcher, an endangered bird.[4]

Such cases were a reminder that wilderness was only one arrow in a quiver of environmental responses. The Nature Conservancy, with its program of conserving and restoring non-wilderness (and often, privately held) lands, was several orders of magnitude larger than the more traditionally focused preservation organizations (such as the Wilderness Society). Northern spotted owls were more likely to keep

national forests roadless than was the promise of wilderness designation.

As it might be necessary to raise-and-release California condors, to save species like Mount Graham red squirrels by putting them in zoos, to train whooping cranes to learn their ancestral flyways, so images of landscape might work to invest aesthetic value into troubled or compromised scenes. No one would live in the wild, and most would never visit a legal wilderness, but the values of nature could be found nearly everywhere we chose to look. Contemporary photographers suggest what we might see, and how we might find aesthetic value.

About the Gallery

BAM: Mark, you come from the tradition of landscape photography rather than wildlife photography or conservation photography. But I'm curious how you see the trends in wildlife and biodiversity conservation discussed in this chapter intersecting with your own interests, and the work of the other photographers in this section.

MK: You're seeing a hole in the picture edit here, because it's true that there is an entire genre sometimes called "nature" photography that specializes on wildlife and conservation related subjects. What we have instead are examples by photographers in the tradition of "fine art" photography. From a practical standpoint, these artists rarely use the same tools as nature photographers, say, preferring the tradition of large format photography over the cameras with telephoto lenses that are necessary to photographing animals at a distance.

SP: Yes, wildlife has its own conservation traditions, quite apart from forests, waters, and rangelands. Reserves for big game preceded those for forests. Even in fire management, the pressure for reforms in the 1960s came from wildlife biologists. I'm not surprised that wildlife has its own photographic heritage.

BAM: So if it isn't nature photography in the traditional sense of supporting a concern about endangered species or conservation, why include it in this context?

MK: Fair question. These photographers explore a personal relationship to wildlife that I think relates to the broader societal and conservation context described in the essay. Terry Falke's picture of a moose in a cage doesn't show a live animal (plate 77). But it seems to my eye to relate to how species are reintroduced to the wild—and yet here the cage is in the California desert, which is ironic. I would think that relates to the debates you must have in your field about where and how species are reintroduced. Barbara Bosworth photographs a swan hunter and his prey (plate 76). This picture comes from an extended series she did, trying to understand hunters and their relationship to the animals they hunt.

BAM: OK, but what should we make of Rebecca Norris Webb's photo of a bison from her car's side view mirror (plate 78)? It's a striking image, no doubt. But what does it mean to you in this setting?

MK: This is the reality of how we often see wild animals from our modern-day equivalent of a horse.

BAM: I can't help but think again of Ed Abbey (in *Desert Solitaire*): "You can't see anything from a car; you've got to get out of the goddamn contraption. . . . "

MK: Well, with all due respect to Abbey, the picture examines how we come to see something, not just what we see. In Norris's case it's important to know that she also has deep family connections to the place she's photographing. Anyway, it might not be advisable to get out of a car that close to a bison.

BAM: You'll get no argument from me on that last point! In fact, there have been more than a few bison encounters in the news in recent years, often due to tourists searching for that perfect wildlife "selfie." So no, I don't imagine that's what Abbey had in mind when he wrote those words. But your point about the relationships and connections implied in these photos is interesting, and of course makes me think of the basic premise of ecology: the interactions of organisms and their environment. It's just that here one of the organisms has a camera.

SP: More three-body problems. It's not just hunter and hunted, photographer and photographed, the interaction between them becomes itself a presence? No wonder the photos are unsettling.

BAM: There's a lot going on in these pictures and it puts them in a different aesthetic and philosophical category than, say, the traditional nature or wildlife photo. Even Annie Marie Musselman's picture of a wolf in the forest, which has many of the trappings of a traditional wildlife image, has a more interesting and personal story, right (plate 80)?

MK: It does. Her work has appeared in many of the traditional venues (such as magazines) for contemporary nature photography. But in fact her relationship to the animals she photographs doesn't result from a hit-and-run approach. She's worked in animal rehab and explores human kinship with them.

BAM: Not just on the outside looking in.

MK: It and the other images in this gallery are a reminder how photographers immerse themselves deeply in their work. For example, Bremner Benedict photographed Quitobaquito Springs along the U.S.-Mexican border (plate 74). It's part of a much larger series she's doing on natural springs in western deserts, work that is clearly shaped by an ecological sensitivity as you mention, Ben.

Photographers can get fascinated by a particular subject in nature and use their working process to learn in great detail about their subjects. Then, through an iterative process of making photographs, learning from them, and going back out to do more work, their work becomes multilayered, and they put that knowledge out into the world in visual form.

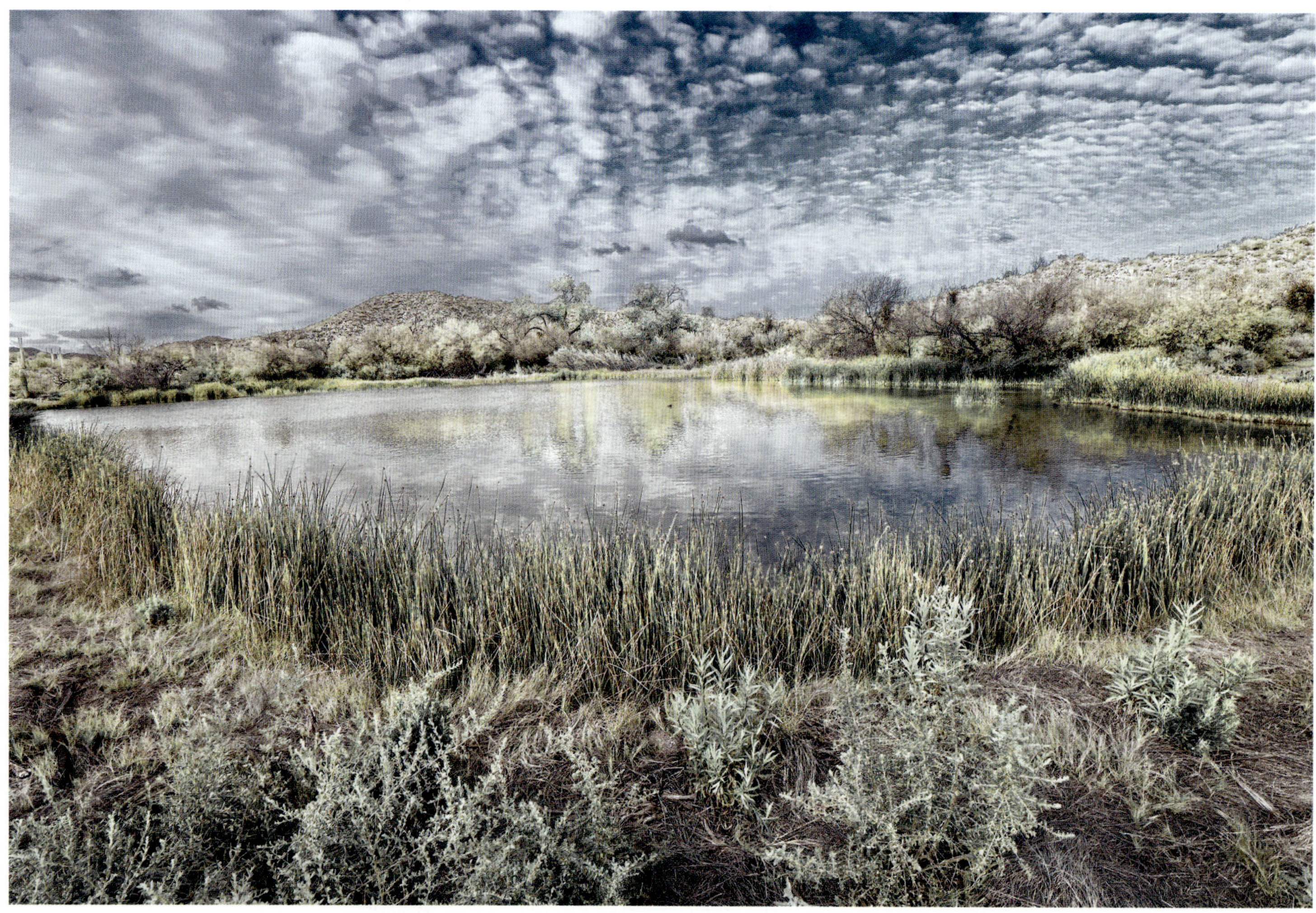

74. Bremner Benedict, *Sonoran Desert—Quitobaquito Springs, Organ Pipe National Monument, Arizona*, 2019

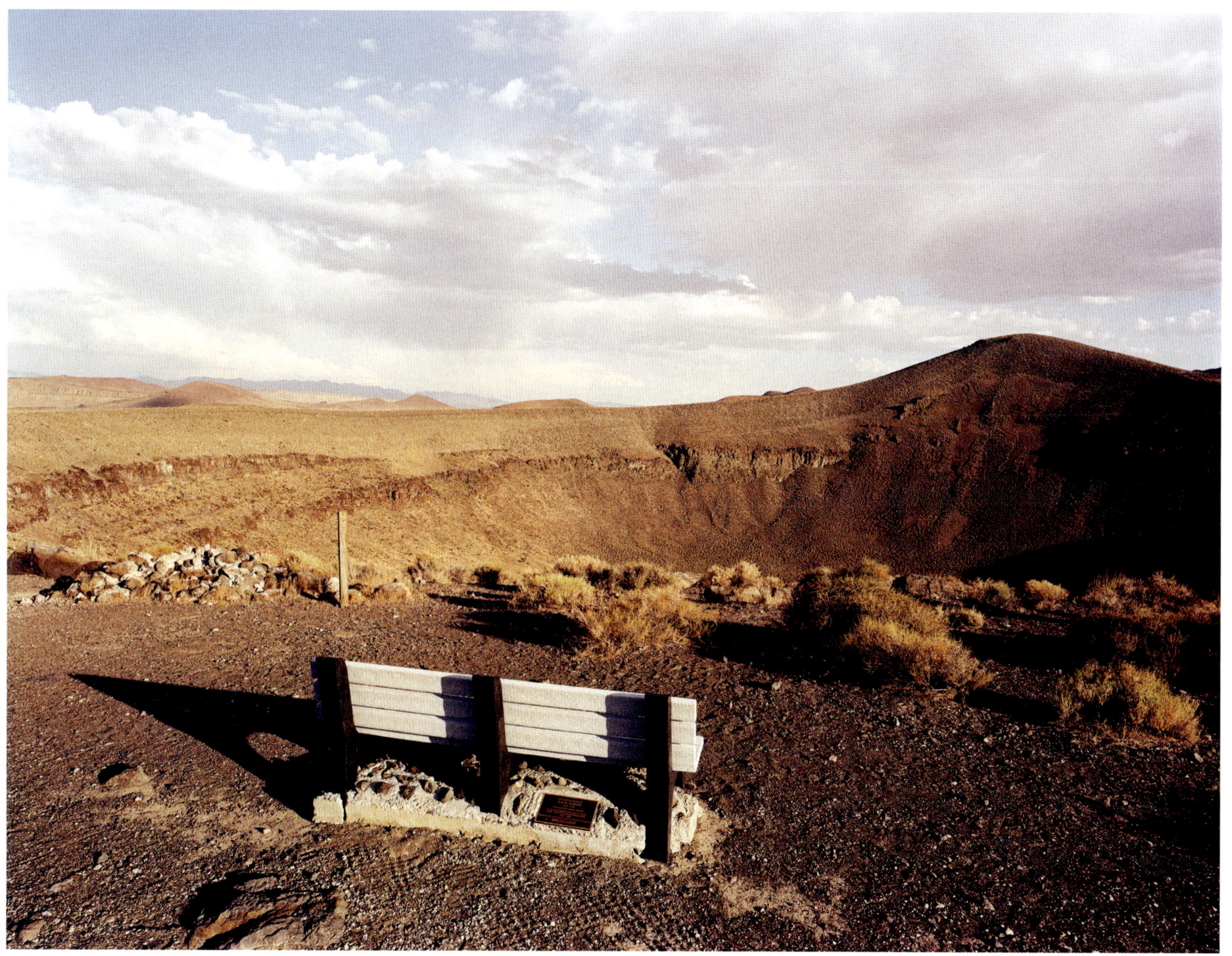

75. John Brinton Hogan, *Lunar Crater National Natural Landmark, Nevada,* 2007 (Courtesy of the artist)

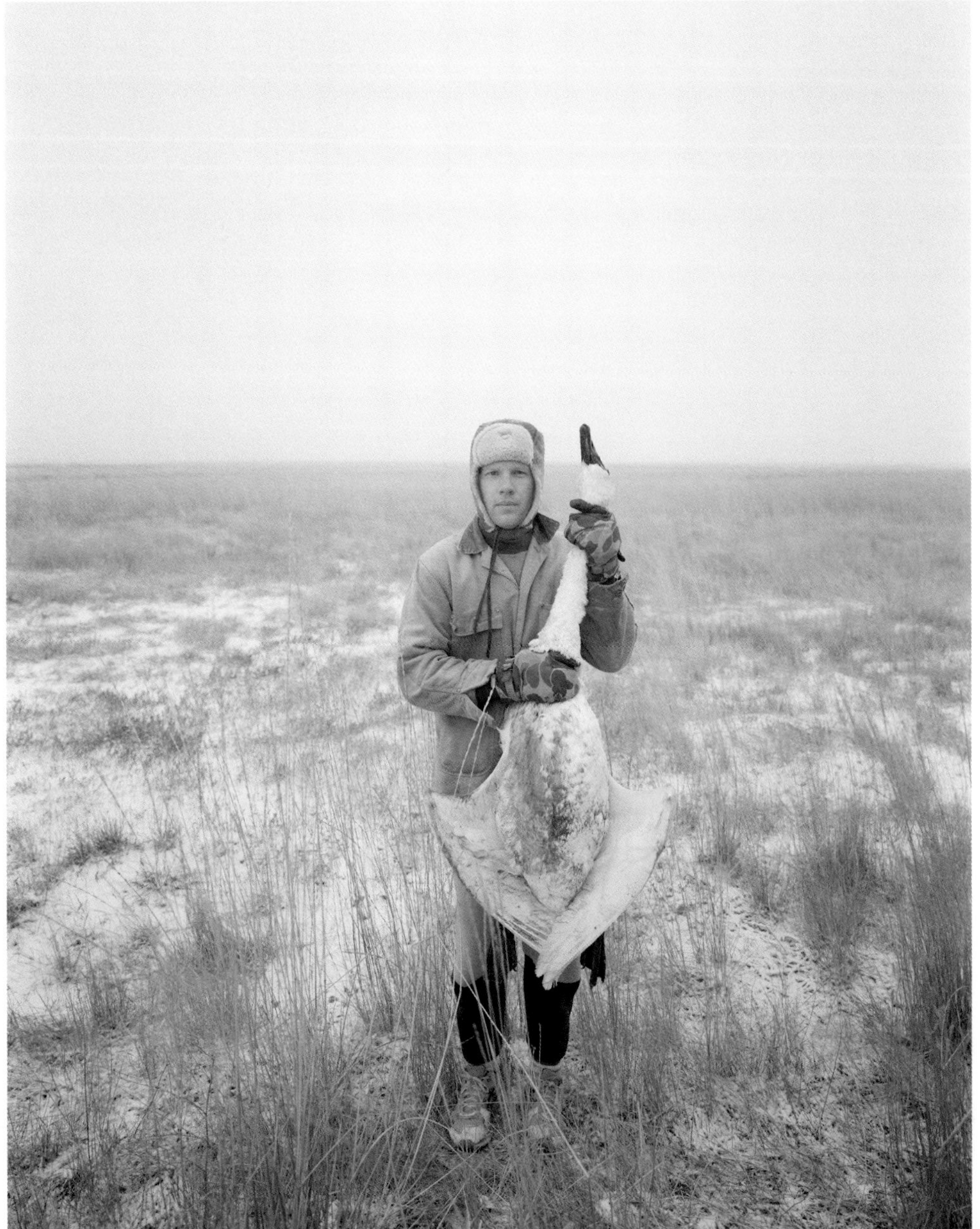

76. Barbara Bosworth, *Swan Hunter,*
Freezeout Lake, Montana, 1995
(Courtesy of the artist)

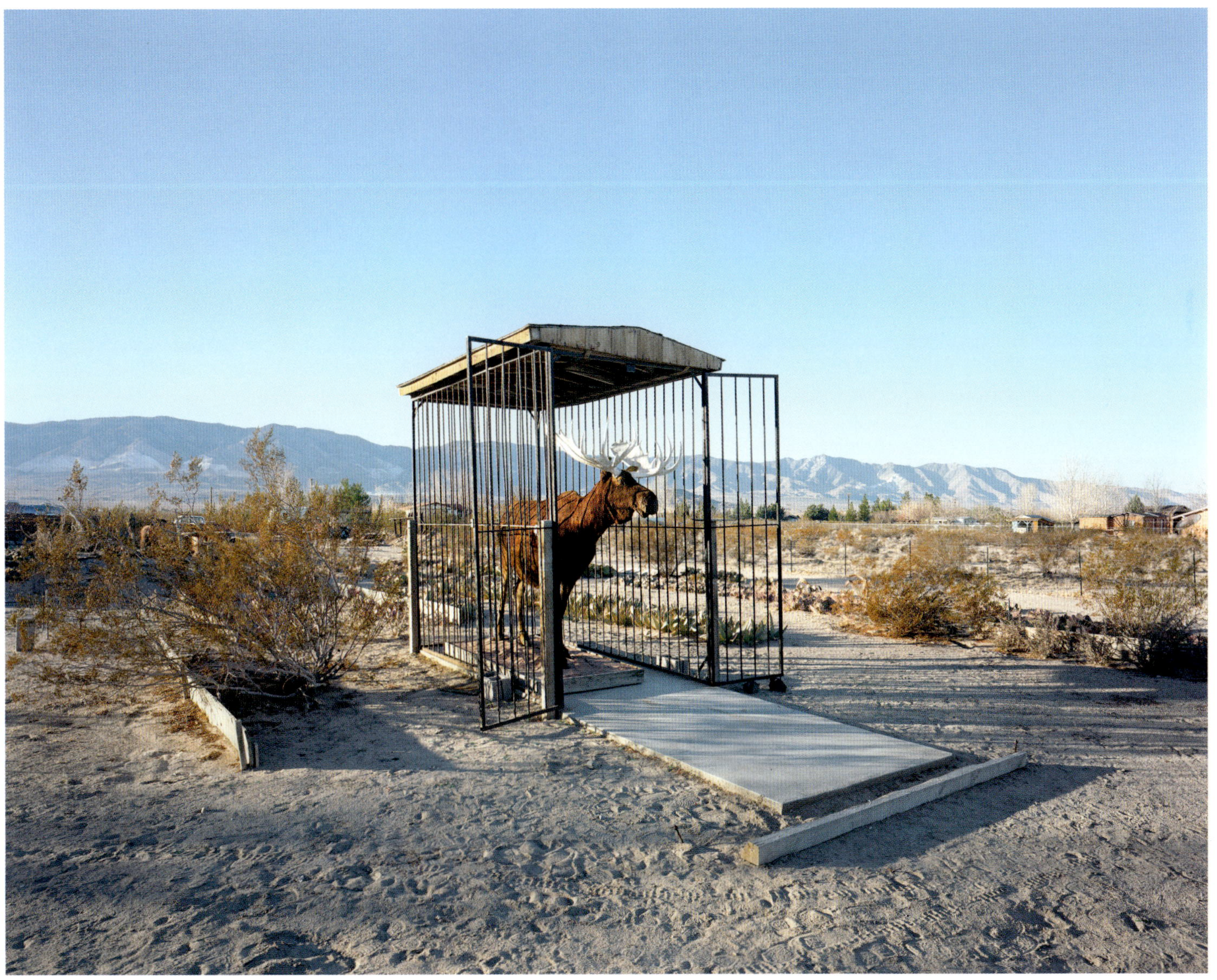

77. Terry Falke, *Moose, California*, 2002

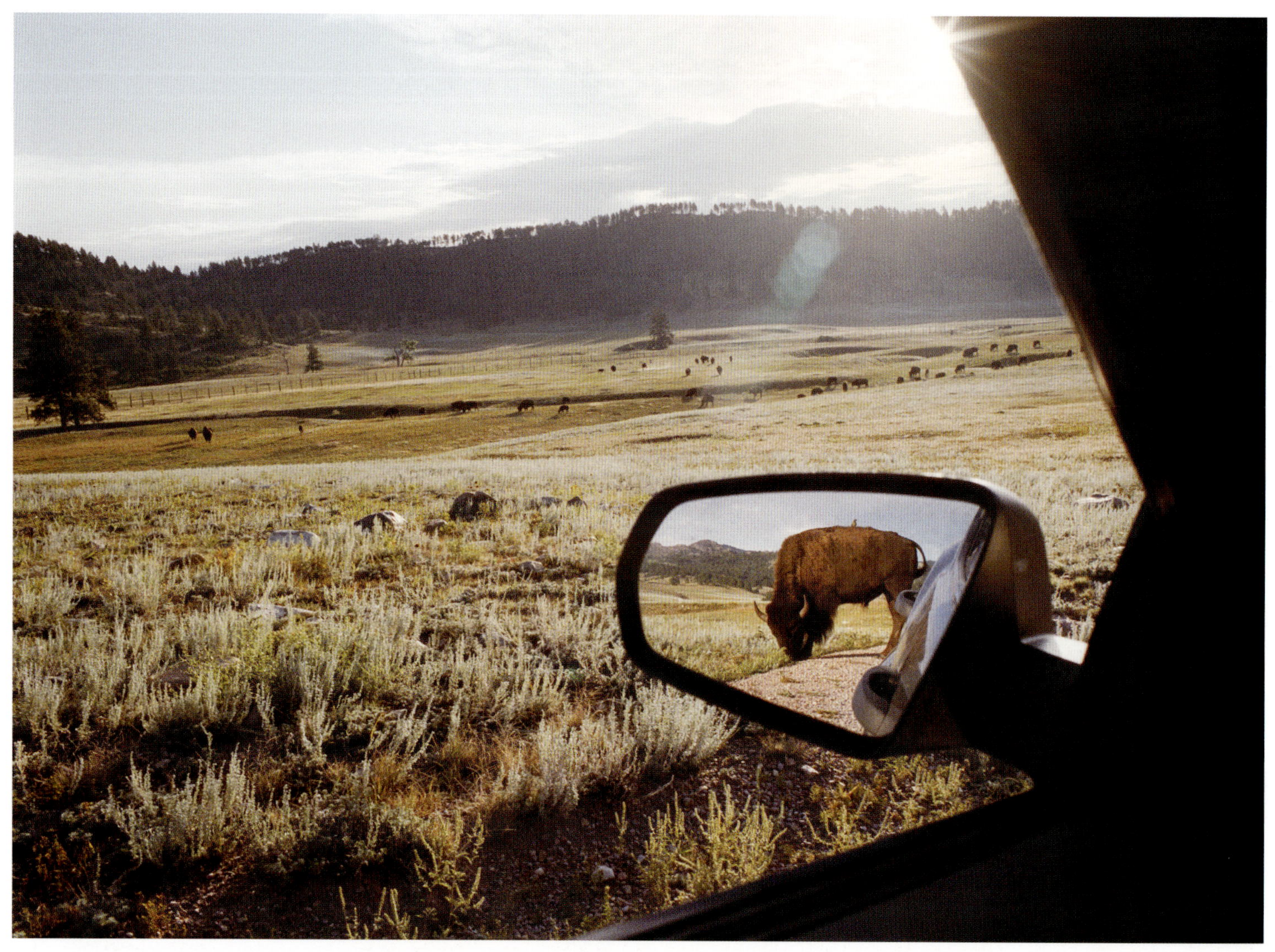

78. Rebecca Norris Webb, *Rearview Mirror,* 2005–2011 (From *My Dakota,* by Rebecca Norris Webb [Radius Books, 2012])

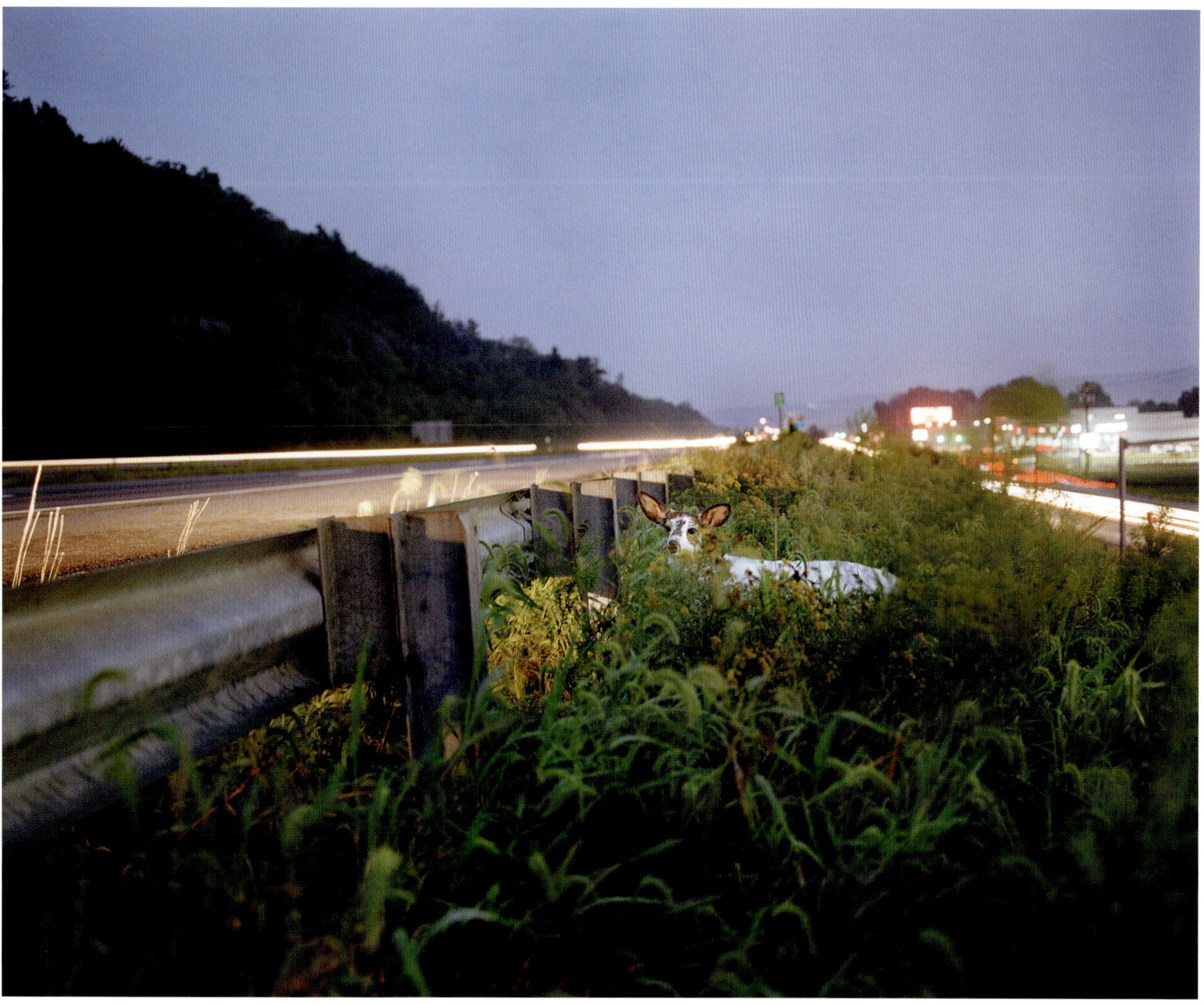

79. Amy Stein, *In Between*, 2005 (Courtesy of the artist)

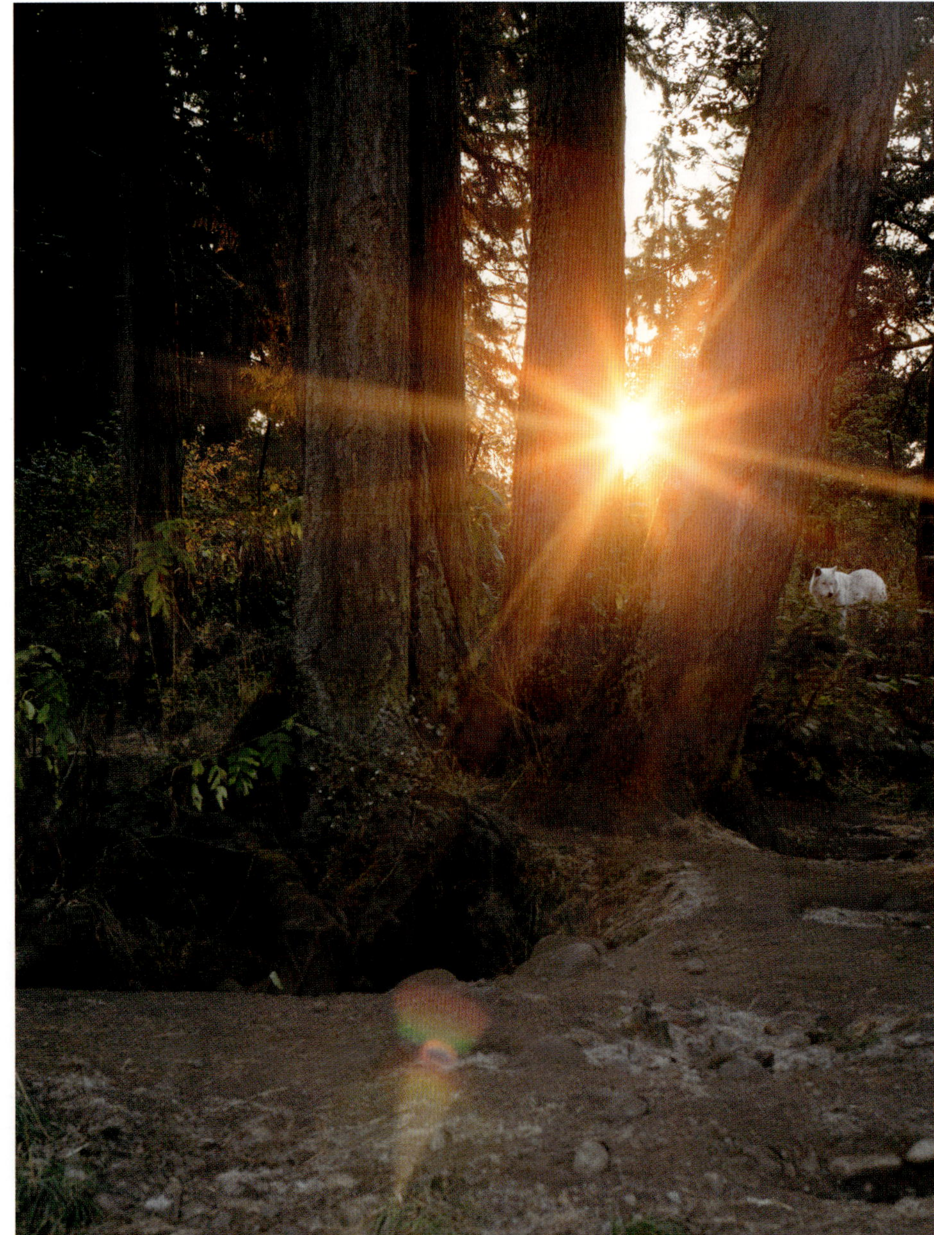

80. Annie Marie Musselman, *Wolf Haven at Sundown,* from the "Wolf Haven" series, 2016

The Storied Wild

In his "Wilderness Letter" of 1960, a manifesto about the value of wild country in American culture, Wallace Stegner wrote that we desperately needed the wilderness, "even if we never do more than drive to its edge and look in."[1] Of course, Stegner wanted us to do more than that; his argument depended on the ability to inspire the public to want to experience wild places firsthand. Like Thoreau, John Muir, and Aldo Leopold before him, Stegner extolled the psychological and spiritual values of the wilderness, especially its role as a fortress of solitude for a society fast becoming disconnected from nature. If we didn't have primitive areas to recharge in (or to take solace in their existence even if we never got there), we might well lose our collective mind. Stegner confessed that he himself would "be very nearly bughouse" if he hadn't been able to spend time in the mountain and desert wildernesses of the American West.[2]

This old idea of a therapeutic value to nature has received scientific justification in studies that document the virtues of even brief encounters with patches of and beings in the natural world, and that warn about a growing "nature deficit disorder" in modern society as our connection to the outdoors frays.[3] It's also been picked up by contemporary environmental philosophers, such as Bryan Norton, who have suggested that encounters with wild nature can not only soothe our psyches, they can enlighten our preferences. In such experiences we find ourselves questioning the very attitudes and values bound up in the drive to exploit nature in the first place.[4] As Norton puts it, "Appeals to the transformative value of wild species and undisturbed ecosystems thereby provide the means to criticize and limit demand values that threaten to destroy those species and ecosystems while at the same time introducing an important value that humans should place upon them."[5] Among other things, this concept of "transformative value" offers an interesting alternative to the traditional view of nature's intrinsic value as something separate from human interests. But it also suggests a more aesthetically and morally infused framing of the instrumental value of the wild, one that regards "use" in terms other than the simple satisfaction of our consumer desires. Most important, it's an understanding that is dependent on the conservation and cultivation of the wild landscapes and species that could trigger these transformations within us.[6]

Norton's notion of transformative value finds earlier expression not only in the thinking of American Transcendentalists such as Thoreau, but (and most interestingly for the present discussion) in the aesthetic and environmentalist vision of Ansel Adams. As Rebecca Senf writes, Adams saw his national parks photography in the 1940s as a way to create wilderness images that would inspire this kind of perspectival transformation in individuals. It was an experience he believed could be promoted through the Sierra Club's campaigns and publications.[7]

Although the therapeutic and transformative value of the wild was presented as a shared and widely accessible good, it inevitably highlighted a private understanding of experience in nature, an intimate and deeply personal transaction between people and place. The search for seclusion, renewal, and grace in the wilderness would become one of the more familiar and durable tropes in American nature writing, from Ed Abbey's southwestern soliloquies and Annie Dillard's meditations on the Blue Ridge Mountains of Virginia, in *Pilgrim at Tinker Creek,* to Cheryl Strayed's story of recovery on the Pacific Coast Trail, *Wild.*

It's a way of thinking, however, that's drawn criticism from a newer wave of more socially and politically driven environmentalists who see in this yearning for wilderness solitude and personal transformation a shamefully bourgeois and exclusionary impulse; an elitist pursuit of the ecstatic. Shoving aside the privileged revelations of Muir and Abbey, they argue for a more pluralistic and inclusive image of American environmentalism and reject the epiphanic ideal of the wilderness for something more prosaic and utilitarian: "coupled social-ecological systems" and their myriad ecosystem services and economic benefits.

Interestingly, landscape photographers have wandered into this debate by reclaiming a compelling form of subjective experience in the midst of criticisms that traditional wilderness ethics and aesthetics are too focused on personal transformation and private perfection. Photographic work in this mode also suggests a cautious and partial reentry to the wild after the rupture of the New Topographic artists—and the deconstructionist arguments in environmental studies challenging the purity of the wilderness idea.

In these pictures the human form is often returned to the scene, albeit in glimpses and isolated moments. Revealingly, the scenic vistas of the classic wilderness photographers are frequently present, but they're shaded by the human perspective and, at times, our physical presence. Here, the wilderness tableau provides a frame for personal experience and contemplation, evincing a mix of moods and emotions, from the mystical and playful to the poignant and critical. It becomes a stage on which, for example, the photographer Taylor James captures the final view of a dying migrant in the Southwest (plate 84); or it serves as a context for exploring cultural and ethnic identity, as in Johnnie Chatman's meditation on black history and celebrated vistas of the American West (plate 88), and Zig Jackson's series of pictures de-mythologizing his Native American heritage and environmental ethics (plate 90). Apprehension of the wild is now bound up with collective and individual human stories and dramas.

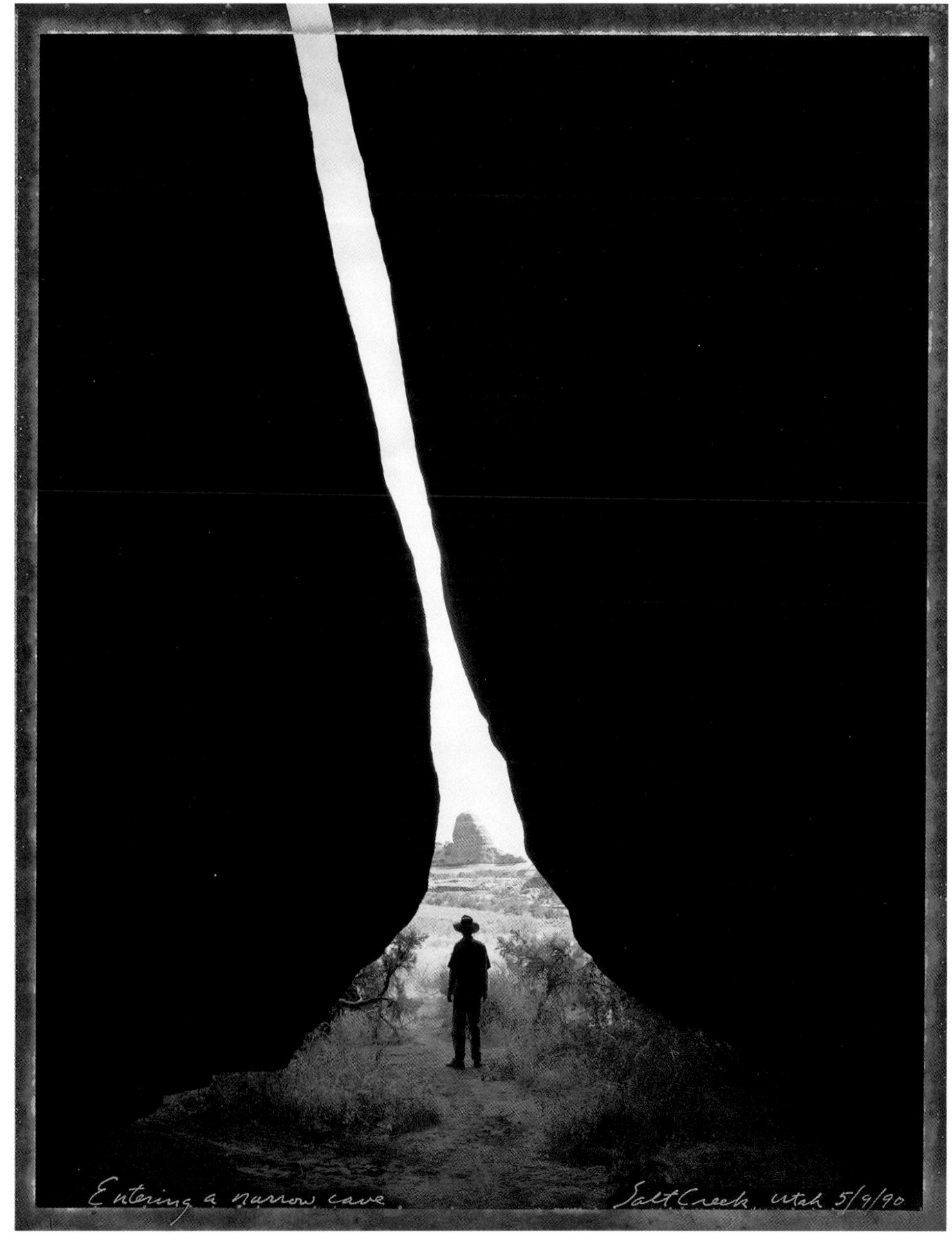

81. Mark Klett, *Entering a Narrow Cave, Salt Creek, Utah,* 1990

"The natural world is a screen onto which we project our own images; without our images there it is as blank as the cold screen of an empty movie house."[8] More than sixty years later, Stegner's words still highlight the inseparable link between the viewer and the viewed, a connection that the visual iconography of Ansel Adams and Eliot Porter often deliberately obscured. The pictures here, though, begin to remind us of the inescapably personal and storied nature of wilderness imagery, its ability to inscribe and make meaning in the wild. Driving to the edge of wild country and looking in is still an option, but even that experience is now captured by the lens.

About the Gallery

BAM: Steve, as we mention in the essay one of the more damning critiques of the traditional wilderness idea is that it reflects an elitist and therefore discriminatory ethic and aesthetic: only those with the time and resources to experience wild country like Wallace Stegner and Edward Abbey would have it are able to take part. The personal and private nature of the "wilderness experience," that is, is part of the problem.

SP: I get that. But I regard solitude as a social good, and as Stegner noted, just knowing wild land is out there has a value. Besides, at some level, all experience is personal.

The elitist critique is trickier, because most of our nature protection has had an elitist component, though that is true for most American reforms. The Grand Canyon as a valorized landscape, for example, did not evolve out of folk sentiment but as a construction by geologists and artists that then became a national emblem. Cultural elites serve a legitimate social role when they elevate our understanding beyond the personal and the tribal. The problem becomes when they are only self-serving.

BAM: You don't think wilderness falls in that category?

SP: It can, sure. But I think that for a multiethnic society wilderness is vital because it presents a shared nature outside blood-and-soil nationalism. It's not truly a-cultural in the sense that it has no cultural character, but that no group can claim it as an exclusive heritage. It can be a blank slate onto which everyone and every group can project their own meanings. There are many arguments for wilderness—this one looms large for me in our present moment.

BAM: That makes sense. But many would of course say that this tabula rasa view of the wilderness was in truth inscribed from the very beginning of the preservationist movement with a particular racial and ethnic identity. It was viewed as the pleasure ground of white Americans, a view that led to the physical eviction and historical erasure of Indigenous communities from some of the great wilderness parks. So it's not just about class, but also race. And of course gender, too: these were often depicted as the privileged provinces of men.

SP: Wilderness is a work very much in progress. Views fifty years from now will likely be as far removed from today's as today's are from the time of the Wilderness Act. Wilderness is not a condition that is reached and then held inviolate. It's an on-going negotiation.

Sure, wilderness was created by a particular group at a particular time, but that is true for American institutions generally. The historical movement has been to broaden inclusion. I expect that will happen with wilderness as well—it's already happening. The gallery images in this book show that, and in recent years recognition of an Indigenous heritage has become pretty common at parks.

BAM: The issue has certainly been on the mind of photographers working in these spaces. They are not only putting people into the scene, but people who have historically been missing. Look at Johnnie Chatman's photo in the gallery as it intersects a classic landscape of the American West with the Black experience (plate 88).

SP: We're in a realm where strength is also weakness, one common to many American institutions. Wilderness requires all groups to lay aside claims of historical identity to a place, which is one reason why it stumbles outside America, and within America, why it falters where cultural identities are strongly rooted and valenced to the land. Not all groups—whether Indigenous, immigrant, or white elites—will agree to cede that tie.

But this tension is not limited to wilderness: it ranges across most aspects of American life. Just as America doesn't have an established church or creed, it can't have an established landscape. It needs a kind of place that no one group can claim as uniquely its own.

BAM: I'm also thinking about the mixture of politics and individual perspective in some of these images. The photos by Taylor James (plate 84) and Zig Jackson (plate 90) certainly appear to be asking questions about the meaning and form of the wild in a time marked by deepening social divisions and inequalities, but the scenes are also deeply personal. Mark, is that how you see this work?

MK: You can see all the pictures in this gallery as referring to someone's personal story about their passage through the land, and those stories are as diverse as the story tellers. But it's also about staking out territory, and responding to the question: "whose land is this, anyway?" The Linda Connor photograph shows the earliest example, a pictograph of a hand created by native people centuries ago (plate 83). Zig Jackson's photograph reveals a more contemporary Native American story, made with ironic humor and, yes, political seriousness and anger, as he overlooks a strip mine on what was once native land. Taylor James's photograph was literally made where a man, considered an undocumented migrant, died trying to avoid detection in the desert. And that, too, has political implications for Southwest borderlands today.

The John Divola photograph shows an abandoned house built in the high California desert as part of an attempt to claim ownership to federal property (plate 85). It reminds me of failed homesteads, and historian Patty Limerick's admonition that the western experience has not always been one of unbroken success (something discussed earlier with the New Western History).

BAM: Some of the photos feature the act of inscription in different ways, which I take it is part of this process of personalizing the wild—and the landscape as a whole?

MK: I think so, yes. Terry Warpinski's image is a more contemporary version of the pictograph photograph, where a picture of the land has been written on by hand in a diaristic manner (plate 86). It's a more personal and poetic approach, as is Erika Osborne's photograph of a man with the topographic map of the landscape he's viewing imprinted onto the skin of his back.

These images seem to be saying that experiences of place literally get embedded into the lives of the people who live there. And I think it's critical to understand the concept of reclaiming the view, and how that has expanded our understanding of whose view this is, which is exactly why Johnnie Chatman's photograph is poignant and relevant today.

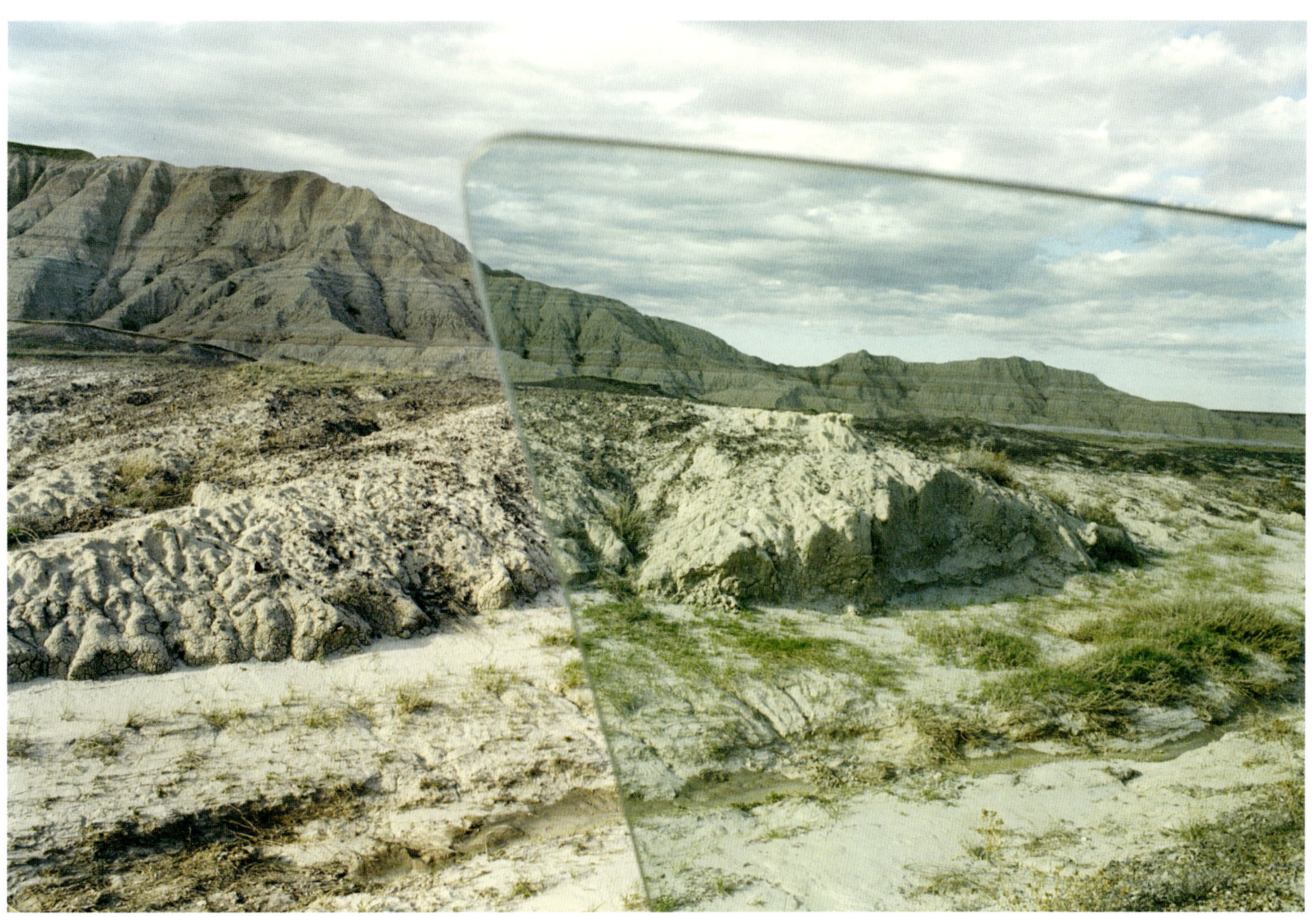

82. Rebecca Norris Webb, *Badlands*, circa 2010 (From *My Dakota*, by Rebecca Norris Webb [Radius Books, 2012])

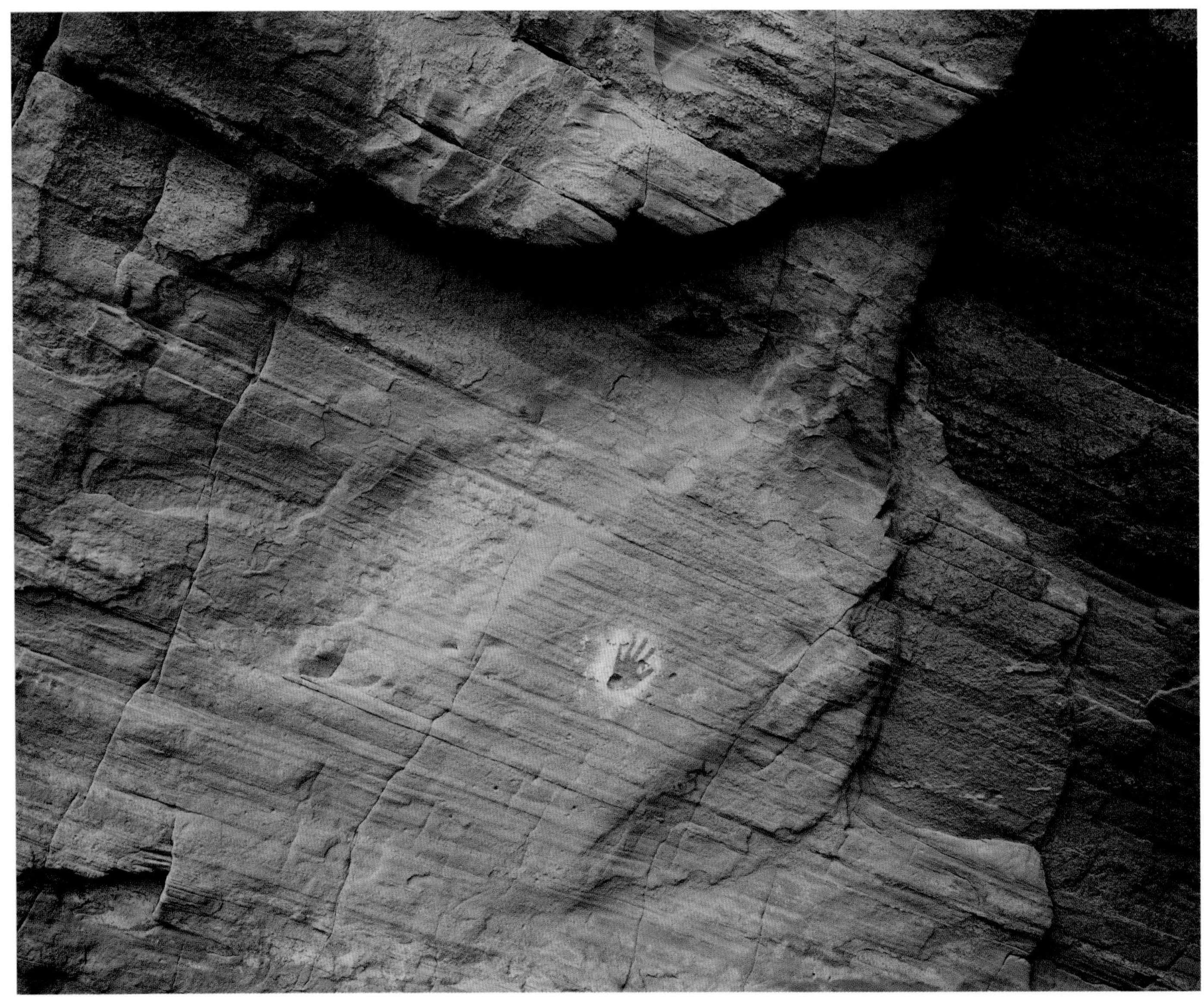

    83. Linda Connor, *Hand, Mystery Valley, Utah*, 1995

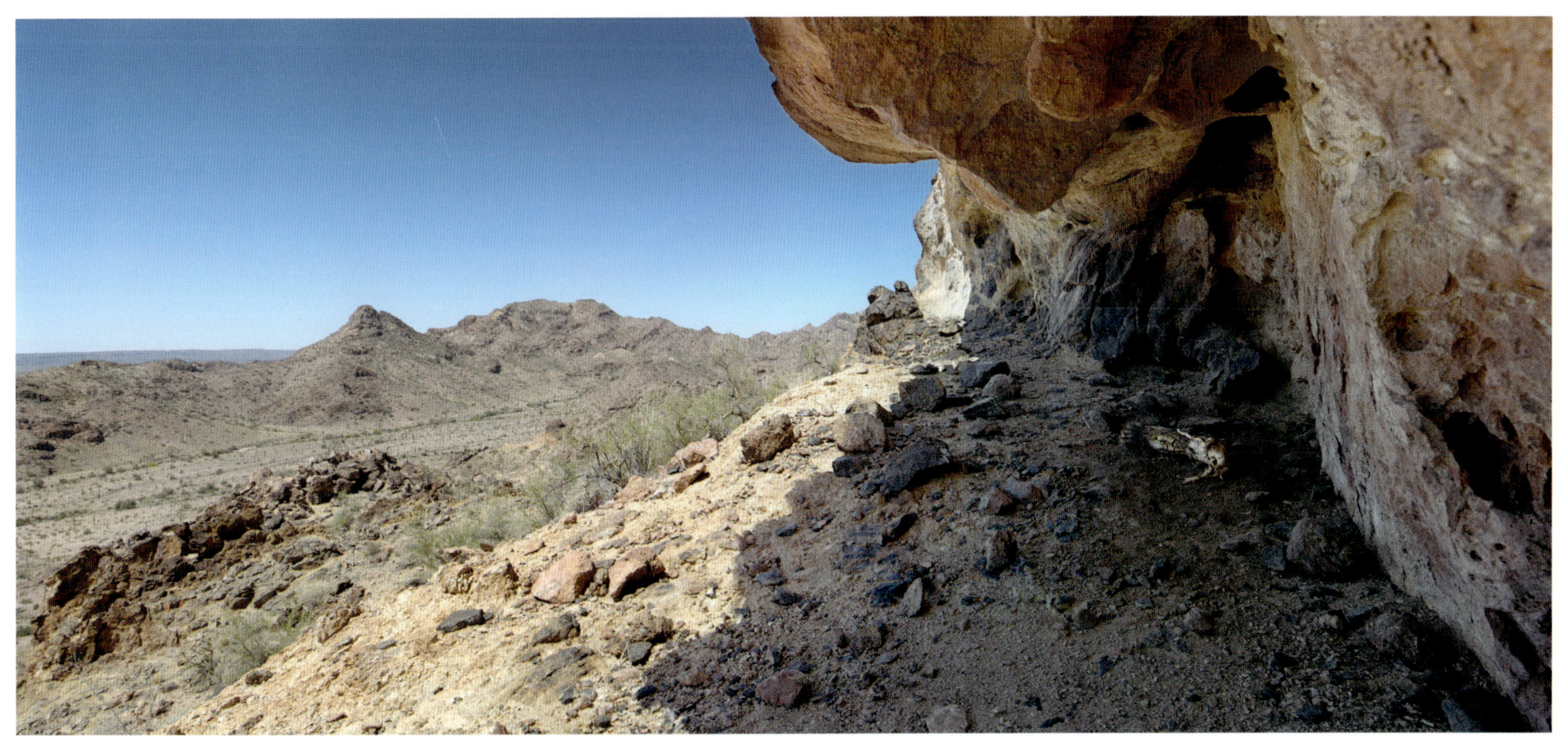

84. Taylor James, *The Last View, Site of a Migrant's Death*, 2016

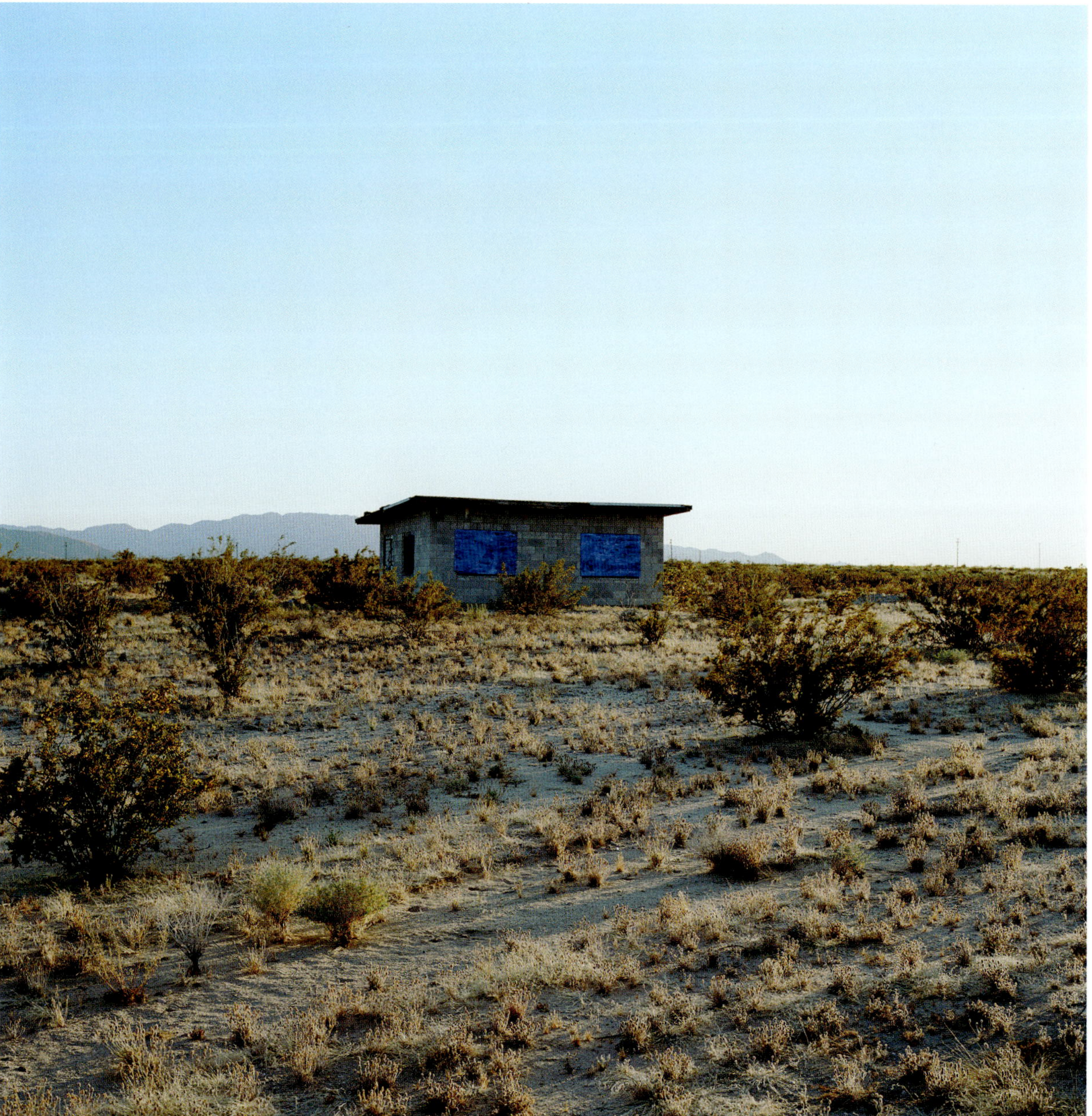

85. John Divola, *N34°10.466′ W115°54.878′*, circa 1995, from the series "Isolated Houses"

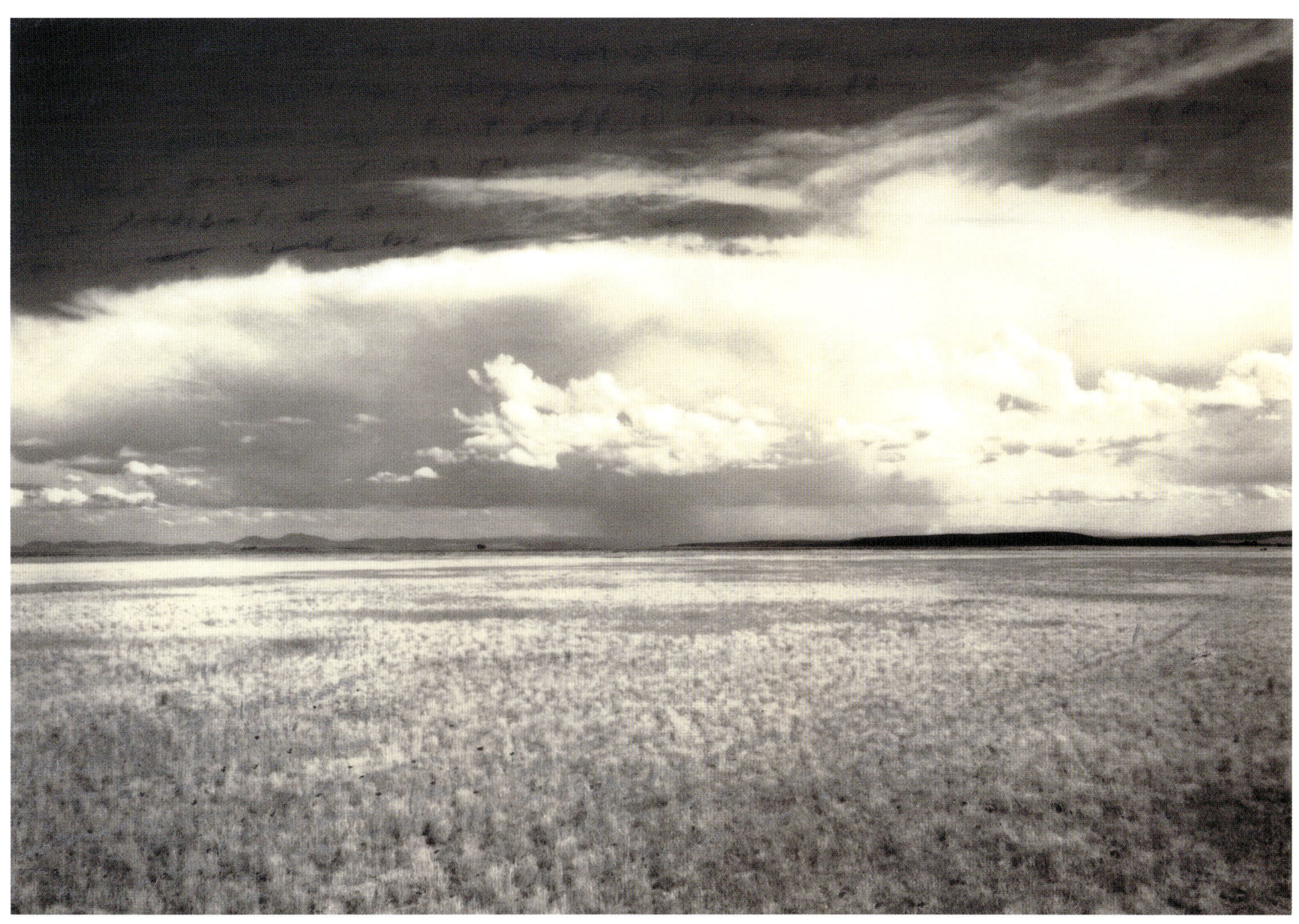

86. Terri Warpinski, *Vanishing Points: Storm, Harney Basin*, 2002

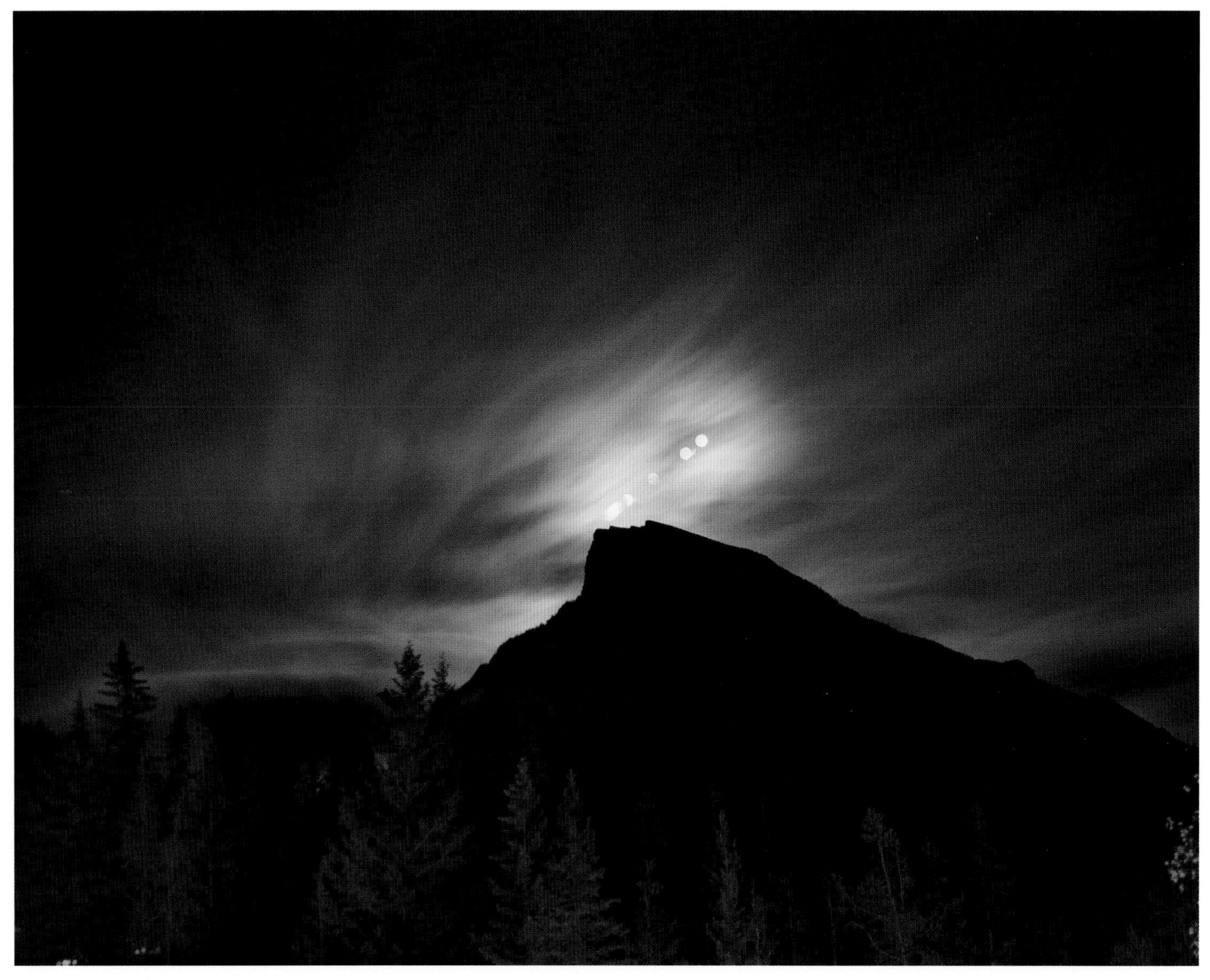

87. Sharon Harper, from her series "One Month, Weather Permitting, 2009"; this image, *Night Sky over Banff, Alberta, September 12–October 10, 2007 (25 September)*

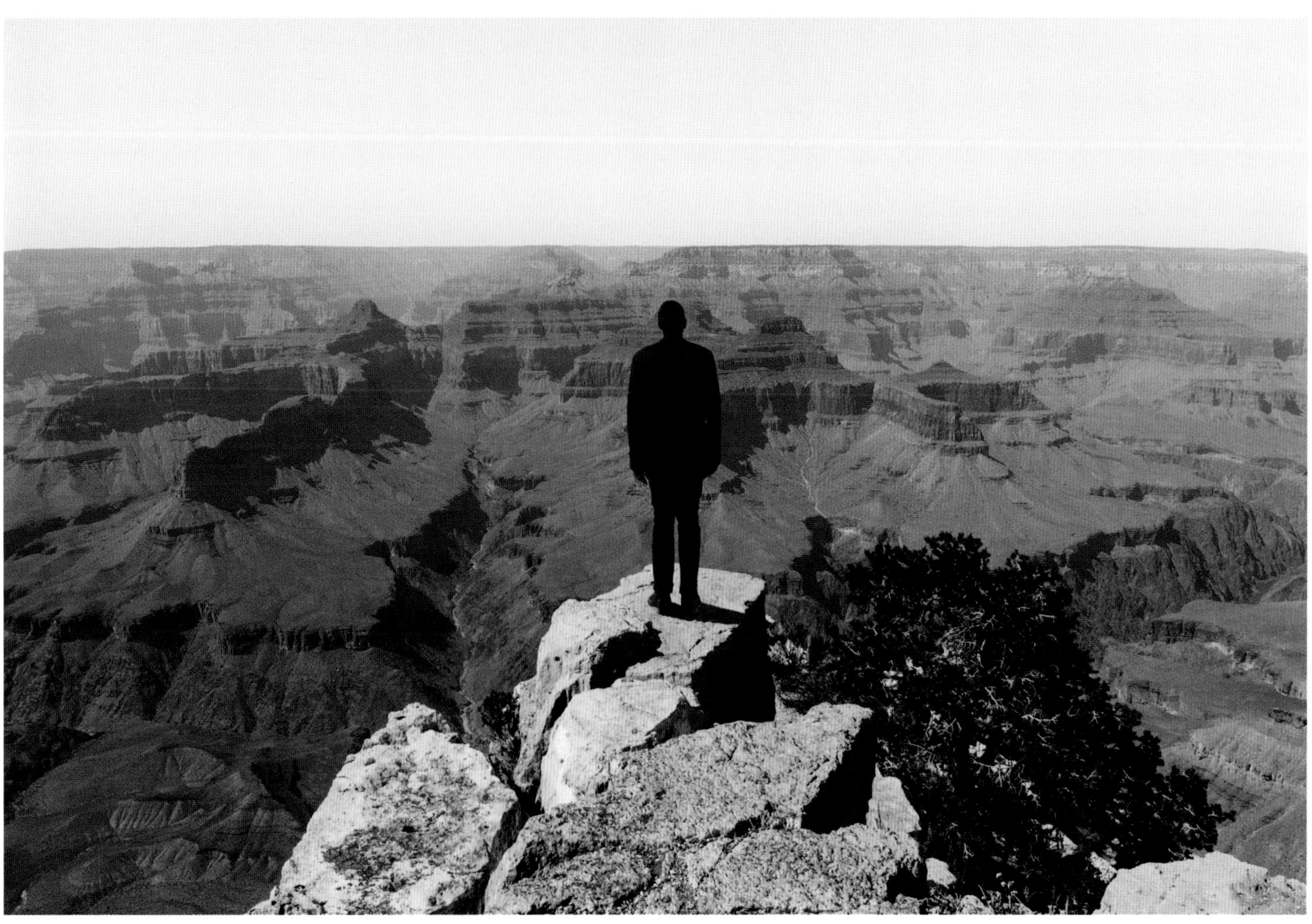

88. Johnnie Chatman, *Self Portrait, Grand Canyon*, 2018 (Courtesy of Johnnie Chatman)

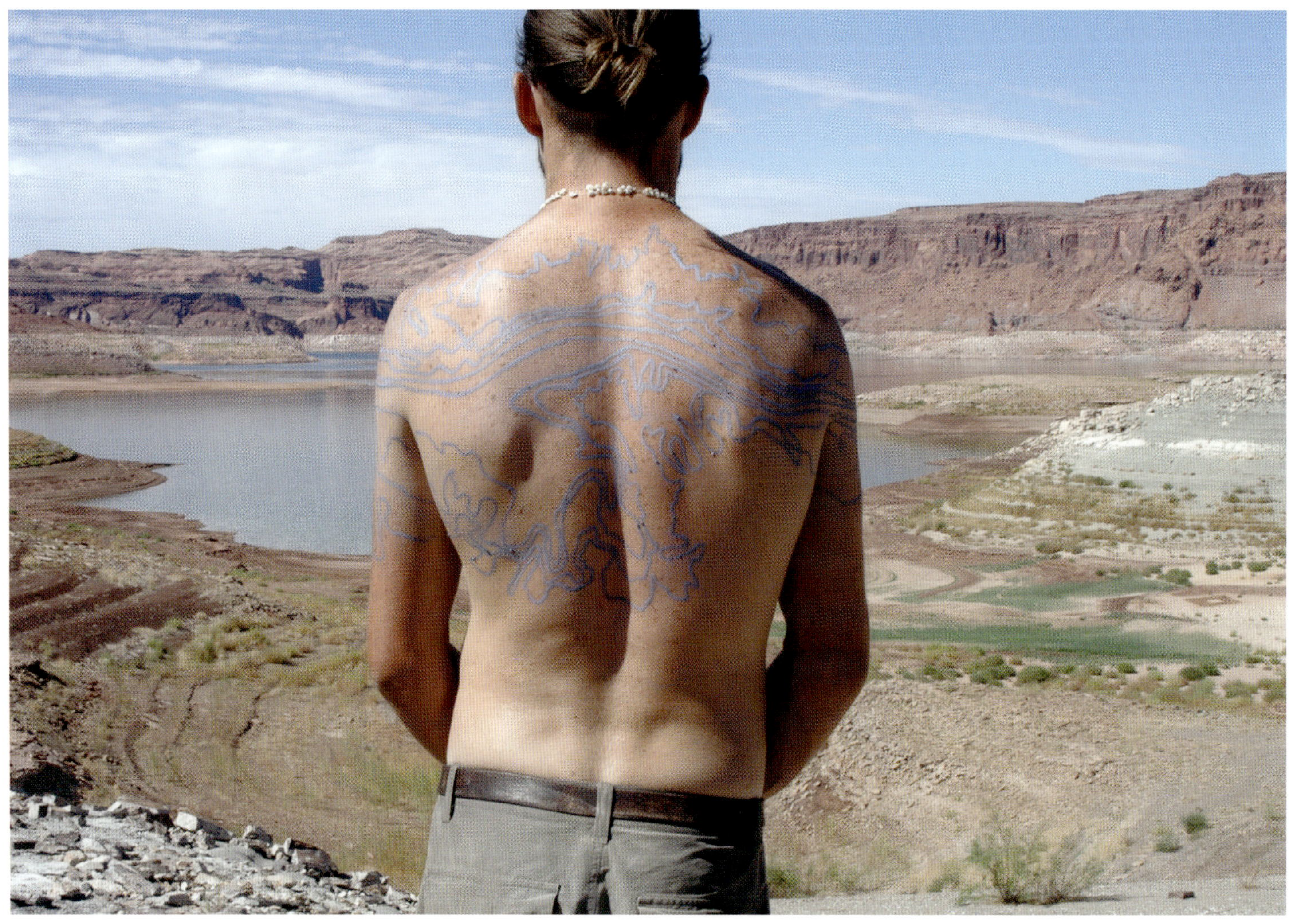

    89. Erika Osborne, *Interpreting Blue Notch*, 2005

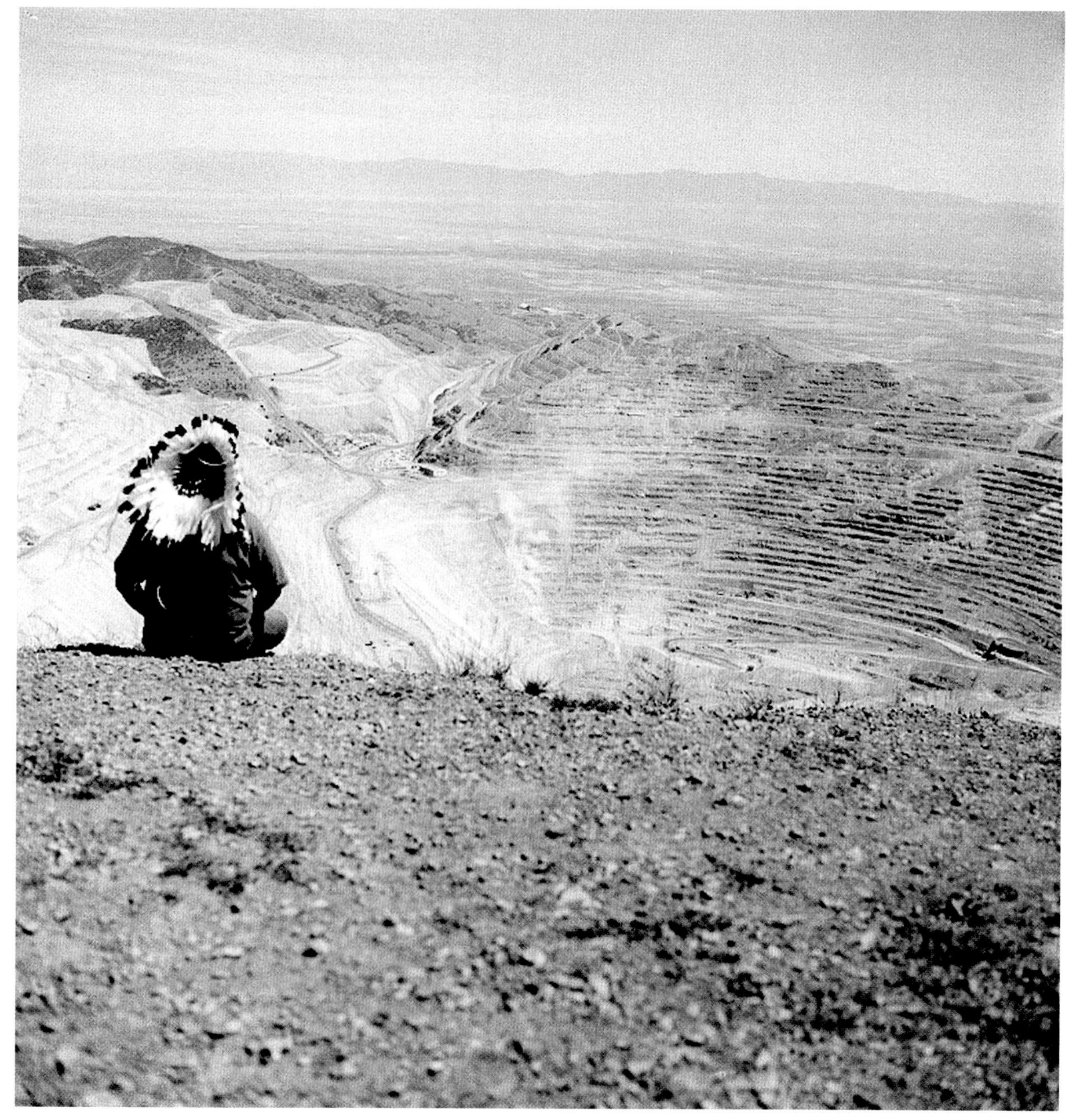

90. Zig Jackson, *Indian Man at Kennecott Copper Mines, Bingham Canyon Mine, Utah*, circa 1994

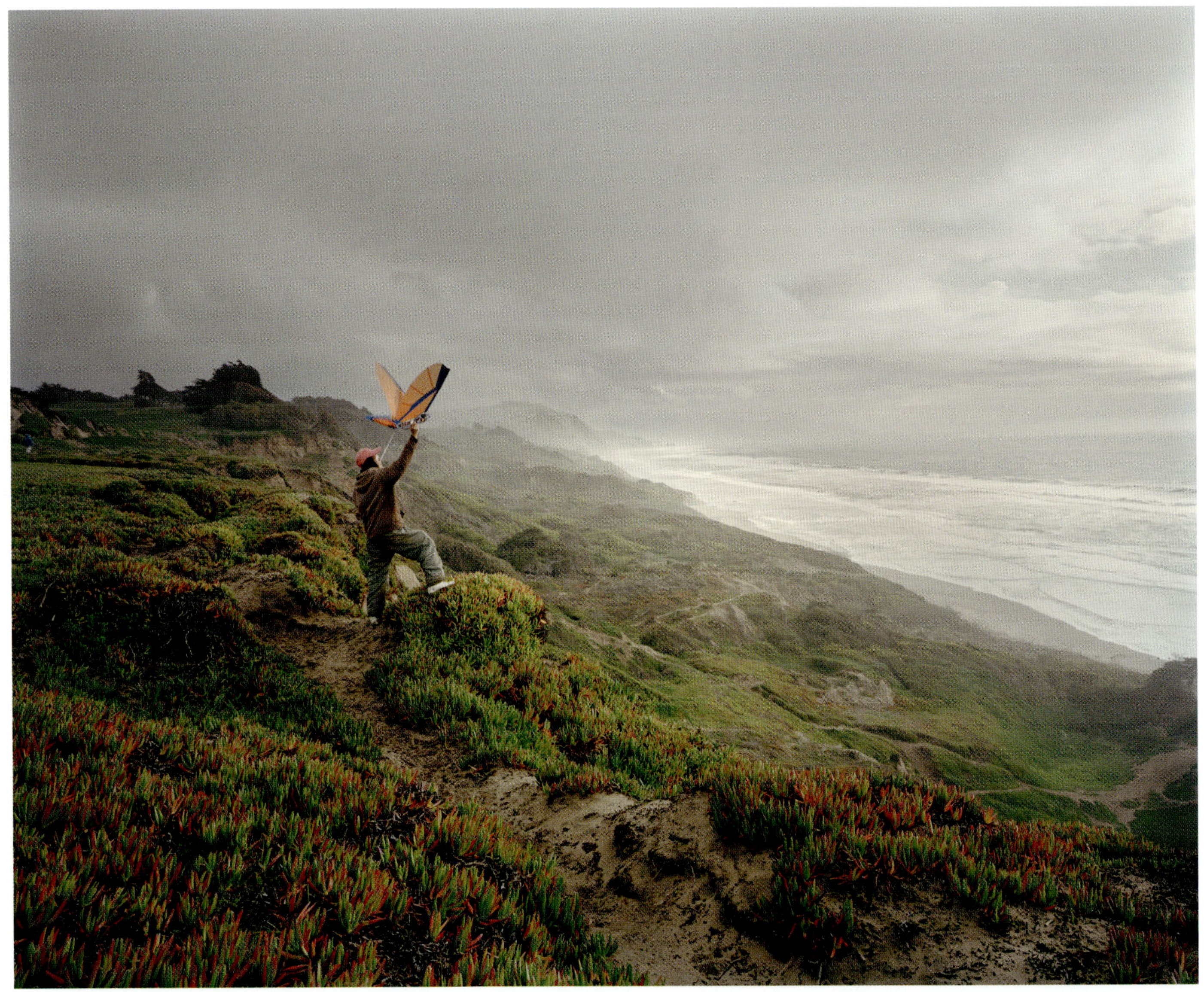

  91. Alex Fradkin, *The Left Coast*, 2011

Managed Wild: Cloud and Smoke

STEVE PYNE

Look warily at these two photos. They depict the same land-scape, Yosemite Valley, but they are not interchangeable. The images might as well be of different scenes (plate 92).

On the left is a classic Ansel Adams piece. A big photo of a big place—a study in the epic. The clouds serve as an emblem of the transcendental, and enhance rather than obscure. The contrasts in light sharpen the image. This can only be Yosemite Valley in its prelapsarian glory. Clarity, purity, the natural wild distilled—the photo can stand for how, in a particular person and time, an aesthetic melded with an idea.

On the right is a more contemporary image taken by Mark Klett and Byron Wolfe. The geology and vantage point are the same, but the impression conveyed by the view is not. Every-thing is blurred. Yosemite Valley seems big, not grand. Where clouds sharpened, smoke smudges. The sacred has become vaguely profane, and the sublime mundane.

The fires behind the smoke have complicated the landscape, not only visually but intellectually. They are a textbook example of how difficult the wild is to administer, and an illustration of the paradox that a place committed to removing people needs people to run it. Some 95 percent of Yosemite is now in legal wilderness. Most of that land will burn—needs to burn. If the National Park Service wishes to maintain ecological integrity, it has to tolerate fires, whether fire officers start or loose-herd them, or just monitor those set by lightning. That means smoke. The smoke from natural fire is as much a feature of the valley as its granite cliffs. Twice wildfires have forced the park to close—once by flame in El Portal, and once by smoke from the Ferguson fire. In principle, both flame and smoke can be managed, but there is no script for reconciling fires lit and fires extinguished with wilderness character. The smoke recorded in Mark and Byron's photo of the valley is an outcome of deci-sions such management requires.

For decades the preferred management choice at Yosemite was to emphasize the view and keep it as uncluttered and pris-tine as possible. The fire visitors saw was the evening firefall

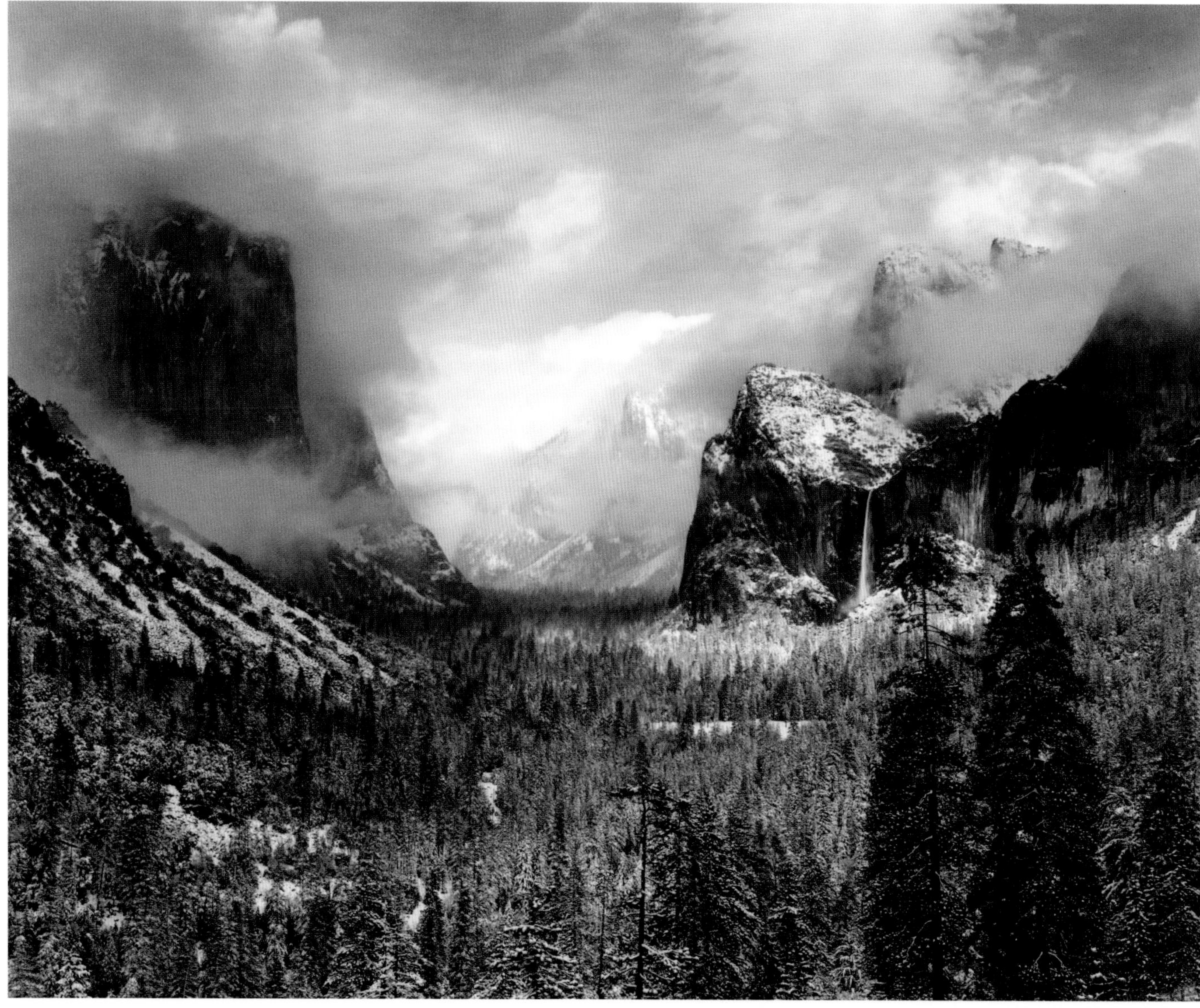

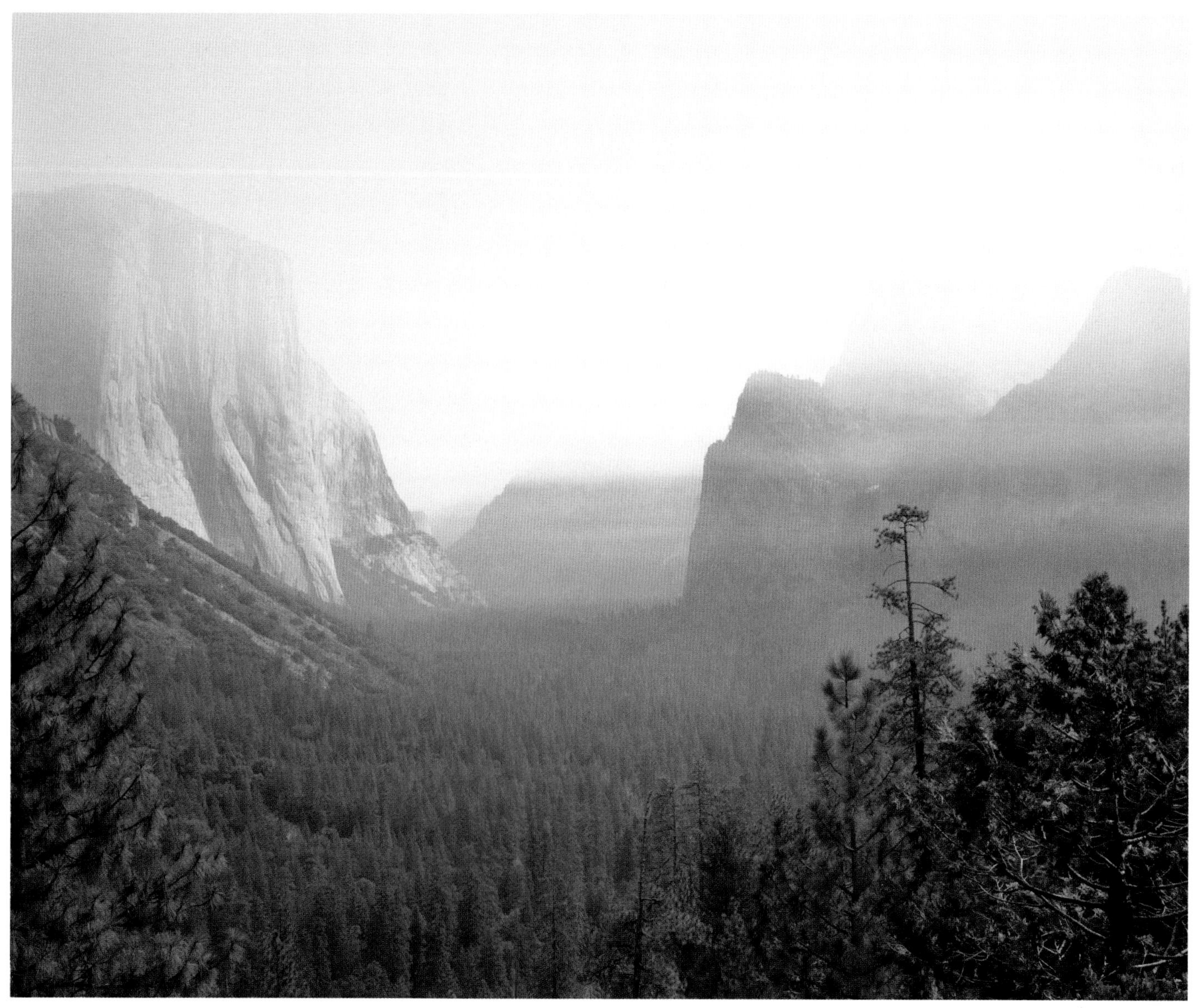

92. Left: Ansel Adams, *Clearing Winter Storm, Yosemite National Park,* 1944; right: Mark Klett and Byron Wolfe, *Clearing Autumn Smoke, Controlled Burn,* 2002

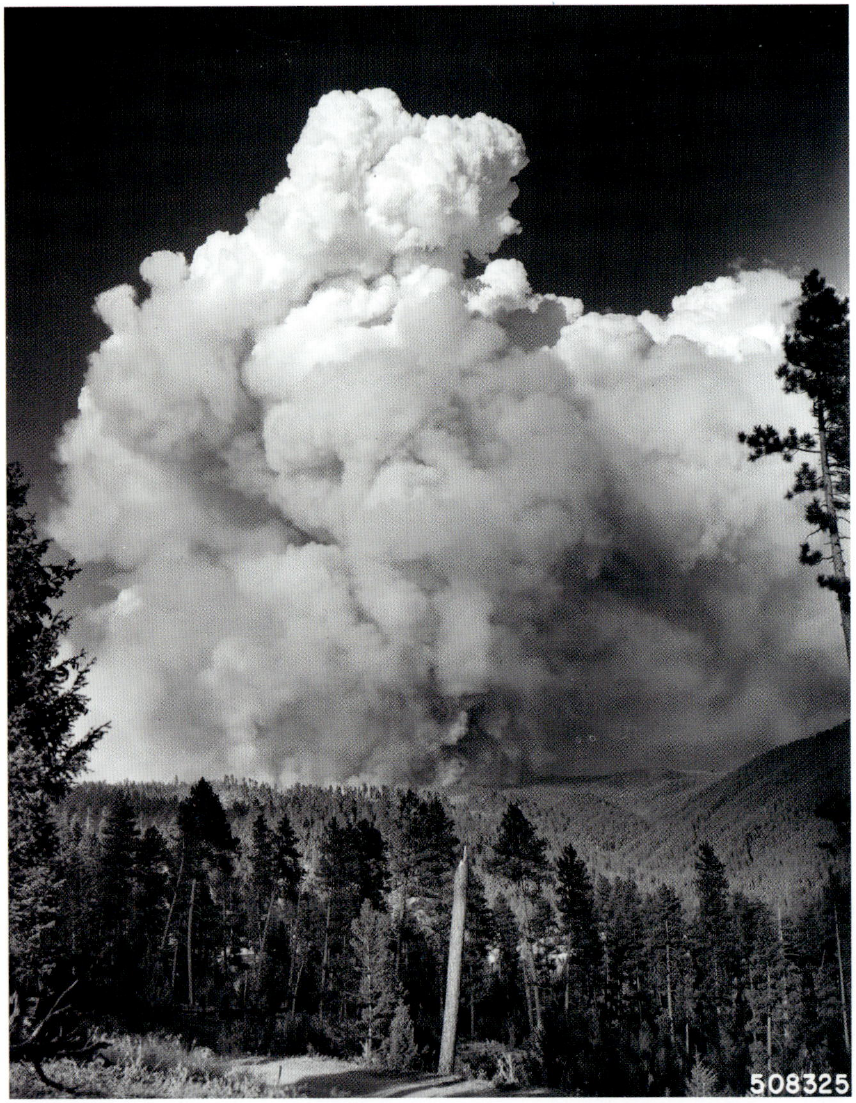

94. A close-up image of a burning yucca, Kinishba Fire, White Mountain Apache Agency, 2003 (Photograph by Kari Greer, courtesy of the artist)

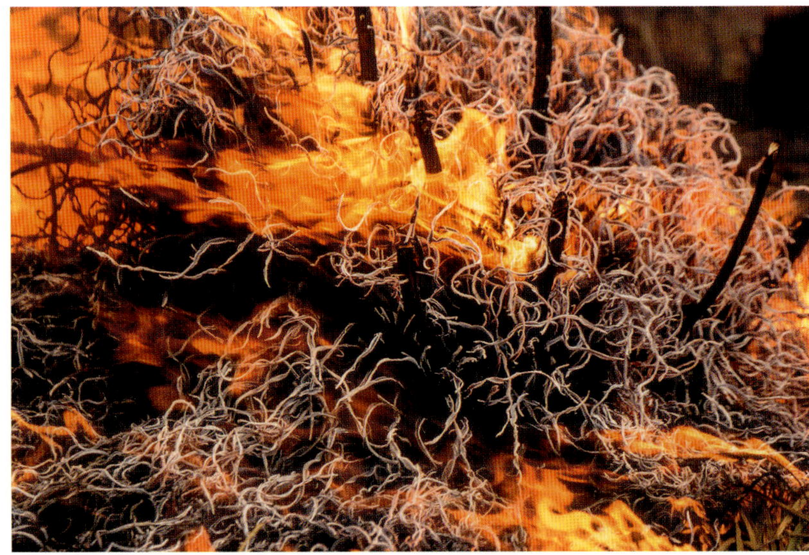

from Glacier Point, a staged event in which the embers from a large burn pit were pushed over the rim to cascade downward in a fiery echo of Yosemite's celebrated waterfalls. In 1968, in keeping with policy reforms to restore naturalness, the firefall was abolished as an artificial spectacle and replaced by the effort to encourage natural burns. (Note the thickening of forest between the Adams and Klett photos, largely a consequence of fire exclusion. Historically, the Miwok people had routinely burned the valley's vegetation.) A curated entertainment, well confined, was being supplanted by backcountry burns that could more or less free-burn and leach their smoke into the valley at inopportune moments.

93. Sleeping Child Fire, 1961, photograph by Ernst Peterson

Fire photographs have traditionally been journalistic. They documented disaster, they portrayed the firefight as a battlefield, and they exploited flame for visual drama. Many were memorable, but few aspired to fine art. When they did, they expressed the prevailing landscape aesthetics of their time. Modernism, for example, has its proponents. Ernst Peterson's image of the pyrocumulus plume of the Sleeping Child fire of 1961 in the Bitterroot Mountains offers an Ansel Adams version of smoke, so perfectly composed it seems almost fraudulent (plate 93). Kari Greer's burning yucca, miniaturizing flame, echoes Eliot Porter (plate 94). If any images can stand for the classic wild, these two can.

But landscapes and fires are becoming more complicated, and so is the pedigree of those who photograph them. John McGolgan's *Elk Bath,* taken during the 2000 fire bust in the Northern Rockies, manages to seemingly domesticate the wild, moving flames from the very icon of terror to background wallpaper, resting as easily in the scene as the elk (plate 95). (Unsurprisingly, the photo promptly went viral when posted on the Internet.)

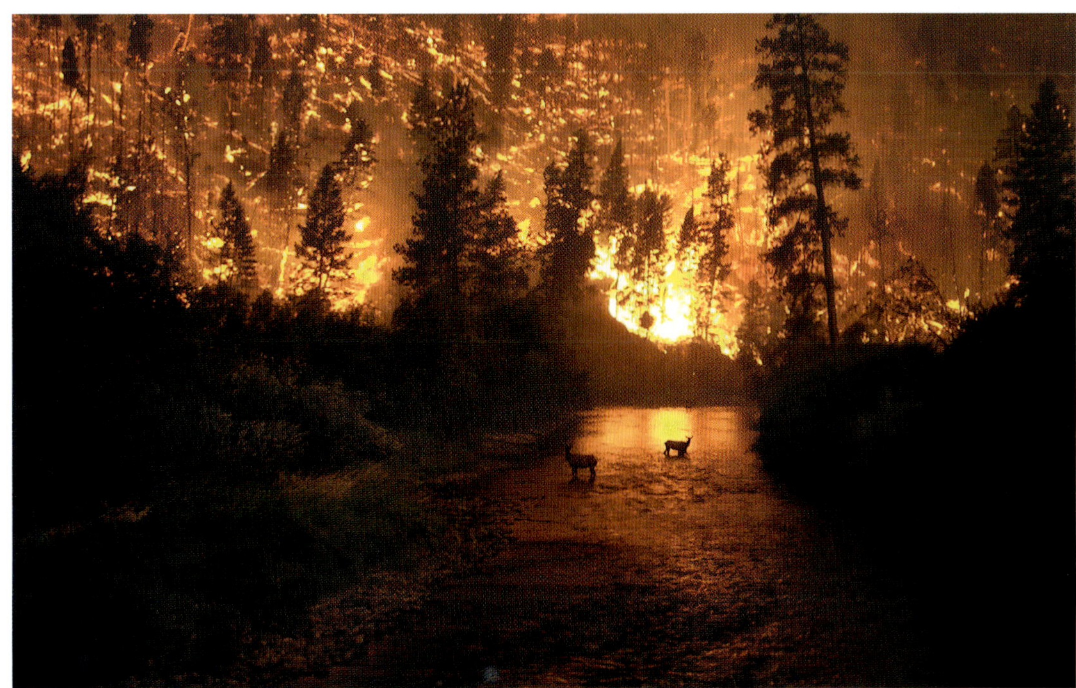

95. *Elk Bath,* Bitterroot River in Montana in 2000, photograph by John McColgan

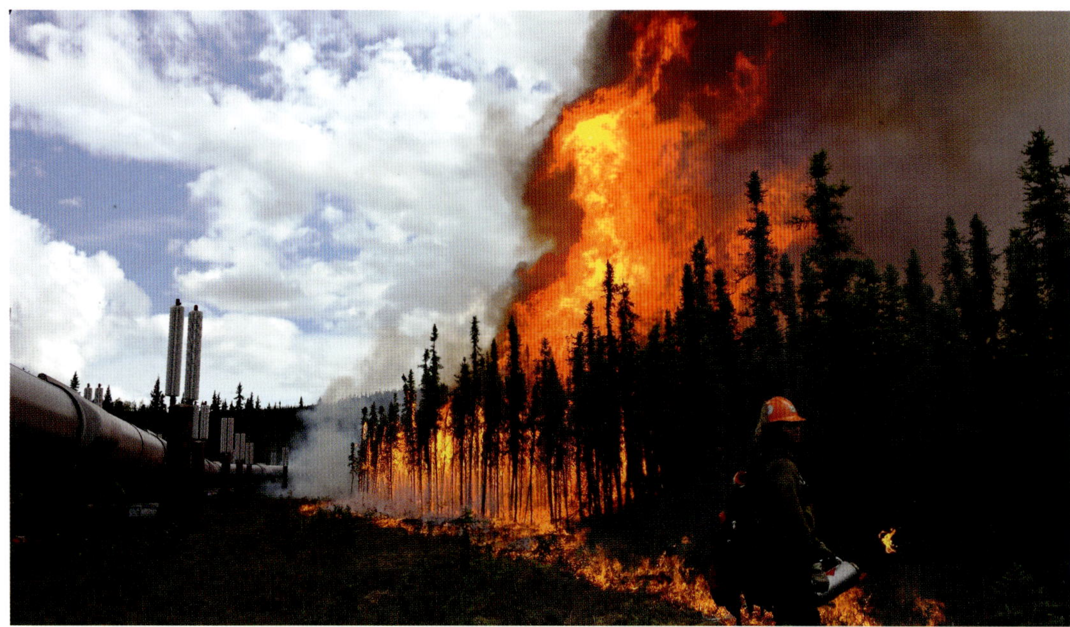

96. The Aggie Creek Fire near Fairbanks in 2015, photograph by Philip Spor/ NOAA

Some of the most striking images are where the built, the natural, and people converge, as with Philip Spor's shot of burnout operations on the Aggie Creek fire in 2015 in Alaska (plate 96). The two drivers of combustion on earth—those from lithic landscapes (oil pipeline) and those in living landscapes— front one another, with a torch-wielding fireman between them. Interestingly, neither McGolgan nor Spor is a professional photographer. They shot the scenes during their duties as members of incident management teams. The fires are not something remote and Platonic, or a commentary on changing aesthetics of photography, but—mesmerizing as they appear—what firescapes now look like when viewed by working fire officers (with a strong sense of pictorial composition) at a time when everyone has a high-definition camera in their phone.

The grandeur in Adams's photo lies partly in the pretense that the scene is not mediated, that the viewer is encountering the wild in its first-contact originality. The attraction of the Klett and Wolfe photo (for me) is that they force us to accept that the wild can also be mundane. It can be hazy as well as heroic. The picture implicitly destroys the illusion of a landscape wholly apart from people, whose presence, even if off-image, blurs the sharpness and definition of the informing ideal. The managed wild is murky. Mark and Byron artistically clarify that murkiness.

BAM: There isn't a separate gallery accompanying this chapter, Steve, but I wanted to ask you about the photos in this essay, which you selected yourself. I assume it's the topic and origin of the photos that interest you in these shots?

SP: Yes, I came upon them as part of my routine research.

Fire photos are as common as Kleenex, but fire photos that have artistic panache are not. Even big wildland fires have historically been regarded as outside the core of national experience, like a freak of western violence akin to a grizzly bear attack.

Now fire seems everywhere every year. Wildland fires are burning into towns, blurring the borders between natural and built environments. Similarly, anthropogenic climate change from fossil-fuel combustion—acting as a performance enhancer and globalizer—is blurring the boundary between the human and the natural. Megafires have joined polar bears as icons of the Anthropocene.

BAM: So wildland fire has become a topic. One that attracts photographers.

SP: Yes, among lots of people. The only fire department on a university campus is traditionally the one that sent emergency vehicles when an alarm sounded. Now many disciplines are looking at fire—fine-arts photographers among them. Contemporary technology helps; it's pretty hard to photograph a blowing-and-going wildfire with glass-plate negatives.

Fire art has a long heritage in painting, but fire photographers have been mostly reporters, chronicling disasters. Now we are seeing photographs with more thoughtful aesthetics that challenge the usual framings and clichés. They result not just from photographers seeking out fire as a topic, but working fire folk with an artistic eye. Again, technology is critical, making everyone with a smartphone into a potential photographer.

BAM: The first image is a diptych joining two photos of smoke in Yosemite Valley, one by Ansel Adams and the other by Mark and Byron Wolfe (plate 92). You discuss the significance of that work in the essay so we don't need to repeat that here. What I'm interested in is your selection of the other pictures in this piece, some of which are not taken by fine art photographers.

SP: Ernst Peterson (plate 93) and Kari Greer (plate 94) are professional photographers who worked for agencies to document fires. They were not primarily searching out fine art possibilities; they were recording events but, being sensitive to artistic possibilities, they recognized and seized the moment in ways that echo Porter's closeups (Greer) and Adams's epic scale (Peterson). They found in fire novel subjects for what we might consider the grand manner of modernism. Kari, by the way, excels in firefighter portraitures, which unfortunately lies outside our focus on landscape.

MK: Ben, we do feature work of landscape photographers in other parts of this book who've taken up the subject from their perspectives, for example Laura McPhee (plate 23) and Victoria Sambunaris (plate 66).

BAM: That's right. So, fire has drawn the attention of both fine arts and professional photographers for a while, then, both as a destructive force and a restorative tool, and in regions outside the traditional ground zero of the American West.[1] But John McGolgan (plate 95) and Philip Spor (plate 96), whose photos accompany the essay, don't fit the description of either fine art or professional photographer, do they, Steve?

SP: No, they were members of fire management teams, working real fires. They represent another variety of inclusiveness, that of people who relate to wild landscapes through their jobs. I find it interesting that a general aesthetic was sufficiently well established that working fire folk, while obviously people with an instinct for composition, could apply it to such a novel setting.

Still, *Elk Bath* shows a pristine nature, if one with flames. The *Aggie Creek Fire* shows a guy burning out with a driptorch, poised between the two kinds of combustion that shape earth today. The image seems to me thematically rich and rife with visual tension. It doesn't have the subtexts that an academic photographer might insert, and it doesn't play coyly with an image that grabs the eye, which a fine-art pro might do with a wink. But I suspect that these photos will be among our enduring images of wildland fire from our time.

The De-Facto Wild

The American wilderness ethic hinges on its origin story, a narrative of raw landscapes shaped primarily by the forces of nature rather than by humans. Although historians, ecologists, and others have challenged this account for decades now, old habits die hard. We can pore over Ansel Adams's well-known photographs of Yosemite Valley and even if we know they depict an area once called Ahwahnee Valley by the Miwok Indians who hunted its forests and fished its streams, the illusion of an original state of nature holds. Mostly, that's due to Adams's artistry and his aesthetic discipline in keeping any hint of people out of the lens. His pictures meet the traditional expectations of what the American wilderness should look like. But then again, they helped shape those expectations.

The question of wilderness origins and authenticity can get even messier for landscapes that present as "mostly wild" to the eye and yet lack the familiar backstory. It's one thing to show that when you peel the wilderness veneer away, a deep record of human influence reveals itself even in places as ostensibly wild as Yosemite. It's another thing to valorize as wilderness landscapes outside the national parks and wilderness system that, while they may seem wild in many ways, still visibly bear the marks of the human activities that shaped them. On the standard view, these places lack the authenticity of (what's considered as) "true" wilderness: they're too "altered" and too historically mediated; impure geographies for a story of the pristine. They may possess many of the aesthetic and physical qualities we usually attach to the wild—such as vastness, remoteness, ruggedness, a general scarcity of humans— but they don't fit the established historical and artistic narratives. They're what you might call the "de-facto" wild.

Consider photographer Mark Ruwedel's images of abandoned rail beds, trestles, and rock cuts in the American and Canadian West (plate 97). Composed in the style of the nineteenth-century railroad and survey photographers, Ruwedel's pictures tell a story about the wages of western development and the play of time on the landscape.[1] Many evoke a sense

of solitude and isolation, and a kind of ghostly splendor—
qualities not out of place in the classical mode of wilderness
photography. And yet these are obviously also part of a chronicle of the drive to "open" the West, the artifacts of human
industry. Interestingly, Ruwedel's photos also convey a sense of
the slow erasure of human activities over time, a kind of geological self-reclamation that partially leavens their suggestion
of environmental ruin.

In other cases, the human presence is even more obvious,
and in the traditional wilderness context, incongruous. An-My
Lê's photos of military operations in the Mojave Desert, shot
in a style that echoes the work of Civil War photographers,
juxtapose the arid landscape's harsh magnificence with the
machines of war (plate 99). And Emmet Gowin's pictures of the
craters pockmarking the Nevada Test Site have an otherworldly
quality; a wilderness-as-moonscape (plate 98). The image mar-
ries two kinds of power, natural and human, within an abiding
sense of desolation.

The barrenness of the southwestern desert and its inhos-
pitable character certainly comes through in most of these
images, a view of the wild that's less inviting than the more
pictorially glamorous locales of Yosemite and Yellowstone.
At first glance they convey a view of the wilderness as a dying
wasteland rather than a bountiful Eden. It's a site to bomb,
to hide prisons in, to prepare for battle. Elsewhere, the wilderness, as Ed Abbey wrote, may offer the purest kind of freedom;
here, the wild appears gnawed on, scarred, and sequestered
by our activities.

This vision of the de-facto wild can be hard to square with
more biocentric attitudes. Some environmental philosophers,
for example, have placed such a premium on "naturalness" as
a cardinal value in environmental ethics that landscapes reflecting such dramatic human interventions can only be part of a
fallen world. Debating the merits of ecological restoration, they
argue that once human design and technology are imposed on
the land, it destroys its original natural value, with the consequence that a rehabilitated mining site or a restored wetland is
tantamount to an art forgery—a "fake nature" of lesser worth
than the pre-disturbance original.[2] It's an ethical position,
though, that's dependent on a strangely binary understanding
of nature and culture, a perspective that defines naturalness
and wild values by their autonomy rather than by their inter-
dependence and co-evolution with human history, practices,
and values.

The impulse toward wilderness orthodoxy also doesn't jibe
with many other conservation trends and values. Since the late
1980s, for example, the conversion of military installations to
national wildlife refuges managed by the U.S. Fish and Wildlife
Service and the U.S. Forest Service has significantly added to
the public land system, especially in the eastern United States
(though also in the Midwest, as Gavin Van Horn's discussion of
the Midewin National Tallgrass Prairie reminds us). Although
these part-wild, part-wasted landscapes can pose significant
challenges, such as the risk of military contaminants for wildlife health and public access, this form of "opportunistic conservation" is another example of the multi-dimensional value
of lands that don't meet the traditional aesthetic and historical criteria associated with the wilderness.[3] In doing so, they
pose an indirect challenge to Aldo Leopold's mature formulation of the function of wilderness as a "base datum of nor-
mality," a template of healthy land to measure the pathology
of the sick.[4] (Though interestingly, they do so while signify-

   RETHINKING, REMAKING

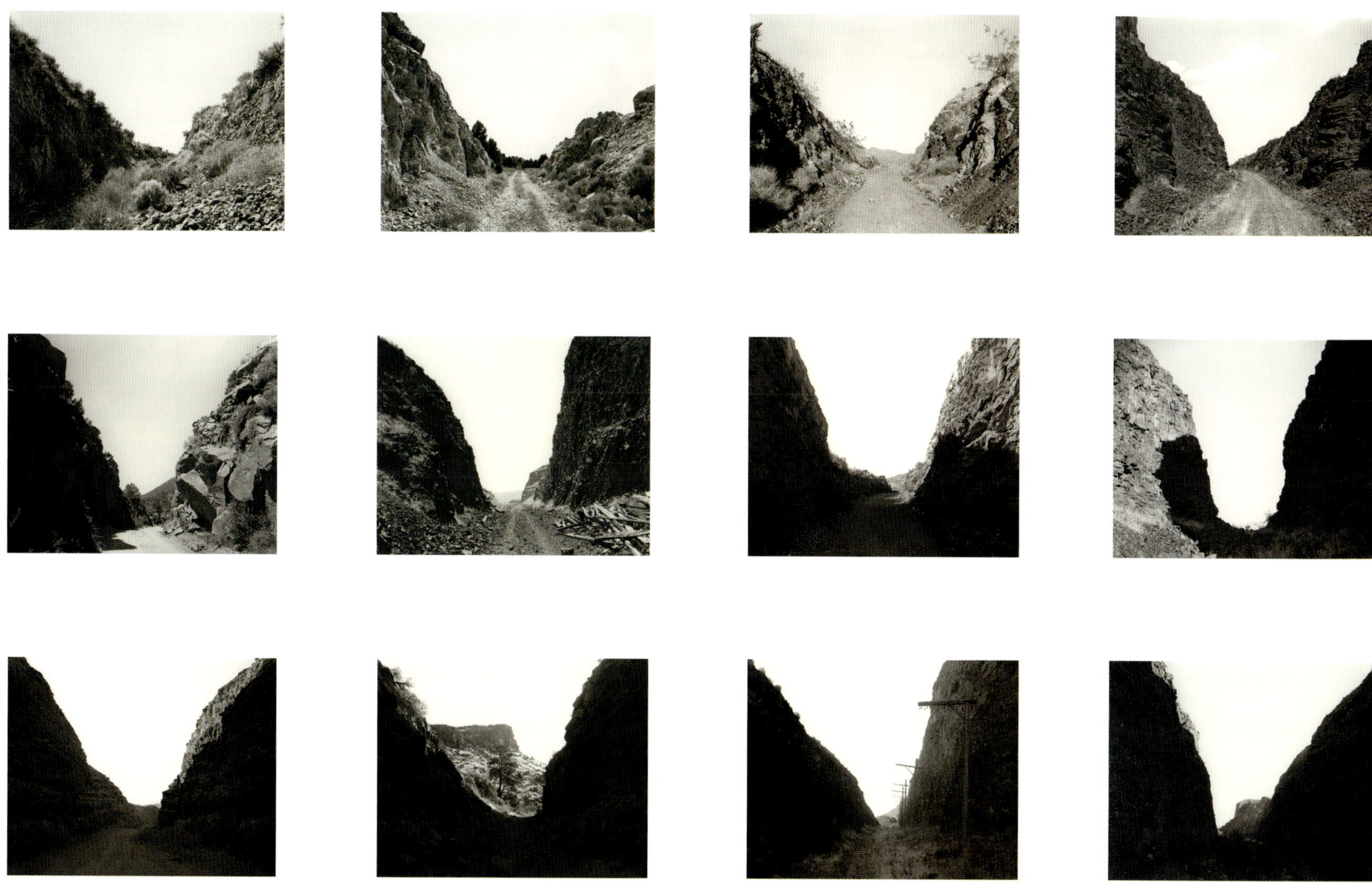

97. Mark Ruwedel, *Westward the Course of Empire (Cuts),* 1995-2005 (Courtesy of the artist and Gallery Luisotti)

ing Leopold's project of restoring degraded places.) Here, the wilderness may not be the picture of Leopoldian land health, but it provides just enough aesthetic, experiential, and conservation benefits to satisfy a more relativistic framing. As we've seen, it's a measured view of the wild that Leopold certainly understood and embraced in his own work.

But even if the "secondary wild" doesn't fit in the familiar wilderness narrative, it expands its reach and diversifies its geography. In doing so, it also shows how wilderness—and wild beauty—can manifest itself in some improbable places. These landscapes may have given up any claims to authenticity, at least in the perfectionist view of the wild, but their damaged, polluted, and extreme qualities don't disqualify them from aesthetic and ethical appreciation. Their condition may even invite and demand active ethical response in terms of restoration and community engagement. Interestingly, the same aesthetic and moral vision can frame both the authentically wild and the "genuine fake."[5] Such degraded lands had a champion in one of the most compelling voices in the annals of wilderness preservation, Wallace Stegner. "I am not moved by the argument that those wilderness areas which have already been exposed to grazing or mining are already deflowered," he wrote back in 1960, adding: "Better a wounded wilderness than no wilderness at all."[6] The medical metaphor is striking for a number of reasons, not least because it suggests restoration as a kind of ecological healing, a partnership with the landscape rather than a relationship of domination and exploitation. In the end, the de-facto wild asks us to set aside privileged framings of "original nature" and instead consider the wild as a shifting and evolving condition. And often a stubbornly resilient one.

About the Gallery

BAM: Steve, it seems to me there are two ideas at play in this cluster of images. As we write in the chapter, the first has to do with the ability of these landscapes to take a punch and (mostly) get back up, from the full blast of westward expansion (Ruwedel's rail cuts) to the literal detonations of military testing. But the other story is of how landscapes that don't fit in the traditional historical and visual narratives of the wilderness can nevertheless become wild in our eyes.

SP: Well, they may not fit notions of wilderness as a site for the sublime, but they are wild precisely because they don't fit in. Maybe they are less wild than feral—the West as neither settled nor unsettled but badly treated. They are not nature "untrammeled" by humanity, but places that humanity should have control over, if not domesticate, and that instead have slipped their leash. They illustrate the wild as not so much a place as a perspective.

BAM: There's also an unsettling political timbre to many of these images, though, as writers like Rebecca Solnit have explored so powerfully. The military and penal contexts of the work by Emmet Gowin (plate 98), An-My Lê (plate 99), and Stephen Tourlentes (plate 100) sit uncomfortably alongside the aesthetics and morality of wilderness preservation, don't you think?

SP: Authenticity is a troubled concept. I'm not ready to accept an Orwellian wild (or a "fake wild"), but these images may belong to a post-truth time. Their power lies in irony, which (ironically) requires a sense of an ideal wilderness and wilderness aesthetic, or else they are just photos of what the world around us looks like. Without our classic notion of wilderness, maybe they are just postcards?

MK: The work does indeed address the wild as a perspective, but these photographs are far more than postcards. When we thought of this section, I was looking for examples by photographers who were deliberately working past the classic notions of wilderness. I've sometimes thought of the places they've photographed as "second generation" landscapes. These are places that have been worked and passed over by humanity yet are increasingly significant to our experience of open land. The photographs comment on the official designation of wilderness as being untrammeled by man.

BAM: I'd say these are definitely trammeled! But you make a good point about the value of these landscapes for how we experience open land and, in that sense, the wild. And as we write in the essay these places are also revealing their conservation value given their remoteness and (mostly) off-limits character.

MK: Compared with other parts of the book this isn't a big section for plates, and yet there's a wide variety of approaches used. Mark Ruwedel made photographs of where the tracks of the first transcontinental railway once lay, now abandoned. These places no longer retain the artifacts of the built environment, but they still show the signs of that intervention. One thinks of empire building in this work, and then what is left afterward. Emmet Gowin and An-My Lê photographed two landscapes shaped by the military. And Stephen Tourlentes's picture is of a prison complex in the high desert at night.

BAM: There's almost a kind of shock value in calling these places "wilderness" given their history.

MK: Right. These examples raise questions about how land can be classified as "wasteland" or deemed unusable because it doesn't fit the normal conception of wilderness, and what happens to these places later. Irony does come into play, because the largest areas of land set aside for military use in the West have also preserved some of the largest areas of wild and uninhabited lands. You touch on this de-facto conservation outcome in the essay.

This section ends with photographs by Michael Lundgren (plate 101) and Michael Berman (plate 102), who address the concept of compromised but preserved lands in a different way. The former's practice involves evoking unexplained mysteries found in the desert, scenes that can be beautiful and terrifying at the same time, examples of a new sublime in unexpected places. The desert in Berman's photograph defies the common belief that desert equals wasteland. We see the extremely diverse ecosystem of a wildlife refuge extending into the neighboring Goldwater Bombing Range.

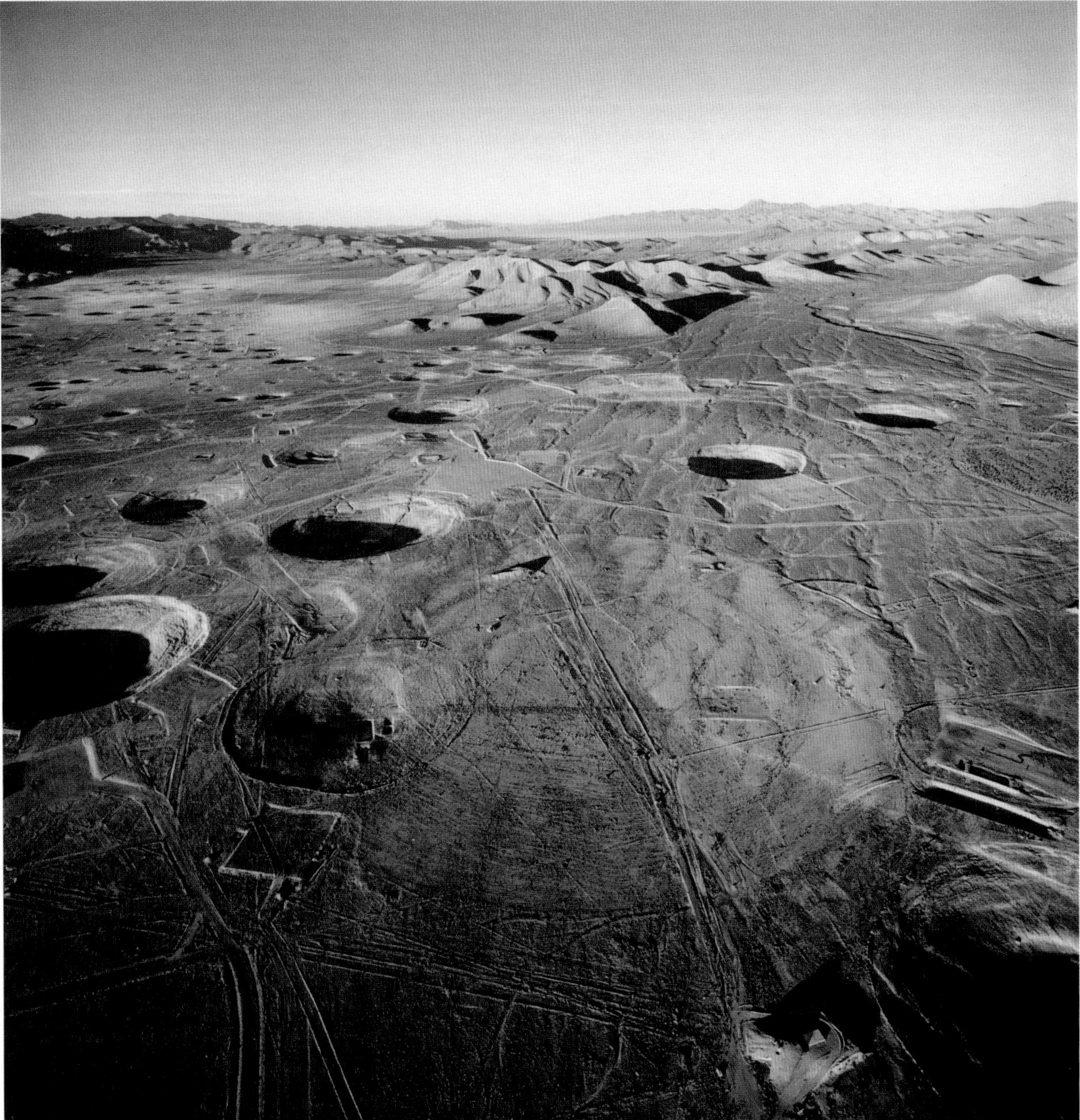

98. Emmet Gowin,
Area 9, Yucca Flat,
Nevada Test Site, 1996
(© Emmet Gowin)

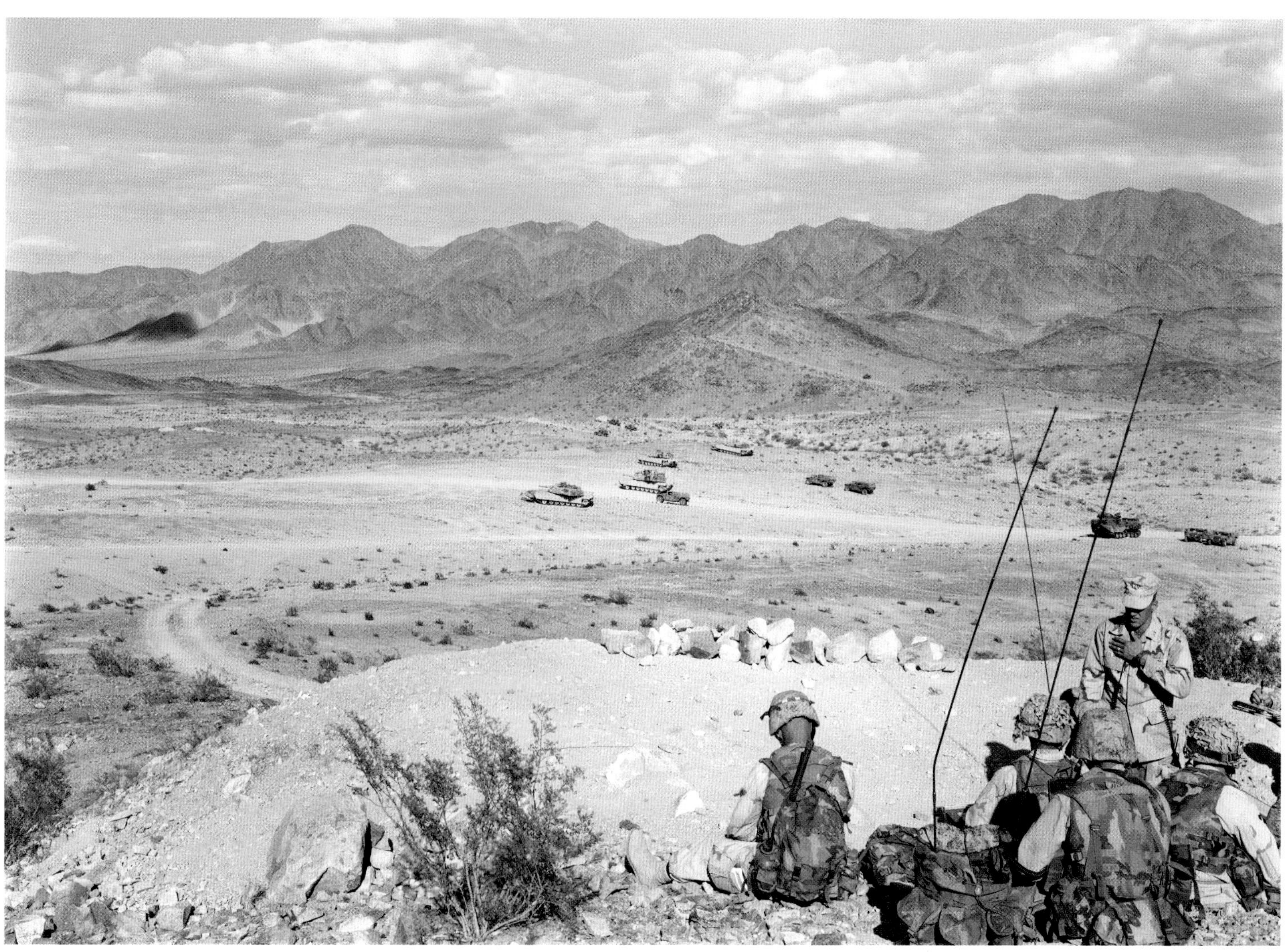

99. An-My Lê, *Captain Folsom,* from 29 Palms, 2003–4 (© An-My Lê, courtesy of the artist and Marian Goodman Gallery)

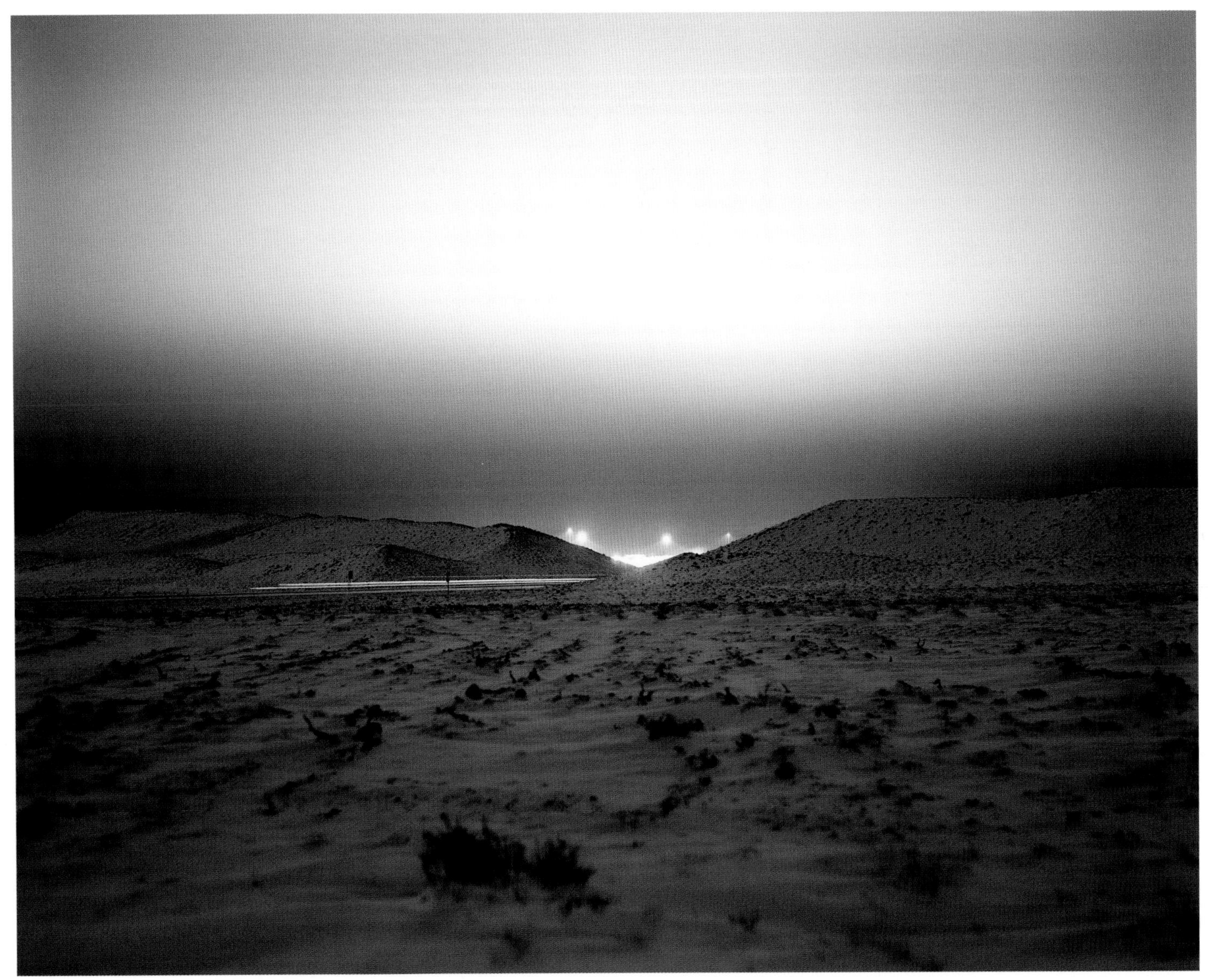

　100. Stephen Tourlentes, *Rawlins, Wyoming State Death House Prison*, 2000

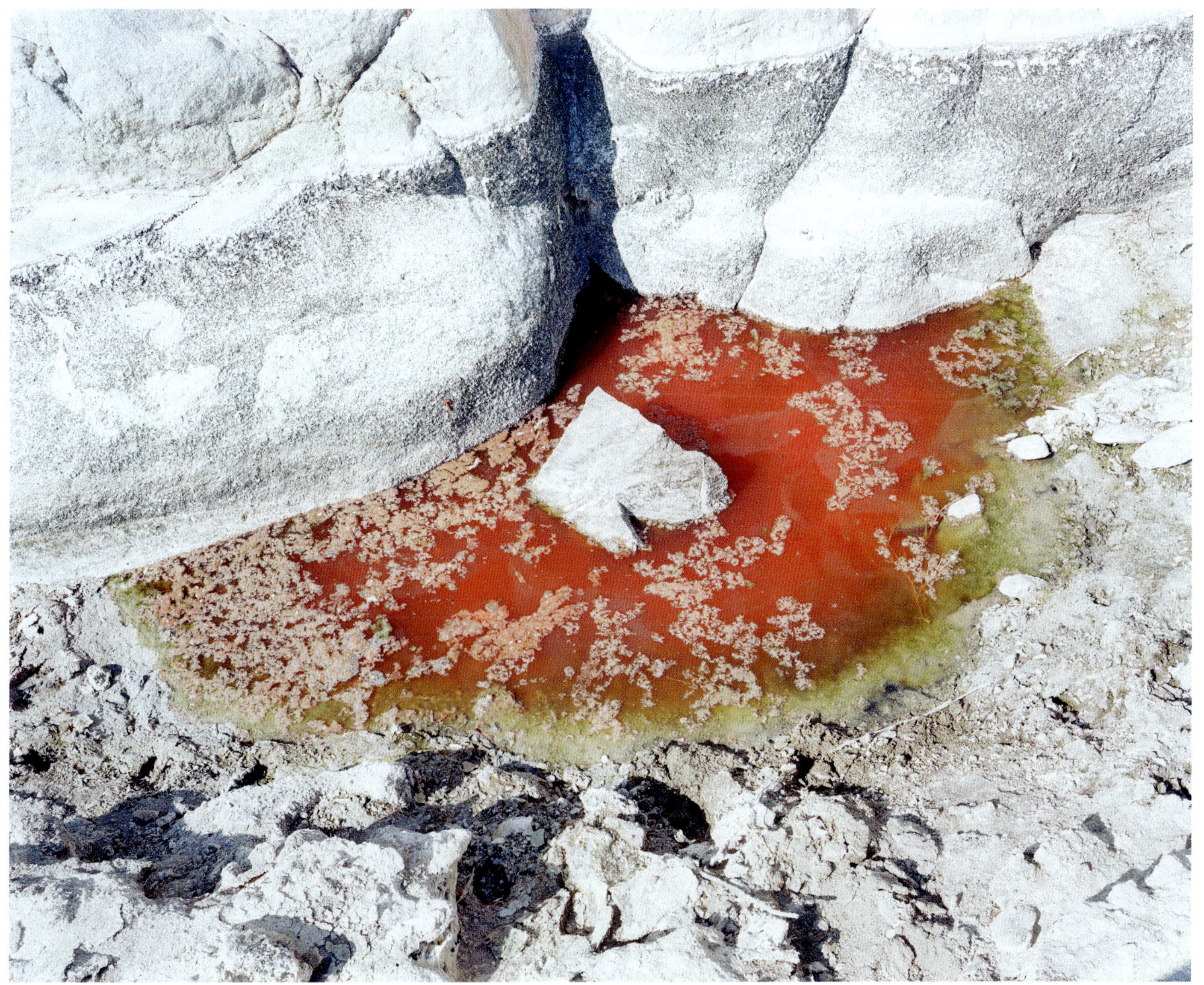

101. Michael Lundgren, *Mano,* 2012

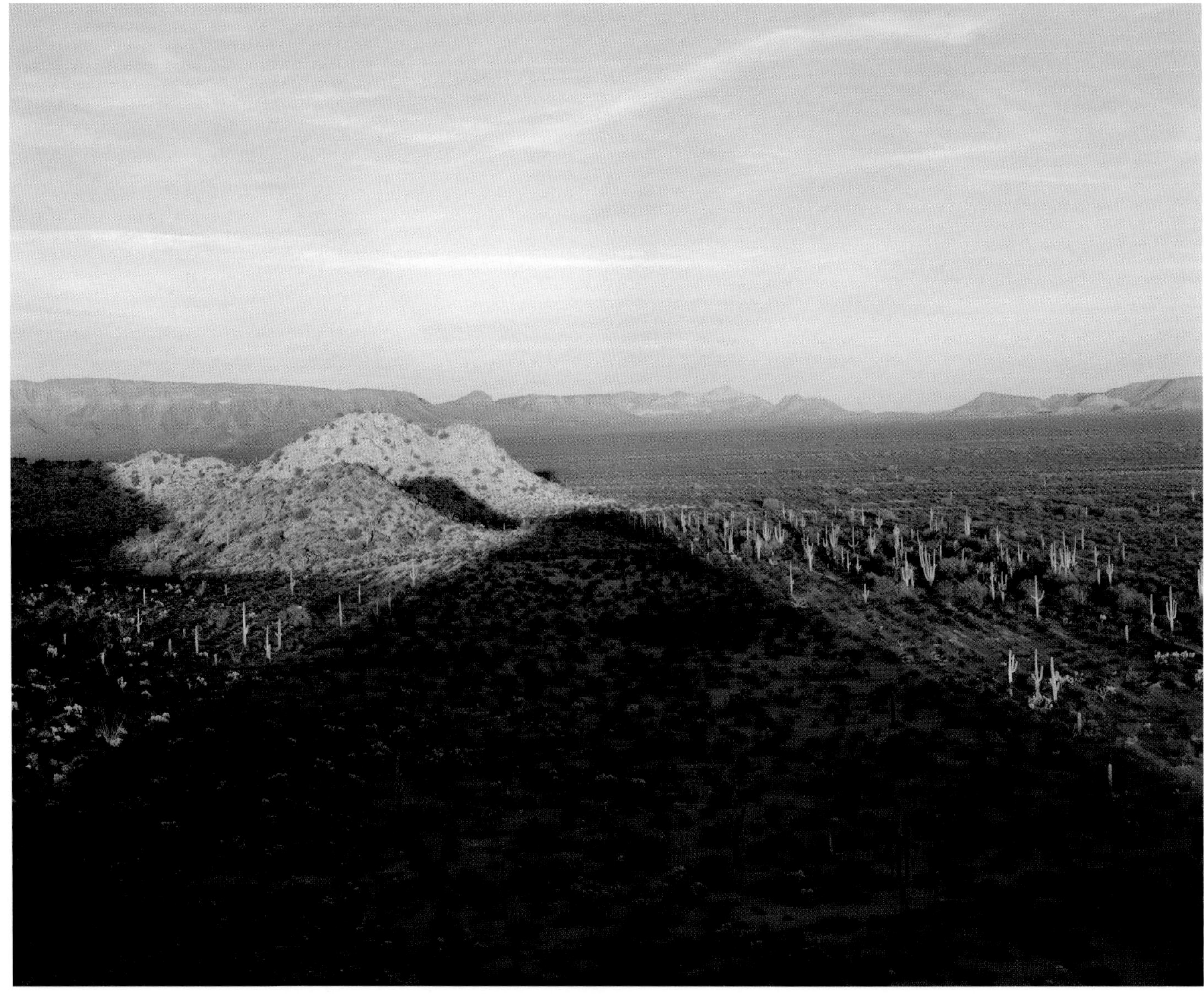

  102. Michael P. Berman, *Shadow, Cabeza Prieta National Wildlife Refuge, Arizona*, 2004

New Ways of Seeing

As we come to a close, it's hard not to see the wilderness idea as caught between two worlds. One is governed by nostalgia for a prelapsarian past in which protection of an unsullied wild remains the ultimate test of our environmental character. The other is driven by the unsentimental vision of a thoroughly humanized planet, a world in which we've outstripped the wild visions that impelled the work and activism of John Muir, Ansel Adams, Edward Abbey, and David Brower. It's a second nature that's fast eclipsing the first, or perhaps a third nature that's eclipsing both—a mashup made possible by a fossil-fueled society that is sublimating fire into electricity, replacing fauna with machines, rewiring geochemical cycles with plastics and petrochemicals, and digitally reimagining human life within such an environment. Modern technology becomes both medium and message for recording that experience.

As a result, preservationists carrying the torch of Muir and company argue that we need the wilderness ideal now more than ever, if for no other reason than without it we'll have nothing left to discipline our craving to cut, pave, and consume. The philosopher William James had it right when he observed that the "trail of the human serpent" is over everything (though he was talking about the inescapability of humanism, not its coronation as an environmental ethic). Still, the more zealous "post-wilderness" environmentalists commit a logical and moral error when they conclude that the preservationist cause has somehow been rendered impossible and inconsequential with the emerging recognition of the Anthropocene. We may be large, but we're not in charge. The ability to disrupt is not the same as the capacity to control. The serpent's trail still isn't the whole territory.

In other words, even if Yosemite isn't a pristine wilderness, it's still a comparatively wild place, one capable of inspiring a romantic sense of awe and wonder among those who see it. That remains true despite its wildness not being absolute—

and as it continues to change under our influence. Its perceived wildness becomes an invitation to consider the layers of meaning and the conflicts that it also holds.

Acknowledging this partly humanized character of the wilderness, though, doesn't require backing off from the view that we should still preserve as much wildness as possible where and when we can. As always, it's a question of degree. Cars, concessions, and parking lots are likely a permanent fixture in Muir's northern California "temple." But that doesn't mean that we also have to welcome drones hovering over Half Dome.[1]

So much is clear. But this split over the meaning and value of the wilderness in a human-defined age is not simply a dust-up over environmental empirics. And it's not just another incarnation of the utility vs. beauty debate that has roiled the American conservation movement for more than a century. The rift over the rightful place of the wilderness in our environmental ethos today is also a struggle over the power of tradition and our relationship to it. That is, it's about how we should continue to value and view wild places and the cultural expressions that have celebrated them when the older myths and images are called out as unscientific, aesthetically passé, and socially regressive. It's about the continuing relevance of the earlier writers and activists that many of us think of as representing the very best of our environmental inheritance, even though our world seems so starkly different from their own, and an appreciation for their good works even as their personal imperfections surface. And it's about the enduring appeal of their defining message of humility and restraint toward the wilderness, especially as our power and impact grows. It's still about place—how to think and what to do about the distinctive configurations of rock, flora, water, and wildlife without a dominant human force at its center—but it's clearer now that it's also about our own moral character; our ability to demonstrate forbearance rather than environmental control.

The old formulation attributed to wilderness values as sanctuary, lab, gym, and expression of American exceptionalism—as a site for spiritual refreshment, as a baseline that can help measure our impact on the earth, as a place for outdoor recreation, and as an emblem of the better angels of the American experiment—are finding updated versions. The sanctuary has become a refuge from a virtual world, a site of approximating something like authenticity. The lab has become a referent against which we can assess the immense upheavals of the Anthropocene. The gym has added climbing walls and yoga mats. American exceptionalism has refashioned from the wild a working expression for a deeply multiethnic nationalism that denies any one group a claim to blood-and-soil patrimony.

The wilderness idea is approaching nearly a century since the Gila Wilderness Area first gazetted the concept—and more than fifty years since the Wilderness Act bequeathed to us a history that can also be seen as a tradition. The wild as idea, as story, as image—these, too, have evolved to adapt to more contemporary circumstances. The idea has matured to accommodate the ever present, if usually invisible, human presence, and so moves beyond irony into paradox. The story, like most modern histories, has morphed from a simple dialectic between the wild and the civilized into a dialogue of a civilization with its past refracted through its natural estate. In the process, moments and images of reconciliation present themselves, as in the idea of the relative wild.[2] It has become a conversation of many natures with many peoples; the wild, it seems, can accommodate a multitude of voices.[3] And the image? That has been the particular concern of this book.

Standing on the shoulders of singular artists like Timothy O'Sullivan, Carleton Watkins, Ansel Adams, and Eliot Porter, landscape photographers today have also found themselves negotiating with tradition as they attempt to represent and evoke wilderness and place in their own time, and in their own style.

They've done so in a variety of ways, from the imaginative retrieval and recasting of nineteenth-century photographic techniques—such as David Emitt Adams's tintype images on oil drum lids (plate 103), Will Wilson's digitally enhanced wet-plate images (plate 104), and Abelardo Morell's camera obscura (plate 106)—to returning to familiar and prized wilderness subjects like Yosemite with fresh eyes and interests. As they report and document the new landscapes before them, a complicated amalgam of the human and the natural, a cultural mashup, their work becomes a bold mixture of aesthetic experimentation, technical innovation, and personal statement. Their landscapes include themes, memes, perspectives, and aesthetics once exclusive to the wild, but now projected elsewhere as well. The awful terror of the sublime can reside in trailer parks and abandoned towns and in unexpected exposures and strange juxtapositions of scenes or of troubled images as much altered by technology as are the lands that are their subject.

Many of these pictures carry forth aspects of the classic wilderness image but dramatically revise and subvert it, making the overt manipulation of the photo a key part of the scene. Colors and features are removed or enhanced, views are taken apart or recreated from digital data. The landscape is still an object of contemplation and appreciation, but it's also become a reservoir of meanings and impressions that take us into new artistic and intellectual territory. It provides an opportunity to rethink, dismantle, and reconfigure the familiar scenes and responses. The artists seem to treat the image as the landscape itself has been treated, perhaps with the intention of at least a partial restoration.

In several of the images we see provocative explorations of the notion of belonging, including deeply personal perspectives on the environmental iconography of the American character. Vietnamese-born Binh Danh's daguerreotypes of Yosemite suggest a visual dialogue about nationalism and inclusion in the national parks and the American photographic tradition (plate 105). And Catherine Opie's photos present a feminist reclaiming of the traditionally male-centered views of the American wild by injecting ambiguity into the recognition of place identity (plate 109).

Elsewhere, features that would normally be hidden from sight are exposed: The satellite trajectories of Julie Anand and Damon Sauer suggest a kind of celestial surveillance (plate 112), which in Trevor Paglen's work evokes a creeping sense of unease, a paranoid irony lurking in the notion of "wilderness solitude" (plate 113). Interestingly, in most of these views technology isn't obscured, it's foregrounded, such as in Mark Klett's and Byron Wolfe's use of social media to create a linear composite of Grand Canyon sunsets (plate 115)—and Daniel Leivick's mining of Google Earth data to create images that pull us into the uncanny valley (plate 118). In pictures like this our grip on the distinction between visual and virtual reality loosens.

In other cases, the camera itself has become expendable. The "Post-Lenticular Landscapes" created by ScanLAB, a group based in the United Kingdom, are produced by a terrestrial laser scanner that reconstructs, in haunting digital arrays composed of countless discrete data points, the historic wilderness views of Watkins, Muybridge, and Adams (plate 121). The work is seen by its creators as a continuation of the tradition of testing the boundaries of image-making and technology associated with these photographic forebears. And Meghann Riepenhoff's camera-less prints formed by waves interacting with photographic materials suggest the power of nature's agency while also exposing the collaborative relationship between the artist and the landscape in picture making (plate 122). It's a striking visual analogue to a line by the writer and biologist Robin Wall Kimmerer: "Listening in wild places, we are audience to conversations in a language not our own."[4] Here, though, the photographer is part of the dialogue.

Taken together, the photos demonstrate the value of engaging artistically and productively with wilderness tradition in a way that leads to new creative possibilities rather than back to the older orthodoxies. While respectful of the choices and legacies of their forebears, these contemporary artists are clearly not bound by them; it's an influence that seems largely free of anxiety. As new ways of seeing the wild landscape, their images also suggest new ways of thinking, both about the wilderness as a privileged place in nature and as a creation continually remade at the aesthetic and cultural intersection of the old and the new. Wilderness as a place may be problematic; wilderness as a tradition can be updated and renewed. Whether these artists can inform the future, as their predecessors did the past, is unclear.

Still, their images show us how it might be possible for wilderness to thrive in the space between the two worlds if we can manage to avoid the excesses of both. In its founding formulation wilderness was defined by what it wasn't. It wasn't roads, tourist lodges, and logging camps. The absence of people let the intrinsic worth of the place shine forth. More recently, we respect the wild for what it reveals about us: it testifies to restraint, which is to say, to humility. Americans have the technological capacity to trash virtually any landscape in their reach; legal wilderness is a declaration that they choose not to. It's a way of thinking about the wild that's stripped of the traditional biocentric metaphysics and marked by a renovated aesthetics. The new wild is about how people position themselves in a place, both in what they do and don't do and in how they might pose for a self-reflective photograph.

Likewise, we have sought to position ourselves within the wilderness tradition, to try to hold both worlds, old and new, in one volume, and to have that volume emulate the Sierra Club Exhibit Format books that proved so influential in promoting the wild. Like a heritage building, this book keeps its predecessors' shape and format, but has replaced the old wiring and furniture with more contemporary experiences and images.

Those images are telling. The old masters of the wild were modernists, whose works stood alone; like the wild, each was whole in itself. The newcomers are postmodernists, rebels who need the old to react against and to define their tweakings, recombinations, and sideways perspectives and who paradoxically need a text to explain the nature of their alterations, for the vision of the wild lies in the mind's eye as well as the camera's lens. It requires the word as well as the image. After all, one word can be worth a thousand pictures.

If it's the right word.

About the Gallery

BAM: Mark, this final chapter provides a summary of many of the book's narrative threads while providing a brief commentary on the work of some of the photographers and visual artists helping to reframe today's wilderness aesthetics and values. As we note in the text, they often do this by returning to the artistic scene of the crime (such as Yosemite), or by manipulating the image, or by mashing up old techniques and new technologies. Some of them do all of that at once. At the risk of papering over the differences among these images, why does this work as a whole speak to you?

MK: Well, I've been trying to pay attention to how photographers have been working in recent years and the shifts in our field. Two things related to methods have stood out: a return to "alternative" or historic photographic processes to make new work, and just the opposite—the use of digital technologies to explore new ways of seeing. Both approaches share frameworks that are grounded in conceptual ideas. The work included here was chosen because it reworks iconic places and themes we've addressed elsewhere in this book, and in some cases because the work intentionally rewires conventional ways of seeing. The photographs in this final section also reflect shifts in vision that can be noted in the work of other plate sections.

BAM: It's interesting to me that so many of these artists go back to Yosemite, which must be among our most photographed natural areas.

MK: Yes, there's definitely an intentional return to Yosemite National Park, where, for example, Abelardo Morell takes in the same scene as Ansel Adams's *Clearing Winter Storm,* but this time projected on the surface of the overlook's pavement (plate 106). He does this by using a device he created that's based on a Camera Lucida, an optical device that was used as a drawing aid that was invented in the early nineteenth century. Dan Holdsworth's image of Half Dome wasn't even made with a camera, instead using data from a digital elevation model (plate 107). And Mathew Brandt's image of Half Dome was made with a process that used mole sauce—think about that for a minute, a delicious view with a Mexican flavor (plate 108)! ScanLAB's image is a twenty-first-century remake of Eadweard Muybridge's view of Veral Falls using cutting-edge Lidar technology (plate 121).

BAM: In the chapter, Steve and I briefly discuss some of the technical innovation of many of these photographs, including this combination of the old with the new. I assume that the experimentalism in this work is part of what draws you to it.

MK: Exactly. Some photographers avoid new technologies and prefer processes that let them interact directly with light-sensitive materials. David Adams uses the nineteenth-century tintype process to depict oil refineries onto the lid of fifty-five-gallon oil drums, referring to the energy source that fueled the expansion of the twentieth century (plate 103). Scott Davis

makes landscapes directly onto photographic materials placed
into the camera, rather than using film or digital capture (plate
114). And as you mention in the chapter, Meghann Riepenhoff makes work without a camera entirely, by exposing and
washing off the paper's light-sensitive blue cyanotype coating
directly in the surf of a California beach (plate 122).

Others comment on celestial phenomena and our relationship to the earth. Chris McCaw uses a large, handmade camera to make a direct image of a solar eclipse onto photographic
paper (plate 110). During the process of creating the image, the
heat of the sun's focused rays actually burned the paper. David
Shannon-Lier tracks the setting of the moon across the horizon
line of his backyard (plate 111). Julie Anand and Damon Sauer
(plate 112), and Trevor Paglen (plate 113), reverse the view, and
refer to the imagery made by satellites ever surveilling the
earth from above.

But this commentary using technology and materials is only
one shift in approach. The other is cultural.

BAM: Let's talk about that. Part of the story of this gallery is
the diversity of the photographers behind the work. I'm thinking particularly of Will Wilson (plate 104), Binh Danh (plate
105), Abelardo Morell (plate 106), Catherine Opie (plate 109),
and Jungjin Lee (plate 116). But others as well.

MK: Right. Several of the photographers in this section are
naturalized citizens (Dahn, Morell), or non-U.S. citizens (Zoe
Childerley, plate 117, and the ScanLAB group), and one (Will
Wilson) is Native American. Danh is originally from Vietnam,
and while his use of the historic daguerreotype process to
photograph national parks is an intentional statement about

our nation's changing ethnic identity, what we can't see in
the reproduction is that the original image is on a mirror-like
surface. The viewer of his original work will see their own image
as well as the landscape shown. Catherine Opie, in her beautiful and out-of-focus view of the Grand Canyon, takes aim at the
historic male-dominated tradition of sharp view-camera landscape photography.

BAM: This attitude of respecting the "received" traditions of
wilderness thought (such as the Sierra Club books, the biocentric appreciation of the wild, and so on) while also turning
the page in these narratives has been a driving theme in our
text. What's really interesting here is that we see this dynamic
playing out photographically.

MK: Many contemporary photographers are challenging conventions and established cultural norms, and in so doing
they've been expanding the baseline of representation by adding
their individual ethnic, gender-based, or other diverse view-
points into a field that, like the wilderness preservation movement generally, has previously been dominated by white males.

This has certainly been happening across photography in
general, and I won't claim that we've adequately presented the
case for that expansion here. But I think it's important to recognize that these changes have been well under way, and they will
no doubt transform the way we see wild places in the future.

SP: When I wrote *How the Canyon Became Grand,* I found a narrative end point just before the cultural consensus about the
meaning of the canyon dissolved into a pixilation of individual
perspectives. The Canyon continued to be viewed and valued,

but the old narrative frame no longer held. I wonder if this chapter is photography's version, except that it continues the story well into the pointillist era.

BAM: The parallels are intriguing, Steve. But I'm also struck by aspects of continuity. As Mark notes, there's clearly an awareness of tradition in many of these photos, and a respect for these places as historical and visual focal points of the wilderness narrative. Yet also an attempt to subvert tradition and inject new personal and cultural perspectives and experiences into the view.

SP: That makes sense. New techniques for old places, old perspectives for new places—even wilderness mingles change with continuity. The three of us value the wild, but we are also creatures of our time.

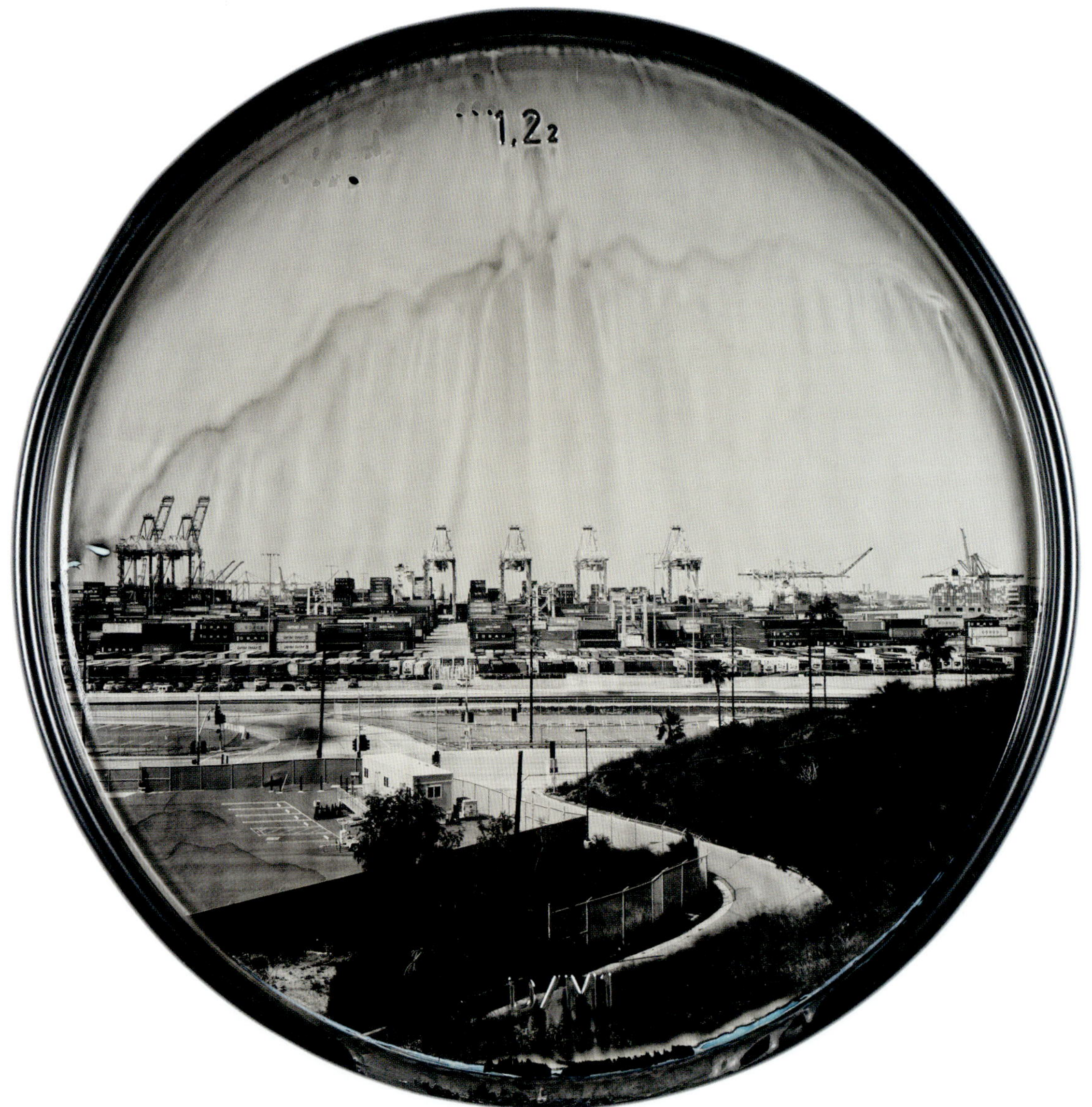

103. David Emitt Adams,
Port of Los Angeles, San Pedro, California, 2015

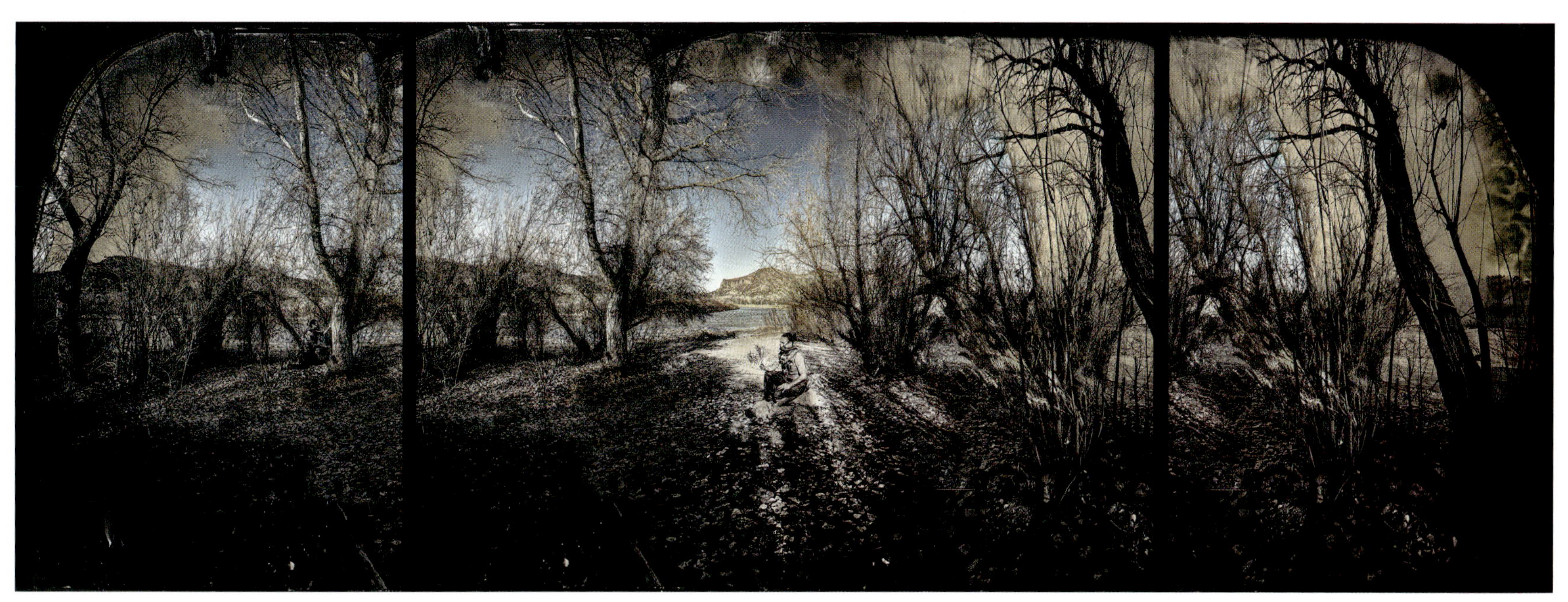

104. Will Wilson, *Auto Immune Response: On the Consideration of Invasive Species, Downriver from Los Alamos, New Mexico,* 2014 (Courtesy of the artist, WillWilson.photoshelter.com)

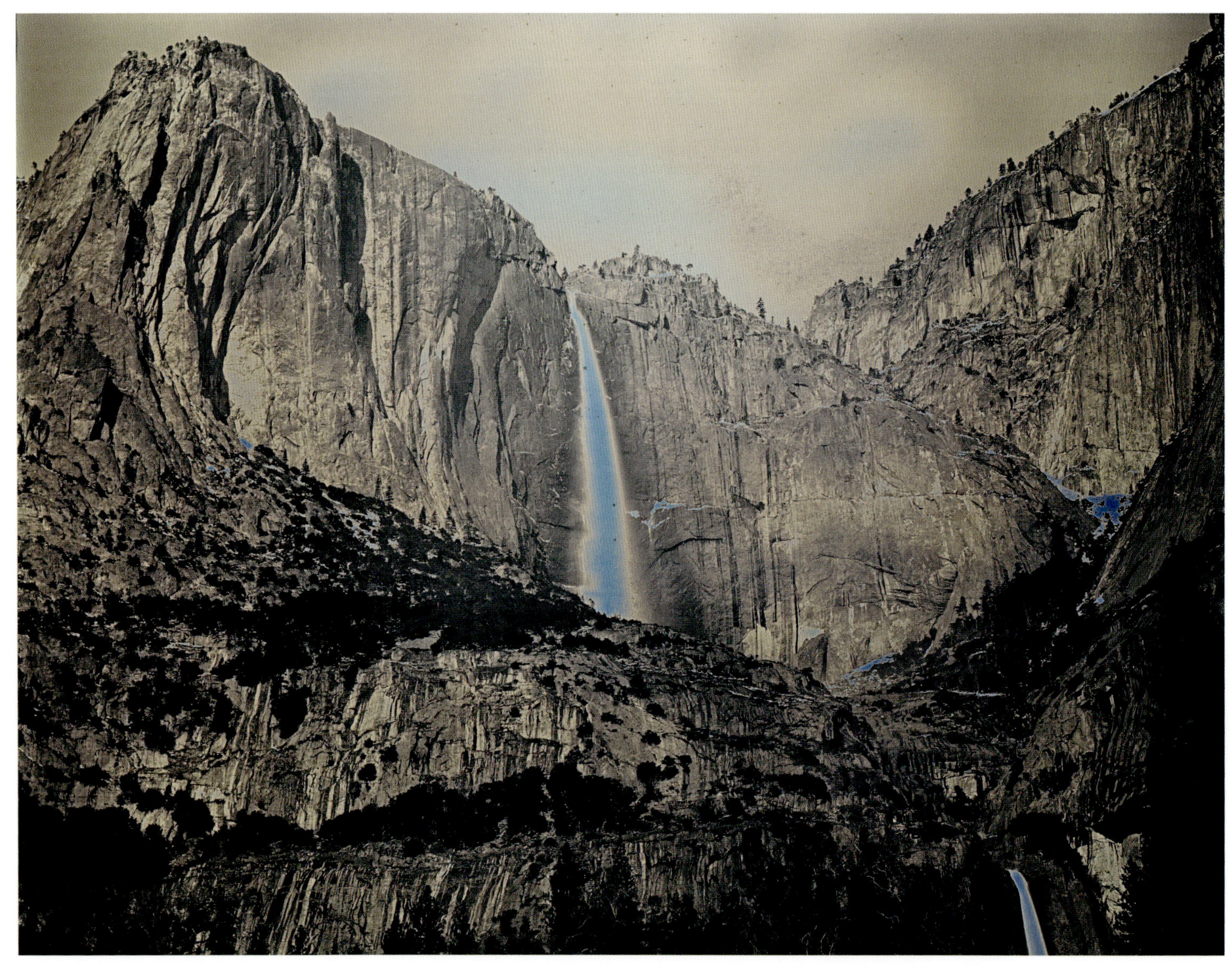

105. Binh Danh, *Yosemite Falls,* 2012 (Courtesy of the artist; Haines Gallery, San Francisco, California; and Lisa Sette Gallery, Phoenix, Arizona)

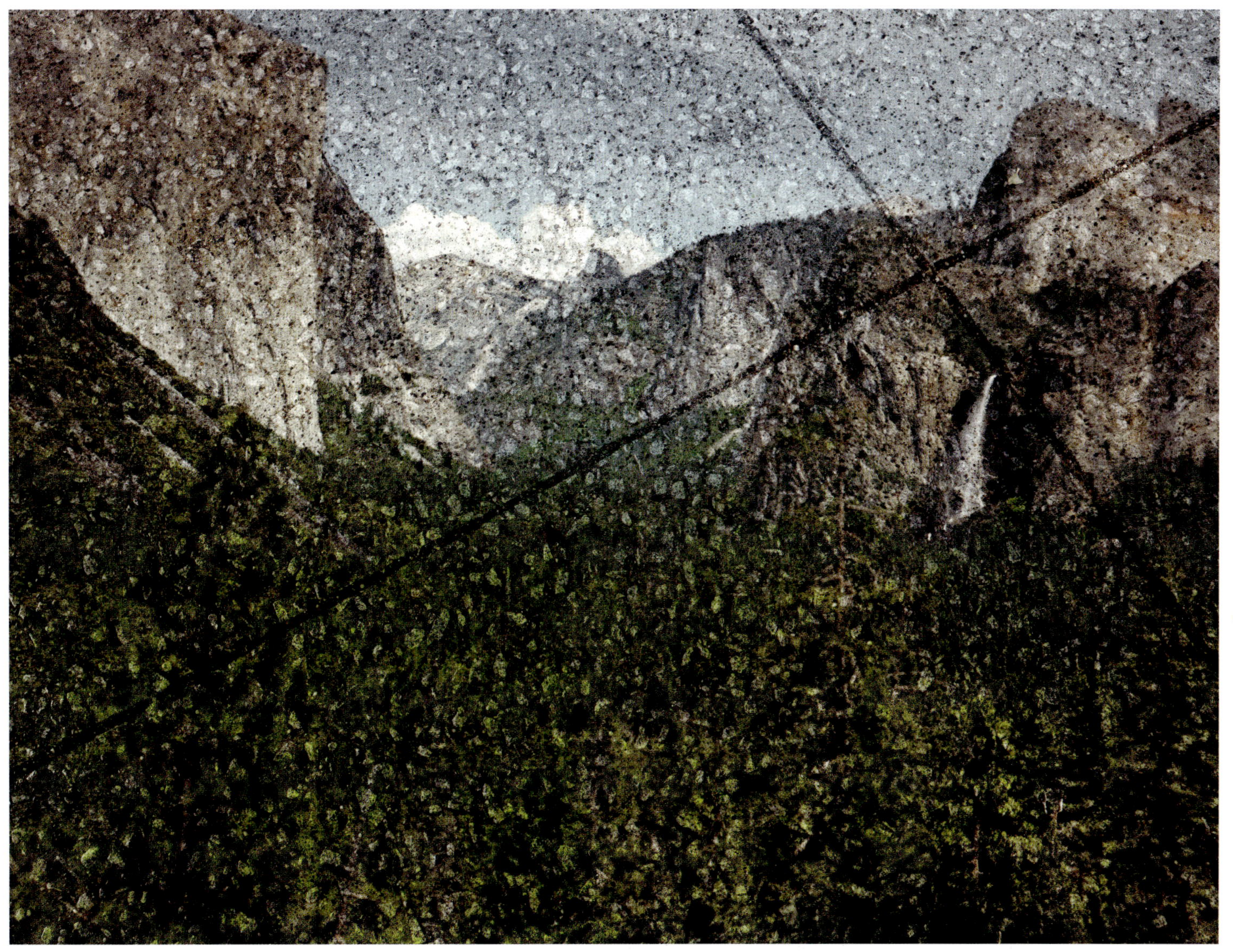

106. Abelardo Morell, *Tent-Camera Image on Ground: View of the Yosemite Valley from Tunnel View, Yosemite National Park*, 2012 (Courtesy of Edwynn Houk Gallery)

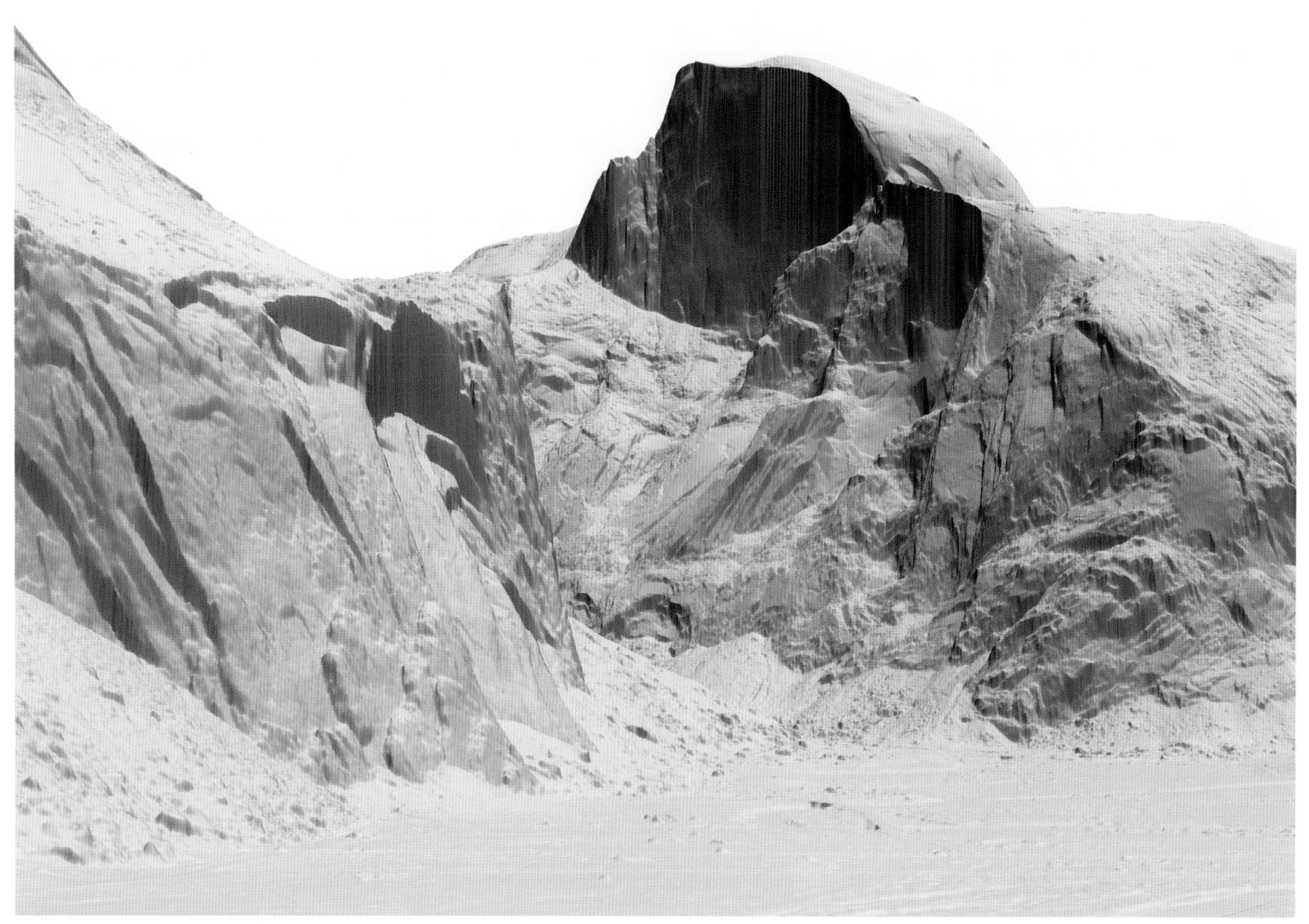

 107. Dan Holdsworth, *Yosemite, C6,* 2012

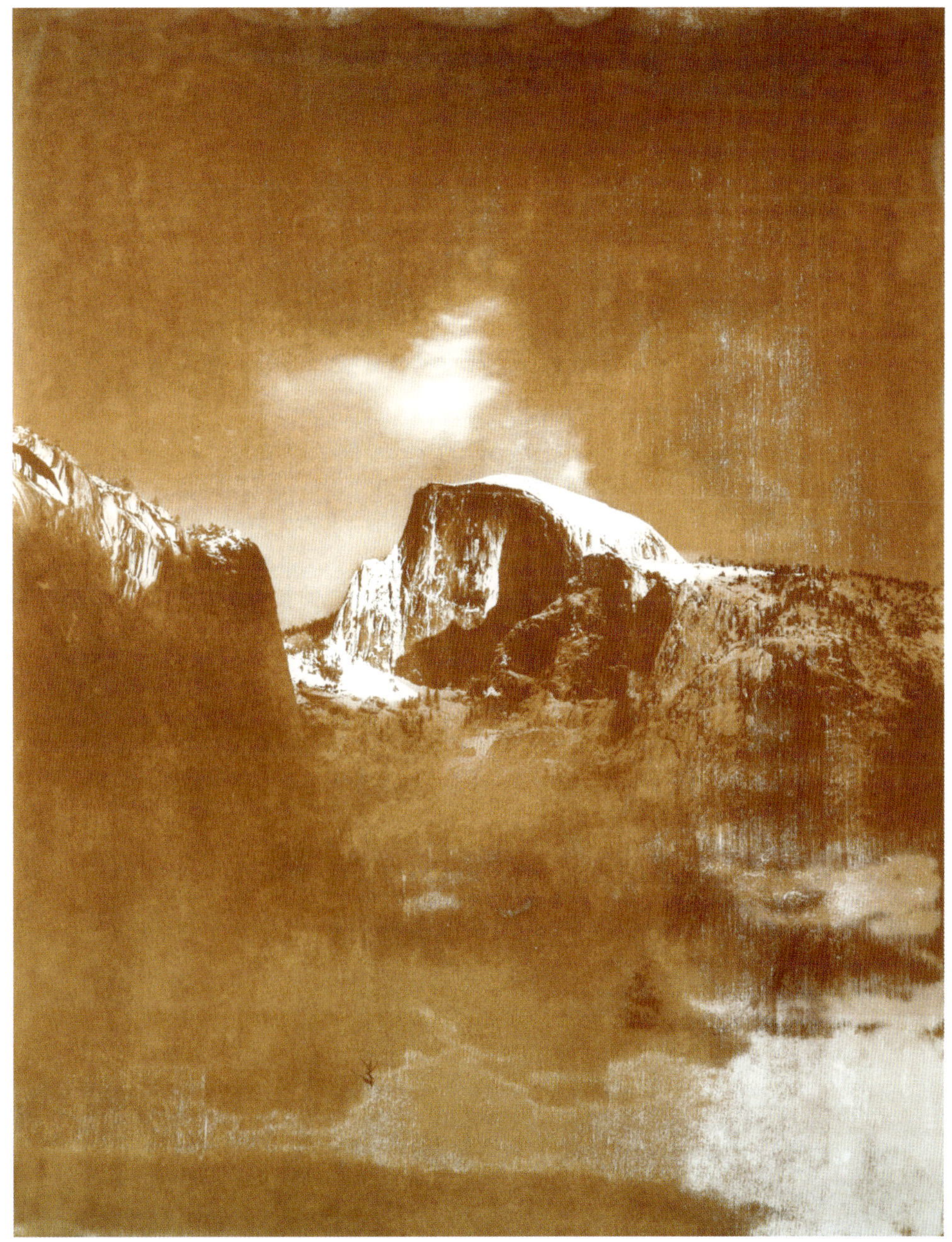

108. Matthew Brandt, *Mole*, 2009, from the series "Taste Tests"

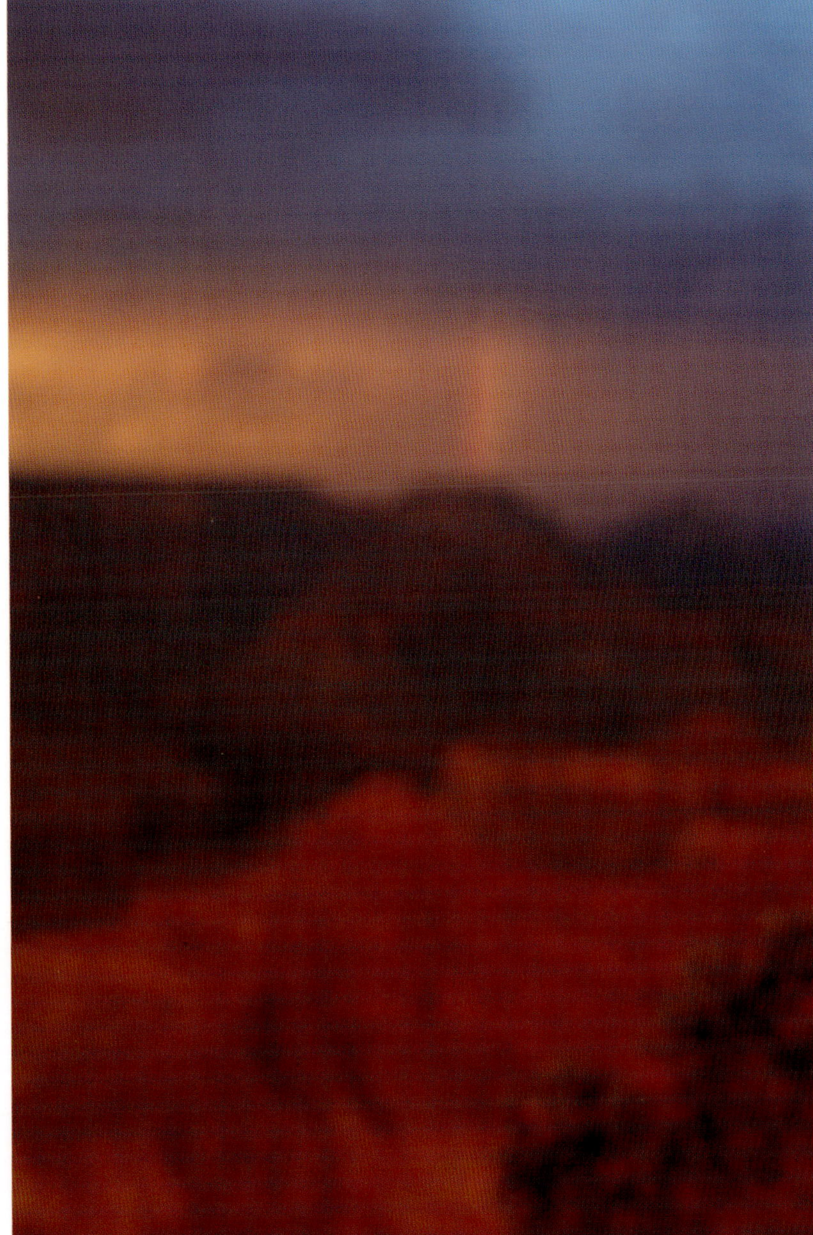

109. Catherine Opie, *Untitled #14,* 2016 (© Catherine Opie, courtesy of Regen Projects, Los Angeles, and Lehmann Maupin, New York, Hong Kong, Seoul, and London)

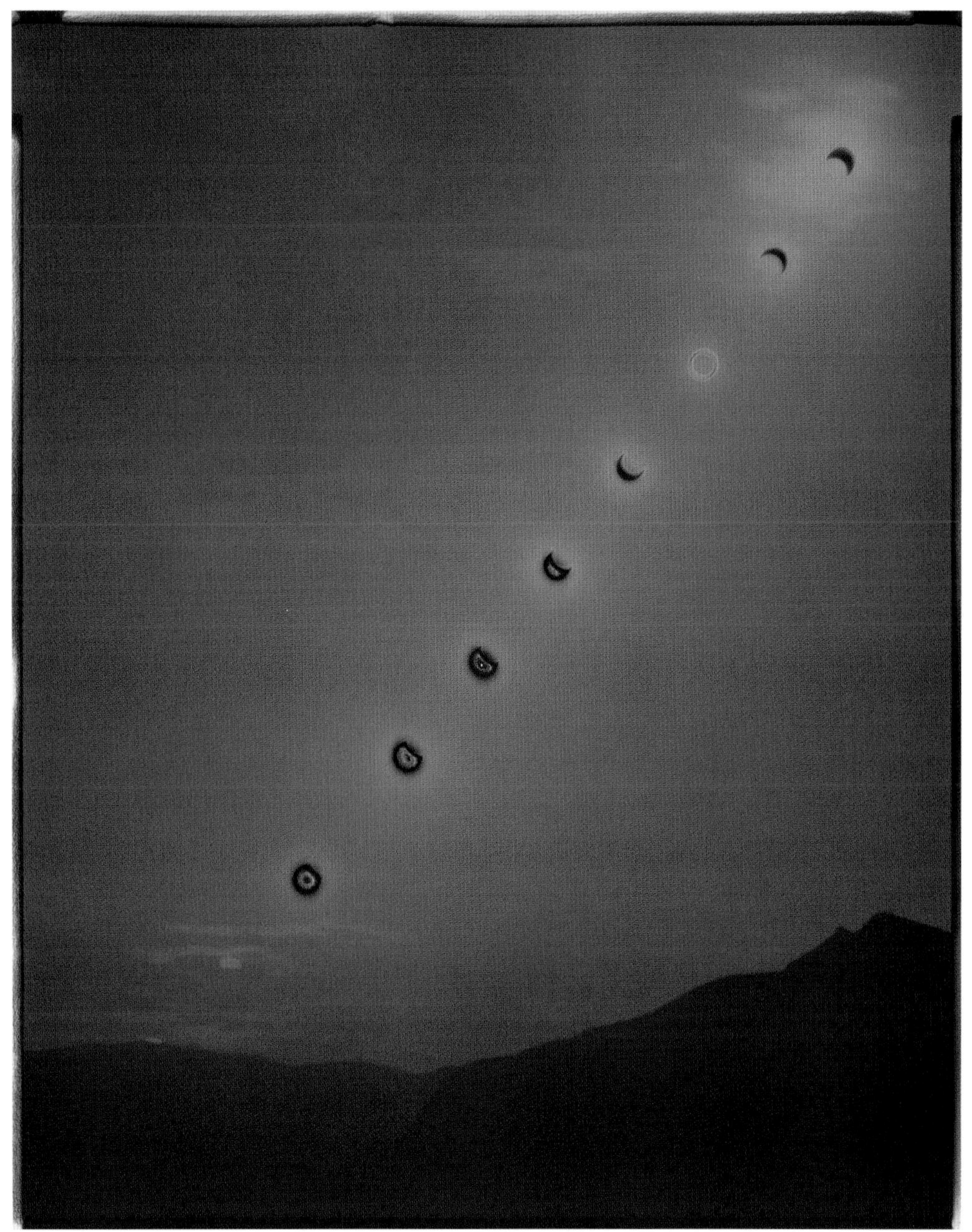

110. Chris McCaw, *Sunburned GSP#576
(Annular eclipse, Nevada),* 2012

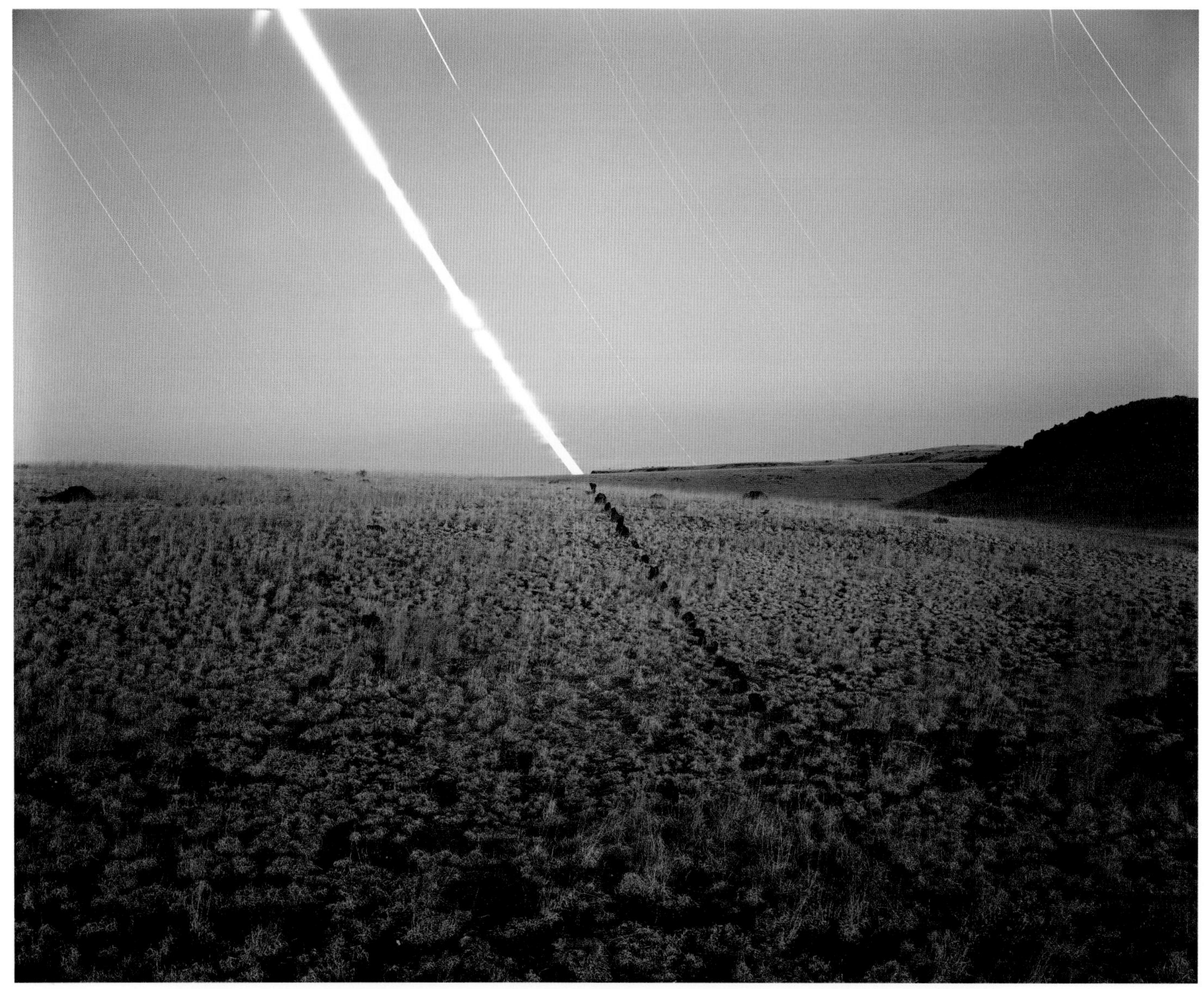

111. David Shannon-Lier, *Grassland Moonset, Gila National Forest, New Mexico,* 2015

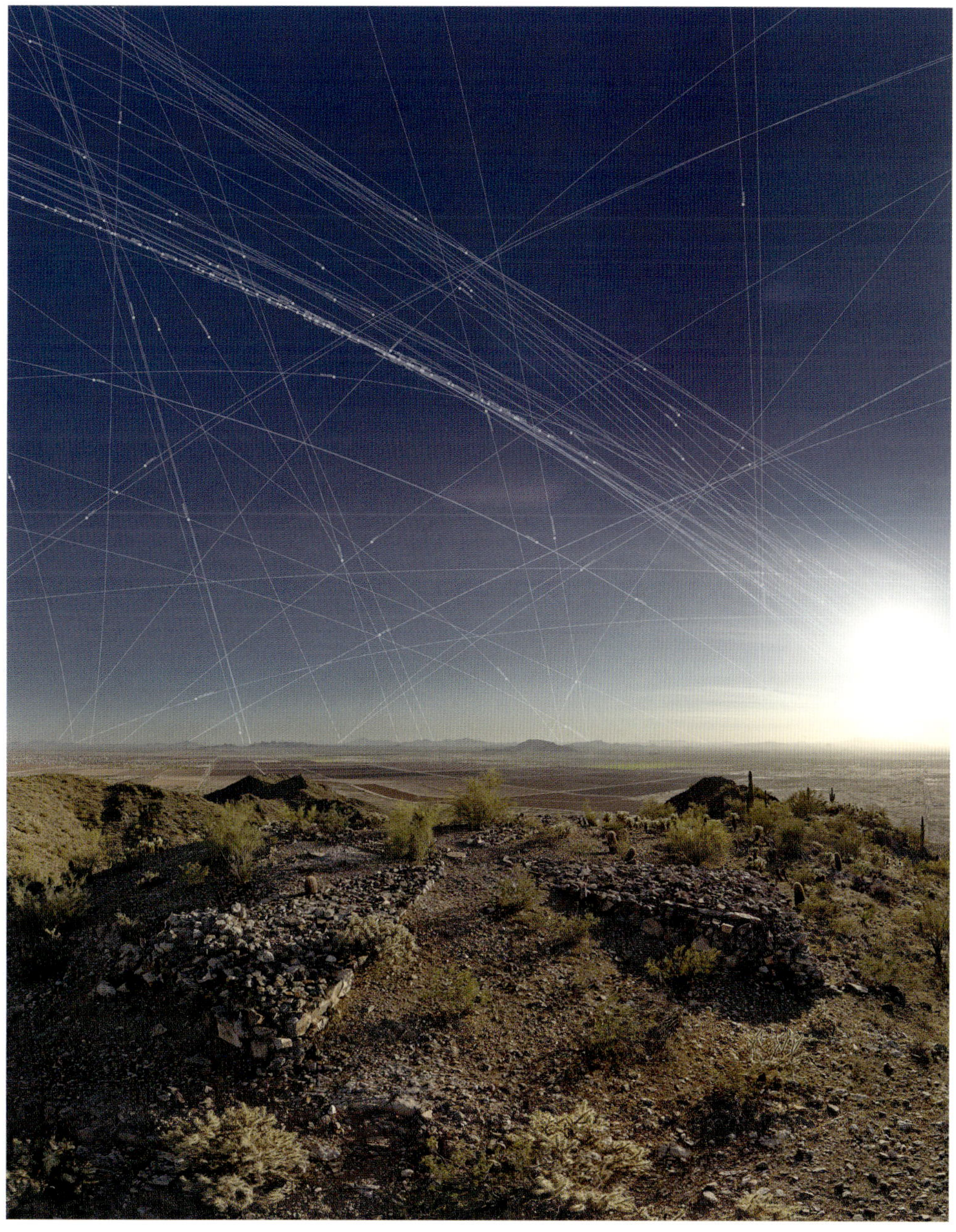

112. Julie Anand and Damon Sauer, *Calibration Mark AF49 with Satellites*, 2015

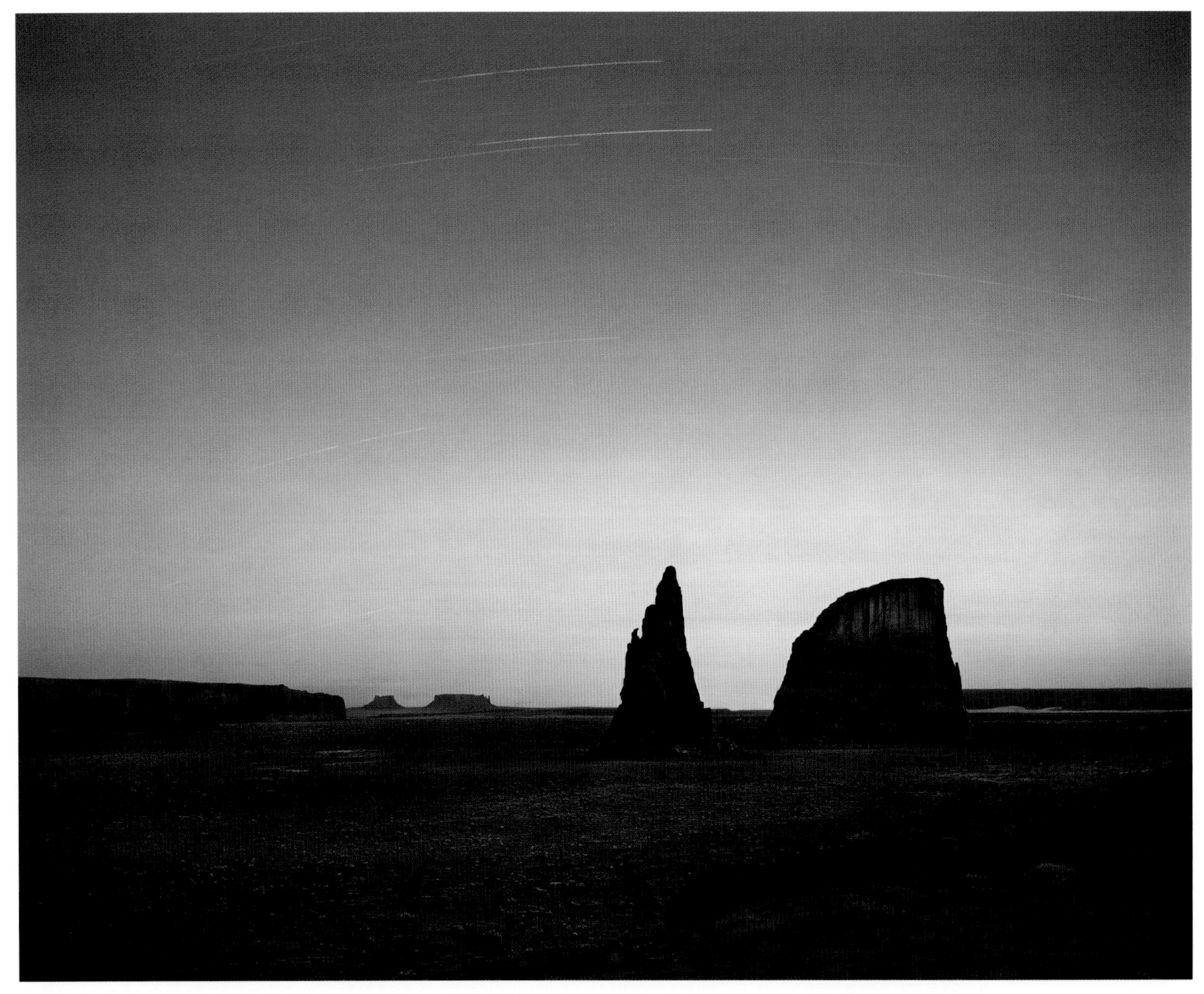

113. Trevor Paglen, *Dead Satellite with Nuclear Reactor, Eastern Arizona (Cosmos 469)*, 2011, C-print (Smithsonian American Art Museum; Gift of Mike Wilkins and Sheila Duignan; image courtesy of the artist, Metro Pictures, New York, Altman Siegel Gallery, San Francisco; © 2011, Trevor Paglen)

114. scott b. davis, *ocotillo, santa rosa mountains*, 2013

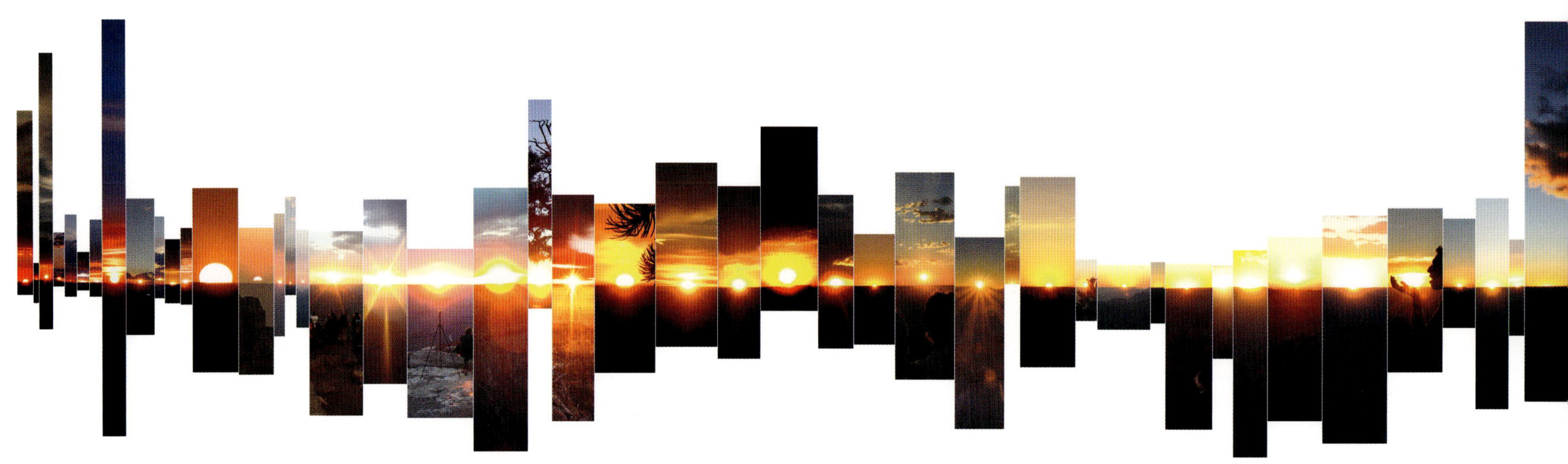

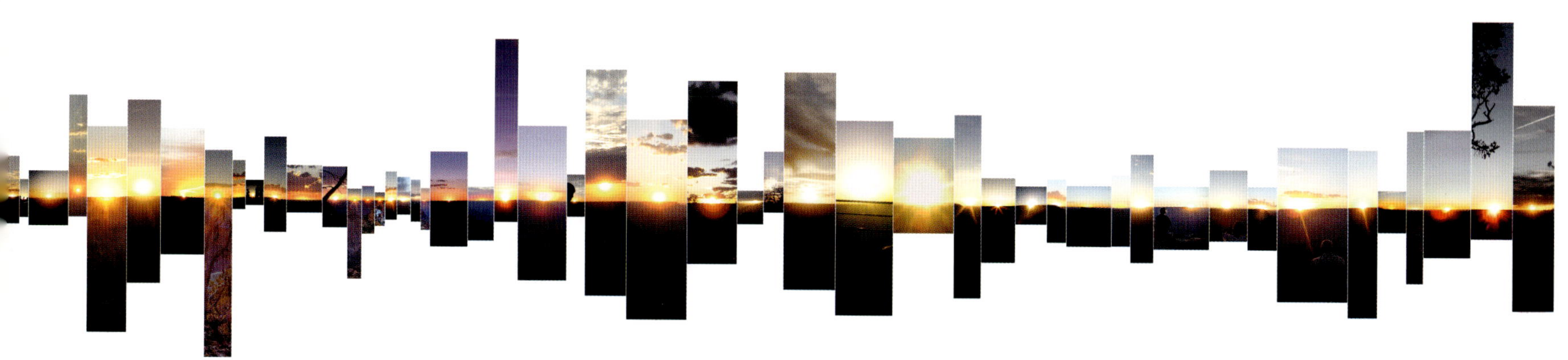

115. Mark Klett and Byron Wolfe, *One Hundred Setting Suns at the Grand Canyon Arranged by Hue; Pictures from a Popular Image-Sharing Website*, 2011

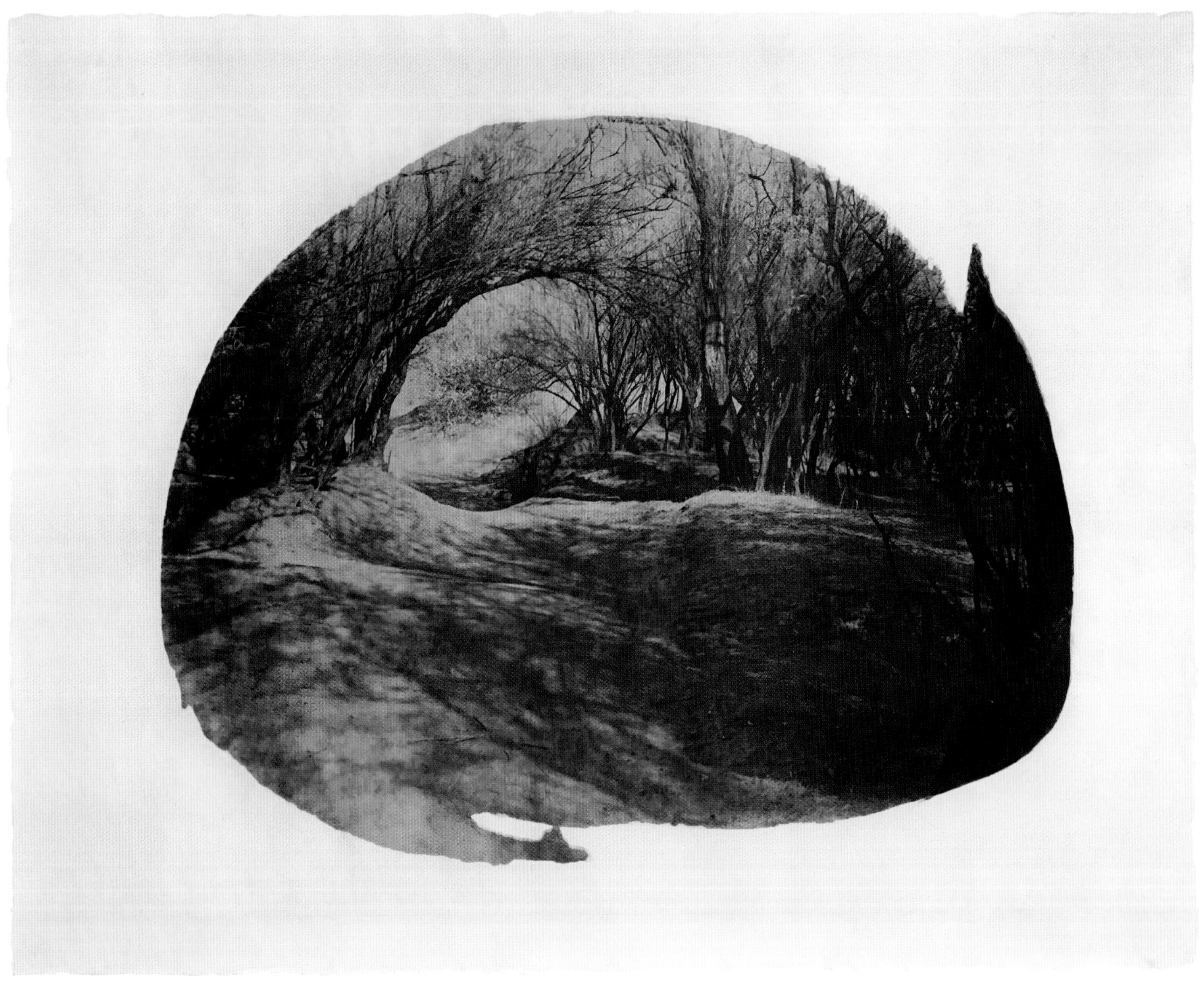

 116. Jungjin Lee, *American Desert IV, 95-13*, 1995

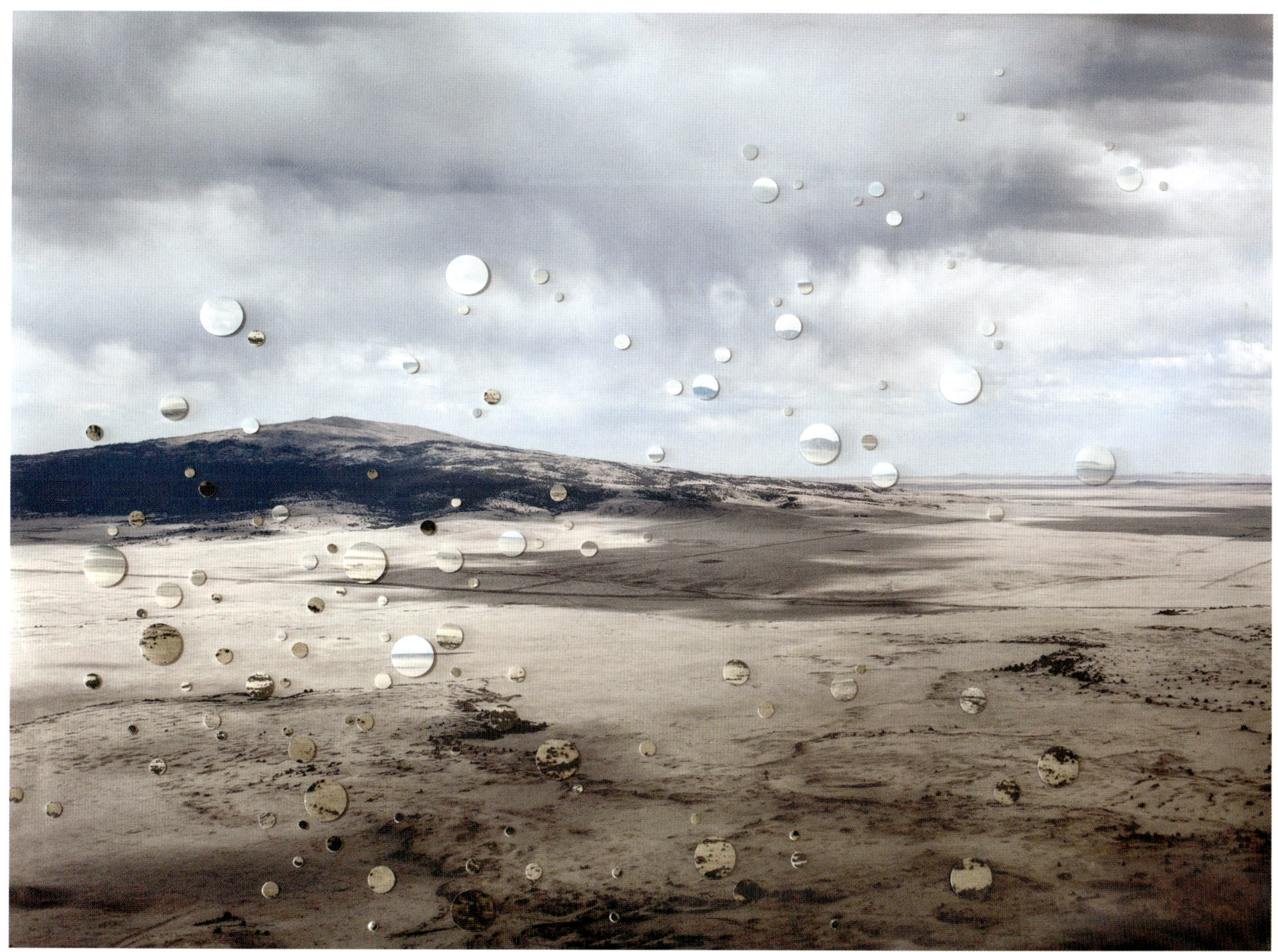

117. Zoe Childerley, *Mapping the Desert, View from Capulin Volcano, New Mexico*, 2014

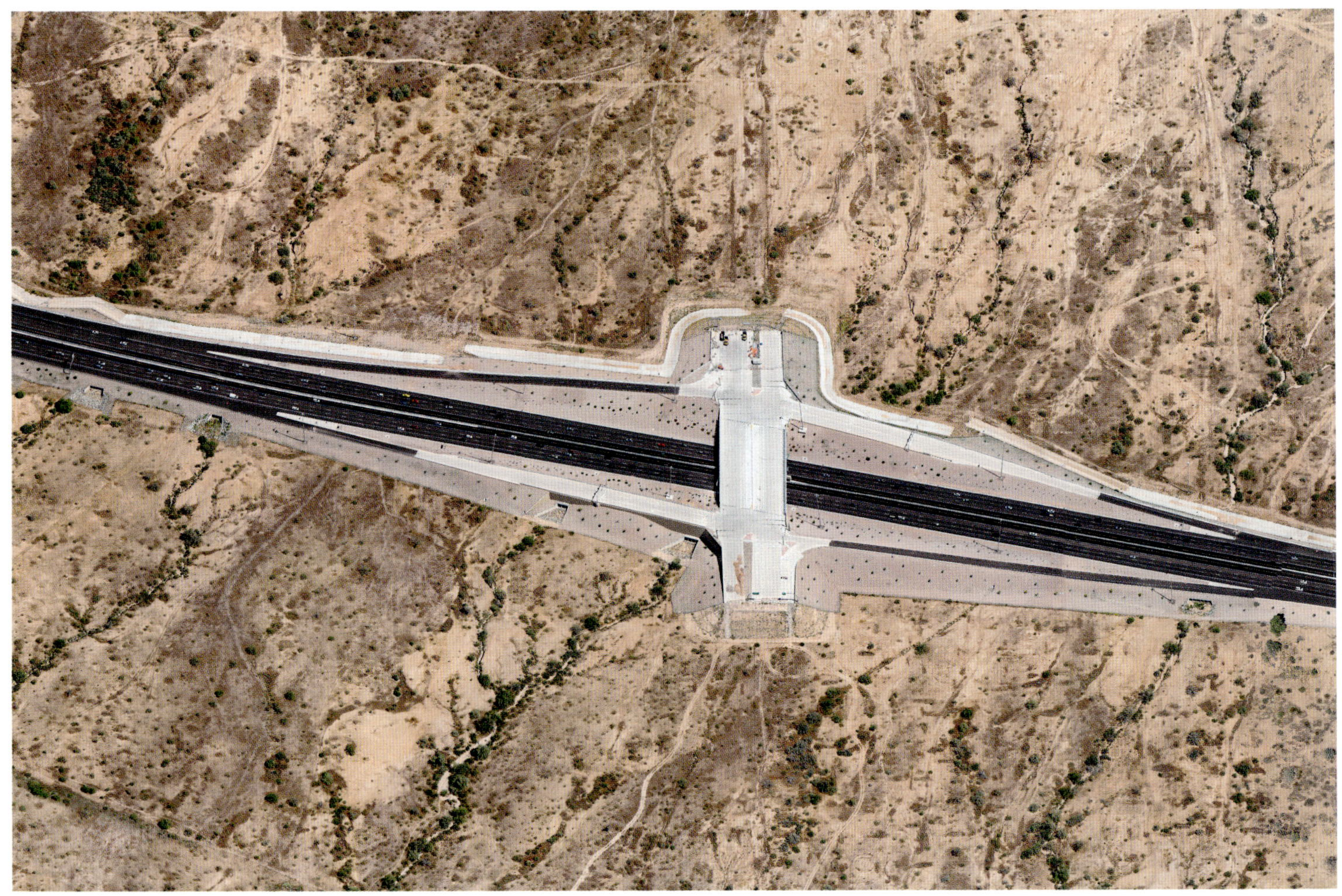

  118. Daniel Leivick, *No Exit*, 2016

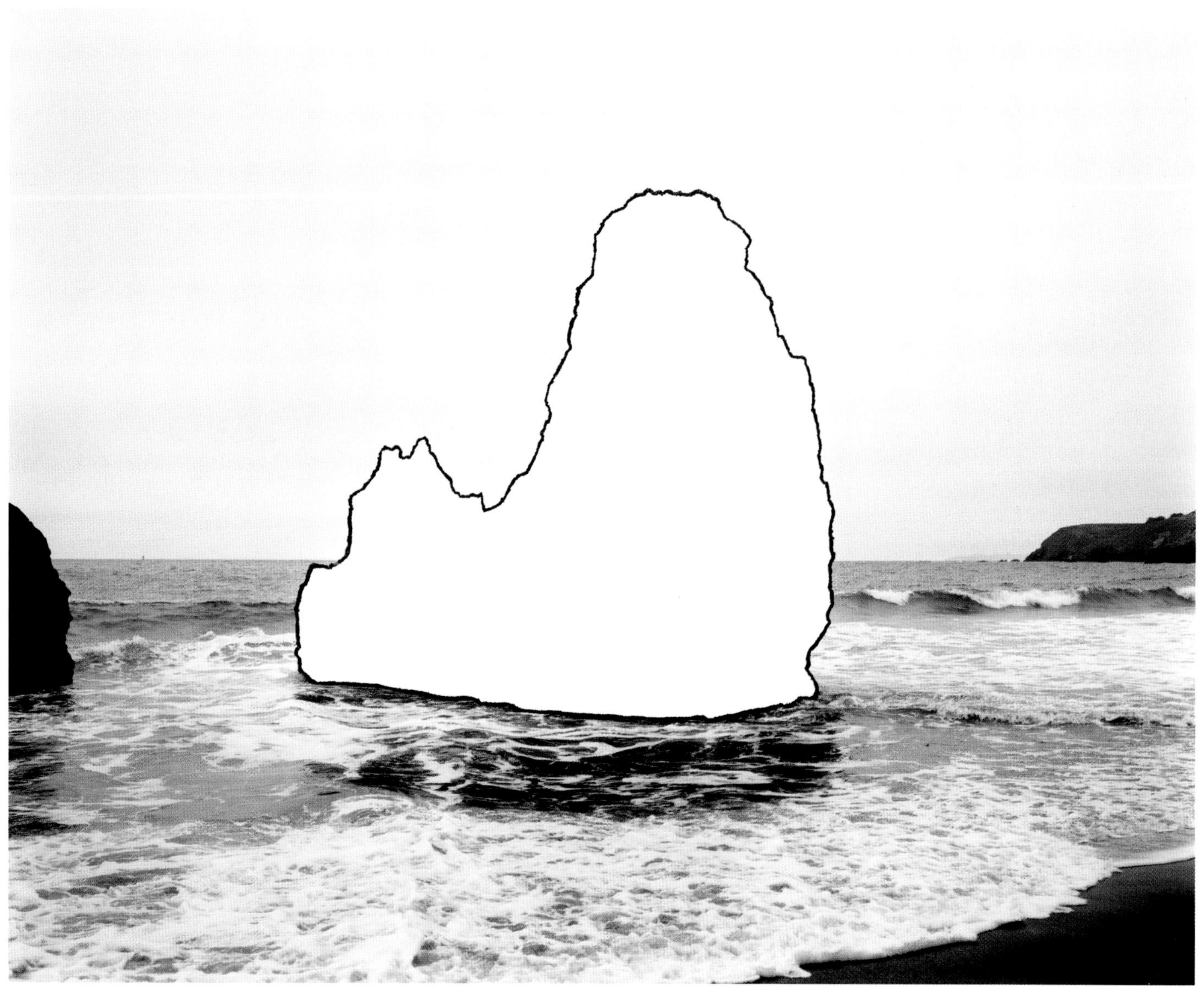

119. Adam Thorman, *Erasure 5*, 2017

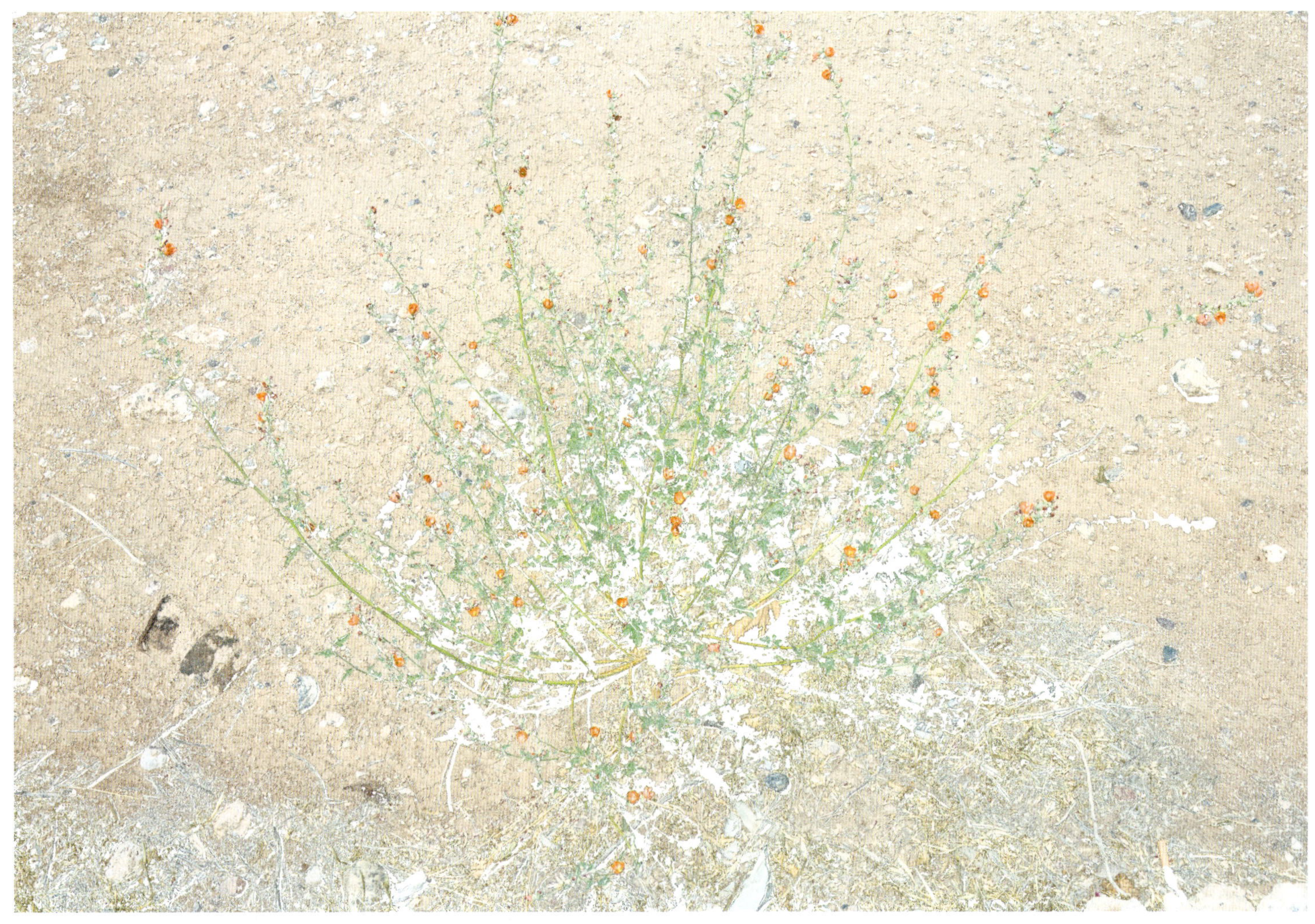

　120. Aaron Rothman, *Untitled (Orange Flowers),* 2012

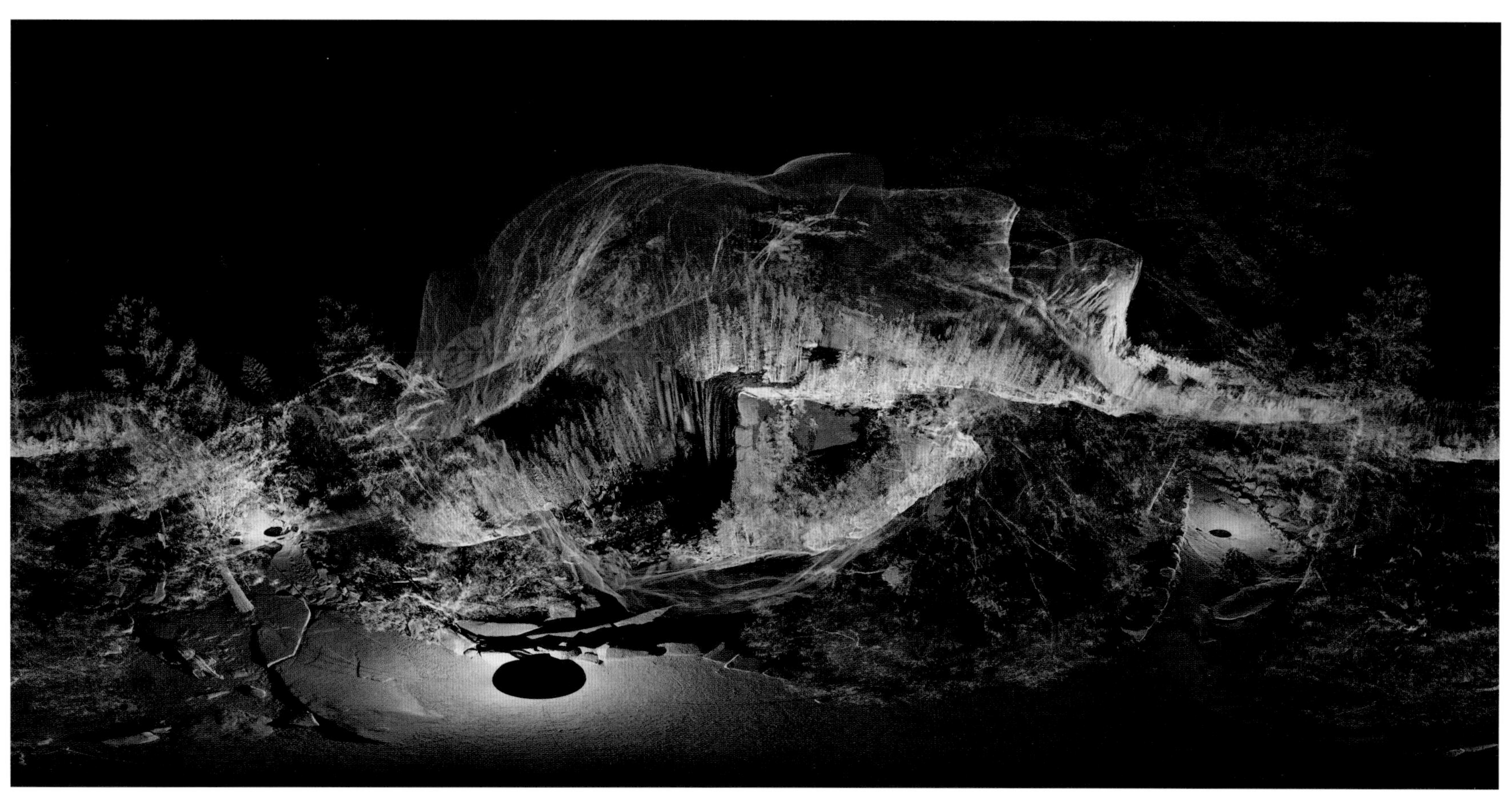

121. ScanLAB Projects, *Equirectangular Landscape 06: Vernal Falls (after Muybridge, Pi-Wi-Ack [Shower of Stars])*, 2018

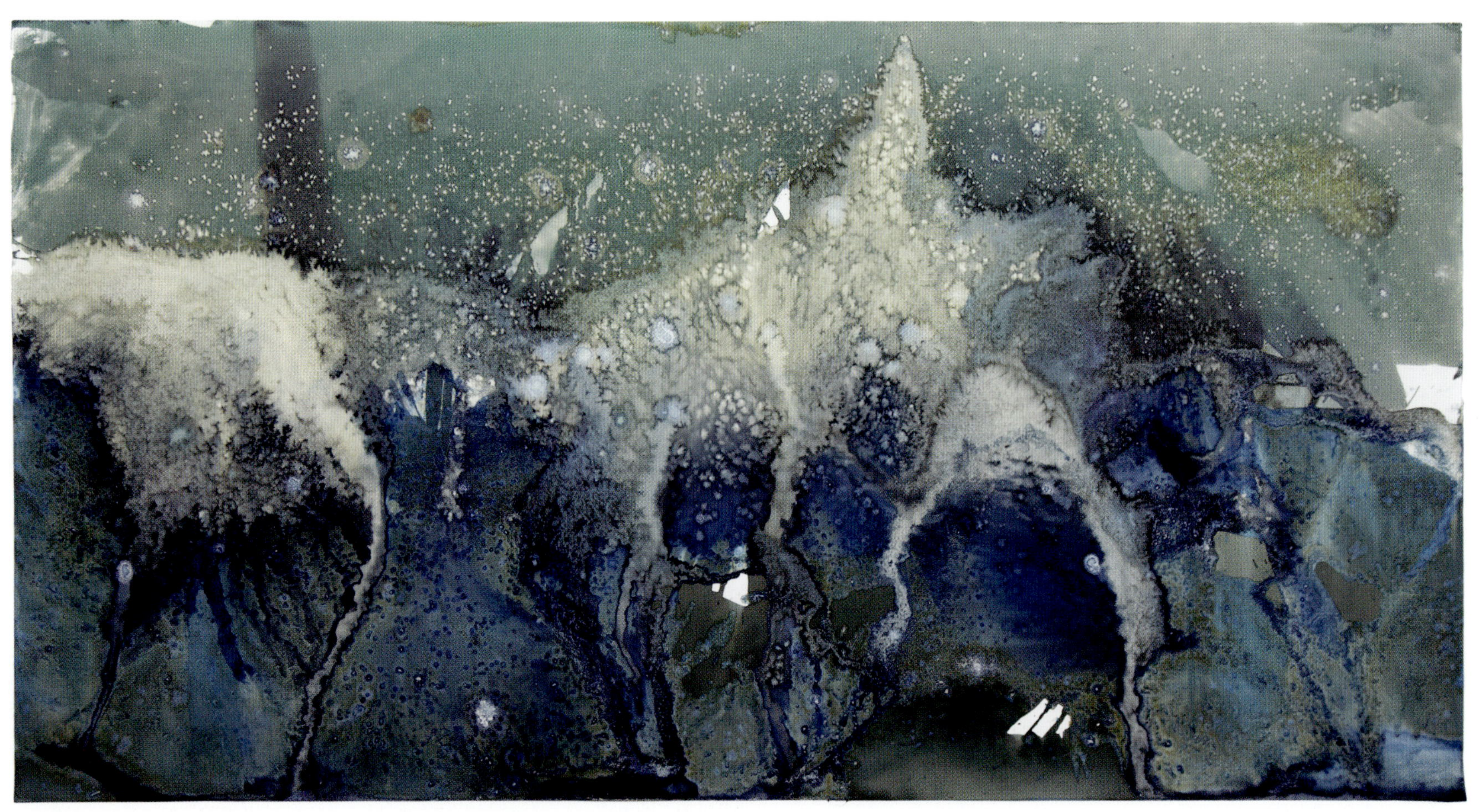

  122. Meghann Riepenhoff, *Littoral Drift Nearshore #502 (Bainbridge Island, Washington 04.01.16, Two Waves and Salt, Scattered and Poured)*, 21 × 42 inches, 2016

Notes

LAYOUT

1. The book was published in 2015 as *Abbey in America: A Philosopher's Legacy in a New Century,* ed. John A. Murray (Albuquerque: University of New Mexico Press).

2. See, for example, Jedediah Purdy, "Environmentalism's Racist History," *New Yorker,* August 13, 2015; and Benton Mock, "The Green Movement Is Talking About Racism? It's About Time," *Outside,* February 27, 2017.

3. Edward Abbey, *The Journey Home* (New York: Penguin/Plume, 1991), 86.

PICTURE

1. The remark is attributed to Benito R. de Monfort, president and founder, Société Héliographique, circa 1851.

CREATION STORY

1. Martha A. Sandweiss, *Print the Legend: Photography and the American West* (New Haven: Yale University Press, 2002), 77.

2. Joni L. Kinsey, *Plain Pictures: Images of the American Prairie* (Washington, D.C.: Smithsonian Institution Press, 1996).

3. See Frederick Jackson Turner, *The Frontier in American History* (New York: Henry Holt, 1920).

4. Roderick Frazier Nash, *Wilderness and the American Mind,* 4th ed. (New Haven: Yale University Press, 2001), 3.

5. Thomas R. Vale, ed., *Fire, Native Peoples, and the Natural Landscape,* 2nd ed. (Washington, D.C.: Island Press, 2013).

6. See Mark David Spence, *Dispossessing the Wilderness: Indian Removal and the Making of the National Parks* (Oxford: Oxford University Press, 1999); and M. Kat Anderson, *Tending the Wild: Native American Knowledge and the Management of California's Natural Resources* (Berkeley: University of California Press, 2013). Although Muir remains a historical pillar of American wilderness thought, nature writing, and advocacy, his embrace of racist stereotypes about Indigenous peoples and African Americans has forced a public reassessment of his legacy, including by the Sierra Club (Muir served as its first president and is often seen as its founder). This more critical appraisal was not exactly new, but it received significant national media attention as part of the broader national reckoning with racism that gripped the nation during the summer of 2020. See, for example, Darryl Fears and Steven Mufson, "Liberal, Progressive—and Racist? The Sierra Club Faces Its White-Supremacist History," *Washington Post,* July 22, 2020 (www.washingtonpost.com/climate-environment/2020

/07/22/liberal-progressive-racist-sierra-club-faces-its-white-supremacist
-history). For a different reading of Muir on this count, see Donald Worster,
"John Muir Biographer: He Was No White Supremacist," *California Sun*,
July 30, 2020 (www.californiasun.co/stories/john-muir-biographer-he-was
-no-white-supremacist).

FROM GRAND MANNER TO GRAND CANYONS

1. Alfred Runte, *Yosemite: The Embattled Wilderness* (Lincoln: University of Nebraska Press, 1990).

2. See Martha A. Sandweiss, *Print the Legend: Photography and the American West* (New Haven: Yale University Press, 2002); and Kevin Michael
DeLuca and Anne Teresa Demo, "Imaging Nature: Watkins, Yosemite, and
the Birth of Environmentalism," *Critical Studies in Media Communication* 17
(2000): 241–260.

VISUAL ART AS REPORTAGE AND ADVOCACY

1. For an excellent study of Adams's early development, see Rebecca A.
Senf, *Making a Photographer: The Early Work of Ansel Adams* (New Haven:
Yale University Press, 2020).

2. Adams was part of an influential photographic movement in the
1930s that branded itself "Group f.64," an artistic community based in
Northern California that also included Edward Weston, Imogen Cunningham, and Dorothea Lange. These modernists emphasized photography's
unique ability to produce images of unmatched detail and sharpness across
the full depth of field—attributes on full display in Adams's work from
the late 1920s on. See Mary Street Alinder's fine study, *Group f.64: Edward
Weston, Ansel Adams, Imogen Cunningham, and the Community of Artists
Who Revolutionized American Photography* (New York: Bloomsbury, 2014).

3. Mary Street Alinder, *Ansel Adams: A Biography* (New York: Bloomsbury, 2014); and Jonathan Spaulding, *Ansel Adams and the American Landscape* (Berkeley: University of California Press, 1995). There is actually
some confusion about the exact year Adams joined the Sierra Club; his
own autobiography says it was in 1919, though other historical studies pin
it down as 1920.

4. Ansel Adams (with Mary Street Alinder), *An Autobiography* (New
York: Little, Brown, 1985), 122.

5. The Cammerer quote appears in William A. Turnage, "The Quintes-
sence of Ansel," in Ansel Adams, *Sierra Nevada: The John Muir Trail* (New
York: Little, Brown, 2006).

6. Wallace Stegner, "The Marks of Human Passage," in *This Is Dinosaur: Echo Park Country and Its Magical River* (New York: Alfred A. Knopf,
1955), 15.

7. See Mark Harvey, *A Symbol of Wilderness: Echo Park and the American
Conservation Movement* (Seattle: University of Washington Press, 1994),
258.

8. Ansel Adams, "The Artist and the Ideals of Wilderness," in *Wilderness: America's Living Heritage,* ed. David Brower (San Francisco: Sierra
Club, 1961), 58.

9. For an in-depth account of the Sierra Club Exhibit Format series, see
Finis Dunaway's fine study, *Natural Visions: The Power of Images in American
Environmental Reform* (Chicago: University of Chicago Press, 2005).

10. See, for example, Rebecca A. Senf, *Making a Photographer: The Early
Work of Ansel Adams* (New Haven: Yale University Press, 2020).

THE POWER OF THE WILD

1. Henry David Thoreau, "Ktaadn," in *The Maine Woods* (1864); collected
in *Henry David Thoreau: A Week on the Concord and Merrimack Rivers, Walden,
The Maine Woods, Cape Cod* (New York: Library of America, 1985), 593.

2. Thoreau, "Ktaadn," 645.

3. Thoreau, "Ktaadn," 645–646.

4. John Muir, *Nature Writings* (New York: Library of America, 1997),
471, 473.

CROPPING THE NARRATIVE

1. Lynn White, Jr., "The Historical Roots of Our Ecologic Crisis," *Science*
155 (1967): 1203–1207.

2. Arne Næss, "The Shallow and the Deep, Long-Range Ecology Movement: A Summary," *Inquiry* 16 (1973): 95–100.

3. Brian DeVore, *Wildly Successful Farming: Sustainability and the New Agricultural Land Ethic* (Madison: University of Wisconsin Press, 2018). We thank Curt Meine for bringing this work to our attention.

WILDERNESS MOVEMENT AS HISTORICAL MOMENT

1. See Paul S. Sutter, *Driven Wild: How the Fight Against Automobiles Launched the Modern Wilderness Movement* (Seattle: University of Washington Press, 2002).

2. See Aldo Leopold, "The Last Stand of the Wilderness," *American Forests and Forest Life* 31 (1925), 599–604; and "Wilderness as a Form of Land Use," in *Aldo Leopold: A Sand County Almanac & Other Writings on Ecology and Conservation,* ed. Curt Meine (New York: Library of America, 2013).

3. Lauret Savoy, *Trace: Memory, History, Race, and the American Landscape* (Berkeley, Calif.: Counterpoint, 2015), 29.

4. For more on Porter and his work for the Sierra Club, see Rebecca Solnit, "Every Corner Is Alive: Eliot Porter as an Environmentalist and an Artist," collected in *Storming the Gates of Paradise: Landscapes for Politics* (Berkeley: University of California Press, 2007); Paul Martineau, *Eliot Porter: In the Realm of Nature* (Los Angeles: Getty Publications, 2012); and Tom Turner, *David Brower: The Making of the Environmental Movement* (Berkeley: University of California Press, 2015).

WRECKED WILD?

1. Two useful discussions of the New Topographic Photography and its significance are Kelly Dennis, "Landscape and the West: Irony and Critique in New Topographic Photography," a paper presented at 10th International Seminar of Forum UNESCO—University and Heritage, "Cultural Landscapes in the 21st Century," Newcastle-upon-Tyne, April 11–16, 2005; and Wendy Cheng, "New Topographics: Locating Epistemological Concerns in the American Landscape," *American Quarterly* 63, no. 1 (March 2011): 151–162.

2. See William Jenkins, *New Topographics: Photographs of a Man-Altered Landscape* (Rochester, N.Y.: International Museum of Photography at George Eastman House, 1975).

3. Deborah Bright, "The Machine in the Garden Revisited," *Art Journal* 51 (1992): 60–71, quote on p. 65.

4. Robert Adams, *Beauty in Photography* (New York: Aperture, 1996), 104.

5. For a cinematic illustration of this historical revisionism, compare Robert Altman's film *McCabe & Mrs. Miller* (1971), with its morally ambiguous characters wrestling with the terms of economic development in a gritty northwestern outpost in the first years of the twentieth century, with just about any of the John Ford westerns of the 1940s and 1950s (except for *The Searchers,* which remains his most thematically mature film in this genre). Aesthetically the difference between the two narrative forms is jarring.

6. On the tenets of the New Western history, see Patricia Nelson Limerick, "What on Earth Is the New Western History?" in *Trails: Toward a New Western History,* ed. Patricia Nelson Limerick, Clyde A. Milner II, and Charles E. Rankin (Lawrence: University Press of Kansas, 1991), 81–88. The quote from Donald Worster appears in his essay "Beyond the Agrarian Myth," in this same collection (p. 15).

7. John Brinckerhoff Jackson, *A Sense of Place, a Sense of Time* (New Haven: Yale University Press, 1994), 90.

8. J. B. Jackson, "Of Houses and Highways," *Aperture* 120 (1990): 64–71.

9. For example, J. Baird Callicott, "The Wilderness Idea Revisited: The Sustainable Development Alternative," *The Environmental Professional* 13 (1991): 235–247; William M. Denevan, "The Pristine Myth: The Landscape of the Americas in 1492," *Annals of the Association of American Geographers* 82, no. 3 (1992): 369–385; and Arturo Gómez-Pompa and Andrea Kaus, "Taming the Wilderness Myth," *BioScience* 42, no. 4 (1992): 271–279. These essays are collected in J. Baird Callicott and Michael P. Nelson, eds., *The Great New Wilderness Debate* (Athens: University of Georgia Press, 1998).

10. William Cronon, "The Trouble with Wilderness; or, Getting Back to the Wrong Nature," in *Uncommon Ground: Rethinking the Human Place in Nature,* ed. William Cronon (New York: W. W. Norton, 1995), 69–90, 89.

11. Worster, "Beyond the Agrarian Myth," 19.

12. Rebecca Solnit, *As Eve Said to the Serpent: On Landscape, Gender, and Art* (Athens: University of Georgia Press, 2001), 93–94.

13. Robert Adams, *Why People Photograph* (New York: Aperture, 1994), 139.

14. Raymond M. Turner, Robert H. Webb, Janice Emily Bowers, and James Rodney Hastings, *The Changing Mile Revisited: An Ecological Study of Vegetation Change with Time in the Lower Mile of an Arid and Semiarid Region* (Tucson: University of Arizona Press, 2003).

EDWARD ABBEY'S WILD VISIONS

1. Edward Abbey, *Desert Solitaire: A Season in the Wilderness* (New York: Simon & Schuster, 1968), 167

2. Edward Abbey, *The Journey Home* (New York: Penguin/Plume, 1991), 139.

3. Abbey's letter is reprinted in *Postcards from Ed: Dispatches and Salvos from an American Iconoclast,* ed. David Peterson (Minneapolis: Milkweed, 2006), 210.

4. See Peter Kareiva, "A New Type of Conservation: Breaking Free of Two Myths About Nature" (www.youtube.com/watch?v=J8w7UI0hmqw&feature=youtu.be&t=2m45s).

5. I thank Steve Pyne for this point.

6. James Cahalan, *Edward Abbey: A Life* (Tucson: University of Arizona Press, 2001).

7. Abbey's remark appears in James R. Hepworth and Gregory McNamee, eds., *Resist Much, Obey Little: Remembering Ed Abbey* (San Francisco: Sierra Club Books, 1996), 56.

8. Abbey, *Desert Solitaire,* 265.

9. Edward Abbey, *Abbey's Road* (New York: Penguin/Plume, 1991), 137.

10. Abbey, *The Journey Home,* 101.

11. Patricia Nelson Limerick, *Desert Passages: Encounters with the American Desert* (Albuquerque: University of New Mexico Press, 1985).

12. Amy Irvine, *Desert Cabal: A New Season in the Wilderness* (Salt Lake and Moab: Torrey House Press and Back of Beyond Books, 2018), 9.

13. Abbey's quip about photographs appears in *Abbey's Road,* 113.

14. Abbey, *The Journey Home,* 139.

WILDERNESS AS PARADOX

1. See Ben A. Minteer, "The Fall of the Wild? Not Really," *Slate,* July 20, 2014 (slate.com/technology/2014/07/wilderness-act-turns-50-is-it-still-useful.html).

CULTIVATING WILDNESS

1. Aldo Leopold, "Wilderness as a Form of Land Use," in *The River of the Mother of God and Other Essays by Aldo Leopold,* ed. Susan L. Flader and J. Baird Callicott (Madison: University of Wisconsin Press, 1991), 134–142; the quote appears on p. 135.

2. Gary P. Nabhan, *Food from the Radical Center: Healing Our Lands and Communities* (Washington, D.C.: Island Press, 2018).

FROM THE WILDERNESS TO THE WILD

1. We thank Curt Meine for helping us fill in this history.

2. See William Cronon, "The Riddle of the Apostle Islands," *Orion* (May/June 2003); and Ben A. Minteer and Robert E. Manning, "Wilderness Preserves," in *A Thinking Person's Guide to the National Parks,* ed. Robert E. Manning, David Harmon, Nora Mitchell, and Rolf Diamant (George Braziller, 2016), 105–115.

3. The Arizona wilderness–bighorn case is well summarized in Sandra Zellmer, "Wilderness, Water, and Climate Change," *Environmental Law* 42 (2012): 313–374.

4. "Tamarisk Eradication Halted to Protect Endangered Bird," CBS News online (www.cbsnews.com/news/tamarisk-eradication-halted-to-protect-endangered-bird), June 22, 2010.

THE STORIED WILD

1. Collected in Wallace Stegner, *The Sound of Mountain Water* (New York: Penguin, 1968), 150.

2. Stegner, *The Sound of Mountain Water,* 150.

3. See, for example, Stephen R. Kellert, *Birthright: People and Nature in the Modern World* (New Haven: Yale University Press, 2012); and two works by Richard Louv, *Last Child in the Woods: Saving Our Children from Nature-Deficit Disorder* (Chapel Hill, N.C.: Algonquin Books, 2008), and *Our Wild Calling* (Chapel Hill: Algonquin Books, 2020).

4. Bryan G. Norton, *Why Preserve Natural Variety?* (Princeton: Princeton University Press, 1987).

5. Norton, *Why Preserve,* 189.

6. A dynamic on display in Gavin Van Horn's essay for this book as well as in the work of writers exploring the reciprocal relationship between cultures and their ecologies like Robin Wall Kimmerer and Gary Paul Nabhan.

7. Rebecca A. Senf, *Making a Photographer: The Early Work of Ansel Adams* (New Haven: Yale University Press, 2020).

8. Wallace Stegner, "The Marks of Human Passage," 17, in *This Is Dinosaur*.

MANAGED WILD

1. See, for example, Jill Metcoff's *Firelines* (Albuquerque: University of New Mexico Press, 2017), which documents prescribed burns in prairie and savannas in southern Wisconsin (including the Aldo Leopold Reserve).

THE DE-FACTO WILD

1. This work is put into broader context in Mark Ruwedel, *Westward: The Course of Empire* (New Haven: Yale University Press, 2008).

2. See, for example, Robert Elliot, *Faking Nature: The Ethics of Environmental Restoration* (London: Routledge, 1997), and Eric Katz, *Nature as Subject: Human Obligation and Natural Community* (Lanham, Md.: Rowman and Littlefield, 1997).

3. David G. Havlick, *Bombs Away: Militarization, Conservation, and Ecological Restoration* (Chicago: University of Chicago Press, 2018).

4. Aldo Leopold, "Wilderness," in *Aldo Leopold: A Sand County Almanac & Other Writings on Ecology and Conservation,* ed. Curt Meine (New York: Library of America, 2013), 166.

5. For an inquiry into the question of authenticity generally, see Lydia Pyne, *Genuine Fakes: How Phony Things Teach Us About Real Stuff* (London: Bloomsbury Sigma, 2019).

6. Wallace Stegner, *The Sound of Mountain Water* (New York: Penguin, 1968), 51.

NEW WAYS OF SEEING

1. See Ben A. Minteer, "The Fall of the Wild? Not Really," *Slate,* July 20, 2014 (slate.com/technology/2014/07/wilderness-act-turns-50-is-it-still -useful.html).

2. Curt Meine, "A Letter to the Editors: In Defense of the Relative Wild," in *After Preservation: Saving American Nature in the Age of Humans,* ed. Ben A. Minteer and Stephen J. Pyne (Chicago: University of Chicago Press, 2015), 84–95.

3. A good illustration of this multivocality of the wild is Gavin Van Horn and John Hausdoerffer, eds., *Wildness: Relations of People and Place* (Chicago: University of Chicago Press, 2017).

4. Robin Wall Kimmerer, *Braiding Sweetgrass: Indigenous Wisdom, Scientific Knowledge, and the Teachings of Plants* (Minneapolis, Minn.: Milkweed, 2013).

Further Reading

Edward Abbey, *Desert Solitaire: A Season in the Wilderness* (New York: Simon & Schuster, 1968).

Jamie M. Allen, *Picturing America's National Parks* (New York: George Eastman Museum/Aperture, 2016).

William Cronon, ed., *Uncommon Ground: Rethinking the Human Place in Nature* (New York: Norton, 1995).

Beverly Dahlen et al., *American Geography* (Santa Fe, N.M.: Radius Books/SFMOMA, 2020).

Finis Dunaway, *Natural Visions: The Power of Images in American Environmental Reform* (Chicago: University of Chicago Press, 2005).

William H. Goetzmann and William N. Goetzmann, *The West of the Imagination* (New York: W. W. Norton, 1988).

John Brinckerhoff Jackson, *A Sense of Place, a Sense of Time* (New Haven: Yale University Press, 1994).

Mark Klett, Rebecca Solnit, and Byron Wolfe, *Drowned River: The Death & Rebirth of Glen Canyon on the Colorado* (Santa Fe, N.M.: Radius Books, 2018).

Aldo Leopold, *A Sand County Almanac: And Sketches Here and There* (New York: Oxford University Press, 1949).

Patricia Nelson Limerick, Clyde A. Miller II, and Charles E. Rankin, eds., *Trails: Toward a New Western History* (Lawrence: University Press of Kansas, 1991).

Paul Martineau, *Eliot Porter: In the Realm of Nature* (Los Angeles: J. Paul Getty Museum, 2012).

John McPhee, *Encounters with the Archdruid* (New York: Farrar, Straus and Giroux, 1971).

Curt Meine, *Correction Lines: Essays on Land, Leopold, and Conservation* (Washington, D.C.: Island Press, 2003).

Ben A. Minteer and Stephen J. Pyne, eds., *After Preservation: Saving American Nature in the Age of Humans* (Chicago: University of Chicago Press, 2015).

Roderick Frazier Nash, *Wilderness and the American Mind,* 5th ed. (New Haven: Yale University Press, 2014).

———. *The Rights of Nature: A History of Environmental Ethics* (Madison: University of Wisconsin Press, 1989).

Barbara Novak, *Nature and Culture: American Landscape Painting, 1825–1875,* 3rd ed. (Oxford: Oxford University Press, 2007).

Max Oelschlaeger, *The Idea of Wilderness: From Prehistory to the Age of Ecology* (New Haven: Yale University Press, 1991).

Stephen J. Pyne, *How the Canyon Became Grand: A Short History* (New York: Penguin, 1998).

Rachel McLean Sailor, *Meaningful Places: Landscape Photographers in the Nineteenth-Century American West* (Albuquerque: University of New Mexico Press, 2014).

Martha Sandweiss, *Print the Legend: Photography and the American West* (New Haven: Yale University Press, 2002).

Rebecca A. Senf, *Making a Photographer: The Early Work of Ansel Adams* (New Haven: Yale University Press, 2020).

Rebecca Solnit, *Storming the Gates of Paradise: Landscapes for Politics* (Berkeley: University of California Press, 2007).

Wallace Stegner, *The Sound of Mountain Water* (Garden City, N.Y.: Doubleday, 1969).

Andrea G. Stillman, *Looking at Ansel Adams: The Photographs and the Man* (New York: Little, Brown, 2012).

Tom Turner, *David Brower: The Making of the Environmental Movement* (Berkeley: University of California Press, 2015).

Gavin Van Horn and John Hausdoerffer, eds., *Wildness: Relations of People and Place* (Chicago: University of Chicago Press, 2017).

Katherine Ware, *Earth Now: American Photographers and the Environment* (Santa Fe: Museum of New Mexico Press, 2011).

Ann M. Wolfe et al., *The Altered Landscape: Photographs of a Changing Environment* (New York: Skira Rizzoli, 2011).

George Wuerthner, Eileen Crist, and Tom Butler, eds., *Keeping the Wild: Against the Domestication of Earth* (Washington, D.C.: Island Press, 2014).

Further Viewing

DAVID EMITT ADAMS http://www.davidemittadams.com

ROBERT ADAMS https://fraenkelgallery.com/artists/robert-adams

JULIE ANAND AND DAMON SAUER http://www.2circles.org

LEWIS BALTZ https://www.icp.org/browse/archive/constituents/lewis
-baltz?all/all/all/all/0

SUBHANKAR BANERJEE http://www.subhankarbanerjee.org

MICHAEL P. BERMAN https://michaelpberman.com/about

DEBRA BLOOMFIELD http://www.debrabloomfield.com

BARBARA BOSWORTH https://www.barbarabosworth.com

KWASI BOYD-BOULDIN http://www.kwasiboydbouldin.com

MATHEW BRANDT https://matthewbrandt.com

LAURIE BROWN http://lauriebrownphotographer.com

EDWARD BURTYNSKY https://www.edwardburtynsky.com

EDGAR CARDENAS http://www.edgarcardenas.com

JOHNNIE CHATMAN http://jchatman.com

ZOE CHILDERLEY http://www.zoechilderley.co.uk

LINDA CONNOR http://hainesgallery.com/linda-connor-works

BINH DANH http://binhdanh.com

SCOTT B. DAVIS https://www.scottbdavis.com

ROBERT DAWSON https://www.robertdawson.com

JOE DEAL https://collections.eastman.org/people/16316/joe-deal

JOHN DIVOLA http://www.divola.com

MITCH DOBROWNER http://mitchdobrowner.com

TERRY EVANS http://www.terryevansphotography.com

TERRY FALKE https://afterimagegallery.com/falkenew.htm

ALEX FRADKIN https://www.alexfradkin.com

GEOFF FRICKER http://ccp-emuseum.catnet.arizona.edu/view/people
/asitem/items@:768

PETER GOIN https://www.petergoin.com

EMMET GOWIN http://www.artnet.com/artists/emmet-gowin

KARI GREER https://www.kariphotos.com

DAVID T. HANSON https://www.davidthanson.net

SHARON HARPER https://www.sharonharper.org

JOSHUA HAUNSCHILD http://www.haunschildphotography.com/#516
_HumphreysPeak_web.jpg#home

ANTHONY HERNANDEZ http://anthonyhernandezphotography.com

JOHN BRINTON HOGAN http://johnbrintonhogan.com

DAN HOLDSWORTH https://www.danholdsworth.com

ZIG JACKSON http://www.risingbuffaloarts.com

TAYLOR JAMES http://www.taylorjamesphotography.com

LEN JENSHEL http://cookjenshel.com

ADAM KATSEFF http://www.adamkatseff.com

SANT KHALSA http://www.santkhalsa.com

MARK KLETT http://www.markklettphotography.com; http://www
.klettandwolfe.com

AN-MY LÊ https://anmyle.com

JUNGJIN LEE http://www.jungjinlee.com

DANIEL LEIVICK https://danielleivick.com

SERGE J-F. LEVY http://www.sergelevy.com

MICHAEL LIGHT http://www.michaellight.net

MICHAEL LUNDGREN http://michaeldlundgren.com

CHRIS MCCAW https://www.chrismccaw.com

LILLY MCELROY https://lillymcelroy.com/home.html

LAURA MCPHEE https://lauramcphee.com

ABELARDO MORELL https://www.abelardomorell.net

ANNIE MARIE MUSSELMAN https://www.anniemusselman.com

CATHERINE OPIE http://www.artnet.com/artists/catherine-opie

ERIKA OSBORNE http://erikaosborne.com/new

TREVOR PAGLEN http://www.paglen.com

JOHN PFAHL https://johnpfahl.com

ANDREW PHELPS http://www.andrew-phelps.com

JANET L. PRITCHARD http://janetpritchard.com

EDWARD RANNEY https://www.photoeye.com/gallery/forms2
/homepage.cfm?id=16689&image=1&imagePosition=1&Door=2&
Portfolio=Portfolio1&Gallery=2

MEGHANN RIEPENHOFF http://meghannriepenhoff.com

AARON ROTHMAN https://www.aarothman.com

MARK RUWEDEL https://yossimilo.com/artists/mark-ruwedel

VICTORIA SAMBUNARIS https://www.victoriasambunaris.com

SCANLAB https://scanlabprojects.co.uk/work/post-lenticular-landscapes

BRYAN SCHUTMAAT http://www.bryanschutmaat.com

DAVID SHANNON-LIER http://davidshannon-lier.com

DAVID BENJAMIN SHERRY https://salon94.com/artists/david-benjamin
-sherry

ALEC SOTH https://alecsoth.com/photography

AMY STEIN http://amystein.com

JOEL STERNFELD https://www.joelsternfeld.net

SHARON STEWART https://www.sharonstewartphotography.net

BUZZY SULLIVAN http://www.buzzysullivan.com

DAVID TAYLOR http://www.dtaylorphoto.com

ADAM THORMAN https://adamthorman.com

STEPHEN TOURLENTES http://www.tourlentes.com/Stephen_Tourlentes
_Web_site/Home.html

ROBERT VOIT http://www.robertvoit.com

TERRI WARPINSKI http://www.terriwarpinski.com

REBECCA NORRIS WEBB https://www.webbnorriswebb.co

WILL WILSON https://willwilson.photoshelter.com/index

BYRON WOLFE https://www.byronwolfe.com; http://www.klettandwolfe.com

Acknowledgments

Multi-authored books are always collaborations, but this project upped the ante. First and foremost, we want to thank all the photographers and organizations that contributed images to this project. Needless to say, we couldn't have done this without their participation and generosity. We encourage readers interested in seeing more work by the contemporary artists featured here to refer to the "Further Viewing" section, where you'll find a list of photographer web resources and can explore their work in greater detail.

A special thank-you to Brooke Hecht, president of the Center for Humans and Nature, for her strong support for the publication of this volume, and to the Center's Gavin Van Horn for contributing to the text. We owe a debt of gratitude to Josh Haunschild for his help overseeing the images, obtaining reproductions and permissions, and assisting us as we pulled the manuscript and images into final shape. We'd also like to thank Jean Thomson Black at Yale University Press for her strong support and careful guidance as we finalized the book. Two reviewers, Curt Meine and Rebecca Senf, provided extensive and expert commentary on and suggestions for multiple earlier versions of the manuscript and photo edit; this book has been vastly improved by their deep engagement, friendly criticism, and thoughtfulness.

Finally, we'd like to acknowledge several publications that carried earlier versions of two of the essays appearing here. "Cropping the Narrative" is based on Ben A. Minteer and Stephen J. Pyne, "Restoring the Narrative of American Environmentalism," published in *Restoration Ecology* 21 (2013): 6–11. Previous and shorter incarnations of "Edward Abbey's Wild Visions" appeared as B. A. Minteer, "Abbey's *Secret,*" in *Abbey in America: A Philosopher's Legacy in a New Century,* ed. John A. Murray (University of New Mexico Press, 2015), and B. A. Minteer, "Why Edward Abbey Still Matters," *Earth Island Journal,* May 15, 2015 (accessible at http://www .earthisland.org/journal/index.php/articles/entry/why_edward_abbey _still_matters). We are grateful to the publishers for their permission to incorporate this material in *Wild Visions.*

Index